Not of

# Not of My Making

*Bullying, Scapegoating
and Misconduct in Churches*

Margaret W. Jones, PhD

First Edition

Pluck Press
Stoughton, Massachusetts

Deb,
It is an honor
to know you and
worship with
you. You are such
a kind person.
Margaret W Jones

# Not of My Making

*Bullying, Scapegoating and Misconduct in Churches*

By Margaret W. Jones, PhD

Published by:
**Pluck Press**
Post Office Box 516
Stoughton, MA 02072-0516

www.pluckpress.com

Copyright 2008
Library of Congress Control Number: 2008925514
ISBN: 978-0-9801491-0-4

Printed in Lowell, Massachusetts

To my husband, Lyndon Jones, and all others like him who will no longer attend church because of all the hypocrisy they have witnessed there.

# Contents

# Foreword

Throughout human history, strong women who have spoken out against injustice have been persecuted. Courageous women who have challenged the status quo and expressed their convictions openly and forcefully have been intimidated by the prevailing powers that be. A sad historical legacy of oppression, marginalization and scapegoating of females is as pervasive as it is incontrovertible. Be it the foot-binding of Asian girls, the specter of the Salem witch trials, or the clitoridectomies still performed across Africa today, the underlying theme remains constant: women must "know their place," suppress their outrage, and never attempt to become empowered. This history of ubiquitous disenfranchisement is particularly evident in the world of male-dominated institutions represented by such realms as business, academia and the church. One need only reflect upon the dispiriting damage inflicted by the well-documented "glass ceiling" to understand the power this barrier possesses. None of these pernicious sociocultural influences, be they enforced legally or more subtly—but surely just as destructively—in rigidly entrenched de facto misogynistic traditions, are of the female gender's own making. What follows is the extraordinary story of one brave woman's stand against this toxic tradition of bullying and silencing, and the cruel diminution of sensitive souls.

Dr. Margaret Jones, like many survivors of emotional, physical or sexual abuse, had an intensely felt need to share her compelling story. The recounting of her painful experiences was an extremely challenging and occasionally overwhelming endeavor. I personally witnessed the toll it often took. Her primary goal was not to excoriate anyone, but rather, to help others who have been subjected to the same painful labeling and shunning, and pressured to conform to stereotypical "good girl" behavior she encountered. Her hope is that others may be spared what she endured; her commitment to creating religious communities that are safe havens for everyone is clearly evident. Margaret was determined to be as accurate as possible in her recollections. It is important for the reader of this memoir to trust in the author's credibility and dedication to honesty. She relied heavily on daily journal entries, emails and letters, while also consulting with family members when written records were lacking. She was not motivated by some hidden desire to extract huge sums of money from an offending individual, church or insurance company. While all such stories are inevitably subjective in nature, her essential integrity is reassuring. What follows are not the crazy fabrications of a deranged mind or disordered personality. As she once expressed to me in a private correspondence, "I didn't imagine this. This really happened." Hopefully, her willingness to bravely share with us her remarkable story of resilience and recovery will inspire others to take up her worthy cause.

Rev. Steven Wiley Emmett, PhD
Scituate, Massachusetts

# Preface

I have debated how best to start this story. Where do I start? What do I include? It hasn't been an easy story to tell. Often I would write a few pages, and then I would have to stop. Overwhelmed, I would curl up on the couch in a fetal position and sleep. I wanted to be as accurate as possible. I relied heavily on my journal entries, emails and letters to reconstruct this story. Where there was no such written record I had to rely solely on my memories and those of family members.

Many people involved in these events experienced things differently and would without a doubt tell the story differently. I wrote to all the individuals mentioned in this book and asked them to make corrections to the manuscript if and where needed. Almost everyone refused. A couple of individuals wanted things they said added. Since I agreed they indeed said what had been left out, I made the correction. Another individual wanted me to replace my perception about an event with hers. I declined to do that. This is my story told from my point of view, not hers. That is the strength and weakness of a memoir.

Like most survivors, I had an intense need to tell my story. I do not want what happened to me to happen to anyone else. I hope, after reading this book, people will talk about adult bullying in churches and seek to put a stop to it. I am committed to creating religious communities that are safe places for everyone.

I do not want to spread the harm done to me. Therefore, to protect people's privacy, I have only used the first names of the main characters. Where there were two people with the same first name, I have changed one of the names.

# Acknowledgements

I would like to thank my husband, Lyndon, my sister, Rita Jo Panten, my daughter, Melissa Jones, and my son, Orion Jones, for all their encouragement and support.

I would like to thank my niece, Rebecca Gorgas, and Steve Emmett, who, in addition to their support, reviewed drafts of this book.

I would like to thank Collen Anctil and Mary Mortimore Dossin for reading and offering comments on an early draft of this book.

I would like to thank Hannah R. Goodman for her professional critique of my manuscript and whose program, Releasing the Writer Within, improved my writing.

I would like to thank Mary T. Hammond, Candace Benyei, Larraine Frampton, Catherine Fairbanks, AdvocateWeb, Mennonite Conciliation Service and Kevin Campbell for helping me when others had abandoned me.

Finally, I would like to thank the many contributors to the Publisher's List for their sound advice and assistance in book design, production and marketing.

# Vulnerability

The first time I was molested I must have been four years old. We were still living in Ozone Park, Queens. In my mind's eye I see myself wandering around the neighborhood dirty and unkempt. All four of my siblings were in school but I wasn't. That is how I know how old I was. My sister, Trish, who is eighteen months older than me, must have been in kindergarten. We were a grade apart. I also remember it was a warm, sunny day. I was wearing thin cotton shorts with a sleeveless top. So I figure it was in early September, just after school started.

The day probably began like any other day. I was awakened by the clinking of dishes and the sound of water running downstairs in the kitchen while my siblings ate their breakfast and made their lunches. I rubbed the sand out of my eyes and stumbled out of bed. I looked around my bedroom floor until I found a sleeveless top and shorts. They were stained and ragged. All of my clothes were stained and ragged. I did my best to button my shirt, but had it cockeyed.

My father, as usual, had caught the train into Manhattan long before I was awake. My mother was still asleep in her bedroom at the far end of the hall. I knew if I disturbed her she would yell, so I left her alone.

Having dressed myself as best I could, I hurried down to the kitchen. My two brothers rushed past me as they ran to the bus stop. Rita, my eldest sister, became impatient with Trish, who was dawdling.

"C'mon," Rita said, "we'll miss the bus." Turning to me she said, "Fix your shirt. You missed a button."

"Bye," I called to my sisters as they walked swiftly through the house and out the front door. I followed them as far as the living room. Scrambling up onto the gray sectional in front of the window, I was just in time to see the big yellow bus close its doors and drive past. I waved but no one saw me.

The house was now quiet. Although I was used to being separated from my three oldest siblings for several hours at a time, not having Trish around was new. I didn't understand why she got to go to school and I had to stay home. My parents, brothers and eldest sister told me I had to wait another year, until I was five. A year was a long time. I didn't think it fair.

Bewildered, I wandered back into the kitchen. My mother rarely got up before ten, and only prepared breakfast on Sunday mornings. Having to fend for myself, I picked through what was left of my siblings' breakfasts. I found a piece of toast that one of my siblings had only taken one bite out of. I finished it. This was the way I usually got breakfast and lunch. I didn't think anything of it. Whenever I saw the pediatrician, he commented on how thin I was. My mother boasted I was an active child who was always outside running around. I had a good appetite and ate the balanced dinners she cooked every night. But I didn't have much of a sweet tooth, and often refused dessert. The doctor appeared to accept my mother's explanation. Not knowing any better, I did, too.

My tummy full, I wandered out the front door that had been left ajar. With the older children at school, the fathers at work and the mothers cleaning their houses, the block was as quiet and empty as a ghost town. I had no one to keep me company. Then I thought of Mr. Stahl.

Mr. Stahl lived behind us. Looking out our back window, you could see the rear of his garage. To the left and cattycorner to our back fence was his grove of peach trees. In the early evenings, I often found my father pruning the hybrid tea roses that lined our property. When he reached the back corner, he would stop and talk to Mr. Stahl, who was tending his peach trees. I liked to climb halfway up the chain-link fence and listen to the men talk about their gardens. Mr. Stahl would soon reward me with a sweet, juicy peach that dripped all over my clothes while I gobbled it up.

So that morning I set out for Mr. Stahl's house. I had been there many times before. After dinner on warm summer evenings, my brothers and eldest sister would take Trish and me around the block to gather with the rest of the neighborhood at Mr. Stahl's. While the adults played cards in the detached garage, we jumped rope on the cement driveway and played I See a Color with Mr. Stahl's elderly tenants who sat on lawn chairs alongside the garden and peach grove. We didn't return home until the streetlights came on.

I found Mr. Stahl sitting in his front window.

"Hello, there," he greeted me.

"Hi," I said, looking up over the bushes planted under the window.

"Alone today?" he asked.

"Yes," I replied, looking at my feet. "Everybody went to school."

"Don't you worry. You'll go to school next year. Would you like some candy?"

"Oh, yes!" I exclaimed as I jumped up and down.

"Come into the house," he said as he stood and walked toward the door. I hesitated. I remembered my parents' repeated admonitions not to go into anyone's house without their permission.

Mr. Stahl opened the door. "Come in," he said, "I will get you some candy."

Eager for the candy, I followed him as he hobbled on his crutches into his living room. His right leg had been amputated above his knee. His trouser leg was folded and pinned up neatly over his stump. It was rumored among the neighborhood children that he had been injured during the war. No one ever said which war.

This was the first time I had been invited inside Mr. Stahl's house. Although it was a sunny day, the room was dark and musky. Feeling uneasy, I hung back, afraid to enter.

"Come in, come in," he urged. "Have a seat on the couch."

Reassured by the sunlight streaming through the kitchen doorway, I sat down. He went into the kitchen and returned with some candy. He took a seat next to me. Before giving me the candy, he slipped his suspenders off his shoulders and unzipped his gray pants. Leaning over with his right hand on the back of the couch to balance himself and his left hand on the seat cushion by my thigh, he pressed his lower body between my legs. I felt something hard. His shirt buttons scraped against my skin while his big, soft belly covered my face. Frightened and gasping for air, I tried to pull away.

"I won't hurt you," he reassured me.

"I need to go home now," I pleaded.

"Sure." He zipped up his pants. "Don't forget this." He handed me two pieces of candy as he walked me to the front door.

As he opened the door, I slipped under his arm and escaped down the steps into the sunshine. No longer caring about the candy, I dropped it on the ground as I ran home.

Fearful of being punished for going into Mr. Stahl's house without permission, I told no one about his strange behavior. I stayed on my side of the block, and only went to Mr. Stahl's when I was with one of my older siblings.

I began having a recurrent nightmare of a pebble falling from the blue sky above my head. As it fell it grew in size, covering my face. I could see nothing else. I struggled to breathe. Each time, I screamed. My mother or father would come into my room. "It's only a dream. You're safe," they said, ignorant of what Mr. Stahl had done. "Go back to sleep."

A year later I began kindergarten at Nativity, the local parish school. Except for one family, everyone living in our neighborhood was Roman Catholic. The church was at the center of our community, giving it cohesiveness and structure.

Once a year, one of the priests assigned to our parish would walk through the neighborhood, blessing our homes. Laughing and skipping, I and the other neighborhood children followed him as if he was the Pied Piper down the concrete sidewalk between the maple trees and the small front yards of our homes. The priest stopped at each house and climbed the red brick stoops to speak to our mothers.

When the priest reached my house, I pushed past the other children and up the steps to stand close to my mother and my sister Trish. With his black cassock billowing in the spring breeze, the young priest raised his right hand and said, making the sign of the cross, "In the name of the Father, and of the Son, and of the Holy Spirit."

"Amen," we responded while we crossed ourselves and placed our palms together.

"Peace be with this house and with all who live here."

"And also with you."

After the priest had blessed all of our houses, he moved on to the next block. The other children scattered, and I was left standing alone on the city street. I wandered back to my house and found my thirteen-year-old sister, Rita, standing with her friends under the maple tree whose branches stretched over the sidewalk toward our parents' bedroom window. I begged her to play with me. Annoyed by the intrusion, Rita chased me away.

When she wasn't playing with her friends, she enjoyed the role of big sister. Often she walked Trish and me across Cross Bay Boulevard and down the side streets to our church, the Nativity of Our Blessed Virgin. We would enter the sanctuary from the side door, light some candles, and kneel in front of the altar. Awed by the dark, shadowy interior with its smells of burning candles and incense, I saw Jesus' face in the tabernacle and felt His protective presence. Here was where I would always be safe.

On school days, my older siblings boarded the bus in the early morning, leaving me alone to wait for the kindergarten bus. Short, timid and undernourished, I was easy prey for the bigger children.

"Whew, you smell. You're ugly," my schoolmates taunted.

When I returned home after school one day, I searched for my mother. I found her in the kitchen with Rita.

"No one wants to play with me," I whined.

"Why don't you help Rita make meatballs?"

I climbed on the chair next to my sister, who was rolling ground beef between the palms of her hands. I grabbed a handful of meat from the ball and copied what she was doing as best as I could. When we were finished we gave the bowl to my mother, who was standing in front of the gas stove.

"Thank you," she said. I watched closely while she browned the meatballs in hot olive oil. When they were done, she took a pair of tongs and removed one of the meatballs. "Here, Peanut, have a meatball." She handed me the brown greasy ball that smelled of oregano, parsley and garlic. I immediately bit into the ball's pink center. The meat juices and fat dripped onto my hands.

"What do you say?" she asked.

"Thank you."

"You're welcome." She handed me a paper napkin. I wiped my hands after I finished eating my treat.

"Now go outside and play."

"Can't I stay here?" I asked. "The other kids are making fun of me."

"Ignore them," she said. "They're just jealous."

Trusting my mother's advice, I tried not saying anything to the other kids when they called me names, but it didn't stop the teasing. Once, while I waited for the school bus at the corner of 133rd Avenue and Cross Bay Boulevard, some bigger children started taunting me, saying, "Piggy, you smell. Take a bath. You're stupid."

"My name's not Piggy," I protested.

"Piggy! Piggy!" they shouted.

Remembering my mother's advice, I looked away and tried to ignore them. The older children moved in closer and got louder. Spotting tears rolling down my face, they began laughing and calling, "Look at the crybaby!"

No longer able to bear it, I threw myself down on the ground crying. A strange man came running across 133rd Avenue from Sam's Candy Store. "Pick on someone your own size," he scolded my tormentors. He set me on my feet and wiped my tears away with his handkerchief. "Are you okay, honey?"

"Y-y-yes," I whimpered.

The man waited with me until the school bus came. Like a responsible and caring parent, he watched me board the bus and take a seat by the window. I pressed my face against the glass and waved goodbye as my rescuer disappeared around the corner, never to be seen again.

When the school bus arrived at Nativity, the nuns dressed in black habits were waiting. As we exited the bus, they placed us in two lines and marched us across the schoolyard, down the stairs into the basement and across the multipurpose room to our classroom. I took a seat with my classmates at a long wooden table. The nuns showed us some religious pictures on a flip chart. I vividly remember a picture of a guardian angel with large, beautiful wings and a flowing white gown. The nuns told us everyone had a guardian angel watching over them. *Did my guardian angel send the stranger at the bus stop to rescue me?* I wondered.

In first grade, I took the same bus as my sister Trish. When we arrived at the parish school, we walked past the black iron gate and onto the cement playground. All the other children, including Trish, placed their books and metal lunch boxes on the line designated for their class. They then ran off to play in the schoolyard, leaving me behind. I was as conspicuous as a blemish on a teenager's nose and equally unwanted. I tried to shrink unnoticed into the sidewalk.

The nuns walked out of the convent that bordered the schoolyard. One of them rang a handbell. The other children came running back. They jostled me as they took their place on the line.

"Quiet, children," our teacher said, and then called each of our names, marking us present in her grade book. She then walked us single file into the red brick school and up the stairs to our classroom. As we filed in, I quietly took my assigned seat along the window and watched the cars go by.

Instead of taking his seat, a boy stood by the teacher's desk mimicking her.

"What are you doing?" demanded Sister as she entered the room.

"Teaching," he replied. I smiled.

Sister's eyes met mine and she scowled. "What are you smiling at?"

I slumped down in my chair, trying to become invisible like a small animal hiding from a predator.

"Nothing is funny. Come here!"

While my classmate took his seat, I walked up to the front of the room. "Tell the class you're sorry."

Confused, I turned around to face my classmates. I didn't mean to smile. It just happened. "I'm sorry I smiled," I whispered, staring at my feet.

For lunch, I purposely brought grapes so I could eat them slowly, one by one, to delay going out into the schoolyard for recess. When I was the last child in the lunchroom, the nuns scolded, "Hurry up. You'll miss recess."

Dreading recess more than the nuns' scolding, I slumped down into my chair and continued to eat slowly.

"What's wrong with her?" one nun asked the other. Shaking her head and turning back to me, the nun started to walk toward me. I shoved the last few grapes into my mouth and hurried out the door and into the schoolyard before she could cuff me.

I wandered around the cement playground between the school, the church and the rectory. The other children held their noses and laughed when I walked by them. I was relieved when the young priest who had blessed our house stepped out of the rectory and onto the schoolyard. His presence distracted the other children, and I was safe while he was there.

"Will you bless my medal, Father?" the children clamored as they gathered around the young priest, holding up their religious medals and crucifixes. While he made the sign of the cross, I hung back.

Seeing me standing at the edge of the group, he asked me my name.

"Maggie," I replied.

"Maggie what?"

"Wandel."

"Josephine's daughter?" he asked.

I hesitated. The name sounded familiar. I wasn't sure. "Yes," I answered.

"Aren't you Francesco Longo's granddaughter?" he asked.

Not recognizing the name of my great-grandfather, I looked at him, puzzled.

"Never mind," he said gently. "Your mother told me about your grandfather and the letter he wrote to the bishop asking for this church to be built. You're from a good family."

I was confused. Who was this Francesco? Why did the priest speak to me? What had I done? He said my family was good. That made them special, didn't it? The priest had to know. He was close to God, wasn't he? Unlike my classmates, he didn't say a thing about my being dirty and unkempt. None of the adults ever did. By the time I reached adolescence, I had concluded that since all my efforts to win my "good family's" love and acceptance had failed, something was horribly and innately wrong with me. When I was nineteen years old, I would try to rectify the mistake of my birth.

Summer vacation released me from the torment of the schoolyard. I was relatively safe if I stayed close to home and didn't wander to Mr. Stahl's side of the block. My mother told my three oldest siblings to watch out for Trish and me. They did so in a haphazard, inconsistent way. Sometimes if they weren't too busy playing with their friends, they would chase away older kids who were picking on us, or they would take us to visit our grandmother in her second-floor apartment. After Grandma buzzed us in, we would climb the dark staircase into her kitchen, where she would feed us roasted peppers and Italian pastries.

On hot days, my older siblings and I walked to the park on Liberty Avenue to cool off under the sprinkler provided by the city. My mother never kept track of where we were, so I doubt she realized we were cutting through the train yard. My brother and sister would grab my arms and hoist me up while I tucked my legs to avoid touching the electrified third rail.

Despite my parents' neglect, there were good times. Family meals, visits to museums and Sunday drives were some of the simple pleasures we enjoyed together. Just before my sixth birthday, my parents loaded my siblings and me into my father's 1952 black Oldsmobile for a Sunday drive along Southern State Parkway. My brother Bill had the coveted privilege of sitting in the front seat with my parents. Rita and my brother Rich claimed the window seats while Trish and I squeezed into the middle.

Driving east along the winding, tree-lined roadway, my parents began sharing what they knew about the area's history. "This highway," my mother said, "is part of Robert Moses' plan for ribbon parks connecting New York City with several state parks on Long Island."

I stood up and held onto the front seat to listen more closely to my mother and to get a better view. Rita looked out the window, barely paying attention.

"Who, Mommy?" I asked.

"Robert Moses. He's the Chairman of the Long Island State Park Commission," she answered.

"Far too powerful if you ask me," commented my father, who rarely had anything good to say about anyone. "Jones Beach was the only original idea he ever had. He just kept repeating it."

As if he had thrown water on a campfire that she painstakingly started, my mother fell silent. Disappointed that the lesson was over, I sat down and didn't ask any further questions.

About one hour after we left our home, we passed some stately pine trees. "Look at those trees!" I said, rising to my knees on the car seat to see better.

"Aren't they grand, Pumpkin?" my mother responded.

"Those trees once lined the driveway to August Belmont's estate," my father said.

"Wasn't he a wealthy banker in the nineteenth century?" my mother asked.

"Nineteenth century?" Rich asked, turning away from the window.

"The 1800s," my mother clarified. "Belmont Lake State Park used to be part of an old estate."

"He purchased the land to encourage his son's interest in hunting, fishing and horse racing," my father, an avid camper and hiker, added.

After exiting the parkway, my father drove north along Deer Park Avenue. There, we joined my mother's girlhood friend Adele and her family at Arlyn Oaks Model Homes. The developer was building tract houses on Long Island's pine barrens to accommodate the burgeoning migration of World War II veterans and their families. Impressed with the model homes, my parents selected a tri-level house to be built on a lot two blocks away from the ranch house Aunt Adele and her husband, Uncle Frank, had chosen.

When my parents told us we were moving, Trish and I were delighted. The suburbs, with their wooded lots and nearby truck farms, were the country to us. Unlike our older siblings, we didn't have any friends we would miss. Even though they would have bigger bedrooms and more privacy, my brothers and my oldest sister were less enthusiastic.

They resented leaving their friends and moving to a town where we had no connection to our neighbors.

We moved to Deer Park in mid-December 1958, and spent Christmas in our new home surrounded by packed boxes. Many of those boxes were moved to the basement, where they remained until my husband and I helped my parents pack for their final move to North Carolina thirty years later.

The parish church that was originally built to serve Polish farmers was too small to accommodate the large influx of Italian Catholics in Deer Park. The Vets Hall, two blocks from our home, was used for Sunday masses and for catechism. On Saturday mornings, my mother would send me by myself to attend religious instruction. Like Grand Central Station at rush hour, the hall was busy and chaotic. I hung back while the nuns hastily divided us into smaller groups, and we were sent to sit with our teacher in a corner of the large hall. I was never placed in the same class twice. After attending a few times and finding the classes boring and the nuns intimidating, it was easier and less scary to bypass the Vets Hall and walk ten more blocks to Geiger Lake, where I played alone in the woods.

This worked well until it was time to make my First Communion. Warned by other children that I needed to attend catechism that Saturday, I walked over to the Vets Hall. The children lined up in front of the portable confessional. From their chatter, I realized I was unprepared.

"What am I supposed to do?" I whispered.

"You don't know?"

"Shssh! Don't talk so loud."

The other children recited the beginning prayer while I tried to memorize it. When it was my turn, I knelt before the priest and began, "Bless me Father." I faltered.

"For I have sinned," the priest prompted.

"For I have sinned. It— It has ..."

"This is my first confession," the priest corrected.

"This is my first confession." Now I had to come up with some sins. That was the easy part. I chose some generic ones, like not listening to my parents. The priest then asked me to recite the Act of Contrition. I had no idea what that was.

"Go tell Sister you don't know how to make your confession."

I stood up and looked around. Apprehensive, I moved toward two nuns who were talking to each other. I looked for a way to escape. Before

I could blend in with the children who had successfully made their First Confession, the priest called to me, "Not that way! Go tell Sister!"

The nuns stopped talking and looked my way. Trapped, I started crying. The nuns came over to see what was wrong. They spoke with the priest and then called my mother.

My mother drove over to the Vet's Hall and picked me up. When we got home, she ordered Rita to teach me the Act of Contrition. Although I didn't understand words like "contrition" and "penance," I did understand that being naughty was sinful and that I was in danger of going to hell. Frightened, I made my First Confession that evening after I memorized the prayer. The next day I made my First Communion along with Tommy, Aunt Adele' and Uncle Frank's youngest son.

After the service, we went to the local diner for breakfast. While I ate my eggs, Uncle Frank entertained the two families with stories about his days as a jockey at Aqueduct Race Track. To everyone's amusement, he taught me to say his full name, "Francis Aloysius McKnight Flynn."

"Francith Alawitcheth McKnight Flynn," I repeated. Everyone laughed.

"No, honey," he said, wiping his lips with his paper napkin. "Francis Aloysius McKnight Flynn."

"Francith Aloywicketh McKnight Flynn," I repeated.

"Break it down," my mother advised while she sipped her coffee.

"Let's try 'Francis,'" Uncle Frank said. "Can you say Francis?"

"Francis."

"Good. Now say Aloysius."

"Aloysius."

"Yes, that's good. Say Francis Aloysius."

"Francis Aloysius."

"Good! Good!" He tapped his fork against his plate, smiling. "Now put it all together. Francis Aloysius McKnight Flynn."

"Francis Aloysius McKnight Flynn." I stumbled over the "s's" but with practice I was able to repeat it without error.

When I heard him proclaim, "You got it!" I beamed with pride and never forgot his name.

When we first moved, Deer Park didn't have a parochial school, so my parents sent Trish and me to the public grade school a block and a half from our new house. My older siblings went to Catholic high schools in different towns. For the first time, my teacher wasn't a nun.

I liked that. It made it more relaxed, less frightening. However, I was confused when the teacher didn't make the sign of the cross at the start and end of the morning prayer. When I went home I asked my parents about it. They told me it had to do with the Protestants in class. I didn't understand what a Protestant was. In our old neighborhood everyone was Catholic. I never questioned it. Apparently, Protestants were some peculiar group who didn't make the sign of the cross. The nuns who taught catechism explained it wasn't the Protestant kids' fault, since their parents hadn't been taught the true religion. God would forgive them if they died before reaching adulthood.

Although there were no longer any nuns to frighten me, I was still taunted by the other children. They ridiculed me for being dirty and unkempt. I went to my teacher, who told me to ignore them. When that didn't stop the teasing, I went to my teacher again. She yelled at me for being a crybaby and a tattletale. Confused and frightened, I choked back the tears. I had no idea how to stop the teasing.

Home wasn't any safer than school. One morning while I was getting dressed for grade school, my sister Trish complained to our father that she wasn't feeling well. Our father unexpectedly flew into a rage and said, "Stop whining and get ready for school!"

Trish returned to our bedroom and got dressed as ordered, but continued to cry. Our father, his belt in his hand, burst into our bedroom. "Maggie, go downstairs!" he ordered.

Terrified, I obeyed, but remained frozen at the bottom of the steps crying. I listened to Trish's screams while he beat her. Trish finally came out to the landing dressed only in her underwear. That was odd. What happened to her dress? I couldn't sort it out. Something was terribly wrong.

Our father came out of our bedroom. "Go to bed," he ordered Trish. Turning to me, he yelled, "What are you crying about? Go to school!"

Fearing a beating, I hurried out of the house.

The lack of nurturance at home made me easy prey at school. My parents rarely told me to shower. Most of my clothes were hand-me-downs that were tattered and stained. No one made sure they were clean and ironed. Desperate for acceptance, I tolerated unkind behavior from my peers. In fifth grade a classmate started talking to me, which I mistook for true friendship. While standing by the school door waiting for the doors to be unlocked, she and the other girls in her clique shared their picture cards of celebrities. At first, they allowed me to stand on the periphery and watch.

"What do you have on your legs?" I was asked when one of the girls noticed I didn't have cotton socks on.

"Stockings," I replied.

"Then where is the seam?"

"They're new. They don't have a seam."

"Those aren't stockings, retard," the girls laughed. "Your mother wouldn't let you wear stockings."

"She said it was okay. She got them for me. See?" I pulled up on the stocking.

"Those aren't—" Before she could finish, one of the teachers opened the school doors. After we filed past the teacher, the girls began whispering and giggling while pointing and glancing at me, saying, "You're ugly. You smell."

"I don't care what you think," I said, and stood as tall as I could while suppressing my tears.

"That's the problem," they replied, sneering. "You don't care if you smell."

Unwanted and unbidden the tears started as I entered our classroom. My teacher called me out into the hallway. "What's wrong? Why are you crying?"

"I don't know," I whispered, confused by my classmates' behavior and wanting to protect one of the few girls who would talk to me.

My teacher, angry with me for not confiding in him, began scolding me whenever I cried. Since it was difficult to suppress my tears, I withdrew. In the mornings, I stopped waiting for the school bus with the other children and walked alone to school. During lunch, I walked home and ate alone. In this way I avoided the teasing that triggered the crying in the first place.

Either my teacher or my parents requested that I see the speech therapist. No one ever explained why I needed this. I probably had a lisp, since the speech therapist had me practice pronouncing "s", "z", and sounds like "th." Once, while standing in the lunch line, my speech therapist stopped to talk to me in front of all the other children. He made me run through one of the speech exercises. "Good, much better," he said, obviously proud of himself and oblivious that he had just humiliated me in front of my classmates.

"What a retard! You don't even know how to talk!" my classmates taunted. When it was time for my next speech appointment, I hid so my teacher would forget and not send me.

Around the same time, Uncle Frank started coming over in the afternoons to visit. My mother, who transcribed court reporters' notes, was in her basement office typing. Trish and I were in the family room watching television when Uncle Frank sat with us on the couch. His breath smelled of beer.

While I was snuggling up against Uncle Frank, he surreptitiously unzipped my jeans and slipped his hands under my panties. At first, it felt pleasant in the same lazy way as having your head stroked. I didn't try to stop him until I became fully aware of what he was doing. I got up and zipped up my pants, then hurried upstairs to hide in my bedroom. As I was about to cross the threshold into my room, I realized Uncle Frank could corner me and no one would hear or see what was going on. I ran downstairs and hid in the kitchen.

Peeking around the doorjamb, I saw Uncle Frank go upstairs. Creeping to the bottom of the stairs, I watched while he peered through the keyhole of my bedroom and the bathroom. When he started back down the stairs, I ran back into the kitchen. Uncle Frank followed me and cornered me by the sink.

Frightened, I stood there frozen while he lifted up my blouse and unzipped my pants. He stuck his finger into my vagina while he sucked my pubescent breast. After he released me, I adjusted my bra and pulled down my top. Our eyes met.

"You aren't going to tell anyone, are you?" Uncle Frank said.

Terrified, I shook my head no.

Shortly after Uncle Frank raped me with his fingers, he moved his family to Lake Ariel, Pennsylvania, where he opened a luncheonette. During a summer visit, Trish and I slept on a bed behind his store. In the middle of the night, I was wakened when he laid down in between Trish and me and tried to slide his hand into my pajama pants. I rolled over onto my stomach, pushing his hand away. His breath stunk of beer.

I tried to stay awake. As my eyelids closed, he tried again to slip his hand between my legs. I stirred and pushed him away again. I was too frightened and too sleepy to call for help. The night was as long as eternity while I struggled to stay awake. My weary body failed me. I fell asleep, no longer able to fend him off. When I woke up in the morning he was gone. I didn't know if he had fingered me or not. I wondered if he had touched Trish.

After my family returned home to Long Island, I asked Trish, "Is Uncle Frank bothering you?"

"Yes," she tensely whispered.

I felt a flutter of anxiety in my stomach. "When he's around, let's stick together."

Uncle Frank's presence in our bed became a secret we shared but never talked about. Years later, I learned that Uncle Frank started raping Trish the summer our paternal grandmother died. I was eight years old. Trish was nine. While our parents were in Washington DC for the funeral, we spent the day at Aunt Adele and Uncle Frank's house. Tommy, Uncle Frank's youngest son, played outside with me. Trish often stayed behind in the house. I remember being puzzled by her absence, but had no idea what was going on. My older siblings, who spent the days with their friends, would pick us up at the end of the day and walk us home, where we would sleep safely in our own beds.

# Rejection

Pushing the memory of the sexual assaults out of my mind, I began junior high in September 1964. For the first time in a couple of years, Lisa, my next-door neighbor, was going to the same school as I was.

At home, Lisa and I were the best of friends. We had taken pride in being tomboys. Together we climbed trees and built forts in the woods. In fourth grade we formed a book club, and sat together on Lisa's patio reading and trading mystery books.

Lisa had been more successful than me in forming friendships at school. As we walked the half-mile to the junior high, Lisa's friends joined us. It wasn't long before the other girls began mimicking my speech as if I still spoke with a lisp. Lisa did nothing to stop them.

Laughing, the others said, "Take a thower! No boy ith going to want to take you out. You're queer."

"Your clothes are ugly," Lisa joined in. "You're so square."

Upset by Lisa's betrayal, I shouted, "I don't want to be friends with you anymore!"

Laughing, Lisa and her companions jeered, "What's wrong with you? You can't take a little joke! What a baby!"

I ran ahead and reached school before Lisa and her friends. Taking my place in line, I sniffled and looked down. Another child noticed and asked what was wrong.

"Nothing," I said as the tears spilled over my lower eyelids.

The other child called out to one of the teachers. When she asked what was wrong, I began weeping. She sent me to my guidance counselor who, after questioning me, said, "I don't see why you're so upset, Margaret. They aren't your friends."

But I thought they were my friends, especially Lisa. Why didn't he understand it hurt to be rejected by them? It must be wrong for me to be upset. My classmates and my father must be right. *I'm a crybaby.* But no matter how hard I tried I couldn't keep myself from crying. I felt the way I felt.

I considered what my tormenters said. Perhaps I am a loser. Hoping to stop the teasing, I began brushing my teeth every morning and taking regular showers. I shortened my skirts trying to look hip. Even though I was cleaner, neater and dressing better, my peers continued to ridicule me. When I cried the kids teased more, so I resolved never to cry in front of them again. Suppressing my tears decreased the teasing, but didn't win acceptance. I walked to and from school alone. I ate lunch alone. After school I retreated to my bedroom, where I read and did my homework. I was never invited to birthday parties, or ever asked to go to a school dance.

Although most kids ridiculed and rejected me, a couple of boys often spoke kindly to me. Dan was one of those boys. As I was walking through the breezeway that connected the old school building with the new junior high, I saw Dan sitting on the ledge with several of his classmates waiting for the school bus. There was a school dance on Friday, and I hoped Dan would take me. I stopped walking and said, "Hi, how are you?"

"Fine, Margaret."

"Do you want to go to the dance with me?" I blurted.

Dan grimaced. "No, Margaret. I'm sorry."

The other children began laughing. What an idiot! Why did I do that? Girls aren't supposed to ask boys out. In shame, I ran out the door.

Sammy, a fat Jewish boy, called me that night and asked me to go to the dance with him. I was delighted to be asked, and quickly said yes. When the other kids heard about it, they started taunting me. "Just because Dan won't go out with you doesn't mean you have to go out with Sammy."

I cancelled my date with Sammy, even though I liked him. I felt ashamed. I hurt his feelings just to gain acceptance by the other kids. It didn't work. I became more isolated. A few years later, I bumped into Sammy at the high school. He had slimmed down and had a small network of friends. I realized I could have been part of that group if I hadn't betrayed him. I vowed never to yield to that kind of social pressure again.

Later that year, my mother drove Dan home from school. While sitting in the backseat, he asked me how I did on the history exam.

"I got an A." I lifted my head, straightened my back and smiled.

"Gee, Margaret, you're smart."

"You're smart, too. What did you get?"

"I only got a B."

"That's a good grade."

My mother stopped the car in front of Dan's house. After he got out, she turned around and scolded me, "Don't ever tell a boy what grade you got. They won't go out with you if you get better grades than them."

Since no one asked me to any of the school dances, including my junior or senior prom, my mother's warning appeared accurate. Ashamed, I hid the date of the junior prom from her and spent the evening alone in my room. A year later, she learned that a friend's daughter was going to the senior prom. "What's wrong with you?" my mother berated me. "Why don't you have a date? There must be someone who will take you."

I fled to my room. The night of the prom, I laid on my bed alone, sobbing. "God, please help me," I prayed.

Gym class was another place where my classmates ostracized me. Whenever I failed to get the ball or make a play, they laughed at me. I came to believe I was clumsy and inept. When teams were picked I was always the last to be chosen, until Gioamia helped me.

I knew Gioamia from grade school. Her father died when she was a toddler. Gioamia's mother, who was blind, supplemented what little Welfare gave her with whatever she could earn teaching piano. After her father's death, Gioamia helped her mother raise her younger sister, who in sharp contrast to Gioamia was a girly girl. Gioamia was strong and muscular. Her arms and legs were unusually hairy for a girl. She didn't shave them. The other children teased her, calling her queer. Gioamia and I were friendly with each other, but since I was in a college track and she in an art track, gym class was about the only class we ever had together.

During a basketball game, I attempted to throw the ball into the basket and failed. The other girls began laughing and saying, "What a dork!"

When the other girls left for the locker room, Gioamia approached me. "Margaret, you can play better than them. You're short, so it's hard for you to get a basket, but you can guard."

I was startled. Gioamia was the first person to ever suggest I had any athletic ability.

"Let me show you how," she said, picking up the ball. "Guard me. Stay close."

Gioamia taught me to aggressively follow the person with the ball, making it difficult for them to score. Whenever I could, I stole the ball

and passed it to Gioamia, who then scored. Whenever the teacher made
Gioamia captain, Gioamia always called me first to be on her team. I felt
good. Having just one ally decreased the verbal assaults from the other
girls.

When it was announced that girls were needed for the cheerleading
squad, I mustered up the courage and went to practice. There were no
adults present.

"What are you doing here, Margaret?" the other girls said, sneering.
"You shouldn't be here."

Crushed, I fled out the back door of the gym and ran across the
athletic field. The rejection by the cheerleading squad further convinced
me no one cared for or wanted me. I was a nobody. Even my father told
me I was "a pill." "No one will ever want you," he said. "You're selfish
and have no sense of humor. No guy will ever want you."

Hattie, like Gioamia, was one of the few girls who didn't reject me. I
remember sitting in the second row from the classroom door when
Hattie, who had just moved into town, was escorted into my ninth grade
algebra class by the assistant principal. Our eyes met and we smiled
broadly at each other. I immediately liked this short, well-groomed girl. I
barely noticed that she was black.

Following on the heels of Italian Americans, black families were
buying houses on the east side of town near the state psychiatric center.
My parents didn't object to the new residents, and welcomed anyone my
siblings or I brought home regardless of race, ethnicity or religion.

I began making the twenty-minute walk over to Hattie's house once
or twice a week after school. Hattie took me into the garage to show me
the big antique car her parents inherited from her grandfather. The
interior was luxurious, and we would sit together in the back the entire
afternoon, talking and sharing our hopes and dreams for the future.

While I don't recall Hattie and I ever discussing race, it would be
naïve to say race had no impact on our friendship. Hattie and I never
went to the movies or did anything else together. We never included each
other in parties or events at each other's houses.

Although social pressures constrained my friendship with Hattie, I
treated the black kids just like I treated the white kids. Perhaps the black
kids respected this, because they never ridiculed or teased me. Or maybe
they left me alone because it would have been too dangerous for a black
kid to harass a white girl. Or maybe their personal experiences with

discrimination enabled them to empathize with my low social status. In any event, they left me alone.

Since none of the white kids would let me sit with them during lunch, I took a bold step and asked Hattie if I could sit at the end of the table where all the black kids sat. After conferring with her friends, I was allowed to sit at their table with one or two seats separating me from their group. From time to time we would talk briefly with each other. This arrangement decreased my loneliness even though I was never fully accepted into their group. We all knew I wasn't black. The racial barrier existed whether we wanted it there or not.

The white kids harassed me and told me I shouldn't be sitting with the blacks, but they never offered me a place at their table. Remembering my mistake with Sammy, I ignored them, continuing to sit in this no man's land halfway between the white and black communities.

My eldest sister, Rita, when she was home from college during spring break, asked to walk with me to the public library. Suspecting that I was having a difficult time at home and at school, she asked, "How are things going? Is everything okay?"

Although I didn't consider the way my parents and peers treated me as abuse or neglect, I did know I was lonely and unhappy. Rita explained counseling to me, and said, "Why don't you speak to your high school guidance counselor? Maybe you could be seen by the school psychologist."

When I went to my guidance counselor, he didn't take me seriously. "You're only going through a stage," he said. "High school is the best time of your life. You don't need a counselor. Anyway, you need your parents' permission to see a psychologist."

Frightened that my parents would ridicule such a request, I never asked them. I became more isolated and depressed.

Simon, like Dan, was one of the boys I had known since grade school and who had always been kind to me. Whenever we were seated next to each other or the other children weren't looking, Simon and I talked about history and other common interests. As long as we weren't too public about our friendship, the other kids didn't harass or pressure Simon. I guess we had a similar arrangement as I had with Hattie.

In our junior year, as we were exiting our American History class, Simon stopped me and said, "Will you go to the dance with me?"

I couldn't believe it. Simon was finally asking me out. I smiled broadly and answered "Yes" without hesitation.

Simon turned back to join his friends from Beta, a local gang that promoted itself as a fraternity. He hesitated, and then turned back to me. "I can't do this," he said. "Margaret, I didn't mean it." His friends started laughing hysterically.

"No one wants to go out with you!" they jeered as I hurried out of the classroom.

*What a fool!* I thought while I hurried to my next class. How could I have fallen for such a joke? What made me think anyone would take me out? How could Simon do that to me? He had never been mean before. Did he have to prove to Beta he wasn't my friend to be accepted into their gang? Was he supposed to humiliate me further by standing me up after I had bought a dress and gone to the beauty parlor? Was I supposed to be left all dressed up on some street corner alone and crying?

Several months later when he saw me at the library, he sat down and spoke to me. "Hi, Margaret, how are you doing?"

"I'm fine," I replied uneasily.

"I am so sorry." His emotional distress was obvious. "I feel so bad about what I did to you. I'm really sorry. Joining Beta was the worst mistake I ever made. I was trying to belong. I quit shortly after that. Hurting you was a big mistake."

"That's okay, Simon, I understand." But it wasn't okay. He had been a coward. Fearing he, too, would be ridiculed and shunned, he concealed his true opinion about me except when we were alone. I should have demanded more from him and not let him off the hook so easily, but I knew what it was like to want to belong. He behaved just as poorly as I had with Sammy.

Oddly, I was also asked to join Beta either before or just after Simon. I was approached by Beta while I was at the local luncheonette on the corner of Lake and Deer Park Avenues. I was startled and excited by the invitation. I was also suspicious. When I got home, I went downstairs to my mother's office and asked her what I should do.

"What do you want to do?" she asked me. "What do you think is right?"

Fearing Beta only wanted me to do their homework, or they were setting me up for a mean trick, I decided to turn down the invitation. My mother was relieved. The other kids were incredulous. No one had ever turned down a bid from Beta before. They laughed at my stupidity.

In my senior year, Beta was at the center of racial tension. Melvin, a talented black athlete and drummer, flirted with one of the white girls from Beta, almost sparking a riot. The school administration considered cancelling the Senior Awards Assembly. Instead, all the teachers nervously patrolled the bleachers and gym floor. If I had joined Beta, I thought, I would have been caught between Beta and the black kids. It was a good thing I told Beta no.

Teachers and other adults had repeatedly told me that college would be better. I wouldn't be taunted and excluded the way I had been the last twelve years. College students were more mature, and I would find acceptance there.

Throughout high school, I clung to the hope this prediction raised. Unable to find acceptance among my peers, I threw myself into my schoolwork, graduating eleventh out of a class of 450 students. I had applied to three colleges, and was accepted by all of them. I chose the one farthest away from home, even though with a Regent's Scholarship I could have gone to any New York State college for free. With no one to advise me I chose the University of Denver, which admitted me to their elite Scholar's Program and granted me a four-year full-tuition scholarship.

As high school graduation approached, Mr. Grodner, my twelfth-grade English teacher, asked me about my future plans. I told him I wanted a career, so I wasn't going to marry and have children.

"Margaret," he said, "you can do both. You should read Betty Friedan's book, *The Feminine Mystique*."

Reading Friedan's book opened up new possibilities and an outlet for my growing rage. While I prepared for college, I began arguing for equal opportunity. Although this garnered more ridicule from my peers, it gave me hope for a better future.

Shortly after my eighteenth birthday in late August 1970, I nervously stood gazing out the terminal window, watching the planes taxi to and from the runway. My parents stood next to me. In a short while, I would be on one of those planes for the first time in my life.

The announcer called my flight. Nervous, I quickly gave my parents pecks on their cheeks and fled down the gangway. I didn't want to miss this opportunity to escape the stultifying confinement of their home. I took a window seat and watched while the jet climbed through the clouds. After flying over the Mississippi River, I looked down and saw the American plains. I had never seen land so flat before. The farm crops of corn and wheat turned the land into one enormous patchwork quilt.

After landing at Stapleton Airport, I disembarked down the stairs and started to cross the tarmac toward the terminal. "Look at that!" I heard another passenger say. I turned and looked west. The snowcapped peaks of the Rocky Mountains rose straight up out of the plain. I was stunned by their austere beauty so unlike the lower, flatter, lush Adirondacks back home.

I took a taxi to my campus dormitory and spent the first week decorating my room, attending freshman orientation and exploring the campus. At the far end of the chapel garden and up a long set of steps stood the campus library, housed in a Gothic structure built in 1932. It quickly became one of my favorite haunts. I would settle into one of the old leather chairs in front of a huge fireplace to study late into the night.

While I was searching through the card catalog that lined a wide hallway with arched windows and a checkered floor, Vance, a classmate from my Scholar's Program art class, stopped to talk. Accustomed to being an outcast, I was surprised and excited that anyone, especially a boy, would initiate a conversation with me.

I smiled shyly. He asked me to join him at the corner deli for Sunday supper since the dorm dining halls were closed. Without hesitation I agreed, and this began our regular Sunday dinners together. Sitting by a small window at the deli, we talked passionately about religion, politics and sex. Thirty years later, an acquaintance would enlighten me that you weren't supposed to talk about those things. My parents, despite their abuse and neglect of my siblings and me, were intelligent people interested in the world around them. Every night at the family dinner table, they passionately discussed religion and politics. During a childhood marred by abuse and neglect, these were treasured moments, bright lights in a dark tunnel. I delighted in having a boyfriend who also enjoyed talking about serious issues.

Vance and I spoke intensely about the Vietnam War and women's rights. But mostly we argued about God. I was no longer certain who Jesus was, or if there was even a God. In fact, I had stopped going to church when I was sixteen. On a Sunday morning in February 1968, my mother woke Trish and me to tell us that our father had a heart attack the night before and was in the intensive care unit at Good Samaritan Hospital. My mother, who never went to church, insisted we attend mass before going to visit him. She drove us through a blizzard to St. Cyril and Methodius in time for the service being held in the church basement. We sat crowded together on folding chairs with our hats and coats on. Although I remember the priest delivering one of the best sermons I had ever heard, I cannot remember anything he said. The sermon had absolutely nothing to do with my life. My father could die, threatening my plans to go to college and start a new life free of abuse and neglect. My mother was obviously comforted by the mass, but it left me feeling numb. I had a deep sense that I no longer belonged there.

Although my attendance at catechism had always been poor, I never questioned Catholic doctrine. I obediently went to Sunday mass with my father and siblings. While my father recovered, I began wondering why God required Sunday worship in a building built by human hands. If God was omnipresent and omniscient, couldn't He hear and respond to my prayers no matter where I uttered them?

Going to mass was like saying I still believed Catholic doctrine when I no longer did. I didn't want to pretend. I made up my mind. I carefully planned what I would do. On a Sunday morning shortly after my father returned to work, I stayed in my room with the door closed. Trish had already gone downstairs. I paced the floor waiting and listening. Sure enough, my father came knocking on the door. I stopped, frozen in the middle of the room.

"Margaret," he called. "Time for church."

I took a deep breath and called out, "I'm not going."

"Oh, aren't you feeling well?"

"I'm fine. I'm not going."

I listened while my father lingered by the door. Was he angry? Would he make me go to church?

I heard him walk away and go downstairs. He didn't yell or scold. He just left. I was relieved.

When my family returned from church, I went downstairs and joined them at the breakfast table. No one questioned me about church. We pretended nothing important had happened. I ate my eggs and bacon. Several weeks later I received a letter from my brother, Rich, who was attending seminary in Hartford, Connecticut. My parents had spoken to him. Rich urged me to go to mass. I wrote back that I could pray at home just as easily as at church.

Fearful I was committing a mortal sin, I was too frightened to renounce Catholicism totally. I continued to identify myself as Catholic.

I waited. Nothing happened. God did not send a lightning bolt to strike me down. I became bolder. Attending college freed me from parental scrutiny, allowing me to openly proclaim myself an agnostic. Whether God existed was irrelevant to my life.

The years of abuse and neglect had left me angry and bitter. I told Vance God wasn't there. "Everyone is alone," I added. "The only thing you have is yourself. You make who you are. If you get knocked down, it is your own courage that gets you to stand up again, not God."

I stopped praying. Prayer never did me any good. It seemed that asking God for something was one sure way not to get it. All the praying, pleading and begging didn't end my isolation. Yet, if I didn't pray to God and ask for His help, whom could I turn to? Who else besides God would listen to me? But maybe God wasn't there at all.

Vance, a devout Christian Scientist, had enough confidence in his own faith to listen to my rants. He challenged my agnosticism and accused me of running away from God. I denied it, but I worried he was right. I was lonely and afraid I would never receive the help I desperately needed.

The night before Vance and I were to leave campus to visit our families for Christmas, I went to his dorm room. We sat on his bed hugging and necking. He moved on top of me fully clothed. I felt his erection through his pants. He suddenly pulled away.

"What's wrong?" I asked, sitting up.

"I'm not sure we should be doing this," he replied.

"Why not?"

"I'm not sure it is right," he replied.

"What's wrong with us loving each other?"

"I'm confused. I need to work something out."

"What's bothering you?" I asked.

"There's someone back home."

"You never mentioned her before," I said. My heart rate increased. My head started spinning. I felt the panic starting, but was able to suppress it and choke back my tears.

"When I'm home, I want to date."

I wanted to be mature about it. I denied my distress to myself as well as to him. "That's all right," I said.

The next morning, I flew home. There were no old friends eager to see me. Long hours sequestered in my bedroom were broken up by solitary walks to and from the public library, giving me ample time to reflect on my efforts to be independent from others, without any strong emotional ties. I was trying to make myself into a machine. I fought with myself. *Yes, I love Vance. No, I don't.* I naively convinced myself that if I loved him, he would return that love.

When we returned to school, we had dinner at the deli as usual. As I placed my fork in the center of the plate, he said, "I just want us to be good friends."

"What are you talking about?" I asked.

"I'm afraid to kiss and hug you. I don't want us to end up in bed."

"What's wrong with that?"

"We need to break up," he said. "I don't love you."

"Oh." I began crying.

"I just want to be friends," he repeated.

"I can't bear that," I said, shattered. My heart was pounding and I felt nauseous. I had been so foolish. "Don't call me any more," I told him as I left the deli.

Desperate for love, I called him a week later. "It isn't natural for us not to be together," I told him.

"I don't love you," he replied.

"Don't say that," I pleaded.

Like Pookie Adams in *The Sterile Cuckoo* I clung desperately to Vance, who eventually told me, "I don't want you to come to me or me to come to you."

All the crying and begging didn't change how he felt. There wasn't anyone I could turn to. I had invested most of my time and energy in Vance and hadn't established a supportive network of friends. Heartbroken, I sat in the small chapel in the center of the garden below the library. I found some comfort in its simple interior of pale pink walls, arched stained-glass windows and polished-wood pews. I prayed, but God didn't send anyone to hold me and love me. What was I to do now?

I couldn't sleep. I tossed and turned each night, waking up exhausted. I considered leaving school. I became apathetic, losing interest in all activities. I began avoiding other people. I sought help from Dr. Valet, the psychiatrist at the college medical clinic. Since I was under twenty-one he could only see me for a few sessions without my parents' permission.

"How are you coping?" he asked.

"I'm reading books, studying and writing in my journal," I replied.

"None of those things includes other people," he observed.

*Other people?* Who was going to spend time with me? There was no one except myself. I hung on until spring break. Feeling disconnected, I called my father and told him I was dropping out of college.

"That's okay," he replied, making no attempt to discourage me. "How can I say anything? After all, I never finished."

After withdrawing from college, I returned to New York and accepted a job as a claims representative for a car insurance company. I was stuck. Vance's rejection proved I was unlovable. I would be alone forever and never be anything more than a secretary. I became more and more depressed. My father said I needed to grow up and stop being such a baby. Late one night, while everyone else in the house was sleeping, I got up and intentionally burned my arm. In November 1971, I was admitted to a state psychiatric center after threatening suicide.

While I was in the hospital, the social worker encouraged me to return to school. She helped me complete my application to the local community college. On my behalf, she also applied to the Office of Vocational Rehabilitation for financial aid. Six weeks later, on December 15, 1971, I was discharged to the care of my parents.

While I was away at college, Trish finally had our parents' undivided attention; our brothers and eldest sister no longer lived at home. Shortly after returning home, I went into the dinette to get my breakfast. Trish was there, standing by the glass door. She turned to me and said, "Why did you have to come home? You've spoiled everything."

# Gifts

Knowing I wasn't wanted, I continued to intentionally burn my arms and began overdosing on my medication. After my fifth suicide attempt, my father took me to see a psychiatrist in the center of town. The psychiatrist told my father I needed to choose my own therapist. I suggested I call Dr. Howard, who I knew from the hospital's rehabilitation center.

Dr. Howard agreed to see me if I would promise to call him whenever I felt like taking my own life. I made the promise and entered treatment with him. With his help and support, I enrolled at Suffolk Community College. Two years later, despite the continuing conflict at home, I graduated with honors, with an associate's degree in general studies.

Although I stopped trying to kill myself, I was still severely depressed and anxious. I continued to burn my arms. I did not make any significant progress until I moved out of my parents' home to complete the last two years of my undergraduate education at Richmond College on Staten Island. The Office of Vocational Rehabilitation paid my college tuition and purchased my books.

For the next two years I lived alone in a studio apartment. Although I excelled academically, I was socially isolated. Needing to save money, I walked to and from school. At first it was a struggle to climb up the steep hill near my apartment. My weight dropped to 103 pounds but I grew stronger. Every Saturday, I traveled by ferry and train to see Dr. Howard. I came to accept my life the way it was and focused on what I had. Without my noticing it, the suicidal thoughts and self-harming behavior stopped. After two years, I no longer felt depressed. I began to think I could handle things myself, and considered terminating therapy with Dr. Howard. I paced the floor for two hours while I thought about not seeing him anymore. The idea of trying to make it on my own, without his support, frightened me.

During my next therapy session, I asked him if he thought I was ready to end therapy. He replied, "I think you know."

Feeling affirmed, I stood up and asked, "May I hug you goodbye?"

He opened his arms wide as I stepped into his embrace. "If you ever need my help again," he said, "I will be here." Neither one of us knew he wouldn't be able to keep that promise.

At his urging, I had begun volunteering at the local state psychiatric center. I co-led a poetry group with one of the staff there. The experience was very positive, and I decided to major in psychology as well as women's studies. After a few months, the hospital staff recommended me for a part-time job. I worked twenty hours on the weekends as a direct care worker while I finished my undergraduate degree.

Although I have no clear memory of it, my husband, Lyndon, tells me we first met during the new employee orientation. He says I smiled constantly. I don't recall seeing him, but I do remember how happy and excited I was to be getting off disability and to finally have a job I enjoyed.

My first clear memory of Lyndon was when he strode onto the ward. Both staff and clients noticed this strong, muscular black man whose erect posture misled people into thinking he was over six feet tall when in fact he was only five foot eleven. He was wearing paisley polyester bell-bottom slacks and a blue nylon shirt with black cuffs and a black collar. Impeccably clean and neat, he dared to wear white-soled shoes that were all the rage that summer. Despite his well-manicured fingernails, Lyndon was a man's man. Other men quickly realized they were outmatched, and never directly competed with him.

I recall standing at the nursing station when Lyndon was first introduced to me. He spoke with an accent I had never heard before. There was a hint of Britain in his grammar, syntax and word usage.

"Where are you from?" I asked.

"Trinidad and Tobago," he replied.

"Where's that?"

"In the Caribbean near Venezuela."

Lyndon's accent was thick. I had to listen carefully. I liked the way he pronounced my nickname: "Moggie." I didn't correct him. Unfortunately Reggie, a coworker, did.

"It's Maggie," Reggie told him.

"Reggie!" I yelled. "Leave him alone. Don't you think if I minded, I would have corrected him myself? I like the way he says my name."

But the damage was done. Lyndon, not wanting to sound different or ignorant, corrected his pronunciation despite my protests.

On a Saturday evening, he and I took a group of clients out to play volleyball. When a ball was hit into a person's area, Lyndon, unlike many men, didn't come charging into their area to get the ball. Instead, he gave each client and staff member, regardless of gender or ability, a chance to play.

I caught myself flirting with him. He was sexy. Frightened by my emotions, I tried to end my attraction to him. I told myself I was looking for trouble if I started dating a black man. Hadn't I had enough trouble? What was I doing?

Concerned about my taking the late-night bus alone, he began driving me home from work. He was always a gentleman. I felt safe with him. He brought stability to my life that I never had before. Realizing I might never have another chance, I put aside my fears and embraced the opportunity for some happiness.

On a sunny Saturday morning eight months after I met Lyndon, I received a telephone call from Mr. Finlay, the director of the rehab center when I was a patient there.

"Oh, hi, Mr. Finlay," I said, even as I wondered, *Why is he calling me?* I hadn't seen him in over a year.

"We've been trying to get hold of you."

"I've been at school. And I work at the state psychiatric center."

"Yes, I know." Mr. Finlay paused, then said, "I'm sorry we didn't get hold of you sooner. I'm sorry, Maggie, but while Dr. Howard was in Manhattan at a meeting, he had a heart attack."

"What do you mean?" Panic rising in my throat.

"He died, Maggie."

"No. That's not true."

"Yes, Maggie, I'm afraid it is true. He died on Wednesday."

"No. You're lying. That's a cruel joke you're playing on me."

"It isn't a joke. I'm sorry. He died unexpectedly."

"No!" I cried.

"We tried to get hold of you before the funeral."

"I was at school."

"Yes, I understand. His wife knew how close you were, so she asked me to call."

"I need to go now," I said, desperate to escape the truth of what Mr. Finlay was saying.

"Are you sure you'll be okay?"

"Yes, I'm fine," I replied, minimizing what I felt. Before Mr. Finlay could say anything else, I hung up. Grabbing my jacket and wallet, I ran out of my apartment and up the steep hill toward the bus stop. Out of breath, I rounded the corner to see the bus pulling away from the curb. Too distressed to wait for the next bus, I started walking toward St. George.

My mind raced. It didn't seem right. It didn't seem possible that Dr. Howard was no longer at his Long Island home, ready to answer my phone calls. There was so much I wanted to say to him, so much that I neglected to say when he was alive. There were unfinished issues. There were questions I wanted to ask about my history in light of what I was learning at school, questions about some of the things he said and did. There were new insights, new joys I wanted to share with him. I still needed him. How could he leave me?

When I arrived at St. George, there were no buses waiting. Too distressed to wait, I walked all the way to the other side of Staten Island looking for Lyndon. When I finally found him, he became angry and wrongly accused me of having an affair with Dr. Howard. He didn't understand that Dr. Howard was a surrogate parent who I loved more than my own father. Lyndon refused to stay with me. He insisted on going to work and going out with friends later. He drove me home, where he left me to grieve alone.

I curled up in my bed and fell into a fitful sleep. The next morning, I took out the journal I had been keeping since I was in high school. Imitating Anne Frank, I treated my journal like a good friend with whom I could confide my most private thoughts and emotions. Numbed by grief, I wrote a brief, emotionless account of Dr. Howard's death. Months later, I would write him a letter telling him goodbye and reaffirming my commitment to never attempt suicide again. I also promised to never burn or cut myself again. If and when I had self-destructive urges, I promised I would find more acceptable ways to deal with what I was feeling.

With Dr. Howard's help, I had survived. He always said life was going to throw trouble at you, and what mattered is how you dealt with it. It was important not to let it get the best of you. Life threw a curve at Dr. Howard and he lost. He was dead. That was the last battle none of us could win, not even Dr. Howard.

The irony was agonizing. Dr. Howard, who loved and wanted his life, died at the age of thirty-seven. I, who had tried so desperately to die, was still living. He saved my life but couldn't save his own. He loved me and had faith in me. He always believed I could make it. Well, there I was, making it. I was happy. I wanted my life just as strongly as I once wanted death. I loved Dr. Howard. His dying broke my heart. But I now wanted my life. That was the gift he had given me.

In May 1975, a few months after his death, I completed my school-work and graduated with honors. Unsure if I wanted to go to graduate school, I accepted a full-time job at the psychiatric center.

Despite intense arguments, Lyndon and I continued to see each other. We became closer as we worked out our differences and misunder-standings. I noticed I was calmer when I was with him. A few months after graduation, he and I decided to have a baby. Believing in natural childbirth, we decided to have our baby at home and not at a hospital. When I was three months' pregnant, we moved into a basement apartment on Forest Avenue, only half a block from Silver Lake Reservoir and two blocks from a small group of stores that included a butcher shop and a bakery. Staten Island Hospital was two blocks in the other direction.

Two weeks before my due date, I was finishing up my last evening shift before the start of my maternity leave. Mrs. Grant, the charge nurse, called to me in her thick West Indian accent as I was walking past the big white counter that stood in front of the staff offices overlooking the dayroom. The staff had nicknamed that counter the White Elephant. It was fairly useless, and created an obstacle that the young, athletic male staff often had to jump over when an agitated client was attacking someone or was about to throw a chair though the floor-to-ceiling plate-glass windows that lined the dayroom. We often joked about the foolishness of the architect who failed to anticipate the behavior of the people who reside at a state psychiatric center.

Mrs. Grant was a tough old authoritarian black woman who you never wanted to cross. I immediately stopped what I was doing and walked around The White Elephant. Like a child waiting to be spoken to, I stood at the threshold of the medication room, where she had been pouring meds. "Come," she said as she removed a container from the small refrigerator and carried it out to the White Elephant. Latoya, the black shift supervisor, walked out of the staff office carrying some white paper bowls and plastic spoons. I watched Mrs. Grant, with her wrinkled brown hands, scoop out from the container vanilla ice cream she had made fresh just for me. While I savored the sweet, cold, creamy treat, Mrs. Grant, a former midwife, gave me some advice about childbirth.

Not having much experience with elders who wanted to share the wisdom they had acquired over their lifetimes, I didn't take her too seriously.

After we finished eating and had thrown away the bowls, Mrs. Grant told me to wait while she went back into the medication room. I was stunned when this woman, who had never been friendly toward me and who I had always been a little afraid of and therefore avoided, gave me a soft, pink, finely knitted receiving blanket that was too beautiful to ever be used. Thirty years later, I still have that blanket safely tucked away in the linen closet.

Latoya handed me two large shopping bags with diapers and baby clothes. "I'm sorry," she said. "We wanted to give you a proper baby shower, but the other staff members refused."

I knew she was talking about the three white males Lyndon had nicknamed the Dodge Boys, but I didn't give it much thought. I hadn't expected any gifts. "This is awfully generous of you," I said.

Later, after my daughter was born, I would connect Latoya's comment with a conversation I had had with the unit's team leader shortly after I began to show. She urged me to talk to the other staff about my pregnancy.

"I'm happy about having a baby," I told her. "It was planned." It never occurred to me that others would object.

"The other staff don't know that," the team leader said.

"It isn't any of their business," I replied. What did my pregnancy have to do with work? After my daughter was born, Rosa, a black coworker, told me there had been quite a lot of gossip. The white staff members felt sorry for me since I was unmarried and pregnant by a black man.

"I asked them," Rosa said, "'Why do you think Maggie's pregnancy is an accident? Maybe they love each other.'"

I left the ward with Lyndon. We drove home in his white 1968 Chevy Caprice to our basement apartment on the other side of Staten Island. We weren't home long when Linda, my good friend and coworker, called. She asked if I wanted to accompany her to the local supermarket to pick up some boxes she needed to pack her belongings. She was moving to a new apartment.

We arrived at Pathmark around one in the morning, and walked up and down the brightly lit aisles snatching up boxes while the store's employees stocked the shelves. After loading the boxes in Linda's car, she drove me home.

Exhausted, I climbed into bed with Lyndon and fell fast asleep. I woke up around four, and became aware of some abdominal pain that felt like menstrual cramps. I picked up from the nightstand the black book on pregnancy my physician had given me and read about labor.

*"Some women describe labor pains as feeling similar to menstrual cramps."*

I put the book down and woke Lyndon to tell him I might be in labor. We waited. The spasms continued but were irregularly spaced. I called my midwife around six. She told me it was probably false labor, but if the pain continued to call her back.

Lyndon got up and dressed for his eight o'clock class at Staten Island Community College. Before he left, I picked up the black receiver of the rotary phone to call Linda who, months earlier, had agreed to be a birth assistant. "She's coming right over," I told Lyndon as I hung up the phone.

He gathered up his books and gave me a kiss as he walked out the door. Linda arrived a few minutes later.

The pain became more regular. I called the midwife again. We were now sure I was in labor. She would be over later. We were to keep her informed via telephone. I walked around our small apartment, occasionally lying down on the bed.

Lyndon returned home around noon. "I'm definitely in labor," I told him.

We hadn't purchased everything we needed for the home birth. I handed him and Linda a list. "I'll be fine. Just come right back."

Lyndon and Linda left for K-Mart to buy a plastic sheet and some other items. When they returned, Linda was chuckling. "It was nuts," she said. "I tried to explain to the cashier she needed to hurry up because you might have the baby any minute. She didn't understand you weren't in the hospital."

Lyndon and Linda stripped the old, worn, cheaply made full size bed Lyndon's mother had given us. After they put on the plastic sheet and remade the bed, Lyndon went out again. He returned an hour or two later with some new stereo equipment just as the solid hardwood crib was being delivered. I moved into the living room while he and the delivery men set up the crib along the inside wall in our bedroom. I then returned to the bedroom and created a nest of pillows for myself. His job completed, Lyndon went into the living room to set up his new stereo.

The nurse-midwife, Hazel, arrived around 4 p.m. Propped up by pillows, I lay in bed talking and laughing in between contractions. I was in rare form, making jokes about what our baby was going to look like. As the labor pains intensified, I called for Lyndon, telling him he was going to miss the birth of his baby. He didn't respond. Linda went and fetched him from the living room and put him to work rubbing my back.

My emotions fluctuated wildly. As the baby crowned I had a strong desire to quit, to give up, to say, "I've changed my mind. I don't want it." But when I saw her, I felt only astonishment and disbelief. *Is she really mine? Is that my daughter?* And then the joyous feeling, *That was really fine. Let's do it again.*

Hazel handed my daughter to me. While I nursed her, I rubbed and caressed her soft, light-brown skin. Melissa Zoe: sweet life. I never thought I could love and cherish a child as much as I did. When I was depressed and suicidal, I avoided children. They were inexorably connected to the life I found too painful to live. Dr. Howard's unconditional love for me changed all that. I was now able to love and to be loved. At a time when I devalued myself, Dr. Howard predicted that someday I would make a good mother. That surprised me. I didn't really see that in myself. But when I cradled my daughter in my arms, I felt the truth of it. Everything had gone better than planned. It had been a peak experience.

Happier than I had ever been, I continued to be oblivious to other people's gossip, but Lyndon paid more attention to the rumors. "People are saying that our not being married means we aren't fully committed to each other," he said.

"What does the legal status of our relationship have to do with our level of commitment?" I asked while I nursed our daughter.

"I don't know," he replied.

He dropped the subject for several months. But as Melissa grew and more people made comments, we became concerned about our daughter's future acceptance by her peers and teachers. In my mind's eye, I saw her being shunned and rudely questioned about her white mother and black father who weren't even married. Not wanting to inflict any unnecessary pain on her, we decided to marry.

Worried our engagement might trigger strong objections from our families, we decided to marry quietly. After we asked Linda and Ray, another friend from work, to stand up for us, we carefully studied the work schedule posted outside the clerical office. We chose a day in late December when three of us were off. Lyndon was the only one who needed to call in sick.

On our wedding day, he and I drove into St. George and parked in the municipal lot across from the welfare office and behind the stores on Bay Street. As we walked down the steep hill past the library, we could see the ferry terminal with its yellow boats anchored in New York Harbor. The cold December wind bit at my face while we crossed the street to Borough Hall, joining Linda and Ray as they approached the building. Together, we climbed the stairs to the license bureau. Lyndon and I handed the clerk behind the counter our completed application and paid the fee. After a short wait, we were ushered into a small, unattractive and completely forgettable room where the justice of the peace, a stout middle-aged woman, waited.

"Who is the groom?" she asked. Lyndon stepped forward. "The bride?" I took my place beside him.

She directed us to stand facing her and the window. I handed nine-month-old Melissa with her brown skin and black curly hair to Linda who, although she had a common Spanish last name, was fairer than I was. Ray, a dark Puerto Rican, stood beside her. The justice of the peace looked at me and then Linda, and then back at me. She appeared puzzled, but asked no questions, just proceeded to read our vows. "We are gathered here to join together this man and this woman in matrimony...."

I hardly listened while I wondered whose child the justice of the peace thought Melissa was. What perplexed her more? Our crossing of racial boundaries, or that we already had a child?

"If any person can show just cause why they may not be joined together...."

My mother objected to biracial marriages. She said she didn't believe in "mixing the colors." My father said the world wasn't ready for it yet.

"... let them speak now or forever hold their peace."

Melissa began to fuss. We shuffled our feet and looked at each other. We all giggled. Straight-faced and solemn, the justice of the peace continued. "Lyndon, do you take Margaret to be your wedded wife to live together in marriage? Do you promise to love, comfort, honor her..."

Good. No *obey*. I wasn't going to obey anyone. We were in this as equals or not at all.

"... for better or worse, for richer or poorer, in sickness and in health? And forsaking all others, be faithful only to her so long as you both shall live?"

This was the important part. Lyndon and I were in it for life. I was no longer fearful of dying alone, unloved and unwanted.

During the early years of our marriage, we had the usual conflicts over the division of chores and childcare. Lyndon at first objected to my returning to work, but came to enjoy the hours he was alone with our daughter. I struggled, like all working mothers, with balancing all parts of my life. I felt guilty that I wasn't with Melissa more. But staying home was intellectually stagnating.

At my sister Rita's urging, we decided to buy a house, but couldn't find anything within our price range in a middle-class neighborhood on Staten Island. We didn't want to raise our daughter in a slum. After Lyndon completed sixty credits at the community college, he transferred to the State University of New York at Old Westbury on Long Island. The college didn't provide campus housing to married students with children. After looking at off-campus apartments, we realized it would be cheaper to purchase a home in Suffolk County. We found a modest colonial in a multiracial community and moved in at the beginning of the summer.

We both transferred our positions as therapy aides from the new and progressive psychiatric center on Staten Island to an old state hospital near our new home. I was soon bored. There was too much idle time for both clients and staff. I needed something more intellectually challenging. After discussing it with Lyndon, I applied and was accepted into a doctoral program in psychology. I was supposed to start in September 1978, but due to my pregnancy with our second child, I was forced to wait until spring.

Starting graduate school triggered a bout of depression. By pursuing an advanced degree, I was moving further way from my family of origin. My father told me I was overeducated. Once again I was overwhelmed by strong urges to self-harm. Lyndon didn't understand what was going on. He tried offering advice, but that wasn't what I needed. I approached the psychologist assigned to the unit where I worked. He referred me to Dr. Robins, a unit director on the other side of the psychiatric center who also had a small private practice.

I had great difficulty opening up and trusting Dr. Robins. We didn't have the instant connection I felt for Dr. Howard and was hoping for again. During most of our sessions, I curled up in a fetal position on Dr. Robins' couch and said very little. When I went home, I would write and send him a letter. In one of those letters, I finally disclosed Uncle Frank's sexual assault.

"Now that we know what the cause of the problem is, we can fix it," Dr. Robins reassured me.

Over the next several years, I learned how to examine and alter depressive thoughts. I also learned to use progressive muscle relaxation to reduce anxiety. With my new skills, I was able to grow and thrive. During a summer visit, my niece commented on how much my family and I laughed at the dinner table. We were truly happy and blessed.

# Rediscovering Church

In 1985, a year before I completed my doctorate, I became aware of a spiritual emptiness that had been masked by my depression. I missed the weekly ritual of attending mass, of being part of something bigger than myself. During my early childhood, Catholicism had been an anchor in a turbulent sea. It was a place where I would always be accepted. Once a Catholic, we had been taught, always a Catholic.

Despite my longing, I chose not to return to the Catholic Church. For the past decade I had moved in a direction that put me at odds with many of the Vatican's moral teachings. I could no longer accept a church dominated by men, and one that didn't recognize a woman's right to control her own body and destiny.

Around this time, I learned from a public radio broadcast that Unitarian Universalism had no doctrine. They prided themselves on openly and freely discussing differences in religious theology, ethics and morality. Hopeful that I would be allowed to form my own opinions and decide what my values were without the dogma I was subjected to as a Catholic, I looked up the local Unitarian Universalist Church in the yellow pages and began attending Sunday services there. Since prior to our marriage Lyndon and I had agreed we wouldn't have our children baptized, I went alone.

The form of worship was very different at the UU church. It was less formal. There were no vestments or rigid liturgical prayers. Communion wasn't offered. The relationship between clergy and laity was also different. I had been taught to revere Catholic priests. When a priest entered a room, I stood up and addressed him formally as "Father." At the UU church, people called the minister by his first name. At first I was uncomfortable with the implied equality. I wasn't sure what the expectations were. Not knowing how to relate to the minister, I avoided him.

I attended a number of adult religious education programs. Through them, I learned that Unitarianism predated Protestantism. Originally Christian, they rejected Jesus' divinity and the doctrine of the Trinity. John Murray, Universalism's founder, rejected the notion of eternal damnation. He believed that in the end, we would all be saved. In the 1950s, Unitarians moved away from their Christian roots and embraced humanism.

After the social upheaval in the 1960s, large numbers of Catholics converted to Unitarian Universalism. When I joined the UU fellowship, I was part of the majority in the congregation who had rejected their Christian heritage. Not wanting to be told when and with whom we should or shouldn't be sexual or whether we should or shouldn't use birth control or have an abortion, we struggled to establish a new religious identity for ourselves and our families. While we rejected God-talk and modified the old hymns, we still celebrated Christmas and Easter while adding Passover and Kwanza. Longing for a world free of hate and violence, we embraced tolerance and strove to be inclusive.

Inspired by Unitarian Universalism's welcoming atmosphere, I approached Lyndon about taking our two children to church. This was a reversal of the position I had taken when Melissa was three months old. At that time Lyndon had approached me, saying, "My mother wants to know when we are going to have Melissa baptized."

"I thought we had decided not to do that," I replied.

"Perhaps we should," he said.

"But, Lyndon, we don't believe in God."

"But it should be done."

"Why?"

He continued to insist we should conform to social expectations. The tension grew between us. Unable to dissuade him, I asked, "Okay, in what church do you want her baptized?"

I knew Lyndon wouldn't have an answer. He didn't, and the issue was dropped. I won. Now, approximately eight years later, I had an answer to that question. I asked Lyndon to allow me to enroll our children in the UU religious education classes.

At first, he balked. He had been baptized in the Anglican Church, but was raised Catholic by his stepmother. She forced him to become an altar boy. The hypocrisy between her piety and her physical and emotional abuse of him contributed to his cynical views about religion and religious institutions.

"All churches do," he said, "is take your money."

"Unitarian Universalism is different from Catholicism," I argued. "The religious education program at the UU church is well run. It draws from diverse religious traditions."

"Some moral education would be good for the kids," he conceded.

Our children began attending Sunday school at the Stony Brook Unitarian Universalist Fellowship while I went to services. By Catholic standards, Stony Brook was a small congregation with only 150 members. Services were conducted in a simple building, with the sanctuary also serving as a fellowship hall. At the end of each service members would stand up, fold their chairs and stack them at the back. The coffee would be rolled in on carts, and the children would come running into the hall, handing their parents whatever they made in class before running off to play in the five acres of woods behind the church.

On occasion, Lyndon came with us. After a few years he became the congregation's youth director. We developed a network of friends who shared our interests and values. We had dinner at the Beckers', attended Super Bowl Sunday parties at the Banks', went on Mother's Day picnics with the Syeds. Every summer our children went to the UU camp sponsored by the Long Island Area Council. Church became an important part of our lives, providing us with supportive friends that filled the void left by the parents who had neglected and abandoned us.

Four years after I completed my doctorate, Lyndon and I accepted jobs in Massachusetts. We investigated the communities near work and chose Attleboro, a small city that was more racially and ethnically diverse than most New England towns. We didn't want our children, now thirteen and eleven, to be the only black kids in the school.

I called the Unitarian Universalist minister in the community we were moving to. He put us in touch with Martha, a spry seventy-year-old woman. Although she had a degree in architecture, for most of her life Martha had worked as a secretary in her husband's medical practice. After her husband retired, she became a real estate broker and bought herself a sporty red car. When we couldn't find a suitable house, she convinced us to purchase a factory-built home, which she modified to fit our needs. She found us a lot within walking distance of Murray Unitarian Universalist Church.

As we settled into our new house, Gretchen, a neighbor and member at Murray, gave us plants for our garden and showed us the path through the woods. Often while walking our dogs, we would pass each other on the trail.

During coffee hour following Sunday services at Murray, Gretchen and some other women urged me to become part of the women's group. Needing some emotional support during the transition from New York to Massachusetts, I readily agreed. I started attending sometime in the spring of 1990.

We met in the John Murray room at the front of the church. The windows along the back wall looked out onto the memorial garden. I always chose a seat on the couch. Gretchen favored an armchair to my left. Three or four other women attended. The group had no identified leader, and no one was assigned the task of moderating. We weren't supposed to discuss each other's personal affairs outside the group.

In November 1990, six months after I started my new job as a supervising psychologist at a state developmental center, layoffs began. Badly needing the rest from the resulting job stress, I decided to spend Thursday night quietly reading and relaxing after I put my children to bed. I had just settled down into the blue cushion of my papasan chair when the phone rang. Sighing, I put my book down and crossed the room to the kitchen wall phone. It was my parents. After barely greeting each other, we chatted about the inheritance they, my siblings and I were receiving from my uncle's estate.

"The money is really going to help Rita," I said. "She'll use it to pay for college."

"Your sister was already in school," my father said.

"It will reduce her student loan debt," I replied.

"How dare you say that!" my father yelled, startling me. "What's wrong with you? You're selfish and inconsiderate!" My mother joined in on the rant.

Holding the phone away from my ear, I recognized for the first time that they were abusive. Although I understood that Uncle Frank had sexually molested me, I hadn't recognized that my parents, especially my father, were emotionally and verbally abusive. I didn't have a model of a healthy parent-child relationship to compare them to. All along, I blamed myself more than I blamed my parents. I was constantly trying to be a better daughter.

My college education also hadn't helped. Post-traumatic stress disorder was just starting to be studied in Vietnam veterans when I was a graduate student. That sexual and/or verbal abuse produced the same or similar symptoms wasn't yet recognized. The psychological impact of trauma wasn't part of the curriculum. Herman's landmark book, *Trauma and Recovery*, was first published in 1997, ten years after I had earned my doctorate.

When my parents' ranting slowed, I told them, "I don't know why you called, but if it's to be abusive, don't call." I hung up.

The following evening, I went over to Murray to attend the women's group and shared the phone call I had with my parents. "I finally realize that my parents are emotionally abusive, and that no matter how hard I try to be a good daughter, they'll never be pleased with me."

The other women, including my neighbor Gretchen, warned, "You'll come to regret this."

"They probably only heard 'don't call,'" Dawn said. "They probably didn't hear the first part."

The following week, a member of the women's group apologized for herself and the others. She realized she had put her own issues in and failed to recognize that severing contact was a positive move for me. I accepted their apologies but my enthusiasm for the group waned.

The following year, the minister of our new church resigned. As part of the search process, the congregation was surveyed. While reviewing the survey results, I was startled to learn that approximately five percent of the members expressed discomfort with hiring a woman or a black minister. I was less startled that twenty percent of the members objected to having a gay minister.

Gretchen, who had volunteered for the pulpit committee, said at a women's group meeting that she wanted the new minister to be black, a woman, or gay. She perceived the congregation's conservatism as out of step with Unitarian Universalism. A few of the other women agreed with her. I said a minister should be chosen based on their qualifications and not their gender, race or sexual orientation.

Gretchen's preoccupation with finding a minister who wasn't white, male and heterosexual was common among Unitarian Universalists, who often are overly anxious to prove they are more liberal and tolerant than other religious denominations. On Sunday while Lyndon and I were exiting the sanctuary, the interim minister, who knew nothing about my husband except his name and skin color, shook his hand and said, "We need more people like you."

Lyndon and I glanced at each other. While we walked through the sanctuary doors and down the hall past the coat rack, I vented to him, "All he wants are more blacks so he can prove how white and liberal the church is."

Another church member overheard me. "What's so wrong with that?"

"When he looks at Lyndon, all he sees is a black man. When I look at Lyndon, I just see Lyndon. I hardly ever think about his skin color."

The man stopped and thought it over. "Oh, I get it. It's like saying we need more men with beards, when what we really need are just people."

After completing the search process, the pulpit committee offered the position to a candidate who turned it down. This unexpected event triggered rumors that pulpit committee members weren't getting along with each other. The search went into a second year.

During the search process, a seminar called "The Welcoming Congregation" was held on a Saturday afternoon. Although I wanted to learn how to be more hospitable to visitors, a competing obligation prevented me from attending. The next morning during coffee hour, several people told me there was a nasty argument between the presenter and some attendees. They felt they had been conned into attending the workshop. The presenter focused on welcoming homosexuals and not on welcoming new members. I agreed the title of the seminar was deceptive.

Several weeks later in mid-December, I locked myself out of my house. I walked over to Gretchen's to ask for a ride to my son's school to get his house key. While I waited in Gretchen's kitchen, she informed me that the search committee had a ministerial candidate to present to the congregation. She expressed anxiety over whether the congregation would approve the pulpit committee's choice.

"Why wouldn't they approve?" I asked while Gretchen gathered up her car keys and bag. "It's rare for a candidate to be rejected unless the search committee ignored the congregation's wishes—" I stopped. I knew what the problem was. "You didn't go and select a gay minister, did you?"

Gretchen didn't reply.

At the next Sunday service, a formal announcement was made that the search committee had selected a ministerial candidate who accepted the call. I thought it unusual that nothing was said about her family. I spoke to Gretchen's husband, Russell, who confirmed the candidate was gay.

"I don't think it wise to hide that from the congregation," I told him. "To avoid a backlash, I really think you should be upfront with the congregation. I have some reservations about having a gay minister, but I'm willing to meet and discuss it."

"You should talk to Deborah. She's the church's moderator," he replied.

I thanked him and headed toward the Unity Room, looking for Deborah. I caught up with her in front of the religious education classrooms. As we walked down the hall together, I expressed concern that the ministerial candidate's sexual orientation was being withheld from the congregation. "It's a mistake," I told her. "The congregational survey indicated a large minority would object to a gay minister. I'm uncomfortable with it too, but I'm willing to discuss it."

"How does Lyndon feel about it?" she asked, disregarding my reservations.

"He's uncomfortable with it too." Why was she more concerned about what Lyndon thought than about what I thought? Was it because she valued having a black man as a church member more than having me, a white woman?

"Ron was on the search committee. He had concerns, too," she said. "You should talk to him."

When we entered the fellowship hall, she immediately escorted me over to Ron, who was talking to other search committee members.

"I have my misgivings about the ministerial candidate, and I don't think I'm the only one," I informed them.

"I had my reservations, too," Ron said, "until I spoke with her. She's really an excellent candidate."

He was as earnest as a new convert. His speech sounded pressured. Did he change his mind of his own free will, or did he yield to group pressure?

"You can't withhold this information from the congregation," I warned him. "When other people figure it out as I have, there could be a terrible backlash. It wouldn't be fair to the congregation, or to the ministerial candidate."

"Do you really think so?"

"Yes. This is a controversial choice. It's unwise to bury it. It would be better to hold forums, where members of the congregation could freely and openly discuss their feelings before Candidating Week. I believe the church should work toward building a consensus while exploring their values with each other."

Ron and the others conceded I had a point. One member of the search committee said, "People will be busy over the holidays. We should wait until January to hold a meeting to discuss the issue with church members."

"Okay. That's fine. I'm busy, too. In addition to Christmas and New Year's, I'll be celebrating my wedding anniversary on the thirtieth."

A few days before Christmas, a member of the search committee left a message on my answering machine. A meeting with the ministerial candidate had been scheduled for December 30.

"I can't believe they did that! I told them I couldn't do it then," I vented to Lyndon while I erased the message.

"They've already decided she's going to be the church's next minister," he replied.

When I attended Sunday services, it appeared people were avoiding me during coffee hour. When I approached, they stopped talking and looked uncomfortable, and quickly excused themselves, leaving me standing alone. Finally, a member let slip that people were saying I objected to the ministerial candidate because I was threatened by her, feared being touched by her, and that I was really gay myself.

How would they know that? I wondered in shock. On what did they base those ideas on? Did they live and sleep with me? Was it my short haircut or my deep voice? Or was it because I objected to the interim minister, who I barely knew, giving me a big bear hug before I could stop him?

It must be Gretchen who was spreading rumors and calling me homophobic, I decided. I called a member of the women's group.

"You really need to talk to Gretchen," she told me.

"Yes, you're right," I replied. I hung up the phone and immediately dialed Gretchen. She agreed to meet with me on Thursday evening. Thursday morning, she left a message on the answering machine: "I'm not feeling well. Ron will meet with you at my house to discuss your concerns."

I had already spoken to Ron, several weeks before. My issue was with her, not him. I saw no point in talking to him again. I wanted to talk directly with Gretchen about the things she was saying about me. I called her back, cancelling the meeting.

The second interim minister gave a sermon regarding true belief. He pointed out that liberalism and conservatism are better viewed not on a straight line, but on a circle, with true believers sitting right next to each other. Regardless of their ideologies, Stalin and Hitler behaved the same way, slaughtering millions who didn't agree with them or who in some other way didn't fit into their vision of the new order.

As I exited the sanctuary, blinking through tears, I begged the interim minister to help me.

"My role as interim minister," he said, "prohibits me from getting involved in any way with the selection process."

I was surprised he didn't see himself as being in the position to stop gossip and encourage dialogue. I shook his hand and walked home through the woods, crestfallen.

In January, just before Candidating Week, another meeting was held after Sunday service to discuss concerns about the candidate's homosexuality. There were at least forty people present. The church leadership responded to people's misgivings by asserting that sexual orientation was irrelevant. A true Unitarian Universalist, they insisted, was tolerant of gays and welcomed them without question.

Not wanting to be marginalized, those holding opposing views stifled any inclination toward dissent. An open discussion of the complex moral and ethical issues was successfully thwarted. The church leadership failed to understand what any good salesperson knows: when a person is asking questions, he's often looking for reasons to make the purchase. When supporters of the new minister dismissed people's doubts as bigotry, they actually undermined their candidate's ministry at Murray, dooming it to failure before it began.

After the meeting, I was told that, as a psychologist, I shouldn't be imposing my values on anyone. It was clear that stating my values had been confused with imposing them, and my professional role and obligations confused with my private life. Although it would be inappropriate for me to preach to my clients, as a parent I had a duty to instill values in my own children. Attending church was one way of doing just that.

One of my children's teachers who was also a member of Murray spoke to me. "You have now had your first disillusionment with UUism."

"I thought they valued open discussion," I replied.

"I've noticed that they only listen around here if you talk in a monotone," he replied. Apparently my emotional demonstrativeness was also politically incorrect.

Friends and acquaintances continued to shun me during coffee hour. People assumed they knew what my position was without speaking to me directly. My adversaries viewed me as having a problem, and attempted to pressure me to seek counseling from the ministerial candidate. Insulted,

I declined. Gretchen and the others assumed that I was uncomfortable with a gay minister because I had no contact with lesbians. They were attempting to apply the contact hypothesis that was once used to racially desegregate schools to homosexuals. What they didn't know was that the contact hypothesis had been modified after a considerable amount of research. The nature of the contact was also important. It wasn't that I had never met a gay person. I knew several. My brother Rich was gay. He came out when I was in my late teens. As president of the Gay Activist Alliance, he was going to be on television, so he told my parents before it was aired. At first it was upsetting, but I quickly got over it. After all, this was my brother, who I knew and loved. Without much thought, I adopted a pro-gay stance. I was liberal, wasn't I? I was against the Vietnam War, pro-choice and a feminist. Supporting gay rights was part of the whole package.

I didn't waver in my support until after a series of negative experiences with gay men and women. My brother was not only gay, but openly bragged that gays weren't possessive like heterosexuals and didn't demand fidelity from their partners. Monogamy was seen as limiting and oppressive. After I married Lyndon and had two children, I began to rethink the issue. Having multiple partners meant you never had to commit to anyone. You could keep everyone at a safe distance. Sex was confused for love.

During my undergraduate years I was active in the women's movement. In the early seventies, lesbians dominated the meetings and conferences. They were often openly hostile to men, and barred men from participating. Heterosexual women were viewed as sleeping with the enemy. Dyke separatists openly proclaimed that in the ideal world, we would only need men for sperm production, and perhaps someday we wouldn't even need that. They envisioned a world populated only by women. They believed such a world would be less oppressive and more peaceful.

When I was a junior in college, I attended a house party hosted by another member of the Women's Studies Department. Her teenage son, a pawn in his parent's divorce, was visiting. In his presence, the women joked about men's inferiority. I looked across the room and saw the pain in the boy's face.

Lesbian feminists encouraged heterosexual women to give up their "dependence" on men and find a female partner. Since I had had so few dates and had often been called "queer," I wondered if my tormentors had known something about me I didn't. I talked to Dr. Howard about it. He told me he didn't think I was gay.

A favorite anthropology professor of mine had left her boyfriend for a woman. She had hoped the problems that existed in her hetero-sexual relationships wouldn't be present in a homosexual one. She dis-covered that relationships have the same problems regardless of sexual orientation. She returned to her boyfriend.

While working at a New York State developmental center, I worked in an all-female building. All the clients and staff except for one supervisor were female. The social worker was a lesbian who regularly harassed the male supervisor, making fun of his masculinity and his Christianity. It was as bad as a group of male construction workers harassing women while they walked down the street. Since then, I preferred environments where both men and women were present.

When I left my state position and went to work for a private agency, I worked with another lesbian social worker. I believed we were working well together. Shortly after she met my husband, who has been described as a man's man, she began gossiping and complaining about me, including innuendos that I was a closet homosexual. I found myself asking the question: Was she angry that I didn't fit her stereotype of a heterosexual woman?

Given these and other negative experiences, I was unsure a lesbian minister would understand the problems confronted by heterosexual families. Further, I feared it would be impossible to criticize or object to anything the new minister did without being labeled a homophobe.

During the weeks preceding Candidating Week, Lenny, a member of the church council, called me. From him I learned that the vote for the candidate would be by a show of hands. I had assumed that a vote on such an important issue would be by secret ballot, since this was how it was done at my last church. Lenny suggested I bring it up at the next council meeting. When I informed him I had to take my daughter to a doctor's appointment, he said he would bring up the issue for me.

The morning following the council meeting Lenny called to inform me that the church council believed taking a paper ballot would be discriminatory against the ministerial candidate, since it had never been done that way before. I didn't understand the logic, and felt they were confusing the issues.

Supporters of the ministerial candidate began speaking privately to church members, encouraging them to set up an appointment with Rev. Melody, the ministerial candidate. While on the buffet line at the potluck dinner that launched Candidating Week, I overheard a church member talking about being "counseled" by Rev. Melody. Although I spoke to Rev. Melody at the various church functions during that week, I continued to refuse to meet with her privately. Just because I had doubts about having a gay minister didn't mean I needed to be "counseled."

On the day of the congregational meeting, Lyndon and I drove the half-mile to Murray. The church's parking lot was full, so we parked at the professional building across the street. Together we crossed busy North Main Street and walked up the circular driveway, entering the church through its heavy oak doors into the vestibule. We said hello to people as we walked down the sanctuary's center aisle. Lyndon chose a seat halfway back from the pulpit on the right side.

The sanctuary quickly filled up. In addition to the familiar faces of regular church attendees, there were people I had never met before. Several of the strangers had white hair. They had probably been church members for decades, but their health and ability to get a ride interfered with their attending church on Sundays. The remaining strangers probably only attended church on major holidays and for important votes like this one.

Russell, the board president, stood at the pulpit. He tapped the microphone and said, "Please settle down. I would like to call the meeting to order."

People stopped talking and took their seats.

Someone made a motion to take the vote for minister by paper ballot. Supporters of the ministerial candidate objected, stating a secret ballot wouldn't keep everyone accountable. They failed to distinguish between the need for transparency in the voting behavior of elected council members with the need for the church's members to vote without intimidation. Their very insistence that people be held accountable for their vote belied their assertion that the church was a safe place. Supporters of the candidate further asserted that a secret ballot was discriminatory against the candidate, and anyone who wanted a secret ballot was homophobic.

At the time, I was unfamiliar with Robert's Rules of Order. I would later learn that a motion to ballot follows the main motion and doesn't precede it. Further, a motion to ballot isn't debatable. After any voice vote, anyone can call for a vote that is more accurately counted. A paper ballot is commonly taken when a motion is controversial and people might be pressured to vote a certain way.

Outmaneuvered by people more skilled in parliamentary procedure, a vote on a paper ballot was taken, and defeated. The vote for the new minister would be taken by a count of hands.

Russell asked, "Will all those in favor please raise their hands?"

Hands went up. I looked around. Ushers went up and down the aisles counting. Clearly a majority of people were voting yes, but more than a simple majority was needed. I had been told by the minister from my old church that it's unwise to accept a call for a church if the vote is less than eighty-five percent, that for a successful ministry, you really needed to have it close to unanimous.

"Will all those who oppose raise their hands?"

Since my desire for free and open conversation about the minister's homosexuality and its impact on the congregation had been successfully thwarted during Candidating Week and I was now denied a secret ballot, I was left with no other option. Lyndon and I raised our hands. I looked around. We weren't the only ones. The hands were counted, and the numbers announced. I sat with my muscles tight and my stomach churning. I couldn't do the arithmetic in my head.

"Wow!" Russell exclaimed. "Seventy-five percent are in favor. Rev. Melody will be our next minister!"

I wasn't surprised by the outcome. But seventy-five percent wasn't a "wow." It was only a few votes over what was needed to carry the motion.

"Can I have a motion to make it unanimous?" Russell asked.

*No!* I thought. *Don't do that! Don't hide the opposition. We lost, but don't take our voice away!*

Someone close to Russell made the motion, and it was seconded. A voice vote was taken. The ayes were louder than the nays.

"The ayes have it," he said. "Rev. Melody has been unanimously chosen as our new minister."

The victors cheered. Tears filled my eyes.

"Let's go," I said to Lyndon.

"Just now," he replied, one of his Trinidadian expressions, and turned to talk to other church members.

"I can't." I walked quickly up the aisle and out of the church, avoiding eye contact because I didn't want anyone to see the tears. I walked home alone.

I stayed away from church for most of the spring. Martha called, suggesting we make a motion at the annual meeting in June to have all future votes for a minister be by secret ballot. She further suggested a friend of hers be the one to present it.

At the annual meeting, Gretchen and Russell opposed the motion. "It will introduce politics into the church," Gretchen argued. "With a hand vote, people will think more carefully about their position. The church is a safe environment, and a paper ballot isn't needed."

With a clarity I lacked during Candidating Week, I stood and said, "The church hasn't been a safe place for me. I've been hurt by the way things were handled."

Gretchen couldn't argue with that. The motion carried. The church's next minister would be chosen by paper ballot.

Murray's last service in June 1993 was lay-led, with members sharing whatever they wanted with the rest of the church community. I decided to attend and read a statement I had written.

To my disappointment, only a handful of people were present. While the other members shared poetry and other readings, I removed my printed statement from my bag. When my turn came, I took a deep breath and slowly stood. My stomach was queasy. My voice faltered as I read the following statement:

> I have been a Unitarian Universalist close to ten years, and have been a member of this particular congregation for three. I am currently ambivalent about maintaining my membership.

> The most important reason I joined the Unitarians was because I believed that I would be allowed to form my own opinions and decide what my values were without the dogma that I was subjected to as a Catholic.

> Last winter after the announcement of Reverend Melody's candidacy for our minister, I expressed to the leadership some of my misgivings, and most importantly, my recommendation that they hold forums where members of the congregation could freely and openly discuss their feelings about having a gay minister prior to Candidating Week. My intent was that Murray should work toward building a consensus. I saw this as an opportunity for

members to explore their values with each other. I thought that was what Unitarian Universalism was all about.

Apparently neither my misgivings nor my recommendations were politically correct. I very quickly found myself being shunned by other members who obviously believed they occupied the moral high ground. Although I was not told directly, I knew I had been labeled homophobic. This was later confirmed in the early spring, when I was told that another member of this church had said I was homophobic and very resistive to a new minister. As my profession, psychology, is a science devoted to understanding and helping others, I object to the use of psychological terminology to demean and injure others. Also, I object to the hidden dogma within Unitarian Universalism.

If there are certain moral stances I'm supposed to take in order to be a Unitarian Universalist, that should have been made clear before I became a member. At least as a Catholic, I knew exactly what I was supposed to believe and what heresy was. The suppression of conflict and the demeaning of those who may hold minority views undermine the unity of this congregation. It is my hope that members of this congregation will stop congratulating themselves on a job well done long enough to take a more critical look at the selection process, how this congregation is governed, and in the way conflict is handled.

Thank you.

After the service, another church member approached me. "You're right," she said. "There wasn't enough discussion."

In the fall, when the new minister started, I was willing to give her a chance despite my misgivings. My friend Molly, who wanted to reengage me in the church and who knew of my interest in shared ministry and lay-led services, urged me to attend a worship committee meeting. My interest in this was long known to the church leadership, especially to Lenny, a church council member.

Although participation in church committees had always been open to anyone interested enough to volunteer, it was announced that only those people the leadership selected would be on the committee. Soon after the meeting, I received a call from Lenny informing me I wasn't selected because I hadn't been involved enough in the church. I immediately called Molly and told her. She called Lenny, and was told I wasn't wanted on the committee because they "didn't want any trouble."

I called the new minister and objected to the way I was being treated. Disregarding my concerns, Rev. Melody insisted on talking about my objection to her candidacy. She refused to talk about my exclusion from full participation in the church.

Rev. Melody's intolerant reaction to my expression of discomfort was the very thing I feared about having a gay minister. Before I could fully voice those fears, I was ostracized. In the beginning, I was willing to consider voting for Rev. Melody but only wanted to discuss my thoughts and misgivings. By the time her candidacy came before the congregation I was opposed to her ministry. During the height of the conflict, I was told the church leadership was acting on her advice. I wasn't certain that was true. I hoped it wasn't. After speaking with Rev. Melody, I realized it was probably true.

I immediately called Faith, the religious education director from my previous congregation. She advised me to withdraw my membership and find another Unitarian Universalist church.

On October 6, 1993, I sent the following letter to Rev. Melody:

> After considerable thought and talking it over with my friends and family, I have decided to withdraw my membership from Murray. Over the course of the last eleven months, it has become painfully clear that what I want out of a religious organization, I have not been able to find at Murray. Your initial denial and that of Lenny that there had been any conflict over the selection process (thereby invalidating my experience and placing all the responsibility on me) has convinced me there is no hope for finding a win-win solution to our dispute. All I ever really wanted was an opportunity to discuss moral, ethical and religious issues in a safe and caring community that acknowledged the right of each individual to form his/her own opinions about those issues. My attempt to discuss my misgivings

about your candidacy and my simple request for a more
democratic vote (i.e. a paper ballot) has led to my exclusion
from full and equal participation at Murray. As I believe
this exclusion is unjust and in violation of the guiding
principles of Unitarian Universalism, I feel that I have no
other choice but to withdraw my membership from Murray
Church, effective immediately.

Resigning my church membership was very painful. I lost another
family. I hadn't realized how conditional my acceptance at Murray had
been. I became frightened of voicing my doubts and concerns, not only
on the issue of homosexuality but also on other issues where I might be
viewed as politically incorrect. I internalized other people's negative
judgment of my character. Even though I had done nothing to harm
anyone else, and rationally, I knew I had only voiced some doubts and
had tried to initiate a conversation about them, I fought feelings of
shame.

Seeking to resolve my pain, I cautiously voiced some of my concerns
on a Unitarian Universalist listserv. The anonymity of the Internet gave
me a relatively safe place to share my story. Reading people's responses
provided some insight into what had happened.

While Unitarian Universalists are quite tolerant on theological
issues, they are intolerant on social and moral ones. When I thought
this through, I realized that Unitarian Universalists were like all other
groups. They were no more virtuous or tolerant. They were relatively
tolerant on theological issues, since such issues were largely irrelevant to
their spiritual identity. However, on issues they felt deeply about, such as
their view of social justice, they were intolerant of any view that wasn't
"liberal."

Yet, it is easy to tolerate something you don't feel strongly about. The
true test of tolerance is when you can accept and not condemn someone
for holding a different view on an issue that touches you deeply.

I considered trying another religion. However, at that point, since I
rejected Jesus' divinity, I didn't regard myself as Christian. I also believed
that the problems I encountered were typical to all organizations. So I
stopped actively searching for another congregation and remained
unchurched for a couple of years.

During this period, a member of Murray and I worked closely
together at the state developmental center where we were both employed.

We shared a dedication to our work and concern for the clients we served. On a bright and sunny day, perhaps in the early spring, he chose to take advantage of the unexpected privacy that an open parking lot provided. He stopped me as I made my way to my car.

"Gretchen is saying terrible things about you."

"I know," I said. Someone was finally confirming the source of the rumors.

"You should come back."

Why was he telling me this? What was Gretchen saying exactly? Why did he think I should attend a church where I was being vilified? I wanted to ask, but like the proverbial deer caught in the headlights, I froze. I lacked the courage to ask the questions I needed answered.

"You must be kidding," I said, walking away. We never discussed it again. I didn't understand the importance of confronting and ending the rumors about me. If we were living in a larger community, this might not have mattered. Four years later Gretchen's view of me would undermine my future church memberships, causing me and my family significant pain.

# Rapid Escalation

Leaving Murray left me feeling empty. I yearned for the connection with others that was denied me when I was a child. Since I was no longer on any church committees, I had free time I didn't know what to do with. I began exploring America Online's chat rooms and found the Unitarian Universe. I began posting, and soon volunteered to host on Tuesday nights. By January 1994, I was exchanging emails with a woman who was active in the Unitarian Universalist Association.

At first I was very cautious, telling her only that I was involved in a dispute over the selection of a minister. We discussed liberalism and political correctness in UU congregations. Eventually I trusted her enough to send her the letter I read at Murray's sharing service. At the time her response appeared supportive, and validated my view that more discussion about homosexuality was needed.

In January 1995, her picture appeared in the *UU World* magazine, clearly identifying her as a lesbian and a staff member at the Unitarian Universalist Association. I wasn't surprised. When she asked me about my family, I told her I had a son and a daughter. She told me she had two boys, but said almost nothing about their father except that he was fair-haired and fair-skinned like her and her boys. I knew she was holding back something. I told her I was a psychologist. She never said what she did for a living.

Despite the deception, the correspondence with this woman helped me put things in better perspective. I came to see I needed to identify what I was looking for in a church, what my expectations, priorities and values were.

In the spring of 1994, I visited a couple of Unitarian Universalist churches with my children. Completely soured on religion, Lyndon refused to come with us. My children and I visited a large urban congregation that proved to be overcrowded and impersonal. Even though I went up to the hospitality table and filled out a card, I never received their newsletter. During coffee hour, no one spoke to me.

The following Sunday I drove eleven miles north to Foxboro. The Unitarian Universalist church there, at the north end of the town common, occupied a nineteenth-century white clapboard building with massive columns and red doors. It had lost its steeple during the 1938 hurricane, and the congregation was never able to raise the money to fix it. Instead, they sold the bell and used the money to repair the roof.

When my children and I climbed the gray wooden steps and entered the vestibule, a black-haired man walked up to me and shook my hand. "Hello, I'm Don. I'm the membership chair here. If you have any questions, I would be happy to answer them."

I thanked him, and then entered the sanctuary. There were fewer than twenty people present. The sermon by the minister was forgotten before he even finished it. But the people were eager to make us feel welcome, and invited us downstairs for coffee. I inquired about their religious education program. It was tiny, with little to offer my children.

A week later, I took my children back to the large urban church where there was a vital and thriving religious education program. I helped them find the Sunday school class for their age group before I went into the sanctuary. When I picked them up after the service, they wanted to leave immediately. They felt snubbed by the other children, who came from more-affluent families and attended private schools. We didn't bother with the coffee hour and left.

I didn't go to church again until the fall. Since my family no longer wanted any part of church, I chose to go to Foxboro Unitarian Universalist Church alone. People were curious about why I wasn't attending the UU church closest to my home. Fearful that sharing that information would lead to another rejection, I skirted the issue.

In November, before the Sunday service welcoming new members into Foxboro UU, I took a seat in the back, away from everyone else. During the service when the new members were called to the front of the sanctuary, my eyes started to tear. The more I tried to stop, the more I cried. The tears just needed to come. Surprised and embarrassed by my emotional reaction I left FXUU's sanctuary in the middle of the service. I had hoped the passage of time would heal my grief over the loss of my church. It hadn't. While my participation in the Unitarian Universe chat room had been helpful, it wasn't enough. I needed to talk to someone face to face.

The next time I attended services, FXUU's minister, Rev. Dick, a short man with a bulging belly, pulled me aside during coffee hour and asked why I had abruptly left the service on Membership Sunday. Sitting in a corner of the church's basement away from the other church members, I told him about my experience at Murray.

"They were trying to convert you!" he said. Understanding my fear of being rejected again, he promised to keep our conversation confidential.

Several weeks later the worship chair became seriously ill. Rev. Dick announced that help was needed with planning one lay-led service per month. Recognizing a chance to contribute to the church while doing something I liked, I volunteered. When Don, the membership chair, learned of my interest, he called me.

"You need to be a member of the church to serve on a committee," he said. I pulled back. I wasn't ready to join a church.

Rev. Dick spoke with Don, and then called me on my business phone.

"Dr. Jones," I answered.

"That's cute," Rev. Dick responded. "What's your doctorate in?"

"Psychology." I wondered what was "cute" about my professional title.

"You can go ahead and help with worship. I told Don you only needed to be a member if you were on the board."

I immediately began planning one lay-led service per month. I attempted to consult with Rev. Dick, but he made it clear he was only part-time. I was to put the services together without his assistance. The church was too small to have a regular standing committee, so each month I solicited help and ideas from other church members. After each lay-led service, people praised me and told me how moved they were. Feeling accepted and valued, I formally became a member of FXUU in the spring of 1995.

Believing much of what happened at Murray was because the majority of congregants were content to allow a small clique to manage church affairs, I decided to learn more about FXUU and how it was governed. I began attending board meetings. When the worship chair died, I was asked to fill her vacancy. I had never considered serving on a church board before. I was surprised that I actually enjoyed it. By the fall of 1996, I was an active member of FXUU's board as well as filling the duties of worship chair and assisting with organizing the music for Sunday services.

Sometime in 1996, I heard a radio broadcast about the Jesus Seminar, a group of Biblical scholars who were studying the historical Jesus and reporting the results of its research to the public. I began to reconsider Christianity. My grandmother and most of the famous people I admired—Martin Luther King Jr., Albert Schweitzer, Abraham Lincoln—

were devout Christians. Gandhi, while not a Christian, was deeply religious and frequently quoted the Gospels. The next time I was in a bookstore I purchased Marcus Borg's Meeting Jesus Again for the First Time, and began my journey back to Christianity.

I wanted to explore Christianity with others. Since Foxboro was too small to offer any adult religious education, I attended ecumenical services and seminars hosted by the local Council of Churches, an ecumenical partnership of Christian denominations in the United States. In addition to fostering my own spiritual development, these activities brought me in contact with laity active in church affairs, and with area clergy.

My first memory of Rev. Karen was when I received a letter from her inviting me to become a member of the committee in charge of planning the seminars. Apparently she had noticed me during a workshop on Christian meditation. I have no idea why she chose to invite me and not someone else. Perhaps it was because she wanted a broad spectrum of churches represented, and I was the only Unitarian Universalist who attended the seminar series.

Welcoming the opportunity to be part of a Council of Churches committee, I accepted the invitation. I hoped the exposure would bring assistance, advice and new members to my own congregation.

The committee met during the summer of 1996 in Rev. Karen's office at Immanuel Lutheran. I was surprised to learn that Immanuel was almost directly behind my home. Set back almost twenty-five yards from the road and with the rear of the church facing North Main Street, I had never noticed it before. The sanctuary was oddly designed, with a flat roof. Cedar shingles came down the sloping sides and overlapped the brick foundation. There were no windows or doors facing the road. Access was gained by parking in a side lot and walking past a modern freestanding bell tower similar to the one that stood in front of Murray. The covered sidewalk passed the main entrance and ended at the entrance to the minister's office and Sunday school wing.

On the day of my first meeting, I was ushered into Rev. Karen's office and took a seat on a large, low, black leather sofa located on the same wall as the door. There were a couple of chairs to the far left circling the coffee table. Rev. Karen busied herself in another office across the hall while other committee members entered and took their seats.

The coffee table in front of me was covered with booklets and a few Bibles. Rev. Karen's desk was positioned cattycorner in front of bookshelves, along the outside wall. There was barely enough space to get around the desk to sit in the desk chair. Apparently Rev. Karen only sat there when she was attending to administrative duties, such as returning phone calls or writing letters.

After everyone had entered and taken a seat, Rev. Karen closed her office door and sat in the rocking chair directly opposite where I was sitting. She reminded me of the East German women that competed in the Olympics, big-boned and sturdy. At first I was put off by her brusque manner, but as we worked together on the committee, I found her to be kind and nurturing.

Rev. Karen asked me to lead a seminar on sexual morality. I gladly accepted the offer. To prepare, I surfed the Internet and read several books, acquainting myself with the positions on sex and marriage of several major religious denominations.

The seminar was held in the library of a local church a mile and a half south from my home. We talked about what different religious groups had to say about sex, marriage and divorce. Following my presentation, Rev. Karen and I talked about divorce while we descended the stone steps that wound through the church's garden to the parking lot. We stopped in front of my red Corolla.

"Although I live in the parsonage with my husband, we've been estranged from each other for nearly ten years," Rev. Karen said. "When he is home, he sleeps in another room."

I was startled by the admission. She barely knew me. Did she feel it was safe to tell me this because I was a psychologist, and not a member of her church?

"I could never live like that," I said, unlocking the door to my car.

"I don't even know where he is tonight. I haven't seen him for days. I think he's with his girlfriend," she continued. "When I retire, I will divorce him."

"Why don't you divorce him now?" I asked.

"I could lose my job at Immanuel."

"Why?" I scrunched my forehead. "Divorce is common. What's the problem?"

"I'm required to inform my bishop and my congregation. They could ask me to leave since I would be breaking my marriage vows. Besides, I don't want him to get alimony. He isn't working. I don't know how he gets his money. When I retire, my income will be a lot less. I would have to pay him less."

*How can she live like that?* I thought. *My house is a haven for me. I am surrounded by my loved ones. Divorce him and get on with your life.*

"When I retire in a few years," she continued. "I will move to Connecticut and live with some friends. I visit them whenever I have a day off."

"That's good," I said, then told her about FXUU and how we were trying to increase our membership. I told her about my renewed interest in Christianity after reading Marcus Borg's books. She had never read them, but she knew what the Jesus Seminar was.

"It's late," I said. "I have to get home to my family. You have a good night." Having lost most of my social connections when I left Murray, I was delighted that a friendship was forming between Rev. Karen and me.

As one of the meetings of the Council of Churches' committee was adjourning, Beverly, a short, obese woman and a member of Immanuel Lutheran, asked Rev. Karen what they would be discussing at Immanuel's Bible study. Apparently they had covered Revelations the previous year. Beverly loved Revelations. Had Rev. Karen read the *Left Behind* series? No, she hadn't. What would they be covering this year? The Acts of the Apostles.

Beverly's loquaciousness had made it easy to get to know her. She was diabetic, and her husband had a life-threatening heart disease. She hadn't expected him to live very long but there he was, disabled but still alive. She had been married for more than twenty-five years. Beverly also emphasized that she had tested low on an intelligence test and had done poorly in school. She grew up in foster homes. She didn't have any children.

After Beverly left, I asked Rev. Karen if I could attend Bible study.

"Of course," she responded. "It's open to anyone who wants to come."

When I first went to Bible study in Immanuel's fellowship hall, I was astonished that the hall was less than half the size of Murray's, and that instead of a full-size kitchen they only had a small kitchenette next to some floor-to-ceiling cabinets.

I was also surprised to see Nancy, a nurse I used to work with, sitting on one of the mismatched chairs that formed a circle at one end of the hall. I was happy to learn that she and her husband had been members at Immanuel for many years. The presence of someone I knew increased my comfort. After Nancy and I greeted each other, I took a seat.

Rev. Karen was warm, welcoming and tolerant of my unorthodox views of Jesus and the Bible. She was fully aware I rejected the Apostles' and Nicene Creeds. Like most Unitarian Universalists, I didn't believe Jesus was God's only son who had been eternally begotten with the Father. Nor did I believe in the virgin birth and the bodily resurrection of Jesus. Although she knew I didn't intend to become a member of her church, Rev. Karen continued to welcome and even appreciate what I had to contribute. I always felt so peaceful and refreshed when I was there.

Determined to do a good job as FXUU's worship chair, I sought help and advice from the Unitarian Universalist Association by attending the Ballou Channing District's 1996 fall conference. FXUU was one of forty-seven congregations within the district. The district's mission was to assist member congregations with carrying out their programs, cultivate cooperative relationships among the member congregations, and advance the Principles and Purposes of the Unitarian Universalist Association. The workshops I attended confirmed what I had already observed. Dying congregations do not participate in denominational affairs, and do not use the services of their district. Growing congregations go beyond themselves into the community and the denomination. I wanted FXUU to be a growing congregation dedicated to building a loving community that was cohesive but welcoming to new members.

A month later, I attended the annual seminar for worship chairs at the Sharon Unitarian Universalist Church. While we were selecting our seats and introducing ourselves to each other, the workshop leader held a brass bowl in her hand while she ran a wooden mallet along its edge. The hum of the bowl drew everyone's attention. The workshop leader explained it was a Tibetan singing bowl, which we could use to enrich our worship services. After lunch we were told that the first step in planning for the coming year was to list all the holidays, both secular and religious, and regardless of denomination.

At FXUU's next board meeting, I suggested the board invite Rev. Terry, the district executive, to conduct a seminar at FXUU. In March 1997, Rev. Terry held a "visioning" session with church members. From this session, three major areas of concern were identified:

1.  A desire to improve our building and space.
2.  A desire for the church to grow but still remain a single-cell

church (fifty to seventy adults attending on a Sunday).
3.    A desire to improve worship, music and adult religious
     education.

Nine months later, in January 1998, Rev. Dick asked the board to
reduce the number of Sunday services he preached per month from three
to two, to give him time to complete a project for the small local college
where he was a full-time philosophy professor. Grateful for all the years
Rev. Dick had worked for minimal pay, the FXUU board was happy to
accommodate him. This meant, as worship chair, I had to take on the
additional responsibility of finding a few guest speakers. Rev. Dick also
asked that I take over printing the order of service for all Sunday services.

Don, who was now the board chair, informed the trustees that Rev.
Dick had spoken to him about his retirement plans and the need for the
board to consider how they were going to replace his services. Don saw
this as an opportunity to negotiate a plan with Rev. Dick to grow the
church. While there was a small growth spurt around the time I joined,
membership had leveled off and was beginning to decline again.

In the spring of 1998, Don and a longtime church member met with
Rev. Dick, who recommended that FXUU hire a seminary student as an
associate minister. When we were unable to meet this person's salary
requirements, he took a position in another congregation.

Shortly after this, Don invited me out to breakfast at a local diner.
Don stirred his coffee. "I am very concerned about our lack of growth."

"It's discouraging," I said.

"And our attrition."

"I joined because I thought the church was growing. Right now it
has very little to offer me." I took a sip of my orange juice.

"You might drop out more and more, or completely, and so might
we. I applaud your staying on, not only with the church, but as worship
chair. You are sorely needed."

"Thank you," I said, flattered.

"Over the last ten years, we've had so little growth in spite of some
really sincere and good work by volunteers."

I dipped my toast into the yolk of my fried eggs. "We've been rowing
upstream."

"It has become clear to me," Don said, picking up his fork, "Rev.
Dick has been FXUU's minister for twenty years, and there hasn't been
any growth, only decline."

"What happened twenty years ago?" I asked. "I've heard a rumor that the church split."

"I haven't been able to find out," Don replied. "It had something to do with Rev. Dick."

"None of the old-timers will talk about it."

"I have always wondered, especially with Emerson and the Bryants leaving, if the master plan was to slowly turn down the flow until the place closed down forever right around the time of Rev. Dick's retirement. When Sharon and I joined in 1989, there were only seven people at Sunday services."

"How many people do we have now?" I asked. "Twenty? Thirty?"

"The growth occurred when I was membership chair," Don replied.

"I remember you greeting me when I visited. It was the reason I came back."

"I'm glad you did." Don smiled. "Have you noticed how Rev. Dick usually says yes to any proposed change, and then never gives it his wholehearted support?"

"Maybe he's burned out," I speculated. "Maybe he just has too much to do. Maybe he can't handle the demands of both his full-time job and FXUU. Several months ago, I overheard him telling someone during coffee hour he had prepared his sermon during the forty-minute ride from his home to the church."

"His retirement could be really good for the church," Don said. "It gives us an opportunity to change things."

"How?"

"What if Rev. Dick continues to do two services per month, you do one, and we hire a guest speaker for the other?"

"Can we afford it?" I asked.

"If we get everyone to raise their pledges a little, we can."

"Rev. Dick's sermons have gotten better now that he's only doing two services per month," I said. "Hopefully, he feels better about that and will agree. We need to treat him with respect. He's well loved by the older members."

"Whatever you do, Maggie, don't leave yet. Give FXUU another year. Would you be willing to schedule guest speakers once a month in addition to doing the lay-led service?"

"Yes."

Having obtained my agreement, Don proposed what became known as "the 2-1-1 plan" at the next board meeting. Rev. Dick agreed to preach one less service per month while receiving the same pay. Everyone raised their pledges so we could hire a guest speaker once per month. This plan was ratified at the annual meeting in June 1998. We were excited about the change and the possibility for growth.

Charged by the Board of Trustees to obtain one guest minister per month, I spoke briefly with Rev. Dick after the annual meeting. I needed to determine which dates we would need guest speakers. Rev. Dick agreed to provide me with his schedule for the coming church year by July.

While waiting to hear from him, I obtained the dates of various holidays, secular and religious, as instructed at the workshop I attended. These included Judeo-Christian holidays such as Yom Kippur, All Souls Day, Advent and Christmas, Chanukah, Lent, Palm Sunday, Easter, Pentecost and Trinity Sunday. The secular holidays of Columbus Day, United Nations Day, New Year's, Martin Luther King Jr. Day, Valentine's Day, President's Day, May Day, Mother's Day and Memorial Day were also included. Using my computer-generated calendar, I constructed a tentative worship schedule with columns for dates, worship leader and holiday, if there was one, and the topic if known. There were thirty-nine services listed in total.

I phoned and sent emails to Rev. Dick, asking for his schedule. I explained I needed to book guest speakers before September. Waiting would put me in my busy work season, and I might not have time to do it then. The longer we waited, the greater the probability that a guest speaker wouldn't be available.

When I didn't hear from Rev. Dick, I emailed the tentative schedule to him on July 8 for his review, suggestions and modifications. I proposed that, on major holiday weekends, FXUU experiment with holding a simple evening service at 4 p.m. When Lyndon and I had visited a Unitarian Universalist minister we knew from Long Island, he boasted of his success in drawing visitors and new members by offering late afternoon or evening services. Since FXUU was already doing one evening service the Sunday before Christmas, I didn't think it was much of a stretch to add one or two more.

Keeping a promise I had made a few months before to Angelina, another member of FXUU's board, I proposed that a communion service be scheduled around Easter or Palm Sunday. Angelina had confided in me how meaningful she found the ritual of communion.

"Communion doesn't interest me much," I told her. "But if you'd like me to include one in the worship schedule, I will."

Around the same time, there was an ongoing discussion of communion on two Unitarian Universalist listservs. Someone made reference to a book published by the Unitarian Universalist Association on communions, that ran the gamut from more traditional communion to flower communion. I decided to buy the book if the FXUU trustees agreed to a communion service.

Toward the end of July, I emailed Don about my plans for getting guest speakers. I also informed him I still hadn't heard from Rev. Dick about the tentative worship schedule. Not wanting to wait until the last minute, I began lining up guest speakers for the fall. I assumed I would be able to work out the details with Rev. Dick at the August board meeting. Lyndon and I then left for vacation.

We returned home from New Mexico a couple of days before the board meeting. I checked my email. There were no messages from Rev. Dick. The evening of the board meeting, I telephoned and let the board know that I would be delayed at work. Don later told me that when he arrived, Rev. Dick's schedule was already being discussed. The board members who were present assumed Rev. Dick had discussed his schedule with me. They were about to make a final decision when Don interrupted and suggested they wait until I arrived.

Peggy, the Finance Chair, said there was no reason that they couldn't have their own opinions in my absence. She wanted to move forward. It was only when Don insisted that the board wait that it was tabled until my arrival.

I couldn't have been more than five minutes late when I entered the church from the basement door and walked across the room past Sandy, Rev. Dick's wife, who was correcting papers near the stairs to the vestibule. I took the only available seat at the opposite end of the table from Harry, a large, affable man who was the new board chair. He frequently boasted he liked and got along with everyone. In contrast, his wife Peggy was a short, thin woman. Her manners were as impeccable as her grooming. She was sitting next to her husband.

Rev. Dick briefly left the table to speak with his wife. Both of them then joined the board at the table. Rev. Dick then said, "I hadn't planned to stick to this schedule tonight, but I've changed my mind. This is the schedule we'll have for the year."

"May I have a copy?" I asked. A sheet of yellow paper torn from a pad was passed to me. On it, Rev. Dick had scrawled the dates he would be preaching. I skimmed it. There were more dates than I expected. I felt confused. It appeared Rev. Dick had disregarded the 2-1-1 schedule. Even though I thought there must be some kind of misunderstanding, my heart rate increased. I took some deep breaths.

"Maggie, may we have your report?" Harry asked.

I took another deep breath. "This is the first time I've seen Rev. Dick's schedule. I need time to review it. May I go at the end of the meeting?"

While Harry moved on to other matters, I could barely listen while I considered Rev. Dick's schedule. He had scheduled himself to do three services per month. But there were no conflicts in September, giving me several weeks to negotiate with Rev. Dick. I relaxed.

When Harry called on me again, I only told the board about the worship plans that didn't conflict with Rev. Dick's proposed schedule, then said, "I'll discuss the schedule with Rev. Dick and get back to the board at the next meeting."

After the meeting, I spoke briefly with Rev. Dick and Sandy in the corner of the church basement by the kitchen.

"There seems to be a mistake," I told him.

"I'm going to continue preaching three times per month," he said, disregarding the time and effort I had put into calling potential guest speakers.

"That isn't what was agreed to last June. Why have you changed your mind?"

"That's the way it has to be," was his only explanation.

The hour was late. I didn't want to argue. "I'll review your proposed schedule and see what I can do with it," I said.

When I got home I was too keyed up to go to bed. I went immediately to my computer and compared the preliminary schedule with Rev. Dick's schedule and the work party schedule. I made a few adjustments, and emailed the resulting calendar to Rev. Dick with this note:

> I integrated your schedule, the preliminary one I developed last July and the work party dates, and came up with the following. Please keep in mind nothing is carved in stone and we can make adjustments as we go along. The All Souls

service last year was extremely well received, and I was asked
to repeat it. I thought you might like to take part. There is
no sermon needed for the service. As I stated in my last
email to you, I was thinking of doing some brief vesper-like
services with no sermon on holiday weekends such as
Thanksgiving. What do you think?

When I checked my email the next morning, I found a reply from
him in my inbox. I clicked on it and began reading.

The idea of trying some holiday vesper services at 4:00 p.m.
is worth experimenting with—

*Good!* I thought. *He wants to try it.*

I read further. He felt there was "little or no interest in a service" the
Sundays after Christmas and New Year's. It would have to be discussed
with FXUU's board. Of course, I already knew that. No problem. I was
uncertain about those dates. *Didn't he see the question mark I put next to
them on the proposed schedule?* I wondered. But I might be away visiting
family anyway. I continued reading.

Communion on Easter is also a delicate matter. I could see
maybe doing one on Palm Sunday if it is wanted, but not
Easter.

*Why not Easter? We wouldn't be the first UU church to do communion on
Easter,* were my first thoughts. But then I thought, *Anyway, it isn't that
important to me. I included it because I was asked to.* I felt I had an obligation
to respond to what other church members wanted. This wasn't just about
me.

Rev. Dick also felt that if the vesper idea was tried, that he, as the
minister, should be the first one to conduct it. *Why?* I wondered. But it
would be great to have him and his support.

On the days for which you said you would like to do the
service with me, I will flex with your idea.

*What does that mean? Flex with my idea?* I was only trying to compromise.
Either way, it didn't matter. I read on. He wanted to keep the other days as
his responsibility, including some that I written as, "Maggie" or "Guest."

I grabbed my calendar and looked up October 18, February 21,
March 21 and April 11.

*Wait a minute. How does that work out? Let me see....*

That still had Rev. Dick doing three services per month. Why was he breaking his agreement?

I looked back toward my computer screen and read,

> Last year I found an occasional "second Sunday off"
> comfortable because of my illness. When we proposed a
> schedule to Peter where he would take one Sunday per
> month, I did not object because I thought that schedule was
> what the group wanted if Peter came. When arrangements
> for an associate minister didn't pan out, I still felt that
> having a little more time off would be desirable. I did not,
> however, envision myself being off twice every month as a
> permanent or consistent pattern.

*What is he talking about? He was present at the board meetings.* Don and Marge, a longtime member of the church, met with him. Rev. Dick knew. Why did he think he could alter the schedule without board approval?

> I am the part-time minister of the church. I have to be able
> to carry out the responsibilities of a part-time minister.
> There is no point to my being part of a part-time minister.

*Wait a minute,* I thought. In my experience, full-time Unitarian Universalist ministers preached three Sundays per month, while part-time ministers preached two. Confused, I pulled out my keyboard and began typing a reply.

> Last spring, the board initiated a discussion with you
> concerning our future plans. At that time, you indicated
> you were happy with the current schedule of preaching
> twice per month. We then spoke with Peter to see if we
> could hire an associate minister. Unfortunately, we were
> unable to come up with the money to pay for it. As a
> compromise, the board raised their pledges and we agreed
> to hire a guest minister once per month (approximately
> eight times in the church year), and that you would do two
> services per month. The schedule, which you are insisting
> on, is contrary to what the board decided last spring and
> unacceptable to me. I have already invested time and energy
> in locating guest ministers. I did not firm up times because

you had not provided me with the dates I needed until last night. The Sundays when there is a guest minister, you could be doing other things, like spending time with Religious Education or whatever you think is appropriate. I don't care which two Sundays you preach and which two you don't. The dates I proposed had to do with trying to evenly divide responsibilities. The only issue I am wedded to is your preaching two Sundays per month, one lay service per month and one guest minister per month. The schedule you shared with the board does not fit that agreement.

I paused to reread his email. He felt too much of his time had been consumed with the "problem" of the church schedule. "Most of today," he wrote, "has been lost to this issue. Your time is valuable too."

*Huh?* I wrinkled my nose and adjusted my eyeglasses. I typed,

I don't know who you spent time talking about this issue with today. You and I only talked for a few minutes. My time is valuable to me, but so is my church involvement. I am committed to improving our worship services. If you have some problem with my involvement, you should say so. You have said to me a few times that I should not assume all the responsibility for the lay services. I never have ... and everyone else that wanted to have participated.

Failing to get Rev. Dick to comply with the board's decision or explain why he changed his mind, I telephoned Angelina, the trustee who had requested communion. I had always admired her poise and meticulous attention to her personal appearance. She was the type of girl I had wanted to be in high school, lean, quiet and beautiful. I was prepared to leave FXUU if the board didn't support the 2-1-1 plan, but Angelina surprised me.

"He has to comply with the board's decisions," she said. "You know, Rev. Dick was trained as a Congregational minister. Congregationalists don't have a tradition of lay ministry. It's uniquely UU."

"Now that you say that, it makes sense," I told her. "Lay ministry is part of the Universalist tradition. American Unitarians and Congregationalists share a common heritage until they split in the 1800s over the Trinity."

"Rev. Dick isn't used to it, but I'm sure we can work it out," Angelina said.

"The UU church I belonged to on Long Island had talk backs and lay-led services," I mused. "Coming from a Catholic background, I wasn't comfortable with it at first. But it's consistent with my approach to therapy: as collaboration between the client and the therapist. I'm a strong proponent of shared ministry between laity and clergy."

"You should contact the other trustees," Angelina said.

After obtaining Rev. Dick's permission, I emailed a copy of our correspondence to other members of the board, seeking advice and direction.

Peggy, the finance chair and the wife of the current board president, emailed Don and the other trustees. Don, as membership chair, she wrote, was "very fortunate" that Rev. Dick was "able and willing to devote more time than he was able to last year" to the church. "The key to retaining good membership," Peggy wrote, "is continuity, which Rev. Dick's three-times-per-month permits."

*Continuity?* I thought. *We have had twenty years of it. Where are the new members? Where's the growth? It is time to do something different.*

As finance chair, Peggy explained, she was especially concerned that FXUU couldn't afford to pay for guest ministers. Money, she wrote, was needed for advertising and church repairs.

Did Peggy forget that people raised their pledges specifically to pay for guest ministers? They didn't do it to pay for church repairs. While maintaining the building was important, if FXUU failed to attract new members, the church would close. The UUA would then sell the building to a developer, who would probably put stores in its place.

Don and his wife, Sharon, came over for dinner Saturday night, August 22. After dinner, we sat in my living room with my husband discussing Rev. Dick's refusal to comply with the 2-1-1 plan.

"I am appalled at his audacity in this," Don said. "He's not in disagreement with your schedule—the schedule agreed upon—he's power playing and stonewalling. You're right, Maggie. There is no change from last year."

"Yeah, Don, I know he's power playing," I said. "He must be feeling threatened by me. I suspect he thinks I'm trying to take over. He's a very poor communicator, and it's been hard getting him to let me know what's going on. He appears to need to be in control."

"Were minutes of the May board meeting and the June annual meeting given out?" Don asked, sipping on his glass of soda. "I didn't get any."

"I don't have those minutes," I replied. "Remember? The church clerk was moving. FXUU would've been the last thing on her mind. She probably didn't send them out. We really need them, though."

"I'm going to email the clerk and see if she has them," Don said. "I'll copy Marge. She's clerk now."

"Do you have a copy of Rev. Dick's contract?" I asked. "When was the last time it was renewed?"

"I don't think there is a written contract," Sharon said.

"That's not a surprise," I said, frowning. "It is my opinion that the board has already voted on the worship service, and that if Rev. Dick wants to preach more, he has to make a motion at the board meeting and get it passed."

"Rev. Dick can't make a motion," Don corrected me. "He's not on the board. He would have to recommend it, someone on the board would have to make the motion, and the board would have to vote."

"So what do we do?" I asked.

"My game plan would be to meet with a select group from the church. This would have to be a secret meeting, without Rev. Dick's or Harry's or Harry's wife's knowledge or involvement."

"I'm not big on secret meetings," I said. "And I don't really think it's necessary. First of all, I already think we have enough votes. I'm trying to remember the new composition of the board, but you and Sharon, Angelina, Sue and I make five votes."

"Everything I stated up until now has been based on my purely emotional response to this," Don said. "If I step back and intellectualize it, I think that we perhaps should fall back a bit and punt—meet initially as a board with Rev. Dick and discuss it openly, maybe for the first time, and come to a compromise. My fear with this is, we've never been able to work together as a board with Rev. Dick, Harry and Peggy that way. And any compromise would still mean losing our involvement in spirit. And worse, in spirit and body! The same could happen to us."

"I think we already compromised and had long discussions with Rev. Dick," I said. "I fear he'll disregard ... or sabotage ... anything that's not what he wants. Though if we reach some compromise, we'll have to make sure it's reflected properly in the minutes *and* in Rev. Dick's contract."

"Maybe you should try calling him?" Sharon suggested.

I looked at Don. "You're more of a diplomat than me, and you've known Rev. Dick longer."

"I'll give it a try," Don said.

After Don and Sharon left, I checked my email messages and found a message to all the trustees from Harry, the board chair.

> As chairman of the Trustees, let me make it abundantly clear—when the minister of the Church is present he is in every way responsible. The minister is the Chief Executive Officer of the Church and he sets the course to meet the objectives....

*What? Who anointed him king?* I was steaming. I thought of all different replies, some unprintable. I considered giving Don a call, but they'd just left our house after a pleasant visit. I didn't want to spoil their positive mood. I assumed Don would check his email in the morning. *Although over his Sunday breakfast, this one could give him indigestion.*

I took some deep breaths. Lyndon advised me to wait before replying. We drove our son back to the Coast Guard Academy where he was a cadet, and came home to bed. The next morning I tended my garden, doing my best to put the conflict out of my mind for a few hours.

Don emailed me and advised me not to reply. "A reply would only dignify it," Don wrote. Harry's email confirmed what Harry and Peggy's position was. "Could it be any clearer??" he asked. "Rev. Dick's response to this will go a long way to telling me what he is really made of. Now is the time for the 'good shepherd' to step in and save the flock! (???)"

Don and I obtained copies of the May minutes, the Chairman's Annual Report, and the church's bylaws from the church's clerk. These three documents confirmed that what I was doing as worship chair was consistent with my obligations, as decided by the entire board in the minister's presence. The minutes verified that Rev. Dick knew and was involved in the process that led to the decision. The congregation had been informed of the proposed changes in the frequency Rev. Dick would be preaching. What Harry purported to be "abundantly clear" wasn't present in any of FXUU's documents.

The By-Laws stated:

> The minister shall have charge of all matters of a spiritual nature connected with the Church; shall keep in touch with community and social affairs, as far as possible. He shall be expected to cooperate in denominational programs, and shall have the assistance of the Church when desired. He will conduct Communion Services when requested by the Board of Trustees.

The Worship Chair:

> ...shall have general supervision of the services of religious worship, including the music program and special religious programs, services and activities.

While the minister was an ex officio member of all boards, committees and organizations of the church, he did not have the right to vote. Don and I interpreted the bylaws to mean the minister's position was subordinate to the board. It was the worship chair's duty, obligation and right to be essentially in charge of the worship program, including all services.

Don and I discussed the possibility that Rev. Dick might resign. Neither of us thought he would leave. We suspected he needed the money, and more importantly, being FXUU's minister met his desire to preach. The problem we faced was how to promote the 2-1-1 plan without doing too much damage to our relationship with Rev. Dick and the older members of the congregation.

If Rev. Dick left in a huff, replacing his Sunday services would be easy. There was a glut of UU ministers. I had had no trouble getting guest ministers. We would have to hustle and make calls but we would get the Sundays filled. The money we paid Rev. Dick would easily pay for guest ministers.

Don planned to speak with Rev. Dick, to gently inform him he would be doing two sermons per month. Then it would be up to him to get either Harry or Peggy to make a motion to change the worship plan agreed to in May.

Prayerfully, I hoped Rev. Dick would recognize that it was in his best interest to work for the good of the church. I prayed that God would grant us the wisdom to deal with this conflict with love and caring. I prayed we would resist the urge to demonize and somehow reach a win-win solution with all parties.

Don asked Harry to call a special board meeting. On August 27, Harry emailed that it wasn't possible due to scheduling conflicts. Ten minutes later, his wife Peggy sent an email stating nothing could

> ... get done because Maggie has an agenda which is so disruptive to all good intentions. ... if Maggie is successful in getting Rev. Dick and us to resign, funding might be academic.

I didn't understand what was happening. A river of hostility was overflowing its banks, and I was caught in the current. But there hadn't been any rain. Peggy was wrong. I didn't want anyone to resign. We were a small church. We needed everyone. I wanted everyone to stay.

How could my motives and character be so misunderstood? When did Peggy come to despise me? I thought she and I had a lot in common. We were close in age, and each of us owned and ran a micro business. We'd talked about managing cash flow during a lunch date in the cafeteria at a hospital where Peggy was a financial consultant. Our conversation then moved to our religious upbringing, and how we came to Unitarian Universalism. Peggy told me about the difficulties she encountered growing up Jewish in Pennsylvania Dutch country.

"It must have been difficult," I told her. "Lyndon and I visited Strasberg with the children several years ago. We had a great time. But I can see how being Jewish in such a conservative Christian region would be hard."

It was at the end of our lunch that Peggy told me she and Harry were especially concerned about preserving and restoring FXUU's church building. "I hope you'll support us in that," she said.

"Yes, I would like that to happen," I replied. "But we'll need more members to do that. To attract them, we first need to improve worship and religious education for all ages."

Peggy and I departed on good terms. A little while later, she and Harry invited Lyndon and me over for dinner. Peggy served us dinner on their screened porch. After we finished eating, she showed us her collection of antique kitchen utensils. She and Harry enjoyed antiquing and always went to the Big E, a large fair in Brimfield, Massachusetts. Harry collected walking canes, and took us downstairs to show them off.

I thought we were friends. What did I miss? The conflict over the worship schedule was the first time Peggy had expressed any hostility toward me.

Wait. Not quite true. Peggy and I had that tiff over "professional" services months before the 2-1-1 plan was ever conceived. She objected to lay-led services, viewed them as inferior. I challenged her. I and other church members had used our skills and knowledge to put together religious services that moved and inspired others. Although we weren't clergy, the lay-led services were professional in every other sense of the word. Don would later say that there wouldn't have been a problem if the services I had planned were poorly done. My competence was the real issue.

The whole thing was crazy. I was just trying to grow the church by making the worship services more meaningful for everyone. Why was Peggy so enthused with Rev. Dick?

Peggy and I must have wanted totally different things. Position and status appeared important to her. Clergy are high-status individuals within our society. Rank, as my father often said, had its privileges. Was Peggy's primary reason for attending church to increase her own status by being close to the minister? The 2-1-1 plan somehow undercut that.

Don said it was about the money. When we raised our pledges, Harry and Peggy were no longer the primary contributors to FXUU, decreasing their perceived power. I had never paid attention to how much people contributed. I didn't think a person's affluence should secure them more power and influence than someone who had less money. Everyone was equal to me. Maybe that upset Peggy.

Wasn't church about building community, deepening relationships, working things through and learning to settle conflicts? I was committed to win-win solutions just as Dr. Robins, my former therapist, had taught me. Couldn't everyone get their needs met if we worked together?

I actually believed in what Jesus and the great prophets had to say. Power and prestige held little interest for me. I was more interested in a just world. One where people weren't victimized the way I had been. That was what mattered to me, creating a just world one step at a time: First in our families, next in our workplaces and finally in our church communities.

Distressed to be singled out in Peggy's email, I replied,

Dear all,

I, too, am saddened by recent events within our little congregation, not by the fact we disagree about the worship schedule but by the way this disagreement has been handled. Wherever there are people, there will be disagreements. What is important is not that we disagree, but whether we can discuss our disagreements openly and safely. If we truly believe in loving and caring for each other, we need to open ourselves up to really hearing, really listening to what someone else is saying, even if it is contrary to a strongly held belief we may have. Character assassinations, deception and scapegoating have no place in a church community.

I feel I have been personally attacked, my integrity questioned because I dared to disagree with some members of this church. I do not wish nor have I ever tried to get Harry, Peggy, Rev. Dick or anyone else to resign. It continues to be my hope that a fair and just resolution can be reached over the worship schedule. In order to achieve that, there needs to be dialogue. All parties to the dispute need to speak to one another. I think the best way to do that is by calling a special board meeting. I am willing to adjust my schedule to be there, even if it means a loss of income.

After the of majority of board members emailed Harry requesting a special board meeting, Harry relented and scheduled one for the coming Friday night, September 4. Three days before the meeting, Harry emailed board members and Rev. Dick with a proposed agenda and preliminary statements. These statements amounted to a significant change in the bylaws, which could only be amended at a congregational meeting, not a board meeting.

On September 2, I received a three-page letter from Rev. Dick. The letter was addressed to all members of the congregation. Instead of trying to first resolve the conflict with the trustees, Rev. Dick expanded the conflict by drawing everyone in. He must have known he didn't have the votes on the board.

The letter started off reasonably enough.

> I am troubled as I know you are ... I regret the pain and distress I have heard. Yet, at the same time, I have heard each of us give and receive the love and civility that characterize our Universalist Unitarian community...

*Were Harry and Peggy's emails civil?* I thought.

> We will heal, I trust, if we continue to speak from our own heart and listen to others with an open mind.

Yes, if we did that, I thought we could still resolve this at the special board meeting. Rev. Dick wrote that he chose to use the US Postal Service to communicate with the entire congregation. Later, I would learn that everyone else's letter contained a personal, handwritten note while mine did not.

Rev. Dick then used his desire to communicate with everyone to justify his refusal to speak to and explain his actions to trustees other than the chair. He was only talking to Harry. I was also sure that included Harry's wife, Peggy, too. Rev. Dick was only speaking to people who supported his position, no one else.

Rev. Dick began his attack on me in the third paragraph. Referring to me only as "the worship chair," never by name, he accused me of replacing a sermon he had prepared for Paul Revere's birthday, "a message I (he) could not use another day," for a talkback (discussion) the previous January.

What was he talking about? I had to think. Then I remembered. The board switched the schedule around to accommodate some event, I couldn't remember what. I printed out the order of service reflecting the change. When I arrived at the church, I discovered Rev. Dick thought he was preaching that day. He hadn't been informed of the change. My fault, probably. I immediately apologized and offered to do the talkback another Sunday.

"No," he replied. "You go ahead. The order of service is already printed."

"Are you sure?" I said, feeling terrible.

"Yes, I can do my sermon another week."

In his letter Rev. Dick wrote,

> I should not have allowed that to happen without expressing my thoughts. By not addressing the event, I believe I gave the impression that I do not care and that my sermons are modular and may be plugged in and out at any time.

Faulting himself for taking a passive role, he then summarized the trustee's failed attempt to hire an associate minister. Apparently he would have been happy preaching only two Sundays per month had we been able to hire an associate. But he was opposed to my proposed worship schedule because it

> ... carried a theological slant of orthodoxy, with holidays and rituals that we have never observed. They characterize, in my view, a move toward traditional Christianity. My own spiritual orientation, while including Christian theological beliefs, encompasses and respects many sources of inspiration.

Hadn't I shown respect by including all holidays regardless of denomination? What about the All Souls/Sam Hein service? Clearly, I had been open to other "sources of inspiration."

He wrote he had "tried to get around the theological issue by insisting on preaching more than two Sundays a month."

So he wasn't opposed to 2-1-1. He just didn't want it to include any Judeo-Christian elements. Why didn't he simply call or email me expressing his concerns? If he had, I would have clarified that I wasn't an orthodox Christian. I was, however, interested in the historical Jesus.

As worship chair, I had attempted to involve all members in lay services, giving them an opportunity to share where they were in their personal spiritual journey. My efforts had resulted in the successful blending of pagan ritual and Universalist tradition during the All Souls/Sam Hein service. After the service, a church member stopped me in the church's basement and asked, "Are you going to become a minister?"

"No," I said. "I already have a profession. I don't need another one."

Don suggested that the five board members who supported the 2-1-1 plan meet, along with their spouses, the evening before the special board meeting. We met at Sue's house, a small cape cod. I entered through the side door into the kitchen. Sue, a heavy woman, was loud and theatrical. She scolded her two children loudly and publicly, shouting, "Get over here! I am going to kill you!" She boasted that her family understood it was *her* kitchen, and they better not make a mess of it. I, myself, have never wanted to take ownership of the kitchen. I never wanted to be the only one cooking and cleaning. My role as homemaker, while important, had never been central to my identity.

Joe, Sue's husband, ushered us downstairs into the basement. It was partly finished, with some couches and chairs in the corner under the casement window.

"This is Joe's domain," Sue informed us while I took a seat on the couch along the basement wall. Besides Joe and Sue, Don and Sharon and Angelina and her husband were there. I was the only one who came without my spouse.

Don chaired the meeting. He thought politically. "Maggie should not be the first one to speak tomorrow night," he advised. "It would be best if she said as little as possible and allowed us to support her position."

I said nothing. I knew I didn't think strategically in these situations. I tended to put too much trust in honesty and reason. I wouldn't have planned our response at all, but simply sought to clarify my position and motives at the special board meeting. I naively believed we could negotiate a win-win solution with Rev. Dick.

Don, however, had more experience with boards than I did, so I agreed to the plan. More than a year later, I would realize that decision robbed me of my voice and cast the others in the role of my protector. Like a child whose parents are embroiled in a bitter divorce, I became a disempowered pawn. Almost a year later, the social support I received would prove to be conditional on my ability to organize and conduct lay-led services. When I could no longer meet my protectors' expectations, I would be discarded and shunned.

When I walked into the church basement the next night, I was surprised to find the table moved from its usual corner to the center of the room. In addition to the chairs placed around the table, there were seats placed in a row between the table and the stairs to the vestibule. Several members of the congregation who weren't on the board were sitting there. Rev. Dick must have told them about the meeting and invited them. I took a seat along the opposite side, several seats away from the head of the table where Harry was sitting.

After everyone had found a seat Harry said, "I call this congregational meeting to order."

"This isn't a congregational meeting," Don said.

"As board chair—"

"You need two weeks' notice to hold a congregational meeting," Don said.

*What difference does it make?* I wondered.

"A congregational meeting would be chaired by the moderator, not the board chair," Don explained. "This is a special board meeting. Only members of the board have a vote."

Harry reluctantly conceded that the procedure to call a congregational meeting hadn't been followed, and that it was, in fact, a special board meeting.

After the purpose and format of the meeting were clarified, the special board meeting was called to discuss the "2-1-1" concept and Rev. Dick's wish to preach more than two Sundays per month. While the board respectfully listened to the opinions of other church members, the bylaws only permitted board members to vote.

Peggy knitted furiously throughout the discussion, at one point saying, "I only attend this church because of Rev. Dick. I am appalled at the disrespect being shown to him."

"We need to be fiscally responsible," Harry said. "It's in the best interest of the whole congregation to have Rev. Dick in the pulpit three weeks per month. This will provide the church with consistency."

Several church members agreed. Helen, an elderly member who lived a block away in the Doolittle Retirement Home, read a letter from her fellow retirees. "It is fortunate to have such good leadership from Rev. Dick," she read. "We want the church to continue in the more liberal tradition."

"It isn't a theological issue," Angelina said.

"As worship chair, Maggie always invited others to help with the lay services," Sue added.

"Don't take a vote tonight," Helen urged. "No one would win. You should contact the district executive."

I looked at Helen. *Maybe we should listen to her. Her husband was a retired minister. She has had more experience with churches than any of us had.*

But we were only voting on what already had been decided on last spring. It wasn't fair the way Rev. Dick, Harry and Peggy had brought this issue up again. Disregarding Helen's advice, the board voted. The 2-1-1 worship schedule was to be implemented.

"Why don't you just give Rev. Dick what he wants?" Marge the church secretary asked as she left the church in tears.

Why was she so upset? I didn't get it. Why was it so important to her to please Rev. Dick? She had grown up in that church. She knew Rev. Dick since she was a child. But still, why was it so catastrophic? Rev. Dick was still our minister. We weren't forcing him out. We just wanted him to honor his agreement. Why was our intent so totally misperceived?

I felt so sad when I saw Marge's tears. What had gone wrong? I never intended to hurt her. I liked her. Tall, beautiful and blonde, she had told me once during coffee hour she liked my hearty laugh. It was then I realized that my laugher and my tears were just different sides of the same coin. They were both part of my passion for life.

Worn, drained and numb, I drove home to the safety of my home. Lying in bed with Lyndon, I shared what had happened at the meeting.

"The abuse in an abusive family," Lyndon said, "does not stop until one or a couple of its members go out of the family unit and seek help."

I sat straight up. "Yes, of course, you're right."

The next morning I emailed Don, Sharon, Angelina and Sue.

> The time has come to bring in more light, more people. I will solicit people to serve on the worship committee next Sunday by putting an announcement in the bulletin and asking Sue to put an announcement in the newsletter. People also need to be educated about why we need a lay ministry and its historical roots in Universalism. John Murray and Hosea Ballou were originally lay ministers. Perhaps a series of newsletter articles will help.

> For the same reason we need to expand congregational participation and increase openness, I urge you to call Rev. Terry. ... Helen suggested we contact Rev. Terry. I think it would be really helpful if one of us called her and asked her why she thinks that might help. She might have other ideas that will help us keep this congregation together. If she becomes part of the solution she will become committed to

it. That is why the five of us were so committed to 2-1-1. We had put so much of ourselves into it.

Don emailed Rev. Terry, the district executive, who responded by telephone on September 6. Don provided him with a history of the problem. Don also shared the view that the board and Rev. Dick had unwittingly been on a collision course over the past several years as the board became more active and the chairs assumed more proactive roles.

Rev. Terry stated this story had been told hundreds of times in Unitarian Universalist churches all over the country. This was merely FXUU's version. If he were to intervene, the protocol was for the board president to contact him requesting he do so. Rev. Terry wanted a cooling-off period. We were to cease discussing the issue until he met with the board. He would then try to bring things back to where they were prior to the start of the conflict.

I welcomed the cooling-off period. I needed a break. I wept while I tended my garden. There were times when I thought we could win and times when I thought we would definitely fail. I kept hoping for someone to pull a rabbit out of the hat. Maybe Rev. Terry would be that person. I believed he would support the future and not the past. He would try to smooth out the edges for people who were resisting. We might have to back up a little and take a deep breath. But we were still the board for the next nine months. We were in the position to influence things, and we already had. I didn't want to make the mistake of thinking Rev. Dick was the most important part of the church. We needed to keep our eyes on our mission to grow the church and work toward that. If we did that, what Rev. Dick did would be inconsequential.

Instead of honoring the cooling-off period, Rev. Dick chose to call Don on Tuesday, the day after Don had spoken to Rev. Terry. Months later, Don mailed me his notes of that conversation. I read them while sitting in my recliner.

Rev. Dick had asked Don, "Where do we go from here? Do we hang in there? Try to please everyone? I truly hope and expect that the church in total will confirm and recognize that the minister is the spiritual leader and not just a community member."

Rev. Dick spoke about what he perceived was my misdirection as worship chair. He said I wanted to observe Pentecost, have a Communion Sunday and observe Trinity Sunday. He said I was being "too assertive" as worship chair. Contradicting his letter, Rev. Dick said I hadn't sent him the worship schedules as I claimed.

Rev. Dick complained, "She has consumed our life. Sandy and I have been unable to write the college history book for three weeks. People are saying that Maggie is calling them to line up sides."

Rev. Dick further questioned whether the church wanted a worship chair "who is willing to act like a layman or one who wants to direct the church."

Rev. Dick informed Don that Harry was very downhearted and physically ill since the special board meeting. He felt he had failed to conclude things in one evening. Rev. Dick went on to say, "People will leave, the church will close, the land and building will revert to the Unitarian Universalist Association, there will be no Unitarian Universalist church in Foxboro. We have never had this before."

Rev. Dick further said, "Maggie wants to be a unilateral decision maker. She wants to push her notions down people's throats—church music, joys and concerns and her personal family news from the balcony, which she keeps doing even though nobody wants it. Board members need to be frank. They cannot be argumentative like Maggie. She acts like she is holding a therapy session. She needles people until they give up and she gets her way. The trouble with Maggie is [she needs] to control people as though they are beneath her. She throws her doctorate around and then she's happy. She needs to settle down and accept people as they are and not try to have the upper hand. Her control is the issue. I cannot tolerate the control aspect of her nature. No minister can. She wants a lay-led church. I cannot talk about these programs with Maggie."

Rev. Dick then asked Don, "If I resign, would the dust settle?"

Don had replied, "It isn't time for anyone to resign."

On Saturday, September 12, Lyndon and I left early in the morning to go to our son's track meet. Returning home late in the afternoon, we stopped at our mailbox to get our mail. There was a letter from Rev. Dick. Standing in the kitchen, I opened it. It was addressed to the entire congregation. My jaw dropped and my first thought was, *Oh, my God!* After twenty-nine years at FXUU, Rev. Dick was resigning effective immediately. No notice. No time for transition. How professional was that?

Rev. Dick wrote he had spoken with the Vice-President of the District Board. I stopped reading. Russell, Gretchen's husband, was currently in that position. Russell was the church member who had declared Rev. Melody's selection as Murray's next minister unanimous. I wondered if he would jump to support Rev. Dick without taking time to listen to both sides as soon as he heard I was involved in the conflict at Foxboro.

Rev. Dick also wrote he had spoken to the Good Offices Minister of the District. I decided that must be the office Don told me was responsible for representing ministers during disputes. Since Rev. Dick was fellowshipped in the United Church of Christ and not in the Unitarian Universalist Association, the UUA's ability to assist him would be limited. Rev. Dick then took credit for securing assistance from Rev. Terry, the district executive, even though Don had made the first phone call.

*Rev. Dick is bailing out,* I thought, *to avoid the mediation process. He must know his position is weak.* Yet, if he cared so much about the church, why wasn't he letting Rev. Terry mediate the dispute and sort it out? What was he so afraid of?

On September 20, a week and a half after Rev. Dick mailed his letter of resignation, Rev. Terry conducted the Sunday service at Foxboro. He met with the board immediately after in the sanctuary. We brought out some folding chairs from the closet that once housed the organ pipes. Like the bell, the organ had been sold decades before to pay the church's operating expenses.

We sat in a circle around Rev. Terry, who stood near the pulpit, two steps higher than the rest of us. When we started to tell him our side of events, he interrupted. "There will be no more bloodletting."

Don said, "But—"

"It would be better for the church not to discuss it anymore," he said.

Don and the others tried to argue with him. Rev. Terry's advice didn't sound right to me either. I thought the meeting was to present our side of things and give the congregation a chance to express their opinions and feelings. Before I could say anything, Rev. Terry turned to me and said, "And you have problems you need to work out with Rev. Dick."

A cloud of confusion engulfed me, and I couldn't think or respond clearly. I had expected Rev. Terry to mediate the dispute. Instead he attacked me, implying the fault was my inability to get along with Rev.

Dick. But I hadn't even known Rev. Dick had any issues with me until a couple of weeks ago. How could I be held responsible for problems I didn't know existed?

Exhausted from all the conflict and not wanting to split the church further, I tearfully urged the board to follow Rev. Terry's recommendation, including that we immediately resign from the board and have a special election.

The following night, Rev. Terry held a meeting with the rest of the congregation. The board sat in pews on the pulpit side of the sanctuary, toward the front of the church. The other members of the church took seats toward the back. They came expecting to voice their views. Instead Rev. Terry cut them off with, "If you don't get together, the church will close."

I felt the eyes of Rev. Dick's allies on me. I knew they blamed me. But they didn't know the whole story, and I wasn't going to be given a chance to tell my side of events. My throat tightened and tears filled my eyes. *Oh, no!* I thought. *Why now? I thought I was handling this. Stop crying before anyone sees.*

I turned my head trying to hide my tears. Sharon's eyes met mine. She saw my pain. I began weeping.

At the end of the meeting, Rev. Terry walked past me. When his eyes met mine, he straightened his spine and looked straight ahead. He didn't acknowledge my tears or offer comfort of any kind. Why was he treating me like I was to blame?

Following Rev. Terry's suggestion, we all resigned from the board pending a special election. Since no other church members came forward to participate, we withdrew our resignations and remained on the board.

Several members who supported Rev. Dick left the church, saying they wouldn't return until I left. Those members who supported Rev. Dick and who stayed were openly hostile to me.

The board asked Joe, Sue's husband, to contact Rev. Dick and ask him to return the water that was used for our annual Water Communion. Sunday after the service, Sue pulled me aside while we stood on the church's porch. She showed me the email Joe sent to Rev. Dick, and Rev. Dick's reply.

*Joe is such a diplomat,* I thought while I read his email. *The board was wise to ask him to handle this.*

After thanking Joe for his sensitive note, Rev. Dick reminisced about how various church members had gathered the water from christenings, a reservoir, and from the rain that fell during his late daughter's wedding. The pain, he said, was great, but he had to resign. He wrote,

> The minister must be the spiritual leader of the church. I cannot be otherwise. When I was manipulated, told what to preach about, told I had to change schedules, saw the sick joke Maggie sent, saw that Don wanted to undercut my ministry in his emails to Terry, and read Maggie's intention of celebrating Trinity Sunday in a Unitarian Universalist Church, I knew I could not in good faith continue to conduct worship with people who acted in such a way.

*Sick joke?* What was he talking about? I didn't remember sending any joke. And if I had, it certainly wasn't sick. I handed the paper back to Sue.

"Look at this other one he sent about you." Sue opened a folded piece of paper. I moved closer. My eyes caught my name and what appeared to be obscenities. I gasped.

"Sue!" Joe snatched the paper from Sue's hands before I could read it. "I told you not to show that to Maggie."

I watched him walk away, grateful for his concern, but I needed to know what I was up against. I didn't need Joe's protection. I wasn't a child. I had handled far worse things than this in my life.

I continued to go to the Council of Churches' committee meetings, but felt numb. After one meeting, I waited until the others had left. Rev. Karen closed her office door. I told her about the events at FXUU.

"I noticed the strain," she said. "I was wondering what was wrong."

I sighed while I put on my coat. "It's been hard."

She walked with me to the exit. "Sometimes I think it's the devil at work in our churches."

I stopped and stared at her. "You can't be serious. Do you really believe in the devil?"

"Yes, I do." She set the door to lock after I left.

"Well, I don't." I pushed the glass door open. "It's just a failure of communication. A lack of good conflict resolution skills. The devil had nothing to do with it."

With the full support of FXUU's board, I began organizing Sunday services. I located and scheduled guest speakers. I planned two lay-led services per month. I typed and printed the order of service every Saturday. If I wasn't at work or at one of my son's track meets, I was working on church services. I wanted to please, fit in and be accepted. I wanted to redeem myself for any fault of mine that might have caused the conflict. But what was that fault? Some people were saying I couldn't get along with anyone. My problems at Murray proved it. How did they know about that? Did Rev. Dick tell them?

Like the major car accident I had been in years before when a drunk driver ran two red lights, I could find no mistakes. It had been completely out of my control. That was terrifying. It meant I couldn't prevent another attack. I was wholly dependent on the good behavior of others.

# Damage Repair

In mid-October, a month after his mediation meeting with us, Rev. Terry realized his intervention had failed and hired Gabriel Ames Associates, experts on church conflict, to investigate and mediate FXUU's dispute. The consultant explained to the board and the rest of the church members that she would be holding small group meetings. She placed signup sheets for the available times on a table. There was only one time that was doable for me. I hesitated. I didn't want to be the only one from the board there. After a brief discussion, someone else from the board signed up with me. I wouldn't have to face my adversaries alone.

On the day of the meeting, I drove from work to FXUU parking along the town common, hurried across the street and entered the church through the red doors into the vestibule. I started to enter the sanctuary, but quickly moved back, out of sight, when I saw that the previous group was still sitting near the pulpit, talking. Thinking, Damn! I looked at my watch. I was fifteen minutes early. Not wanting to intrude, I withdrew and chose a seat on a bench as far away from the doorway as possible.

Tired, I closed my eyes and rested my head against the wall. I took some slow, deep breaths.

"Maggie should go to speech therapy to cure her of her cackling."

I sat straight up. It was Katherine, a former teacher who lived at the retirement home next door.

Memories swirled in my head. I was back in school, standing in the hallway with my speech therapist. My classmates were laughing, "You don't know how to talk." They mimicked my deep voice. "You're stupid." I was such a moron. I couldn't even laugh right.

My heart rate increased. My breathing became shallow and quick, my actions automatic. I raced toward the red doors and placed my hands on the cold gray panic bar. But I didn't push. Quiet, I thought. What would they think if they knew I was out here? I took some slow, deep breaths. My heart rate slowed.

Why should I leave? What did I do wrong? What does the way I talk and laugh have to do with the dispute with Rev. Dick?

For an educated woman, Katherine was mean and petty. Why did Katherine think it was okay to say such things? She must have expected support from the others.

Katherine had never spoken to me about my laughter. Once, during coffee hour, she made a rude comment about my biracial marriage and my children. When I went home I vented about it, but eventually dismissed it because of Katherine's advanced age. Whenever I spoke to her I was cordial, polite and respectful.

As I walked back to the bench I heard, "Shssh! She's in the vestibule." It was Sharon, Don's wife. She must have seen me when I first arrived.

I heard the moving of chairs as people stood up and prepared to leave the sanctuary. I quickly sat back down on the bench and wiped my tears. Taking a deep breath, I tightened my face and took refuge behind a stony façade.

Katherine pushed her walker across the vestibule toward the door nearest me. She stopped in front of me. I pushed my shoulders back while focusing on slowing my breathing. Katherine might have apologized. My memory isn't clear.

"It's too late," I said. "The harm has already been done."

"Katherine didn't mean it," Sharon said, trying to smooth things over. Who was she trying to protect? Me or Katherine?

I did not intend to seek speech therapy to cure me of my "cackling." I wasn't interested in becoming a proper New England lady with two sticks up her ass, unable to laugh heartily. I was fine the way I was.

After Sharon, Katherine and the rest of their group left the church, I entered the sanctuary. The consultant looked at me sympathetically but offered no words of solace. I took a seat. The rest of the group arrived, oblivious to what had just happened.

A couple of the long-term members of the church told the group that the previous April, Rev. Dick told them he was feeling uncomfortable. He felt there was a movement to fire him, similar to one that occurred twenty years before, when several congregants questioned his ministry. Just as the current board had done, the possibility of getting an associate minister was discussed at a congregational meeting. The idea died due to lack of funds. The congregation split, with the majority of members resigning en masse and joining the Congregational church next door.

A week after the group meeting, I attended the North Atlantic Regional Gathering of the Unitarian Universalist Association in Providence. I bumped into Russell in the exhibition hall. We briefly discussed Rev. Dick and FXUU.

"We were trying to be so careful," I emphasized.

"Why so careful?" Russell asked.

He sounded suspicious. Didn't he understand we tried to be sensitive to Rev. Dick and the older church members? We had crafted a plan for church growth while acknowledging and respecting the needs of the older members. Before I could answer, Russell was called away.

The next day, t he Unitarian Universalist Christian Fellowship hosted a seminar on Christianity within the UUA. I took a seat in the back. They were discussing when, where and with whom communion could be administered.

"Can someone other than a minister give communion?" someone asked.

"That's an interesting question."

Tears filled my eyes. Embarrassed, I stepped out into the hall. I bumped into the consultant.

"How are you doing?" she asked.

The tears streamed down my face. "I was scapegoated."

"I know," she replied.

Grateful for the validation, I relaxed. She saw what I knew.

Shortly after the regional gathering, the consultant wrote her report and presented it to the congregation. She wrote that my involvement in lay services filled "a definite void in the congregation" and,

> No one else wanted to do it, and Maggie enjoyed doing and organizing the services. Most of those who talked about the services said they enjoyed them, and that they had heard good reports of the services. By all accounts, there were a variety of people involved in the services and many issues, theological perspectives and topics covered in these services.

The consultant further wrote she was amazed at how fast the issue escalated. This suggested things "had been festering for a while" and that theological orthodoxy was not the real issue. The worship schedule I had proposed was not atypical of Unitarian Universalist churches. The consultant concluded, "Disagreement with the calendar should have been an opportunity for reasoned dialogue. Unfortunately, assumptions were made and accusations followed."

The recommendations the consultant made had either been tried unsuccessfully before or were largely unworkable in such a small congregation. For instance, her recommendation that a new board be formed with a "neutral moderator" failed to recognize that no one except the existing board members were willing to serve, and that there was no neutral person in the church. She also didn't recognize that it wasn't the board that was refusing to meet, but Rev. Dick's supporters.

Inexplicably, even though she recognized I had been scapegoated and had done a good job as worship chair, the consultant further recommended that I resign my position as worship chair as if the conflict was started by me. In conversation, she referred to me as a "lightning rod." Her solution was to support my enemies' efforts to push me out of the church.

I would have gladly allowed someone else be worship chair, but no one volunteered. Rev. Dick's supporters didn't want me there but weren't willing to assume any responsibility. They had served on the board and its committees for years. They merited a break, but unrealistically wanted the new members to do the work just as they had without making any changes.

Although most of the consultant's recommendations were un-workable, the board did adopt her recommendations regarding the process for selecting and hiring a part-time minister. In close consultation with the district executive, the guidelines of the Unitarian Universalist Association were largely followed and a formal contract developed that stated the responsibilities and expectations of the minister. Four months after Rev. Dick's resignation, Rev. Terry provided the FXUU board with the names of two retired ministers who were willing to serve as interim minister. The board scheduled interviews with both.

I remember very little about the interviews except one of the candidates' response to questions about her theological stance. "It isn't possible to know if there is a God," Rev. Dorothy had said. Was she emphasizing her agnosticism because she had heard of my interest in Christianity?

"I do not believe Jesus Christ is my personal savior," she said

"Neither do I," I replied.

While she spoke, she appeared vaguely familiar. Had we met before? I asked.

"I don't think so," she said. She had been district executive a number of years before. Now she was retired.

Was she the woman I met a year and a half ago at the district's fall gathering? I vaguely remembered sitting down to eat my lunch when a slender, shorthaired woman in her sixties or seventies joined me.

"We can't have you eating alone," she had said.

The woman and I talked about FXUU and Rev. Dick. She made a point of stating he was not fellowshipped in the Unitarian Universalist Association. I was offended but said nothing. Her remark was irrelevant, and disparaged Rev. Dick. He was well respected by FXUU members, especially the older ones. It wasn't until months later, when efforts to grow the church failed, that I questioned Rev. Dick's competence. I didn't realize an important layer of oversight and accountability was missing when a minister wasn't fellowshipped in the same denomination as the church he served.

Was that woman Rev. Dorothy? Yet there were many older women who, following their divorces, became UU ministers. I could be mixing them up, I decided.

Rev. Dorothy was hired as FXUU's interim minister. After a second meeting to work out the details of her contract, she and I spoke in the church's vestibule. Guarded, I asked her, "What have you heard about me?"

"Nothing."

I doubted that. Later I would learn she was good friends with Gretchen, attending writing classes in her home every Monday night. Certainly Gretchen had shared with her the conflict over Rev. Melody, although perhaps Gretchen didn't mention my name. Rev. Dorothy also knew Rev. Dick well. She used to babysit his children when they lived next door to each other in Ohio. The coincidence made me uneasy. Could she be trusted?

On Sunday, February 21, Rev. Dorothy conducted her first service at FXUU. An elderly woman and long-time church member praised Rev. Dick during the Joys and Concerns part of the service. I bit my lip and said nothing.

After returning home from church, I felt nauseous. Nothing I ate helped. I worried I was coming down with a stomach virus. By late afternoon, I realized I was crashing. During the crisis at FXUU, the other board members had praised me for not losing my temper. None of us realized how much I had shut down emotionally. Like a robot, I had mechanically performed my duties as worship chair. With the emergency behind us, fear overwhelmed me.

I emailed Rev. Dorothy late that evening.

> Thanks for the service today. I thought it went very well. I
> just wanted to share with you how difficult it is for me to sit
> quietly every time someone brings up a farewell service for
> Rev. Dick. I have kept quiet when anyone has asked about
> Rev. Dick or someone else sings his praises, thinking it will
> be okay with time. If I were to explain to them why I now
> feel the way I do about Rev. Dick and his wife they would
> probably take that as confirmation that I was up to no good
> from the very beginning. Anyway, it is the feeling that I
> have to be quiet about what I know and understand that
> ends up distressing me. I have been experiencing mild bouts
> of anxiety. ... I am uncertain what will make it better.
> Sometimes I think time will take care of it. Other times I
> think your efforts will do it. Other times I think that maybe
> I should go talk to someone, that it would be beneficial to
> talk to someone where I could share it all and connect the
> dots. Then I think I am overworked and exhausted and just
> need a weekend where I can veg. Or perhaps it is all of the
> above.
>
> I am uncertain why I am writing this note or if I should
> trust you or not.

I met with Rev. Dorothy in the church basement the next day. I told
her the expectation that I remain quiet about Rev. Dick and not defend
myself was like blowing up a balloon and never letting any air out.
Eventually it pops. I never had any desire to "take over the church." I
wasn't even sure what people meant by that. I just wanted to be an
accepted member of the church community. There were times I felt
responsible for what had happened. I feared it would be better for me to
leave. Maybe that would satisfy Rev. Dick's supporters and they would
return to FXUU.

Rev. Dorothy told me it wasn't uncommon at the end of a church
conflict for church members to develop problems. She offered to provide
me with pastoral counseling. I told her I needed to think it over. Later
that evening, I emailed Rev. Dorothy asking for some names of therapists.

She provided me with three names. Standing in my kitchen I picked
up the wall phone and dialed the only woman listed. I was told she had

moved out of state. I fumbled with the paper. The second name sounded familiar. He worked in Taunton, where I frequently consulted. Worried that I knew him, I called the third name on the list. It was his home number. A woman I assumed was his wife gave me his office number. I took a deep breath and dialed. His answering machine picked up. Relieved I was temporarily off the hook, I left a message.

Around noon, Rev. Steve Emmett, PhD, a licensed psychologist and an ordained Unitarian Universalist minister, returned my call.

"I got your name from Rev. Dorothy," I told him anxiously.

"Rev. Dorothy? Oh, yes, Rev. Dorothy. I haven't seen her in a while. How is she doing?"

"She's fine. She's the minister at my church."

"Can you make it tomorrow at 11 a.m.?" he asked.

I hesitated while I mentally reviewed my schedule. "Yes." I paused, then blurted, "I'm a psychologist too."

"I bet it's been a long while since you've been in therapy," Dr. Emmett replied.

I relaxed. "Yes. Ten to fifteen years."

The next morning, I drove south into Seekonk. Dr. Emmett's office was located in an old cape cod whose yard had been made into a parking lot. Strip malls surrounded it. I entered through the front door. To my right I saw a counter. Behind it stood shelves filled with shampoo and conditioner. Women were sitting on chairs along the front window. I stood still, thinking I was in the wrong place.

"May I help you?" a woman asked.

"I'm looking for Dr. Emmett's office."

"At the top of the stairs." She pointed to a stairway that was right in front of me. I hadn't noticed it.

I climbed the steep stairs to a narrow hallway with white walls that needed painting. There were three doors. Slightly to the left was one with Dr. Emmett's name on it. It was closed. I was a little early. I paused, uncertain what to do. Was there a waiting room behind that door? Should I wait, or knock?

Fearful that I would miss my appointment, I knocked. A man with gray hair stuck his head out. I caught a glimpse of an older man sitting on a couch.

"I'll be right with you," he said.

Clearly, this was Dr. Emmett. "Okay," I replied while he shut the door.

There was no waiting room. No place to sit. I walked a few feet to the right. There were two other doors. One was probably a bathroom. I stood there while my stomach churned and I thought of escape. I glanced at my watch and waited.

At exactly 11 a.m. Dr. Emmett opened the door, and the older man left. Dr. Emmett invited me in. The room was small and narrow. A white dilapidated couch lined the wall opposite the door and an old, shabby club chair stood between the door and the desk. There was a small window at the end of the room overlooking the parking lot.

Uncertain where to sit, I chose the couch. Dr. Emmett sat directly opposite me. With his knees only a few inches from my own, it was uncomfortably close.

Understanding without being asked what was expected, I told him the basic facts of my life. I was married with two grown children. I was the youngest of five, born to an alcoholic mother. I was hospitalized almost thirty years before when I was nineteen. While I talked, he took out a yellow pad and began taking notes. Occasionally he would ask a question. I told him how I knew Rev. Dorothy, and what had happened at FXUU. I also told him I was sexually abused when I was a child.

"It appears the church conflict triggered a reoccurrence of post-traumatic stress disorder. Do you agree?" he asked as he stood.

"Yes." I was surprised the session was ending. Had it been fifty minutes already?

He opened the door as I walked toward it. I stopped. He was too close to the door. He looked at me, saw the fear in my eyes and stepped back, creating a safe distance for me to exit.

Once through the door, I raced down the steps and out the exit without looking back. When I reached my car, I slid behind the steering wheel and pushed the button for the power locks. Safe, I leaned my head against the headrest. I felt confused. How long was the session? I looked at my watch. It was ten to twelve. When did I leave Dr. Emmett's office? Five minutes ago? Oh, *that's right*, I thought. Insurance companies were now paying for forty-five minutes instead of fifty.

While I rested in my car, my mind raced. I wished I didn't need therapy again. After all these years, I found myself dealing with issues I thought I had resolved years ago. I was sure I would recover quickly. I expected to be out of therapy in a couple of months.

My cell phone rang. It was Lyndon.

"How did it go?" he asked.

"Okay. I don't know if I like him."

"It's only the first session."

"I know."

"Where are you going next?"

"I have an appointment at a group home in Taunton."

"Okay. Talk to you later."

"I love you."

"Me, too."

The next day a client cancelled, giving me a late-afternoon break. Weary, I stretched out on the brown plaid sofa in my office. Dozing I smelled the beer on Uncle Frank's breath as he slid his hand into my pants. I pressed my legs tightly together and moved my knees up to my chest, protecting my body from his prying hands. If I cut my arms, I thought, the evil poison infecting my body would run out with my blood, relieving my pain.

*Oh, my God!* I sat up. *What was I thinking? I am in serious trouble.*

The next session with Dr. Emmett, I sat in the club chair opposite the sofa. I avoided eye contact. Toward the end of the session, I mumbled that I was thinking of harming myself.

"What did you say?" he asked.

I froze. I stared at my hands in my lap.

"I need you to repeat what you said," he insisted.

"I've been ... I have been wanting to ... cut," I whispered.

"If you need to I can be reached—"

"Don't," I pleaded. "I'm not going to—"

"You can call 781—"

"No, please."

"You know I have to do this," he replied.

I looked at him, and then away. He finished telling me how to reach him in case of an emergency. His voice sounded far away as I suppressed the urge to run. I wanted him to stop, this whole thing to stop. This couldn't be happening to me again.

During our next sessions, Dr. Emmett urged me to call him or Rev. Dorothy whenever I was on the verge of harming myself. I resisted. I didn't want to bother anyone with my problems. I didn't want people to think I was crazy. He eventually convinced me, and I began calling Rev. Dorothy a couple of times per week. She told me about her own sexual victimization. "It was only once, but it was severe," she said. The demons that were haunting me were the same ones that had haunted her.

"You have gotten your figure and ground confused," she said "Your past has become the figure, when it belongs in the background."

I understood the metaphor taken from Gestalt psychology and visual perception. I had confused my past with the present.

Besides conducting worship services, at the request of the board, Rev. Dorothy began contacting disaffected members, including Rev. Dick. Rev. Dorothy had lunch with him and his wife on February 27. On March 8, she read her report to the board.

> Much of my conversation with Rev. Dick concerned the need for an event that can celebrate his ministry here and bring it to a fitting closure. At first he said he didn't want such an event at all, and expressed apprehension about interactions with some of the people who might attend....

*He must mean me,* I thought. *I'm uneasy too.*

> As I explained to him, there are many people in the congregation who feel the need for such an event, and that their needs should be considered. He wavered, but still wasn't convinced. Finally, I asked him if he didn't feel the need for closure himself. Again he started to say no, but his wife intervened and said she was sure he did both need and want something of the sort for his own satisfaction. He acquiesced. Later, I asked him what sort of event he would like to have. His stated preference was for one last Sunday-morning service with him. We could then plan a special coffee hour afterward.

I sighed. Contact with Rev. Dick was the last thing I wanted.

"I think," Rev. Dorothy continued to read, "it is important to have this event in the church as a kind of symbol of the possibility of everyone coming together again."

"I suppose," I said. "It would be the right thing to do."

"He could use that service to stir up the conflict all over again," Don said. "We should see his sermon before the service."

After a brief discussion, a motion was made. We all voted in favor of the special service.

"I would like all of the trustees to attend," Rev. Dorothy said.

I didn't say anything. Sitting at a church service to honor a man who I had lost respect for and pretending everything was okay didn't feel right. I wasn't sure what to do about it. I discussed this with Dr. Emmett, who supported my desire to do what was in my own best interest.

It continued to distress me that what might be best for me was in conflict with what Rev. Dorothy thought was best for the church. I wanted to find a way to keep myself safe while supporting her efforts to bring some healing. To sort some things out, I asked her some questions about Rev. Dick. In her conversations with him, I asked, did he ever explain why he changed his mind about preaching two Sundays? He expressed regret about his resignation. Was it because he realized how unprofessional and harmful that was, or was it because he felt by doing so he allowed us "evil people" to take over the church? Had he ever said he was sorry for advocating that I be forced out of the church, or for the nasty things he said to Don about Sue and me? Did he ever apologize for that vicious email he sent Joe? Did he recognize in any way how badly he hurt me? Or did he continue to blame me?

Dr. Emmett asked me if it would help if he gave Rev. Dorothy a call. I wasn't sure. I emailed her, asking her if she was interested in speaking to Dr. Emmett. She agreed. I then gave Dr. Emmett blanket consent to speak with her whenever he wanted to coordinate his treatment with the pastoral care Rev. Dorothy was providing me.

She informed Rev. Dick that the board wanted to see his sermon prior to the farewell service. He viewed this as an intrusion and declined. A formal service marking the end of his ministry at FXUU was never held. Instead, he opened his home to anyone who wished to talk to him. I don't know if anyone ever did. Perhaps some of the older members who were able to travel did so. Maybe he visited them in their homes. I never called him even though I was tempted to do so. I didn't think he would ever tell me why he broke his agreement.

At the March 1999 board meeting, Rev. Dorothy handed out a letter she intended to send to every member of the congregation. She read it to the trustees while we sat at a collapsible table in a corner of the church's basement.

"One of the obligations of an interim minister," Rev. Dorothy read, "is to 'speak the truth in love' to people of the congregation. This letter is my attempt to do that."

I sipped a cup of water while I listened intently.

"What I am seeing here at FXUU is a classic case of the road to hell being paved with good intentions. Most of you know that I have known Rev. Dick since we were both growing up in Ohio. I know the spirit that motivates him. However, that spirit has contributed to the difficulties here. Back sometime ... I don't know when ... there was an arrangement whereby Rev. Dick became the pastor here at a very minimal salary. In addition, Rev. Dick gave much, if not all, of that salary back in the form of a pledge to the church. Rev. Dick, along with his wife, has been the largest single pledging unit in the congregation."

Although I had heard some of this at the tense emergency board meetings we had during the conflict, seeing it in print clarified the details and their import.

"To put it bluntly, Rev. Dick literally bought this pulpit and his position as minister. Let me say again that I know Rev. Dick acted out of generous impulses...."

For twenty years? And only after half the church left in protest over him? I think being minister met some need in him. Perhaps he needed to be admired and fawned over.

"Rev. Dick could not have done this without the collusion of the long-term members of the church. From their perspective, this was a good deal: cheap ministry for them. It also meant they didn't have to accept the responsibility for the health, particularly financial health, of the church. This went on for many years without much friction, but when there was a fairly substantial influx of new members..."

*That would be all of the trustees sitting here,* I thought.

"Strains were put on the arrangement. The new people were not party to the agreement, if they ever knew about it."

Not until now. It had never occurred to me to ask what Rev. Dick was paid. Was there even a contract?

"They were willing, even eager, to take on the responsibilities of the institution, and thus became a threat to the long-term members who saw their arrangements being challenged."

Yes, I was eager. I enjoyed doing the lay-led services. I thought I had something of value to offer. Why was that such a threat? Wouldn't we all benefit if the church grew?

"This was an institutional explosion waiting to happen, and the personalities involved didn't cause all the difficulty. If it hadn't been these particular people, it would have been someone else. This does not excuse the unkind, even cruel things that were said. But the stress of the situation put pressure on everyone."

I didn't feel stressed until Rev. Dick refused to honor his agreement.

"I am saying that you are all responsible for what has happened. I am saying that you all need to recognize that responsibility and act to remedy it."

Sounded reasonable, but what could we have done differently? The new members didn't know there was a problem until things exploded. By then it was too late. Shouldn't Rev. Terry, in his role as district executive, have warned us about this when he met with us about growing the church? Shouldn't he have shared his knowledge about church conflicts and how to handle them before things erupted?

"The long-term members of the church abandoned the church when their arrangements were threatened," she continued. "The new members were angry and rebellious."

Rebellious? Against whom? Rev. Dick? We were all adults here. We were not teenagers. We were exercising our legitimate authority granted to us by FXUU's constitution. Rev. Dick and his supporters never communicated honestly with us.

After sending out her letter to the congregation, Rev. Dorothy sent me a letter about how I handled anger. I can only speculate what prompted it. It came out of the blue. From our telephone conversations, I knew she believed I was depressed even though I explained to her I was severely anxious. She also believed depression was caused by unexpressed anger. In her letter she wrote, "Anger is a very powerful and energizing emotion. It can accomplish a lot when used constructively. It can be devastating when used destructively."

Of course. No argument. Why was Rev. Dorothy lecturing me about things I already knew, and that weren't a problem for me?

I immediately called her and left a message on her voicemail. Concerned that I hadn't clearly stated what I intended and how it sounded to her, I sent her a long email.

> First, I want to thank you for all the time you have given me. I am aware that it can be taxing dealing with someone who is falling apart, decompensating. I do not want to overburden you and cause you to burn out. We certainly

need you at FXUU. I am optimistic that this emotional
rollercoaster ride is almost over for me.

Responding to her question as to how I handle anger, I wrote,

As for how I handle anger—within my own household,
extremely well. I fully understand the constructive use of
anger. I am often at my best when I have found my anger,
when I have been clear what I am angry about. Outside
the house, during the conflict at Murray and FXUU, I
bottled up my anger for fear it would intensify an already-
nasty situation. I am now paying the price for suppressing
my anger for such an extended period of time. It is way
out of character for me to engage in personal, derogatory
attacks at home or outside the house. I assume Rev. Dick
was the person who accused me of "sending nasty emails."
I swear to you that my emails to Rev. Dick and everyone
else were always respectful. I did not engage in character
assassinations.... If someone is accusing me of sending a
nasty note, ask them to produce it. I would really like to
know what they interpreted as "nasty"...

Further, I acknowledged,

I think it is difficult for reasonable people such as yourself
to believe that the nastiness was one-sided, since in most
fights, both sides of the dispute do something they later
have to apologize for. In the dispute at FXUU, myself and
the other board members consistently chose the high road
and did not get down and dirty. I do not regret anything I
said or did during the dispute except for not contacting the
district executive sooner.

Rev. Dorothy also wrote, "My guess is that the people at Murray
shunned you because they were uncertain about how you use your
anger." I doubted that was the reason I was shunned. I was mistreated at
my old church because I expressed politically incorrect views. I failed to
adequately defend myself. I didn't become overtly angry and aggressive.
Quite the contrary, I retreated and cried at home.

In her letter, Rev. Dorothy advised me, "If you are hurt and angry at
the people at Murray for shunning you, why not use that anger to build

up the FXUU church to show the Murray people what a great, effective, dynamic person they pushed out?"

I replied,

> I thought I was already doing that. I can't imagine putting any more energy than I already do into FXUU. Very few of my needs, spiritual or otherwise, are being met there, but I stay because of my loyalty to my friends and because I believe we now have an opportunity to build a better, healthier church.

A few weeks later during one of my urgent phone calls to her, she suggested doing a prayer service for me. At first I hesitated. I worried it was a dumb, self-centered thing to be doing and I should refuse. I didn't really deserve to have this done for me. I wasn't a good enough person, and my problems were really rather insignificant in the scheme of things.

Rev. Dorothy couldn't be serious. After all she was the agnostic, wasn't she? She probably didn't expect me to take her up on her offer.

"You are correct," she said. "I don't really expect you to take me up on the prayer service. Not because I don't want to do it, but because I thought you would think it smacked too much of superstition and Catholic traditions."

"Yes, I do see a lot of Catholicism as superstitious," I replied. "But there are parts of Catholic ritual that I actually miss. Like the use of incense for instance. It's Catholic theology that troubles me."

My daughter and another member of the church encouraged me to do it. Thinking it over I realized accepting Rev. Dorothy's offer was consistent with my therapy goal, to seek out and accept help from others. I was also aware that religious participation could help decrease my anxiety by fostering positive social connections. As a teenager, I did a lot of self-isolating. Enough to know it wasn't healthy.

Don, as chairman of the board, got the private prayer service confused with the politics of the larger church community. On Sunday, in response to his concerns, Rev. Dorothy announced that she was willing to do private prayer services for anyone who wanted it. She respected my desire for privacy, and didn't divulge for whom she was doing a prayer service.

I invited my family and other board members, clearly telling them I regarded it as a private matter. I didn't want my current mental health problems shared with anyone else.

On the last Friday in April, Rev. Dorothy conducted the prayer service. I don't have any clear memories of it, except that the small group I invited gathered in the sanctuary in the early evening. Some candles were lit. At Rev. Dorothy's request, I chose some favorite music that would "reach into my heart." We sat quietly together. Someone read my favorite verses from Walt Whitman's *Song of the Open Road*:

> Afoot and light-hearted I take to the open road,
> Healthy, free, the world before me,
> The long brown path before me leading wherever I choose.
> Henceforth I ask not good-fortune, I myself am good fortune,
> Henceforth I whimper no more, postpone no more, need nothing,
>
> Done with indoor complaints, libraries, querulous criticisms,
> Strong and content I travel the open road.

# Breaches

On May 2, two days after the prayer service, church members milled around the vestibule during Sunday-morning coffee hour. While I poured myself a cup of juice, I saw Rev. Dorothy step outside onto FXUU's veranda to speak with Don. I thought it odd. What was going on? Was it a private matter, or did it have something to do with me or the church? When Don came back into the vestibule, I overheard him ask another board member when Rev. Terry's term as district executive ended. So, it had something to do with the church. I wondered why the rest of the board, including me, had been excluded from the conversation. *If it's important*, I reassured myself, *we'll be informed tomorrow night at the board meeting.*

Twelve hours later, when the day was over and my chores completed, I laid in my bed waiting for Lyndon to finish brushing his teeth. I reviewed the events of the day. It was odd the way Rev. Dorothy called Don out on the veranda. What were they talking about? Were they talking about me? I hoped not.

Lyndon climbed into bed and I turned off the light. He fell asleep almost immediately. I snuggled up against him and closed my eyes, thinking. *What do I have scheduled for tomorrow? What day is tomorrow? Monday, the third. That's it!*

I opened my eyes and moved away from Lyndon. Rev. Dorothy was going to decide by May 3 whether she was going to continue as interim minister next year. She must have told Don her plans. She must be leaving. If she were staying, she wouldn't have kept it secret. There would have been no reason to. *But if she's leaving....*

Unable to sleep, I put on my glasses and went downstairs to my study. My computer clock read 12:30 a.m. I sent Rev. Dorothy a short note: "Are you staying on next year? What happens to our relationship? I would like to know before the board meeting, to give me time to sort out how I feel in some privacy."

The next morning, she called. Yes, she was leaving. She hadn't known how to tell me. Why don't we go out for coffee after the board meeting tonight? I bit my lip. Okay. Thanks for letting me know.

That evening at the board meeting, she handed the trustees her report. She wouldn't be able to continue as interim minister when her contract expired in June. She no longer had the energy and stamina to do ministerial work. She was too old. She offered to work toward finding another minister. She hoped there was a possibility of sharing a minister with another church. Since she knew all the churches in the district and the leadership in them, she believed she could work out such an arrangement. She had talked to the district executive, who would also be helping with FXUU's search for a new minister.

Rev. Dorothy also decided that she wanted to become a regular member of FXUU in the fall, after a summer hiatus. She wouldn't be leaving us, but would be changing her role in our church community. She stated she had come to love all of us so much, she didn't want to leave. She wanted to contribute to our future growth and development.

After the board meeting, she and I went out for coffee.

"I'm not abandoning you," she reassured me. "We are, well, sort of attached."

"Nothing changes?" I asked.

"Nothing changes."

With Rev. Dorothy's and the district's help, the board began a search for a part-time minister. She checked with the district and two other local districts for recommendations. On May 10, 1999, the board met to discuss committee assignments for the coming year. It was assumed I would be taking worship again. I said something about wanting a change.

"Then who will do it?" someone asked.

Afraid to displease my friends, I acquiesced.

I emailed Don after the meeting. He responded the next morning.

> I am very sorry you had a bad time at the meeting last evening... I did my best to keep the focus away from your difficulty by moving away from the subject and going on to other areas... please do not fret over Worship next year. I want you to begin thinking that YOU ARE NOT GOING TO HAVE TO CARRY WORSHIP NEXT YEAR.

Later that day, I was working near Rev. Dorothy's small duplex. While I drove past her street, I wondered if she was home and if it would be okay to stop by to talk to her. I turned the car around and drove the quarter mile to her house. As I parked my car, I fretted. What would she say? Would she be mad at me for dropping by like this? What if she saw me sitting out front?

I placed my hand on the key in the ignition. I had been here once before. Using my cell phone, I had called from outside the group home where I consulted, saying, "Rev. Dorothy, this is Maggie. I'm in Taunton today. I see some clients here. Anyway, I have a couple of hours free. Would you like me to come over and help with that email problem?"

"Yes, that would be fine," she had replied. "Come right over."

Since I was just down the street, I was there in a few minutes. It was a duplex. I didn't remember her telling me that. The lawn was mowed but weedy. The soil appeared poor. When I arrived, she ushered me up the stairs directly opposite the front door. Her computer was in a small bedroom that she used as a study. Books and papers were strewn everywhere. The New English Bible was sitting on the floor near her computer. I didn't feel comfortable. I felt I was intruding.

Now, I took my keys out of the ignition. Had she spotted me sitting in my car? On the off chance she might have, I couldn't turn around now.

I walked up to the front door and rang the bell, and she was right there, so quickly, she must have noticed me drive up. She opened the door and ushered me into the living room.

The room was small, with a double window facing the street. It was furnished with a stiff, formal sofa with a chair opposite. There was no sign the sofa or chair had ever been sat on. I wondered if she ever used this room. Did she ever have guests? I knew her son visited sometimes. Perhaps the living room was just for show: and for Fred, her cat. His hair was all over the throw blankets neatly draped over the sofa.

She appeared neither pleased nor displeased to see me. I don't recall her offering me a drink or anything to eat. Nor were the throw blankets covered in cat hair removed. Uncertain what to do, I took a seat on the edge of the sofa. She sat opposite, on the chair.

"I'm not sure I can do worship," I said. "I'm exhausted."

"You walked into it Monday night," she replied. "You never said what you wanted to do. That's part of the information that should be taken into consideration when plans are made for the coming year."

"The group expects me to do it. Will they be mad if I refuse?"

"They will support whatever you want to do."

As I was leaving, she handed me my copy of Laura Davis' *The Courage to Heal Workbook*. As part of therapy, I was asking family and friends to write dedications to me on any available blank page.

"Thank you," I said.

"Have a good day."

"You, too," I replied, hurried to my car and drove over to the park. Opening the workbook, I flipped the pages, passing the dedications written by my family and friends until I found what she had written on the bottom of the page opposite the chapter titled, "Creating Safety." I began reading.

Rev. Dorothy had watched me struggle with the events at FXUU, and acknowledged how hard I had worked to keep my life "on the even keel." I read further, "My prayer for you is that you learn just how valuable and precious you are, and how you deserve to find all the happiness, good things, love and respect this life can offer...."

I took a deep breath and read it again, trying to accept its truth. I was working hard. My life was valuable. I pressed the yellow workbook against my chest. Her dedication contradicted my parents' message, especially my father's, that I was stupid, lazy and selfish. During one of my therapy sessions, I had told Dr. Emmett, "My father said no one would ever want me."

With a truth that was so obvious I hadn't seen it, Dr. Emmett replied, "Well, he was wrong."

A few days later, I spoke with Rev. Dorothy on the telephone. She offered to do a Gestalt empty chair exercise with me. I had learned about this therapeutic technique in college but had never done it, or ever used it with any of my clients. I hesitated. I wondered about her qualifications. She assured me she was trained to do it. I told her I would think it over.

I emailed her on Sunday night.

Hi, Dorothy,

On the drive to and from New London (Orion [my son] was home on liberty again), I was thinking about our conversation on Friday and your offer. When the conflict started last August, I was very much aware how angry I was with Rev. Dick. During the conflict, any inclination I may have had to express that anger was thwarted by Rev. Dick's resignation and by what Don saw as politic. While this may have been in the best interest of the church, I don't think it was what was necessarily best for me. By the end of the conflict, when Dr. Emmett asked me if I was angry with Rev. Dick, I told him no, and had become unaware that my anger had turned into rage. Now I am left with trying to figure out what to do with all that pent-up, impotent anger without self-destructing. I am not really sure just what it is that you are proposing, and am also uncertain that it will help. I also fear making things worse. So to help me figure out what I want to do, why don't you clarify what it is you want to do and why?

Two days later, she replied and explained how she would conduct the exercise. I agreed to do it, but feared I would just shut down. Although I remembered the conflict clearly, I was unable to remember how I felt. The visual memory of Rev. Dick and his wife cornering me in FXUU's basement near the kitchen was vivid and clear. But how was I feeling? My stomach churned and tightened. Uncle Frank flashed across my mind's eye. He had blocked my escape from the kitchen.

I met with Rev. Dorothy in FXUU's basement on a Wednesday afternoon. While we were opening two metal folding chairs, we heard the church's basement door open and close. I straightened up and looked at Rev. Dorothy. We turned toward the door as Angelina walked through the doorway.

"Hi," she said, unaware she was intruding.

*Oh, no!* I thought. My heart rate increased. I felt exposed. There was an awkward silence.

"Good afternoon, Angelina," Rev. Dorothy said.

"I'm here to do the bulletin boards." Angelina crossed the room and walked up the stairs.

"I didn't expect anyone to be here," Rev. Dorothy said, turning to me.

"I didn't either. She's upstairs. It will be okay."

Rev. Dorothy sat down behind me. I took a seat on one of the chairs, turned toward the empty chair and said, "Why, Rev. Dick, did you break your agreement with the board?"

Angelina came back down the stairs. I stopped talking. Why didn't she use the front door? She was intruding again. As she crossed the room, she said goodbye and left.

I began again. As I talked, my rage erupted. Yelling, I stood and flipped over the empty chair. Rev. Dorothy and I looked at each other.

"Well," she said.

The next two days I felt pretty good. I appreciated Rev. Dorothy's support and compassion. After the Gestalt exercise, for the first time in months, I had moments when I actually felt happy. I was sure I was going about my recovery in the right way. Rev. Dorothy affirmed my ownership of my story, my right to choose how I tell it, when I tell it and who I tell it to.

I loved Rev. Dorothy like she was my mother. I thought I had finally found a maternal figure who truly loved me. At first I was suspicious and distrustful. Her willingness to provide pastoral care was perplexing. Growing up Catholic, my relationship with priests was distant and respectful. They never offered and I never sought any pastoral care.

I was uncertain what the limits and ground rules were in a pastoral counseling relationship. I was uncertain how they differed from my therapy relationship with Dr. Emmett. I only saw Dr. Emmett in his office. He never came to my home. Rev. Dorothy I saw at church, at my home and on rare occasions, at hers. No fee was charged. There were no time limits to our meetings or phone calls. The ambiguity made me anxious. I worried that I was bothering her. I was uncertain how long the relationship would last. If Rev. Dorothy needed to end the relationship, would she tell me or would she just disappear? Could she be trusted not to abandon me?

Rev. Terry provided FXUU's trustees with a list of candidates for FXUU's part-time minister position. In addition to these candidates, Rev. Patience, a minister who wasn't yet fellowshipped in the Unitarian Universalist Association, contacted Don, who was coordinating the interviews. She wasn't on the list Rev. Terry gave us. We didn't know how she learned of the position.

During her interview with the board, Rev. Patience informed us she hadn't completed her internship requirement so she wasn't yet fully ordained. In exchange for little pay, she offered to devote twenty hours per week growing our small congregation. To me it sounded suspiciously like the deal we had just ended with Rev. Dick.

At the annual church picnic in June, board members sat around a table in the church's backyard discussing the ministerial candidates that had been interviewed. Since the district executive originally did not refer Rev. Patience to FXUU, and she admitted during her interview to having some problems with her previous churches, I had serious reservations about her.

"Be sure to check references," said Rev. Dorothy, who was sitting next to me.

Don passed the salad. "I'll call Rev. Terry to clarify why she wasn't on the list of potential candidates."

"Why is that necessary?" Sue asked. "Let's hire her."

"That's not wise," I said. "We could end up in the same situation we just got out of."

"Don's right, Sue, Rev. Terry should be consulted," Angelina added. I appreciated her good sense. Something Sue's bombastic style often lacked.

"Be sure to check references," Rev. Dorothy said again.

I turned toward her. Was she trying to warn us? UUA rules didn't allow Rev. Dorothy to directly influence who the board selected as her replacement. Later in a private conversation, Don told me he thought Rev. Dorothy was trying to tell us to hire Rev. Patience. Whose interpretation was right? Mine or Don's? I trusted Don's conversation with Rev. Terry would straighten it out.

Two days after the picnic I received some angry emails from Angelina and Sue. In an earlier email, I had written that if we hired the candidate who held a doctorate I would enjoy having a peer at the church. Angelina and Sue misinterpreted the remark to mean I disparaged their level of education and accomplishments. Angelina had a bachelor's degree while Sue had a high school diploma. Both of them had chosen not to work while they were raising their children. I had made a different choice for myself. While I loved and cherished my family, I was proud of my doctorate. I saw my degree and the honorific, doctor, as similar to the badges earned in Girl Scouts. It was a mark of personal achievement, and was never intended as a comment on Angelina and Sue's achievements.

As I wrote an apology and explanation, I remembered my mother admonishing me not to tell others about my high grades. A knot twisted in my stomach. Like a dirty little secret that I enjoyed alone in my room, I was supposed to hide my accomplishments. Otherwise people wouldn't like and accept me. *Nerd, egghead, stuck up.* I heard those voices echoing in my head. I feared I didn't really belong, and would be better off resigning from FXUU. I had a good cry, and telephoned Don's wife, Sharon.

"One of the things I like about you is your vulnerability," she said.

While I appreciated her emotional support, I didn't want to be vulnerable. Experience had taught me that being strong and independent was safer than being vulnerable.

Don reported that he had spoken to Rev. Terry, and Rev. Patience's references were good. I was surprised. The majority of the board supported hiring her as our permanent part-time minister. I emailed Don that I was concerned we were repeating the same mistake made with Rev. Dick. Rev. Patience was promising more ministry than what we were paying for. Realizing, however, that I was outvoted, I supported the board's decision.

One month after the board had negotiated a contract with her, Rev. Patience reopened negotiations, claiming she was unable to fulfill all the duties in her contract because she needed to be home to care for her frail mother. I suspected a bait-and-switch maneuver. During her interview, Rev. Patience promised more than she could reasonably deliver and once hired, renegotiated her contract to less than what we needed. The majority of the board saw this as a result of unforeseen circumstances. I wasn't so sure.

Rev. Patience's contract was renegotiated. Her salary was decreased to reflect the reduction in hours she would be working, but an additional allowance for a personal computer was added. This would allow her to maintain contact with members of FXUU via email.

Around the same time, Rev. Dorothy told me that Unitarian Universalist guidelines for ministers required her to inform Rev. Patience that she had been providing me with pastoral counseling, and that she needed to ask Rev. Patience for permission to continue our relationship. Rev. Dorothy couldn't continue to take my phone calls, reply to my emails or assist me with my emotional problems without informing Rev. Patience first. This was necessary, Rev. Dorothy said, so as not to undercut Rev. Patience's ministry at FXUU.

I protested. I didn't want Rev. Patience to be told anything about me. It was my personal business. I wanted Rev. Patience to get to know me first and form her own opinion of me. Although I understood Rev. Dorothy's desire to follow her profession's ethical guidelines, the UUA rules appeared more concerned about Rev. Dorothy's relationship with Rev. Patience than with my right to privacy. The rules also usurped my autonomy. I was an adult, not a child.

Faced with losing Rev. Dorothy's support, I acquiesced. "Okay," I told her during a phone conversation. "But I want to be the one to tell her. Not you. It's my business, not yours."

"Fine," Rev. Dorothy replied.

Immediately after speaking with Rev. Dorothy, I telephoned Rev. Patience and left a message for her to call me. She returned my call and left a message: "My mother is in the hospital. I have sent you a letter."

Unable to talk to her directly, I decided to send her a short note, only telling her that Rev. Dorothy was providing pastoral care for some personal issues. I asked her permission for that relationship to continue. I mailed the note midday on Friday, July 16.

After I mailed the note to Rev. Patience, I called Don. I wanted to check out how much people at church cared about me. Rev. Dorothy kept saying they did. Don was a bit frustrated with me over my ambivalence about my staying at FXUU. He let slip that he had shared with Rev. Patience that I was going through a bad time and spoke with Rev. Dorothy often. That upset me, although I didn't say much to Don about it.

The next morning while Lyndon was in the shower, I laid in bed thinking things through. I realized that no one shared any information with Rev. Patience with any malicious intent. In *The Courage to Heal*, Laura Davis encourages survivors not to keep things a secret anymore. And I was doing just that by sharing with Don, Sharon, Sue and Angelina. Of course, once I did, that meant it really wasn't a secret anymore. Since I decided weeks before that I wasn't going to keep it a secret, it was kind of foolish of me to be upset that Rev. Patience needed to be told. The abuse was part of my past and had contributed to who I was. I felt relief when I finally got out of bed.

Don called after I was up to continue our conversation from the previous day. We discussed what was driving my desire to withdraw from the church. I told him it was just hard for me to believe that I wouldn't eventually be hurt and betrayed. I was a lot more comfortable with people being nasty to me than when they were nice. I trusted that more. I knew how to respond to it. Being with a group that cared about me put pressure on me not to hurt myself anymore. I had to take their feelings into consideration.

After I got off the phone with Don, a letter from Rev. Patience arrived. It was deeply personal, revealing Rev. Patience's own struggles with sexual abuse and self-harming, a heartfelt letter from one survivor to another. She was offering her help. But I didn't want or need her help. I didn't know her. I didn't trust her. Besides, I was getting all the help I needed from Rev. Dorothy and Dr. Emmett. Rev. Patience wrote that Dr. Emmett knew about her life—

*Wait a minute. How did she know I was seeing Dr. Emmett? Who told her?*

I looked at the date on her letter. July 15. Two days ago. Who told her about the sexual abuse and the self-harming? Not me. I only wrote in my note that I was receiving pastoral counseling from Rev. Dorothy, and would like it to continue. Besides, this was written the day before I wrote and sent my note. It would take at least a day, maybe two for Rev. Patience to receive it.

I felt exposed. I wanted to withdraw from everyone who knew that I had been abused. I had an urge to burn or cut myself. I took some medication and began writing in my journal. As I vented my distress, the urge to self-harm diminished and my thinking became clearer. I reminded myself that no one shared any information with Rev. Patience with any malicious intent. However, it was my story, and I wanted to be the one to decide who was told what and when.

Reflecting on my own profession's standards of practice, I concluded I should have been informed of the Unitarian Universalist rules prior to my first private conversation with Rev. Dorothy. Rev. Dorothy also should have given me the choice of informing Rev. Patience or terminating our pastoral relationship.

I called Rev. Dorothy, who denied telling Rev. Patience. "It was probably someone on the board," Rev. Dorothy suggested. "No good will come from trying to figure it out."

That was odd. Approximately one month before, Rev. Dorothy had urged me to contact my sister, Trish, to find out what she remembered of Uncle Frank's sexual assaults on us. At that time, Rev. Dorothy thought it important to pursue the truth.

After I got off the phone with Rev. Dorothy, I called Sharon to discuss who had been sharing my personal history with Rev. Patience without my knowledge or consent. Sharon also denied breaching my confidences.

I had just gotten off the phone when Rev. Patience called. She had just received my note. She wanted to reassure me no one was going to interfere with my relationship with Rev. Dorothy. When I asked her who had told her about my abuse history, she said she didn't remember.

My head was spinning. I had lost control over my own story. Too many people were being freely told I had been sexually abused. I couldn't concentrate, and again started thinking of injuring myself. I laid down for half an hour. I had to force myself to get up and take the anti-anxiety medication prescribed by my physician. I called Rev. Dorothy and spoke to her while I waited for the medication to kick in.

That night, I had difficulty falling asleep and staying asleep. Sunday morning I woke up anxious. I was really terrified about people beyond my small, trusted group knowing my story. While I was eating breakfast, I started thinking that all I needed to do was cut my arm, and if I did it well enough, all the dirt and badness would run out and I would be all right. I took another pill and called Rev. Dorothy.

Later that evening, I read my journal and came across a letter I had written to Dr. Howard after he died.

> Goodbye George Howard. I haven't forgotten the commitment I made to you. I promise never to attempt suicide again and I also want to add one more thing. I'm making a new promise never to physically injure myself by burning myself or whatever again. When I want to be self-destructive I will find a more acceptable way of dealing with what I'm feeling. So you take it easy. I loved you and your dying broke my heart but I have my own life and I want it now.

*Oh, my God!* I thought. *I broke my commitment to Dr. Howard.* I didn't mean to. I had forgotten I had finally promised I wouldn't harm myself anymore. Desperate, I called Rev. Dorothy, who suggested I write Dr. Howard another letter. I never did, but I knew Dr. Howard would understand.

On Wednesday, July 21, I saw Dr. Emmett. As I was taking my seat he said, "Rev. Patience called me. She thinks you should be in a group for trauma survivors. Do you know of any?"

*What the hell?* I thought as I straightened up in my chair. My back muscles tightened. I never gave permission for her to speak with him.

"Does it matter what I want?" I asked, looking directly at him.

"Of course," he replied.

"I'm not interested."

After leaving his office, I ruminated. I was very angry with Rev. Patience and whoever disclosed my personal business to her. I was angry with Dr. Emmett. When Rev. Patience called him, it was a violation of confidentiality for him to even acknowledge that I was his client. I had never given Dr. Emmett permission to speak with Rev. Patience about me.

I wrote Dr. Emmett a letter, telling him if Rev. Patience should ever call him about me again, to please tell her he couldn't discuss me with her. Dr. Emmett called me immediately after receiving the letter and reassured me he wouldn't discuss my case with Rev. Patience unless I gave him permission.

I also telephoned Rev. Patience and told her I didn't want her calling Dr. Emmett or discussing my sexual abuse history with anyone.

"Why did you contact Dr. Emmett?" I asked angrily.

"I wanted to help," she replied.

"Why didn't you speak directly to me?"

"I don't know," she replied. "But I will do that in the future."

"Who told you about the sexual abuse?"

"I'm not sure. I think Rev. Terry."

"Who told him?"

"I don't know."

"Okay. Thanks." After I hung up, I dialed Rev. Dorothy.

"Did you tell Rev. Terry about what was going on with me?

"No."

"Then who did?"

"It could be anyone."

Someone was lying. Why? I proceeded to call everyone at the church who knew my history. I called Don.

"You don't need to investigate your friends," Don told me.

"Would you want Rev. Terry to have information about your childhood?"

"No. I see what you're saying."

"How else can I find out who is lying?" I asked.

"You know some people are willing to say whatever is politically expedient. Rev. Dorothy might be one of those people."

"Yes, she can be political, but I'm sure she wouldn't lie to me."

Next, I spoke to Sue. She expressed anger with me for not trusting her and felt I was accusing her, though I wasn't. I just wanted to know who breached my confidentiality and why.

I remembered the times I would walk down the halls of my school. Often my classmates would talk among themselves, glancing at me as I walked by and giggling. They wanted me to know I was a reject. Since no one would stand up for me, the only way I could protect myself was to reveal as little about myself as possible. If they didn't have the information then they couldn't use it to hurt me.

Sue had also told me she spoke with Don about my concerns about how Rev. Patience had obtained personal information about me. Worried that Don and his wife, Sharon, were also angry with me; I called them and left a message. When I didn't hear from them, I called them two more times. Still no response.

On Thursday, July 22, I emailed Rev. Terry.

> I'm sorry to bother you now that you are no longer district executive.... This week it has come to my attention that you may have shared some personal information concerning me with Rev. Patience. Since we have never spoken directly to each other about my personal life I assume you obtained that information from someone else, perhaps Rev. Dick. I would like the opportunity to speak with you and find out what it is you think you know about me and why you felt it necessary to share that information with others. I am not trying to stir up trouble. God knows this past year has been painful enough. I am trying to piece the puzzle together and heal from all that has happened.

I also informed Rev. Dorothy and Rev. Patience via email that I was contacting Rev. Terry.

The next morning while I was in my study checking to see if Rev. Terry had responded, the phone rang.

"Maggie." It was Rev. Dorothy. "I was the one who told Rev. Terry."

I began crying. "You lied to me."

"Yes. Last March, I was overwhelmed. I needed to consult with someone about what was going on."

"You could have asked. I would have understood. How did Rev. Patience find out?"

"Rev. Terry probably told her shortly after she was hired."

My hands were sweaty and my ear hurt from pressing the phone up against it. "May I come over?"

"Yes."

I grabbed my car keys and rushed out of my house. The drive to Rev. Dorothy's duplex took thirty minutes. We sat on her back porch. The vegetable garden she often talked about was along the fence to the right. I was surprised how small and struggling it was. I didn't see any of the big, juicy tomatoes she boasted about harvesting. I wept. I repeated all the things I had ever told her about the sexual abuse and my father's verbal assaults. I told her about all the losses in my life. How unloved and unwanted I had been. She listened.

When I had no more tears left, no more tales to tell, I prepared to leave. Walking through her dining room, I saw the plant I had given her for Mother's Day. It was dead. It looked like it had never been cared for. My eyes met Rev. Dorothy's. Without saying another word, I left.

I drove to a local restaurant for a lunch date with a Department of Mental Health case manager. I had been working with several of her clients for many years. One of the exercises in *The Courage to Heal Workbook* was to select people you trusted and tell them about the sexual abuse. I had started with my friends at FXUU and was now expanding my circle of confidants to colleagues.

"How did you get to be such a kind person?" she asked me as we ate our lunch.

When I reached home at the end of the day, I wanted to share this positive experience with Rev. Dorothy. I called her and left a message for her to call me when she got the chance.

She didn't return my call until midday Saturday. Before I could share my good news, she said, "You are making too many demands on my time."

"My calls to you have been decreasing," I said.

"No they haven't," she replied.

"My phone bills prove it," I said.

"You're too much," she said.

"What do you mean?" I asked.

"You know what I mean," she replied.

"No, I don't," I said. Upset I told her, "Don't call me anymore." I hung up crying.

She called back a few minutes later. "I want you to talk to me after you calm down."

"No. I need time to think."

"How much time?" she asked.

"I don't know. Don't call me." I hung up again.

Again she called me back. "Leave me alone," I told her, hanging up for the third time. She finally stopped calling.

After a few hours, I called her. "I'll talk to you on Sunday or Monday," I said. "I owe you that much." Then I hung up.

On Sunday, I called her and told her how angry and hurt I was. She wasn't being fair. She wasn't giving me a chance.

She said she needed to think how to reply. We agreed to talk on Tuesday morning.

Wired, I bickered with Lyndon. I retreated to our bedroom and laid on the bed. I brooded, lost control and hit myself. I called Dr. Emmett.

"Rev. Dorothy called yesterday," he said. "She said you've been demanding too much time from her."

The muscles in my neck tightened. My heart rate increased. "She lied."

He wasn't listening. He accepted what she told him. He didn't know there was more to the story. He thought I was upset that she wanted to limit contact with me.

"She lied," I repeated.

"What do you mean by that?" he asked, finally hearing me.

"She was the one who broke confidentiality."

"How do you know that?" he asked.

"She told me yesterday."

"Dorothy should have told me the entire story," he said. He believed me. He understood. I relaxed.

"I don't want you talking to her anymore about me," I said.

"Okay. I understand," he replied.

Later that day, July 25, I finally received a reply from Rev. Terry stating he had no knowledge of my personal life from anyone except that I was in counseling to work on some life issues. He denied being told what issues. He stated he wouldn't have felt it concerned him. He further wrote,

> In any case, I am sure I passed on to Rev. Dorothy and Rev. Patience, as I would to any new minister starting in a new congregation, the advice that they find out from church leaders and previous ministers any information that might affect congregational life. In doing that, ministers will hear a lot of stuff. I advise them that not all they hear is true, and less is accurate. Because of that, I urge new ministers to talk to people directly about what they hear.

I replied late Sunday night.

> Since sending you the email on Thursday, the 22nd, Rev. Dorothy has admitted that sometime in late February or early March she not only told you that I was in therapy but

> also that I was a sexual abuse survivor and was, at the time she spoke to you, engaging in self-destructive behaviors which were triggered by the FXUU conflict. In response to direct questions, Rev. Patience informed me that she obtained information about my abuse history from you. I never gave Rev. Dorothy permission to share personal information about myself with you, and I certainly never gave you permission to share any personal information about me with anyone else. I understand that no one except for Rev. Dick meant me any harm and were only trying to help. However, it is for me to decide when, where and to whom I want to share that kind of information. Therefore, I am asking you to obtain permission from me before you share any personal information about me with anyone. This includes divulging to anyone that I am or have been in therapy. This also means that if anyone should ever approach you asking you about me that you not confirm or verify any information that person may or may not have.

Monday morning, Rev. Terry replied that he had no memory of hearing anything about me. He understood my need to deal with the process of recovery in my own way. He promised me no one would hear anything from him.

The next day I received a letter from Rev. Patience.

> Thank you so very much for the beautiful card you sent me.... It was a reflection of your sensitivity and spirituality.
>
> I am glad that you were comfortable in calling me to say you were angry with me. I was deeply sorry that I had hurt you. I will probably make other mistakes, hopefully not the same ones, and I think you can come to me and tell me when you're hurt and angry....
>
> Thank you again for the beautiful card, for your gracious forgiveness of my errors...

On Tuesday, Rev. Dorothy called as promised. She apologized for hurting me. She promised not to share confidences with anyone without my consent ever again. She stated she wanted to preserve the relationship. I hesitated. I wasn't sure that was possible, but completely losing the relationship would be too painful. Maybe we could build a better, more equal relationship. I agreed to stay in touch.

Later that day, while I was eating lunch with a colleague, I burst into tears and told her what had happened with Rev. Dorothy. She viewed it as re-victimization and wanted to know why I continued with "this church thing."

How could I explain it to her? How could I explain this striving, this need for something bigger than myself?

The next day, anxious that Don had not returned my phone calls, I sent him an email.

> Where have you been? I have called three times and have not heard from you. Have you been busy or is there a problem? I spoke to Sue, who without my knowledge spoke to you about my concerns about how Rev. Patience obtained personal information about me. Sue expressed anger with me for not trusting her. She thought I had been accusing her, which I wasn't. That was her interpretation. We talked about it. But it raised concerns that maybe you are similarly annoyed with me. Would love to touch base and clear any misunderstanding if one exists.

Don replied. He had tried repeatedly to call me but kept getting a busy signal. Melissa must have been tying up the line. Don wrote,

> As far as us being annoyed—absolutely nothing I can think of from either of us. I do think that you and Susan need to work through some stuff and that both of you approach things very differently so that is problematic at best—but I think you can....

Don was right. Sue approached things very differently than I did. We had very different perspectives on life. This became really clear to me when she and I had gone out to lunch the previous June.

Sitting across from each other at a local restaurant, she said, "You think too much. You really should try yoga and just let your mind go blank. Don't think about the abuse."

"And just pretend it never happened?"

"Just don't think about it. It is better if you don't."

While I used meditation almost every morning to help calm and center myself, my approach to life was a lot more analytical than Sue's. Sue believed in intuition, a mysterious process that could never be fully understood. Trained as a scientist, I was more interested in examining the objective evidence and discovering how something worked. I saw intuition only as an unconscious synthesis of an individual's observations, experience and learning. There wasn't any magic.

In August 1998, just before the conflict with Rev. Dick began, Lyndon and I had vacationed in New Mexico. We spent a couple of nights at a ranch just south of where Georgia O'Keefe, my favorite American painter, had spent the last years of her life. Our hostess, an Irish American, noticed I was reading a book on Judean Christian heritage. Sitting in the house's dining room, we shared our religious faith. Raised Catholic, she had converted to Islam several years before.

"There's a mosque around here?" I was surprised to find Muslims living in the American Southwest.

"Just look at the landscape," she said. "Wouldn't you, if you came from the desert of the Middle East, feel at home here?"

"Yes, now that you point it out, of course."

Following a route recommended by our hostess, Lyndon and I drove north through the high desert and past the mesas. Unlike Long Island where I grew up, the sea didn't limit the New Mexican landscape. Instead, it literally went on as far as the eye could see. I was unsettled by the land's hugeness and immensity. Standing at the base of the white cliffs painted by Georgia O'Keefe, I knew I was in God's country.

That August night, sitting in our room at a bed-and-breakfast, I read my book's discussion of the Ten Commandments. I knew them, of course, but hadn't really reflected on them since leaving the Catholic Church. As I read the first commandment, "I am the Lord, your God, thou shalt have no other gods before me," I remembered one of my first conversations with Sue. My sister Rita and Sue were standing in the back of the sanctuary talking. I joined them.

"I think my views would upset people here," Sue was saying.

"UU's have no creed," Rita explained.

"You can believe what you want," I added.

"Including paganism?" Sue asked.

"Yes," Rita and I replied.

"I think it is just as likely for there to be more than one God as there is to be only one," Sue asserted.

"That's fine," I said.

Now, I blinked and dropped my book in my lap. Leaning back into my chair, I wondered, was it really okay? Sue's polytheism was a violation of the first commandment. In my desire to be tolerant and open, I had supported Sue's idolatry the previous October when I suggested to Sue we transform the All Souls service I was planning into an All Souls/Sam Hein service.

After Rev. Dick resigned in September 1998, I wondered if Sue sensed my changed perspective. I was no longer willing to participate fully in the pagan services as I once had. Perhaps getting her cue from Rev. Dick's letter that accused me of moving FXUU toward traditional Christianity, Sue began dropping any reference to All Souls when talking about the All Souls/Sam Hein service. She also began taking full credit, ignoring my contribution. I privately wondered why it was okay to do a pagan service but not a Christian service complete with communion.

The relationship with Sue became more strained during our struggle to rebuild the church. During Sunday coffee hours, she often misrepresented my beliefs to visitors even after I had repeatedly corrected her. If I mentioned God while talking about my own beliefs, Sue would interrupt and correct me by saying "goddess."

"I don't see God as being male or female," I explained to Sue. "In the Bible there are many feminine references to God."

"I'll make a pagan out of you yet," Sue said.

Offended, I walked away. Other members of the church began noticing the tension between us. Don's email was the first acknowledgement of the problem. On July 29 I wrote Don back.

> That's a relief! Within the past two weeks I have uncovered who breached confidentiality (no one on the board) and have been dealing with the emotional aftermath, which was what I wanted to talk to you or Sharon about. I felt I needed your direct and clear thinking on this...

> Yes, Susan has a very different approach to life than I do. That became real clear when I went out to lunch with her last spring. Rev. Patience may be useful in working out the current situation with Sue.

Don replied later that day, promising to talk about it more when I telephoned. He didn't think Sue and I would ever be "very accepting of each other." I wasn't sure why he thought that, but at the end of his email he wrote that Sue and I could "work it out better than you might think." I was certain that was so. After all, despite our differences, Sue and I were friends.

A week later, I received an email from Rev. Dorothy. In it she quoted Clarissa Pikola: "Part of healing from a secret is to tell it so that others are moved by it. In this way a woman begins to recover from shame by receiving the succor and tending she misses during the original trauma."

Yes, I agreed with that. And I was doing that when I told people I trusted about the sexual abuse.

Rev. Dorothy further wrote, "I think this is what is happening in your interactions with the people at the church, and it seems appropriate and healing. People are offering you succor and tending, and you can only benefit from it."

Rev. Dorothy wasn't getting it. It isn't "succor and tending" when others tell your story without your consent. It is a betrayal. People's intentions did not excuse their breach of confidentiality. What I needed from Rev. Dorothy and the others but never received was a sincere apology and a conscientious effort never to do it again.

# Coffee and a Little Spirituality

Desperate like a small child lost in the mall, I called Rev. Dorothy once per week. My feelings fluctuated wildly. At times I felt really angry and bitter. Other times, I just felt sad. No matter how much I tried I couldn't trust her anymore. With the loss of trust, I no longer felt close to her. The love had died.

I reminded myself that a year before I was happy and strong. I didn't know or need Rev. Dorothy then. I didn't need her now. I had plenty of resources. I could cope. I could survive. The odd thing was that after pursuing who had lied to me, I was less anxious. Instead of passively accepting breaches of confidentiality, I asserted myself and insisted my privacy be respected.

When I saw Dr. Emmett, I tearfully told him I believed Rev. Dorothy wouldn't call me if I didn't call her.

"Why don't you test your assumptions?" Dr. Emmett asked. "Wait. See if she calls."

"Okay. I will."

While I drove to my office I promised myself I wouldn't call Rev. Dorothy until she called me. During a break between clients, I curled up in a fetal position on my office couch brooding over her, the things she said to me, her emotional reactions and her behavior. It was confusing. Did she truly care for me? Did she know me at all?

Dr. Emmett was going to be away on vacation for two weeks. He had arranged for a colleague to take his urgent calls. I didn't know her. How could I call a stranger? Without knowing me, how could she understand? Rev. Dorothy knew me. She had understood in the past. After an hour, I forced myself to get up and give her a call.

Rev. Dorothy sounded glad to hear from me. "Would you've called me if I didn't call you?" I asked.

"Eventually," she replied. "Aren't you worthy of friendship? Do you believe Don and the rest of the board are your friends?"

I hedged and said only, "I don't know."

Silence. Was Rev. Dorothy my friend? Did she value her relationship with me?

"How do you feel about the way the relationship between us has worked out?" I asked.

143

"Fine," she said without hesitation.

Fine? How could she be fine with it? Didn't she feel the distance between us? The distrust?

"How are you with it?" she asked.

Feeling it wasn't safe to share the truth, I lied. "It's okay with me too."

I hung up the phone and looked out the window. The leaves on the trees shimmered in the late-afternoon light of the summer sun. Was Rev. Dorothy ever worthy of my trust? When Dr. Emmett first encouraged me to use her for pastoral care, I warned him it would backfire. Just as I predicted, I became a bother to her and others at FXUU. They felt the conflict was over and wanted to move on. My recovery was too slow. I needed too much support. They didn't understand why I was stuck in the place that I was. Perhaps my colleague was right. Perhaps I should end my involvement with the church. There had been just too many painful experiences.

I picked up my journal from my desk and began to write. I imagined I was talking to a good friend.

"It really hurt. I wasn't ready for others to know," I wrote.

"Others already knew. What difference did one more make?" my imaginary friend replied.

"She was a stranger. There was no trust. I was terrified."

"Terrified of what? What did you think would happen? Rev. Patience wasn't trying to harm you."

"There was no malice. But I wasn't ready. I still feel shame. And I want her to know me as a strong, independent person. Not weak and needy."

"You are weak and needy right now. What's wrong with that?"

"It makes me the identified patient. While it gets me nurturing, it also leaves me open to scapegoating."

"When everyone perceived you as strong you got scapegoated anyway."

"Rev. Dick used his knowledge of my vulnerabilities to hurt me."

"He would have done that no matter what you had shared with him previously. The problem is you don't defend yourself well. The solution is not to keep your vulnerabilities secret but to stand up for yourself better. When you sought information and contacted Rev. Terry and wrote Dr. Emmett and called Rev. Patience, you were standing up for yourself."

"Yeah, you're right. I let Sue bully me a little. I need to get better at defending myself."

"Don't worry. You will get there."

"When I speak to Don, I must remember not to be bullied. I might call Sue and let her know how I felt about the things she said. And finally, the abuse is not a secret or something to be ashamed about, but I have a right to decide how and when people are told."

I set down my pen. I felt better. I was getting stronger.

Like most other Unitarian Universalist churches, there were no Sunday services held at FXUU during July and August. I decided to attend summer services at Immanuel Lutheran, Rev. Karen's church. Beverly, who sat on the Council of Church's committee with me, invited me to sit with her. She showed me how to follow along in the book of worship, which made me feel welcome.

In early September, shortly after the August board meeting, I retrieved a voicemail message from Sue. She said she needed to talk to me. She sounded upset.

I returned Sue's call the next morning.

"Don called me. He says there are significant problems between you and me. He said your negative reaction at the August board meeting to the change in the meeting time from Monday to Wednesday was just an example of it. You wouldn't have reacted so negatively if it was anyone else making the request."

"There are some tensions in our relationship," I replied. "But that has nothing to do with my frustration over the change in the meeting time. The change conflicts with my work schedule. I see clients on Wednesday nights. It will be difficult to change my appointments. One has nothing to do with the other."

Surprised, Sue said, "I guess I was the only one who didn't think there was a problem."

"It's a minor problem," I told her. "We can easily work it out."

"Don," Sue informed me, "said you are willing to do deep psychological work on yourself and I'm not."

*Oh, no!* I thought. *How could Don say such a thing?* "Sue, we need to stop all the gossiping and work out how we're feeling now that the crisis is over."

I immediately called Rev. Patience. We talked briefly. She suggested a meeting. I agreed. She said she would get back to me. In a second phone call to me, Rev. Patience said she had talked to Sue and calmed her down.

At the FXUU's work party that Saturday, Rev. Patience spoke briefly with me and asked how I was doing. She informed me she had scheduled a meeting next Sunday for the board to discuss their issues with each other.

Sue called a few days before the meeting, wanting to talk about what I saw as the problem. I told her since we had a meeting scheduled, I would rather wait until then. Sue told me she had again spoken to Don. *Great,* I thought, *we're having the meeting before the meeting!*

After the church service on September 19, 1999, we gathered in the church basement. We each took a seat on one of the metal folding chairs that had been placed around one of the portable tables used for Sunday school. The table had been lowered for the children and was placed in the center of the room. Wearing long dangling earrings and a flowing black dress over her tall and slender frame, Rev. Patience sat at the head of the table nearest the kitchen. To her left sat Angelina, Sue and Joe, with their backs to the outside wall. Angelina, as always, was neatly dressed in a style that I call collegiate. Sharon was seated at the end of the table opposite Rev. Patience. Unlike Angelina, her clothes were disheveled with her shirt only partly tucked in her pants. I sat to Sharon's left with my arms crossed and my legs stretched out, trying to get comfortable in a chair whose seat was a little too high for my short legs. The stairs to the vestibule were behind me. Don sat to my left with a cup of coffee.

Rev. Patience called the meeting to order and set the ground rules. "We will go around the table. Everyone will be allowed to talk for five minutes. When the next person speaks, I want them to paraphrase what the speaker before them said."

*That's an odd way to do it,* I thought. *It will stifle dialogue.*

"I want everyone to use 'I' messages," Rev. Patience continued.

"Five minutes is too long for anyone to accurately paraphrase," I said. Others agreed.

"Okay, three minutes."

People nodded agreement. *Still too long,* I thought. It was good that Rev. Patience wanted us to listen first before speaking, but at best, individuals can paraphrase up to three separate thoughts or ideas at a time. *It's Rev. Patience's meeting, not mine,* I thought. *We'll see how it goes.*

Angelina went first. She said something about my reaction to her last pregnancy but was glad when my comments stopped.

I stared at Angelina, puzzled. "When was this?"

Rev. Patience interrupted. "Repeat what Angelina said first."

"It's okay," Angelina said, jumping in. "I can see Maggie is confused." Turning to me, she said, "I didn't want to confront you at the time. You were so emotionally fragile."

"I'm sorry, Angelina. I don't remember. I wish you had said something at the time."

Sue went next. "I am open and honest."

*No you're not,* I thought. *You're crude and vulgar.*

"I like to bust balls," Sue boasted. "People like it except when it's directed at them. It is just the way I am. I mean nothing by it."

Leaning back in my chair, I grunted, thinking, *She means everything by it. It's how she gets away with saying angry, hostile things.*

Weighing each word, Don spoke next. "I think Sue busts balls as a cover for her own insecurity."

I sat straight up. *What does that mean?* I looked to Rev. Patience, waiting for her to ask Don to talk about his thoughts and feelings and not analyze others. She said nothing. Sue didn't say anything in her own defense either. *What's going on here?*

Speaking next, I leaned forward, wrapping my feet around the front legs of my chair. "Sue, I need to set some limits, some boundaries with you."

"That won't work!" Rev. Patience interrupted.

"How do you know that?" I shifted my gaze from Sue to Rev. Patience.

"It won't work," she repeated.

*Why is she interrupting me and not the others?* "Yes it will," I said. Annoyed, I waved her off. "It isn't okay with me that Sue busts my chops—"

"I said *bust balls,*" Sue snarled, making a point that she preferred the reference to male genitalia.

"I don't care what you call it. I don't want you to do it anymore." I focused on Sue, unaware of how the others in the group were reacting.

"Maggie, please explain what you mean," Rev. Patience asked.

"Sue, do you know what I mean?"

"Yes," Sue replied.

"Be more specific," Rev. Patience insisted.

"Sue, I no longer want you to insert 'goddess' when I'm talking about my religious beliefs. I also don't want you making derogatory remarks about Christianity in my presence, and I don't want you telling people that I am 'very Christian'."

"I introduce myself as very pagan," Sue retorted.

"That's fine." I took a deep breath. "You can self-describe yourself any way you want, but it's inaccurate to describe me as 'very Christian.'"

"You have trouble with my being pagan," Sue said, shifting the focus off her behavior.

"If that's true, why did I invite you to do a combined All Souls/Sam Hein service? Why did I help you with the drumming service?"

Without answering my question, Sue replied, "I know you have problems with paganism. That's why you don't get along with your brother."

I sat straight up. What was she talking about? What did that have to do with my relationship with her? "How do you know that?" I asked.

"You told me," Sue replied.

When did I talk to her about my brother? My heart rate increased. It was hard to think clearly. When was the last time I saw Rich? It was a couple of years ago. He was up from New York for a few days. We had a good time together until the last day, when he and I argued over the Catholic use of holy water. I saw it as verging on superstition. He saw it as calling on the mysterious and the divine. After he left, I spoke to Sue on the phone about our plans for worship. During the call, I vented about Rich's behavior. Sue got it wrong. I didn't care that Rich was now a pagan. It was his goading and provocative behavior that upset me.

"That's incorrect," I told Sue.

"No, it isn't," Sue replied.

"Yes, it is." What? Was she mindreading? What made her think she knew more about my relationship with my brother than I did?

Stunned, I looked to Rev. Patience to step in. Wouldn't this be the time for her to ask us to paraphrase each other? Rev. Patience did nothing. Sue continued twisting and misinterpreting our private conversation in front of the other board members.

"Stop," I said, and pushed back my chair, increasing the distance between Sue and me. I looked at Rev. Patience. Still she did nothing.

I looked at the others. Why weren't they saying anything? Why weren't they telling Sue to stop?

"I know I am right!" Sue insisted.

"Stop!" I said, louder. My relationship with my brother really wasn't any of her business.

Sue continued her attack. My eyes darted around the room. People were just silently watching. *Step in. Help me. Tell her to stop. Don't just sit there.*

This was another betrayal. I could feel myself coming apart. My insides were imploding. My very survival depended on getting Sue to stop. Desperate to end the pain, I yelled at the top of my voice, "Don't speak for me!"

The room fell silent. Sue backed off. Rev. Patience finally said, "The two of you need to work this out later."

Everyone shifted uneasily in their chairs. My heart was pounding. I focused on breathing slowly. There was a feeble attempt to talk about something else.

Don finally said, "We should deal with the elephant in the room."

"That is not a good idea," Rev. Patience said.

"It is never appropriate to raise one's voice," Angelina admonished me.

"I don't see anything wrong with raising your voice when you're angry, so long as you don't use putdowns or curse," I said, defending myself. "I didn't attack Sue. I didn't use obscenities. I just wanted her to stop insisting she knew better than I did what the cause of friction with my brother was."

Sue and her husband remained quiet while everyone else in the room disagreed with me.

"Sue was way over the line when she threw my brother in my face," I told them. "I'm angry."

"You're not angry, Maggie," Rev. Patience insisted. "You're hurt."

"No," I said, tightening my lips, "I'm angry."

Joe, Sue's husband, whispered to her. She said, "I'm sorry, Maggie, for saying that about your brother, but ..."

She threw in a dig, negating her apology. I don't remember what it was. Everyone in the room voiced their disapproval. Sue apologized again.

Angelina turned to me, "Maggie, please apologize to Sue."

"No. I didn't do anything wrong."

Sue sat up. "You mean she isn't going to apologize to me? Then I take my apology back!"

I already knew she wasn't sincere.

"Apologize, Maggie," the others demanded.

"I won't apologize just to apologize. I was only defending myself. Sue had no right speaking for me. She understands nothing about my relationship with my brother."

"I think Sue and Maggie should meet with me to work this out," Rev. Patience said.

"Okay, I'm willing," I said.

"No. I'm not going to do it," Sue replied.

"That's it," Don said. "We've failed."

*What? How could Don be saying that! What is going on here?*

"It is too soon to know that," I said. My heart rate increased. *Give it time*, I thought. *Sue and I will work this out.*

"Maggie stood up," Angelina said.

Did she mean that metaphorically? I was still sitting.

"Maggie never stood up," Sharon replied.

Rev. Patience ended the meeting. Sue stood and moved toward her, crying. Everyone went over to Sue, ignoring me. Baffled, I stood up and watched as they put their arms around her. Why were they siding with her? *What about me? Don't you care about me?*

Suppressing the desire to cry, I escaped up the stairs into the vestibule, grabbed the letters for the wayside pulpit from the table and went outside through the red doors. I changed the sign, and then returned the extra letters to the vestibule. The others were still downstairs. I walked out the red doors and around to my car. Through the basement windows, I could see and hear everyone still talking to Sue.

As I was turning my car's ignition, Sharon came out to get something from her car. She looked at me but said nothing, just went back inside. I pulled out of the church's driveway. While I drove around the town common, I dialed Rev. Dorothy on my cell phone. I cried when I told her what had happened. She promised she would help me fix things with Sue and the others. We agreed to have breakfast together the next Sunday morning.

The following morning, I felt angry. While I showered and dressed, I worried that Don wasn't talking to me. I called him at noontime, and was relieved and surprised by his warm greeting. We discussed what happened at yesterday's meeting.

"I'm sure we'll find a way to resolve things," he said.

Encouraged, I called Rev. Patience and left a message for her to call. When she returned my call, I struggled to find some common ground on which to start the conversation. Rev. Patience took offense. "Talk to Rev. Dorothy or your therapist!" she said, and hung up.

I started weeping. I was expecting a client in thirty minutes. I needed to get control of my tears. I called Rev. Dorothy.

"Rev. Patience hung up on you?"

"Yes. She didn't even give me a chance."

"I don't know what to say." She listened to me cry. "It will be okay. Take some deep breaths. We'll work it out."

"Thanks." I wiped my face and blew my nose. Expecting my client, I said goodbye to her. When my client didn't show, I used the time to write.

> Rev. Patience, if you don't want to talk today that is okay. But at some point you and I need to have a private conversation to work out our differences. I am a member of the church and one of the people you have to deal with. I just want to find a way for us to understand each other better.

I then called Rev. Patience back, expecting to get her answering machine, but got her instead.

"I wrote out this brief thing—"

"I can't take any more negativity," she said. "You guys are mired in conflict. I don't want anything to do with it. I am setting limits." She hung up on me a second time.

The level of my distress tripled. I was confused. Why was Rev. Patience treating me this way? Had she formed an opinion of me based on the rumor mill, or was she harboring resentment after our conflict over her unsolicited phone call to my therapist?

Sobbing, I called Rev. Dorothy, who once again assisted me in regaining my composure so I could see my evening clients.

At 10 p.m., I sent Angelina an email asking her if she was angry with me. I apologized for saying anything in the past that might have upset her. The following afternoon, she replied that she could no longer deal with conflicts at church. I felt blamed. Why did raising my voice make it my fault? Ironically, at the September 19 meeting, I was the one most in control of my emotions and behavior. Although I was enraged by Sue's remark about my brother, I remained seated. I never threatened her or called her names.

Rev. Patience and the others allowed Sue to break the rules and misuse personal information. Then, after Sue apologized, from some sense of balance and fairness, the others demanded an apology from me. For what? What had I done? Yelled? No way! I wasn't sorry. I was proud. I had finally stood up for myself. They should have applauded. Months of therapy had taught me that whenever I allowed others to silence me I become anxious and suicidal. That was too high a price to pay for acceptance. I was never going to apologize.

But what part of it was my responsibility? I tried to be respectful and tolerant of Sue's religious beliefs. Even though I was increasingly uncomfortable with paganism, I encouraged her participation in the planning of worship services. Clearly, she sensed my discomfort and felt threatened. She began "busting my balls" whenever we talked. Her negative comments about Christianity were like rags stuffed in my mouth. I spoke less and less freely of my renewed and growing faith in God. Perhaps if I had responded more directly and immediately whenever Sue made an offensive remark, the conflict would have been resolved before it exploded. But it wasn't only my responsibility. Sue, also, had been unassertive, and hadn't shared with me her belief that I was intolerant of her paganism.

On Wednesday, I emailed Sue. I informed her that I intended to contact her at some future point in time so the two of us could talk and work things out. I was confused how a small problem between us became such a huge problem. I was certain that, with time and patience, we would be able to work things out.

Sue responded a few hours later. She had decided our friendship was detrimental to her emotional health and asked me not to call her.

That was that. I was intensely disappointed. I liked Sue, but we would never be friends. We saw the world too differently. I grieved the loss. All my efforts to resolve things were turning out badly. Lacking any bright ideas on what else to do, I decided to let things go for a while. I would no longer bring up the issue unless they did. I remained willing to discuss it at any time.

I decided to distance myself from FXUU by limiting my involvement to my current obligations. I wasn't going to extend myself any further. I had concerns about being part of a community that condemned me for standing up for myself. I considered leaving, but felt I had no church that I could join. Anyway, I had fought and worked hard for FXUU. It was as much my church as anyone else's.

Don called on Friday, when I had just left my client at the group home. I parked my car behind a convenience store, and we talked for half an hour. He didn't understand my point of view about the argument with Sue. "All of us can't be wrong and you right," he said.

"I didn't know right and wrong was decided by a popular vote," I replied.

"Well, I'm willing to set our differences aside and still be friends."

"My beef isn't with you."

While I drove home that night, I found myself feeling angry and bitter. I wasn't sure how much longer I could remain at FXUU. I had ties with Rev. Dorothy and Don but in the end, the only people you can really trust are your family.

On Saturday, Lyndon and I attended our son's cross-country track meet. When Orion heard what Sue had said about my relationship with my brother, he said, "Mom, let's call Uncle Rich."

I looked at my son, puzzled.

"Now that Sue has told us what the problem is, we can fix it."

"Oh." I smiled. "Isn't it remarkable how Sue, without knowing much about me and my brother, has figured out what the problem is?"

"Yep, some people are really talented that way."

"I wish I could've used humor just as you're doing now," I said.

"That's hard when you're in the middle of something," he replied.

"I guess if it was easy, I would've figured it out long ago." I hugged him while we laughed at Sue's arrogance.

Before church on Sunday, Rev. Dorothy and I met at the café on the common for breakfast.

"I've never been here before," I said, taking my seat at a square table for two.

"It's really quite nice," Rev. Dorothy said. "It can be hard to get a table on Sunday morning, though."

After our eggs arrived, we began discussing the argument I had with Sue.

Rev. Dorothy stirred her coffee. "I don't understand why Sue's remark made you so angry."

"She took a confidence, twisted it and threw it back at me," I said, and broke my yolk with a piece of toast, realizing I still liked my eggs the way Uncle Frank used to cook them for me.

Rev. Dorothy changed the subject. "I spoke to Gretchen as promised."

During the summer months, Rev. Dorothy and I had discussed over the phone the conflict at Murray over calling a gay minister. I told her I had been looking for a way to reconcile with Gretchen, that she and I were neighbors and we saw each other from time to time at UU functions. I wanted to reduce the tension between us. Since Rev. Dorothy and Gretchen were friends, Rev. Dorothy agreed to ask Gretchen to meet with me in the fall.

"What did Gretchen have to say?" I asked.

"She won't meet with you." Rev. Dorothy sighed.

I stopped eating, "Oh. Did she say why?"

"She prefers to communicate via email."

"Email is not the best way to discuss emotionally charged issues. Did she say anything else?"

"It is best that I don't repeat it." Rev. Dorothy fell silent.

"That bad?"

"You have significant problems getting along with other people. You fail to take responsibility for your end."

I put down my fork and tightened the muscles in my face so I wouldn't cry. What did Gretchen tell her? "I never had a conflict at the Unitarian Universalist church I attended on Long Island," I reminded her.

"I'm not sure that's true." Rev. Dorothy wiped her mouth with her napkin. "You're in denial and have a rationalization for everything."

What? How would she know? We didn't know each other then. She never lived on Long Island. Did she even know anyone there? Rev. Dorothy had been reading too much Freud, I decided.

"I have thought through my end of things," I said.

"Have you?" She raised her eyebrows.

*What did Gretchen tell her?* I held fast to my truth. "I have come to a different conclusion than you have."

While we were paying the bill, Rev. Dorothy said, "We never did discuss what to do about last week."

"We'll be late for church." I put on my jacket and walked toward the door.

The next day was quiet and productive. In the evening I went to Bible study at Immanuel. Rev. Karen and I spoke briefly afterward about the events at FXUU. We agreed there was a lot of dysfunction at my church.

"There was nothing wrong with you raising your voice," Rev. Karen said.

"I was really angry," I said.

"Why do you stay?"

"Where can I go? Several people at Murray have asked me to come back whenever I bump into them, but I don't think I'm liberal enough to fit in."

During our Tuesday morning sessions, Dr. Emmett and I talked about the argument with Sue and the reactions of Rev. Dorothy and the others.

"Rev. Patience didn't do a lot of moderating, did she?" Dr. Emmett said.

"No."

"If you were happy, would they ask you not to smile?"

"No, of course not."

"When people are angry, they yell. Maybe you should write a letter to Rev. Patience and tell her how you feel?"

"I'm not sure she'll read it."

"Oh, she'll read it."

"I'm thinking of leaving the church and not joining another," I told him.

"Spirituality is important to you. You shouldn't isolate yourself. Surround yourself with people with whom you can be open and honest."

Wednesday morning, I called Rev. Dorothy and tried talking to her again about my relationship with Sue.

"Why did Sue's remark about your brother make you so angry?" she asked.

"She took a personal confidence and distorted it." I was puzzled by Rev. Dorothy's failure to understand. She must have had someone do that to her at some point in time. Hadn't she learned how important it was to me that people not break my confidences and allow me to tell my own story?

Even though she didn't understand me, I felt better when I got off the phone, believing that I was holding fast to the validity of my own experience.

Wednesday evening, FXUU's board meeting went surprisingly well. There was actually less tension than in the past. A little tiff occurred between Don and Sue. I don't recall what it was about. I thought, with time, people would understand my reaction to Sue better.

Thursday morning I woke up with no anxiety. Standing up for myself had decreased my fear. The following week was a mix of rough and good moments. However, by Friday I was in a panic. On Sunday I would be seeing Rev. Patience for the first time since the argument with Sue. I tried calling Dr. Emmett, but he was away. Rev. Dorothy and Don were out. There was no one I could talk to. I called Lyndon.

"I'm struggling," I told him.

"It will be okay."

Saturday, Lyndon, Melissa and I went to Orion's track meet. I walked through the woods overlooking the Connecticut River with Melissa.

"Mom," my daughter urged me. "Why don't you join the church in Providence? You'll meet better educated people there, people who share the same values and interests."

Despite the tension at FXUU I decided, with trepidation, to email Gretchen explaining my desire to resolve any misunderstandings that occurred between us when Murray Unitarian Universalist Church called Rev. Melody to be their minister. Lyndon objected, because he believed honest communication with Gretchen was impossible.

In response to my email, Gretchen forwarded the email she had sent Rev. Dorothy, the one Rev. Dorothy thought best not to share with me. In it, Gretchen stated Rev. Dorothy's involvement felt "like triangulating" that would keep the issue from being resolved. She also wrote she didn't need anyone to "take her inventory," but then proceeded to take mine, stating that the problem wasn't about her and me, but how I "can learn to function in and belong wholeheartedly to a faith community. It's about how Maggie can be loved and be at ease and make a contribution to a group and be valued and accepted."

So she thought the problem was mine alone. Was she saying she didn't need to make any changes or take any action?

The next day, before I could respond, Gretchen emailed me again. She wrote that she had moved on and had forgiven me as well as herself. She further stated, "You need to handle this mostly on your own or with a therapist, as I did with my therapist in the years since."

So she believed she fixed her problem. Perhaps, but the content of her emails suggested she had no understanding or appreciation of my point of view. I was offended by her telling me what I needed to do to grow as if she were wiser and more knowledgeable than I. My request to meet with her was not for her to tell me what I needed to do but to resolve our differences together as equals. I never wrote back.

People at FXUU continued to side with Sue, refused to discuss the September 19 meeting and shunned me. During coffee hour, I stood by myself watching them talking to each other. I found that hard to bear. "Their reaction to you is very shaming," Dr. Emmett said.

I remember nothing about the Sunday service on October 3 except that I was moved to handwrite a brief letter on a note card to Rev. Patience. After telling her what I liked about the service, I asked her to meet and talk with me about the argument with Sue.

"That's beautiful," Dr. Emmett said when I showed him the letter.

Rev. Patience replied via email the very day she got the note. She thanked me for the card but made no mention of my request. I forwarded Rev. Patience's email to my eldest sister, Rita, who replied,

> I find Rev. Patience's response to your letter more of an insult than if she ignored it altogether. I hope that she will take the time to think things over and seek a rapprochement. If she chooses not to do so it will most certainly be her loss. I know this has been and will continue to be very painful for you. You have had to endure so many losses in your life. I wish this were not so but as you said ... you are a survivor. As difficult and painful these experiences are they are, the raw material of the overcoming and increasingly healthy person that you are. I love you very much and count myself lucky that you are my sister.
>
> No matter ... hold fast to the knowledge that as in the letter to Rev. Patience you are on the right track. You are responsible to do the very best you know to do. You have

always endeavored to live your life with integrity. That
others fail to do the same or are unable to do better than
they do is beyond your control. Surround yourself with
people who will lift you up and stay strong.

Rev. Patience's continued refusal to talk to me was not very spiritual
or forgiving. She and the other board members were punishing me for
refusing to apologize to Sue. Although I yearned to regain my place in the
church, I knew an apology would give them permission to continue to
break confidences and misuse my personal information. By surrendering
what I knew to be true and just to their distorted view of reality, I would
become their lackey and lose myself. That was just too high a price to pay
for acceptance.

On October 6, three days after Rev. Dorothy's seventy-fourth
birthday, I wrote her a letter.

> I have had great difficulty picking out a gift for you since I
> am unsure what you already have and because I wanted it to
> be the right gift to express my gratitude. Since we first met
> eight or nine months ago you have given a lot of your time
> and energy to helping me through my recent crisis. You
> have been very supportive as you listened to a lot of painful
> stuff. Your willingness to do this made it a lot easier for me
> to get through the day without injuring myself. I thank you
> for your kindness and your ability to be firm when the
> situation called for it. Regardless of how our relationship
> changes now that I am stronger and healthier, I will always
> be in your debt.

> Since I value your friendship I am concerned about the
> current strain in our relationship caused by our discussions
> about my recent argument with Sue. I have thought
> through and discussed the argument and my conversations
> with you about it with my family, including my eldest sister,
> and with Dr. Emmett. Since the conflict with Sue, I don't
> feel listened to and understood by you. I believe your view
> of me may be lopsided since so much of what you know
> about me you have learned while I have been in crisis and
> while my judgment and perceptions have been distorted.

But there is a lot you don't know about me. You haven't seen much of the strong, healthy side. Those who have known me a lot longer than you and who have stood by me while I went through the crises during my youth will tell you I have survived and I have survived well. What has happened to me this past year is not about misdirected anger. It has largely been about fear and feeling powerless to protect myself from the emotionally abusive behavior of others. It is bewildering to me when you call my hard-won insights into myself as "rationalizations." I think it is a mistake to assume to know more about a person than a person knows about herself. Although our relationship has been intense, you still have only known me for nine months. Please do not pass judgment on me and analyze my behavior. What I need and want from a friend is a kind and listening ear.

The next day was a bright, sunny fall day. It started off slowly with a cancelled appointment. I used the time to clean off my desk. Later I saw a Puerto Rican client who had had a good week. She was smiling and laughing. She gesticulated wildly as she talked, reminding me of my Italian heritage. She had had an argument with a coworker who attempted to bully her. She stood her ground and yelled. The coworker cried.

"Did you apologize?" I asked.

"Why should I? No. She was wrong but I did feel sorry for her."

I felt connected to my client. She was a kindred spirit who valued emotional expression as much as I did.

I was increasingly ambivalent about remaining at FXUU. During our many telephone conversations, Rita pleaded with me to leave FXUU and join Immanuel Lutheran where I was accepted.

I considered dividing my time between FXUU and Immanuel Lutheran. This would allow me to be with Don and Rev. Dorothy while getting my spiritual needs met at Immanuel. *Yes, that is what I will do!* I thought, then, *No, I need to begin a search for a new religious community where I can find kindred spirits just like my daughter and sister want me to do.* But I had invested so much into FXUU. I couldn't decide. No choice was safe.

Lunchtime Friday, I was sitting in my car at the lake listening to classical music on public radio. The sun was shining warmly through my car window. I picked up my pocketknife from my car's ashtray and considered cutting myself. I reminded myself I could always relieve my anxiety that way if I wanted to, if it became too unbearable. I could also take my medication or call someone. I chose to call my husband. Just hearing his voice reassured me. I was going to be okay.

Rev. Dorothy's accusation that I must have had problems at my Long Island church haunted me. She was wrong, definitely. I had friends there. Faith, Kate and Shirley valued and accepted me. While we were preparing to move to Massachusetts, Shirley asked if she could write to me. I was confused. Why was she asking? Why didn't she just do it? I was so overwhelmed by the move. A letter would have been welcome. Why didn't I tell her that? She misunderstood and never wrote. I was disappointed. Why didn't I stay in touch? A longing seeped into every cell of my body. Would my old friends be happy to see me?

In the early morning, I moved my body up against Lyndon, skin next to skin. He stirred, and with his muscular arm moved me even closer.

"Lyndon," I whispered, "please take me home."

"When?" he asked.

"Soon."

Later that morning I emailed Kate, an old friend who was now the minister at our former church. She immediately wrote back, inviting us to stay at her place.

On Columbus Day weekend, Lyndon and I left early on Saturday morning and returned home late Sunday. We ate some New York pizza for lunch, did some shopping and drove by our old neighborhood. We stopped to talk with Mrs. Forest, who was bringing groceries into her house. We shared what our children were doing.

Mrs. Forest said, "Malcom is attending college in Springfield."

"Orion is attending the Coast Guard Academy. Melissa is in college studying interior design."

After our brief conversation, we drove to Kate's house where we ate dinner and spent the night. We had so many years to catch up on. Why did we stay away so long? Kate was doing well. She was in a new relationship. Our old church was thriving. Kate was empathetic to my situation and advised me to seek another church.

On Sunday morning we went to services, and were warmly greeted by old friends and acquaintances. *Why did we stay away so long?* I thought. After services we visited with Faith, the religious education director. Faith was warm, concerned and empathetic to all that happened to me at FXUU. She had been involved with a bitter church conflict herself.

My memories confirmed and validated, I decided to leave FXUU and find a spiritual home where I was truly accepted.

The day after we returned I had a session with Dr. Emmett, and told him about my trip to Long Island. "I have decided to leave FXUU."

"How do you feel?" he asked.

I hid my tears and avoided his question. I wanted him to shut up and leave me alone. I didn't want to cry today. The session felt long. I wanted to escape.

I also showed him the emails I received from Gretchen. He saw them as less negative than I did. I was defensive, distrustful and angry. *What's the point? Is there no place on earth for me?* I wondered.

"The only people you can trust is your family," I said.

"I hope that also includes your therapist," Dr. Emmett replied.

"I'm tired of having a therapist. I'm not interested in growing."

"Growth is my business," he said.

I wanted to be left alone. I wanted to quit. Retreat. Disappear. Stay home with the people I trusted. I didn't want to trust Dr. Emmett.

That night after a long day, I went to bed early. Despite my exhaustion I couldn't sleep. I laid awake brooding. I felt angry and mistrustful. I felt that nothing mattered. Despite my best efforts I had failed. *You can't trust anyone outside of your family,* I told myself, *including your therapist.* Dr. Emmett really wasn't on my side. He probably sided with Rev. Dorothy. He wasn't being honest with me. If he wasn't my therapist he would more openly betray me.

I began scratching myself. I knew I should stop and seek out Lyndon. Maybe take some medication. Grab hold of my teddy bear. Go cut my nails. I didn't want to. I didn't think it was worth it. Since doing my best didn't work, why control my self-destructive impulses? At least I would feel better afterward.

I fell asleep after I did it. I would have done more overt damage if Lyndon wasn't around. He would surely spot any self-inflicted wounds on my body. I didn't want to deal with his reaction. Even though I knew I would tell Dr. Emmett, I didn't care what he had to say about it.

Don called me on Thursday, wanting to talk about public relations. "I can't talk right now," I replied. "I have clients."

"Please call me on Friday."

I hesitated. My Friday schedule included several seriously mentally ill clients. It was hard enough dealing with them when I was feeling good. It was almost impossible when I was feeling bad. They demanded a lot from me. I didn't want to call Don. "I'll be busy."

"Call on Friday," he repeated, insistent.

"Okay." I hung up, relieved to be off the phone. I wasn't quite ready to tell him about my decision to leave. On Friday, while I drove from group home to group home, I decided it would be better to email Don and tell him I would call on another day. Don, however, called me on my cell phone before I could do that. He tried to engage me in a conversation about public relations. I didn't want to commit to any new project. He must have suspected something was up. I wasn't at church on Sunday. I hadn't called to say I would be away. He wanted to know what was going on.

"I have decided to leave."

"What?"

"I need a break."

"What about Sue?"

"I don't know." *What about me?* I thought.

"What are you going to do about Sue?"

"Nothing. I am leaving."

"What about Sue?"

He was boxing me in. I pushed my way out. "I don't give a rat's ass about her."

Later that evening when I was home, I emailed him and asked him not to tell Rev. Dorothy. "Give me a few days to contact her and speak to her personally," I wrote. "I don't want her to think I wasn't going to let her know. I owe her that much respect."

The next morning he replied, "See if you can handle it today. Since Sharon and I both know, I don't want either of us to be in a position to have to keep this secret tomorrow. I'm sure people will be asking for you ... especially since this will be two weeks that you've missed without saying anything."

I felt pressured. Why couldn't he just tell people I was taking a break or encourage them to call me if they wanted to know why I wasn't at church? Didn't he understand I needed time to work things out?

"We're leaving for the cross-country meet right now," I emailed back. "I will try to reach her this evening. Hopefully she will be in. Don't feel you have to keep this secret. If she asks and you tell her I would appreciate it if you also tell her I intend to talk to her directly. Thanks."

When Lyndon and I returned home from our son's track meet, I found Don's reply in my inbox. He said he wouldn't make a campaign of telling everyone of my decision. However, when Rev. Patience called him asking what was going on, he told her I was leaving.

There was also an email from Rev. Patience.

"I respect your decision," she wrote, "and understand that you need to do what is best for you. May God's healing love be with you always. I sincerely wish you well."

*No you don't, you twofaced hypocrite,* I thought. *You don't give two hoots about me. I'm giving you what you want. I'm leaving. I wish I could stay, but I need to retreat to a safe place so I can heal and get beyond the tears.* If Rev. Patience had wanted me to stay, she would sit down with me and work things out.

Fearing Rev. Dorothy would hear of my decision from someone else, I called her immediately and told her about my decision to leave FXUU. She sounded tearful but was supportive. She made it clear I was still her friend. She wanted me to promise not to make it irrevocable. That was easy. Until I died everything was revocable, every decision could be changed. I didn't want to hurt her. I would miss going to church with her.

On Sunday I attended a healing service at Immanuel Lutheran and lit a candle for everyone at FXUU. I emailed Don and informed him I would be writing a letter to people at FXUU.

Don emailed back. He misunderstood my intentions. Referring to our last phone conversation, he wrote,

> I also heard what you said about not giving "a rat's ass" about the "the rest of them." I let all that go, attributing it to your self-defenses kicking in as you make this very difficult decision—and I understand that. If you are going to send that kind of thing in a letter to the entire congregation

though—I would hope that you do not. If you are gone, let
us go on without having to really dislike you.

How could Don get it so wrong? I didn't want to burn any bridges. I
just wanted to express my gratitude to individuals who had been
supportive in the past and say goodbye in the most constructive way I
knew. I had no intention of writing a letter to the entire congregation.

I wrote back,

> Don, yes, you heard anger. Anger is a healthy emotion. It is
> a reasonable self-protective response to a threat to one's
> physical and emotional well-being. It is not dangerous.
> Anger does not necessarily lead to violence. I have never
> harmed anyone but myself. Just because I was enraged by
> Sue's breach of a personal confidence and her use of it as a
> weapon, that does not mean I am easily enraged or
> habitually lose my temper. How many times in the last four
> years have you seen me that angry? Actually, I usually do the
> opposite. I shut down and retreat. Please do not pass
> judgment based on the one incident.

The email exchange with Don left me feeling anxious. Sunday night,
I tried to stay strong and optimistic. I took some medication and went
into my study, settling into my tan corduroy recliner with my journal. In
an effort to sort things out I rewrote the emails Gretchen sent me,
removing or rewording the parts I found offensive. I also wrote an
apology to my body for all the times I tried to intentionally injure myself.

By bedtime I was more hopeful and decided to retain my
membership at FXUU while resigning from the board. I planned on
attending services at other churches and considered organizing a local
chapter of the Unitarian Universalist Christian Fellowship.

Monday morning I received an email from my sister Rita.

> I have always found writing letters to be a superior way to
> say things that may be difficult to express. It gives distance
> to the writer and the receiver. You do a particularly good
> job of expressing yourself via the written word. If Don
> doesn't like it he doesn't have to read your letter. I am glad
> that Rev. Dorothy at least had a positive response. In spite
> of some bumps in the road she sounds like a person that is
> really trying to be a true friend to you. I know you have had

too few of those, especially in Massachusetts. Take care and write as many letters as you need to write and mail the ones you feel good about.

Her email set the tone for the rest of the day, and I was able to enjoy simple pleasures. At lunchtime I was delighted to find some leftover stew in the refrigerator. I poured it into a bowl and reheated it in the microwave. Sitting at the kitchen table, I took pleasure in finishing the stew and wiping out the bowl with a piece of whole wheat bread. I then sat in the living room near the window and wrote in my journal,

> At tomorrow's session with Dr. Emmett I would like to be able to apologize to him for not calling and for allowing myself to sink into that dark, illogical space where I trust no one and it is perfectly all right to try to injure myself. I don't know why I allowed it to happen last Tuesday night. I am ashamed of it and would do it differently if I could. I wish I could promise never to do it again, but I fear I would break that promise if conditions were right for it. When I get like that I am in another world, another reality. I am not thinking about my family or friends or any promises I have made. I and my misery are the only things that exist.

On Tuesday, Dr. Emmett supported my decision not to resign my membership from FXUU. As soon as I got home from my session I went into my study and sent an email to Don, who was now the membership chair.

> Given that I have already met the requirements for membership this year (i.e. made a contribution of record, attended church services and volunteered my time), I have decided not to withdraw my membership at this time and would like to remain as a member.

I sent a second email to Sue, the current president of the board.

> Due to health and increasing professional obligations I regret to inform you that I need to resign from the board of FXUU effective immediately. I will no longer be able to assist with printing the order of services, the newsletter, PR or any of the signups. I will, however, maintain my membership at FXUU.

I sent copies of both emails to Rev. Patience and the other board members.

Don called after receiving my emails, asking, "What are you doing!" He implied I was disrupting the church. He kept telling me how supportive everyone had been. It was peculiar. It was as if he was saying, "Maggie, you shouldn't be anxious and distressed. What's wrong with you? Why aren't you better after all the support we gave you? Where's your gratitude?"

Discounting the work I did as worship chair, they felt I didn't give enough in return. They didn't realize I was depleted and had very little left to give. I tried to show my appreciation with greeting cards. It didn't satisfy them.

Rev. Patience responded an hour later.

> When we understood from Don that you had decided to leave the church, everyone I spoke with was relieved. You are not welcomed as a member. I have made it clear to the board that if you return, I will resign as minister. In my years of ministry, I have never experienced a member who has caused so much destruction to a church as you have. Do not send me any emails. I will delete them before I read them.

Weeping, I called Dr. Emmett. He wasn't available. I left a message. I called Rev. Karen, who asked me to come over to her office at Immanuel. I left immediately. When I arrived, she asked, "Do you know the Lutheran minister in Foxboro?"

"No. I've heard of him but I've never met him."

"I wasn't going to tell you this but now I think I need to. Last week I went to a meeting. While I was getting out of my car he came running over. He told me that Rev. Dick telephoned him and warned him about a member of FXUU who had assaulted another member and was now attending a Lutheran church."

"What? How did he hear of the argument?" My chest ached from the pounding of my heart.

"Rev. Dick called him."

"How did he hear about it? He wasn't there."

"I don't know. Tell me again what happened."

I gave Rev. Karen a quick summary of the argument. "I was on the opposite side of the table. I never went near Sue!"

"Did you threaten her?"

"No. I was very angry but I was in control. What was meant by 'assault'?"

"I called Rev. Dick and asked him if he meant you had actually hit someone. He said no."

"I didn't even threaten anyone. How did he hear about the argument with Sue? He wasn't even there!"

"I don't know. He didn't say. Maggie, you should consider speaking to a lawyer. Several years ago when I had a problem with some malicious gossip I had my lawyer send a letter warning them to stop."

Rev. Karen informed me that it was a common practice for clergy to warn each other of problem parishioners. I told her I felt that was unethical, since it involved disclosing personal information without a person's knowledge or consent. It also didn't give a person a fair chance to explain their side of things.

I checked my watch. I had to go. "Rev. Karen, thanks for telling me."

When I returned home I found another email from Rev. Patience. She had written to the new district executive and forwarded a copy to me.

> As you are our new district executive and a representative of the Unitarian Universalist Association, we appreciate your information on an official level and your support in this matter. To reiterate what you said, a church had the right to remove any member who it feels is harmful and destructive to the organization of the church. Further, you confirm that membership is a privilege and not a right. It was helpful for us to know that we have the right to inform such a person that they are not welcome at the church and will be removed from the premises if they come. First and foremost, you have affirmed for us what we already knew, that the well-being of the church is what is most important.

I was sobbing when Dr. Emmett called. I read the emails to him and told him what Rev. Karen said. "Can you come back to my office?" he said.

"No."

"Why not?"

"I have to work."

"Okay. I'm here if you need to talk."

While I was up in my bedroom getting ready to leave, Sharon, Don's wife, called.

"Sharon, I can't talk to you now."

Oblivious to my emotional distress, Sharon said, "You lost my support when you wrote you could no longer put the church before your emotional health. People are saying you gave nothing in return for all the support they gave you."

Sobbing, I said, "You don't know what's been going on. I really, really can't talk to you now."

Ignoring my tears, Sharon replied, "We just want to come to church on Sunday, have coffee, get a little spirituality, have some fun and go home."

# Descent into the White Space

The harsh message in Rev. Patience's emails played over and over in my head: "Everyone was relieved when you left. You're destructive. You will be removed if you come back."

My father was right. No one wanted me. I didn't belong or fit in anywhere. The fault must have been mine. Depressed, I called Rev. Dorothy.

"You know," she said acidly, "the story about Rev. Dick isn't true."

My stomach churned. Did she think Rev. Karen lied when she told me Rev. Dick had accused me of assaulting Sue?

"You don't think this is right, do you?" I asked. My throat tightened as I suppressed my tears.

"Who is to say what is right?" Rev. Dorothy responded.

"I have to go." I hung up the phone. Not even Rev. Dorothy was on my side. What had happened? Why did she doubt what I told her? How could she think so little of me? I thought she knew me.

I went upstairs to the master bath and took out my pill bottle. My physician had given me a large supply of sedatives. I wondered if that was really wise of her. What would happen if I took all of them at once? Would I die?

I took one pill and laid down on top of the comforter on my bed. Curled up into a tight fetal position I pulled the afghan my grandmother made for me over my head and tried to rest. I ruminated. Why did Don, Sharon, Angelina and the others overreact to my anger? Was it because I spent six weeks in a mental institution twenty years ago? Did they think I was crazy and dangerous? I sighed. *I am the only person I have ever harmed. What do I do about the stigma?* I didn't want to go back to keeping a secret. Doing so would deny an important part of me. Weepy, I called my sister Rita.

"The church used you. When they no longer needed you they discarded you like an old shoe."

That night I dreamed that as my family entered God's temple, the guard blocked my way. "I'm with them," I told him as I tried to sidestep him. He was bigger and faster than I was. Hearing my voice, my family turned and stared blankly at me. They didn't acknowledge me.

"You don't belong with them," the guard said.
I awoke. Lyndon wrapped his big, strong arms around me as I wept.

I withdrew into myself and didn't want to see Dr. Emmett anymore
or do any more work in *The Courage to Heal Workbook*. What was the
use? Like many of my colleagues, I considered my need for therapy and
my phone calls to Dr. Emmett as evidence of pathology. Shortly after
my hospitalization, my need for emotional support was denigrated as
attention seeking by the psychiatrist treating me. I berated myself for
not being able to recover without professional help. Why, with all my
skills and education, couldn't I get over it more quickly? I felt so stupid.
I was a sham. How could I help other people when I couldn't even help
myself?

The psychic pain impaired my ability to use well-learned coping
skills. I couldn't think clearly enough to evaluate what had happened.
When I tried taking a walk through the woods, all I could think of was
burning my arm. I feared everyone, including Dr. Emmett, would
eventually abandon me. I would say or do something that they would
find unforgivable, and then they would stop talking to me. There was no
way to predict what would trigger rejection.

My niece Rebecca called. "It is hard to lose a church," she said. "You
lose a whole support system."

Dr. Emmett was the first person to tell me that my desire to call and
reach out was my healthy side. In my more rational moments I understood
that just as surgeons cannot operate on themselves, I couldn't climb out of
the abyss without someone supporting me and showing me the way. I
dreaded therapy, but by the end of the week I was desperate to talk to Dr.
Emmett.

The drive to his Providence office took twenty minutes. Fearful I
would get caught in traffic and miss my appointment, I would leave half
an hour earlier than I needed to. Worried that arriving early would
meet with disapproval or appear foolish, I parked my car on the street
where it couldn't be seen from his office and fed the parking meter.

I waited fifteen or twenty minutes before walking across the Brown
University parking lot and into the back door of the nineteenth-century
wood frame house that had been converted into offices. After climbing
the narrow, winding back stair, I waited anxiously by the window, fearful
he wouldn't be there. Right on the hour, he opened his office door. As

his earlier client exited, Dr. Emmett invited me in. I passed his other client, avoiding eye contact.

After greeting Dr. Emmett, I took a seat across from him in a chair that was too high for me to rest my feet on the floor. He looked directly at me, waiting for me to start. I squirmed and looked down at my lap. I clutched my journal, debating whether to share it with him or not. Finally, unable to bear the silence, I thrust my journal into his hands and showed him which entries to read.

Shifting nervously in the chair while he read, I looked around. If I tried to use the exit behind him, would he get up and allow me to pass or would he block my escape? If he did, could I escape through the door behind me? Where did it go? What about the window? I couldn't see out of it. Did it let out onto a roof? Could I make my exit that way? Was I quick and agile enough to run straight for the door and evade any attempts to stop me?

The fear made me lightheaded. I floated in the room. I was aware he was talking, but couldn't make out what he was saying. He was so far away. I couldn't reach him. I was trapped. Nothing mattered. I did not weep. I considered driving to a remote wilderness area to find a cave or a crevice where I could die quietly. But my husband sensing my mood, had been watching me too closely. I couldn't figure out how to deceive him long enough to succeed.

I didn't share these thoughts with him. He said something about my journal entries. I shrugged my shoulders. The session ended. I moved toward the door, but stopped. He had gotten up to show me out, but was too close. He observed my hesitation and moved away.

"Goodbye, Maggie. Have a good week."

I rushed out the door and down the steps. Dr. Emmett's next client, a young dark-haired woman, was standing on the small wooden deck taking a final puff on her cigarette. We made eye contact. Damn! We had intruded on each other's private agony. What to do now? I panicked. I didn't want anyone, not even strangers to know I had been there. But this woman was a fellow sufferer who I had seen before and would probably see again. I couldn't just ignore her.

"Hi," I whispered, then turned left toward the parking lot. I barely heard her return greeting as I hurried toward my car. I tried to slow my pace. I didn't want anyone to notice me. When I reached my car, I slipped into the driver's seat and locked all the doors behind me, then sat still allowing my breathing to slow and my head to clear. I plugged my headset into my cell phone and drove away. I called my husband.

"How did it go?" he asked.

"Okay," I said, reassured by the familiarity of his deep Trinidadian voice.

I made all my weekly appointments with Dr. Emmett. I was never late and never cancelled at the last minute. I was responsible. Besides, I was desperate.

Week after week I sat there shrugging my shoulders, avoiding talking about things that hurt, saying I was fine when I wasn't, saying I didn't care when I did or that it didn't matter when it did. Then, after a long drought, my eyes darkened like rain clouds until the tears they could no longer contain overflowed. Dr. Emmett gave an audible sigh of relief. Neither one of us moved from our chairs as we sat face to face. He kept silent vigil while I sobbed alone.

"I'd hug you," he said at the end of the session bridging the chasm between us.

My eyes met his for a second, acknowledging his kind words.

High levels of anxiety continued to trigger and intensify my desire to burn or cut myself. Like a jumper clinging to the ledge of a Manhattan skyscraper, I looked down into the abyss and saw only white. If I let go and fell into the white space, I would enter another dimension that had its own bizarre logic, its own rules that could only be understood by its inhabitants. Family and friends didn't exist. They were beyond my awareness. I didn't consider their needs. All that mattered was my desire to injure myself severely enough to purge all blame. Like an addict, I would begin a frantic search for matches or sharp objects that could inflict enough physical pain to release me from my suffering and bring salvation.

Dr. Emmett tried to talk to me about the self-injury. "There's no point in discussing it," I told him. "It will always be part of my life."

"How do you feel about it?" he asked.

"I'm okay with it." Tears exposed my lie.

In between sessions, I searched for answers. Following a suggestion in Richards and Bergin's A Spiritual Strategy for Counseling and Psychotherapy, I imagined God being with me when Uncle Frank sexually assaulted me. I tried to imagine God protecting me. Instead, I was flooded with an image of God stroking my hair and whispering as Uncle Frank raped me, "Don't be afraid. He is only going to love you."

Devastated and numb, I went to the healing service at Immanuel Lutheran. I allowed Rev. Karen to anoint my forehead with oil and lay her hands on my head. Her touch was gentle and loving. I was comforted.

Almost every week after Bible study, she and I would talk privately in her office. She would sit across from me in her rocking chair while I sat on the black couch. She told me she liked me and I was always welcomed at Immanuel Lutheran even though I didn't believe in Jesus as Savior. I shared my childhood history of neglect and sexual abuse. We discussed why God had allowed me to be abused. I told her about my struggle with self-harming behaviors. I even showed her the scars on my arms that came from burning myself in my early twenties.

"It's easier to hurt myself," I told her.

"Easier but not better," she replied.

Dr. Emmett suggested I read Elie Wiesel's *The Night Trilogy*. While I went about my daily routine, I was haunted by the image of the hanged child as God. I was uncertain what Wiesel meant when he saw God in murdered children. Were they Christ-like figures, or did evil kill God, or is God with the oppressed? It was disquieting. The Nazis turned their captives into godless, wild, hungry animals. Did clinging to God and love help a prisoner maintain some dignity, some humanity?

I didn't have any answer for where God was when children were being raped or abused. If evil was the work of the devil, why didn't God, who was more powerful, stop him? How could God stop it? With a lightning bolt? By yelling at Uncle Frank to stop? How? How could God intervene without us losing our sense of self? Is evil the price we pay for free will?

I needed to believe God valued me and didn't want any harm to come to me. But where was God? Was I, as Elie Wiesel asked, a mere toy for God to play with? Surely God didn't want to harm us, any more than a parent wants to hurt their child. There are things that happen, painful experiences we cannot protect ourselves or our children from. Maybe God, like a good parent, knew that you often have to allow your children to work things out by themselves.

Where was God? I remembered St. Augustine's words: God is always with me even though I have not always been with God. God hadn't abandoned me. Uncle Frank was not with God. God must have been weeping.

I tried controlling my anxiety by keeping myself busy. I had plenty to do. I had clients to see, bills to pay and errands to run. With considerable effort, I calmed my fears for brief periods. So long as nothing reminded me of my old church, I was okay. On an errand to the mall, I saw Sue's daughter looking at jewelry while I rode the down escalator. She didn't see me. I felt irritable for the rest of the day. By Friday, I was extremely anxious.

At lunchtime, I picked up some fast food and drove to the lake to eat. While sitting in my car, I tried to alleviate my anxiety by reading, and by listening first to a tape on anxiety and next to a relaxation tape. Inexplicably, the anxiety increased. I felt a strong urge to pick up my pocketknife and cut myself. I was convinced that sooner or later I would do it, if not then, sometime in the future. It was destined to happen. The anxiety peaked and then subsided. I picked up the knife and put it in the glove compartment. I continued listening to the relaxation tape. I took out the knife again, opened it, and pressed the sharp edge against my calf. I gained control. Closed it and held it tightly in my hand. It felt warm and comforting, like a teddy bear. I put it in the tray under the cup holder and drove to my next appointment.

Dr. Emmett suggested keeping a knife in my car was like an alcoholic keeping a bottle of whiskey. Whenever I felt like hurting myself he asked me to write in my journal instead. When I arrived home, I moved the pocketknife from my car's ashtray to the kitchen drawer. With ready access to my pocketknife eliminated, I considered using my keys, a screwdriver, scissors or any other sharp object to cut myself. While searching for a sharp object, the urge would dissipate, allowing me to regain control.

At my next session, I handed Dr. Emmett a letter as I took my seat.

> Last Tuesday, I missed the early signs that I might lose control. Looking back on it, I suppose I should have called you, Pastor Karen or Lyndon before I sat down in my recliner. I thought I could distract myself by reading. I didn't realize my emotions were escalating so rapidly.

> It is always a debate within my head about when, at what point I should call you. How early in the chain I should call you or someone else. I don't want to be a pest by wearing people out with my problems. I feel I should be able to manage things on my own.

Tuesday I obviously didn't cope very well. I really whacked myself pretty hard this time. I cut my nose and injured my finger. I couldn't bend it for a few days. I also had a superficial scratch on my right wrist from where I took a can lid across it.

I looked down at my hands while he read the letter. He looked up and handed the letter back to me. "Maggie, will you pledge to call me whenever you feel like hurting yourself?"

I hesitated. I wanted to please him, but wasn't sure about making such a promise. Last week, I had been stopped by the custodian in the vestibule of the building where I rented office space. In the dim light of dusk, he confided in me that his grandfather had committed suicide years ago, and his father had killed himself a few months before. He had thought about suicide. After getting his assurances that he would call his therapist, I left him standing alone in the shadows.

A week later, while I was locking my office door, another tenant stopped and spoke to me.

"Did you hear the custodian hung himself?"

My heart sank. I quickly reviewed the last conversation I had with him. Had I taken enough time with him that night? Was there anything I could have done?

Twenty-plus years ago, I stood on the stoop of my childcare provider's home with my infant daughter in my arms. "My father was an alcoholic," my babysitter confided. "My mother died from cancer when I was ten. A few months later my father killed himself."

"Oh, I'm sorry," I replied.

"What was wrong with him?" she asked plaintively. "He still had me. Didn't he love me?"

"Perhaps you are not ready." Dr. Emmett's voice penetrated my consciousness. "Often you have been denied a voice...."

Fearing disappointing him and not wanting to leave my family a similar legacy as the custodian or my childcare provider's father, I interrupted. "Yes, I promise."

After I left his office, I felt defeated and dejected. It was hard to admit I couldn't manage things without professional help. During my childhood, I had learned it was better to solve my own problems and not disturb others. When I was in my late teens, I was having problems with the thread tension on the sewing machine. Following the instructions in the machine's manual, I tried adjusting the screw on the bobbin case. That didn't work. With the case in my hand, I got up and went to my mother, who was in the kitchen. As I was explaining my problem, she began yelling as she hit me, "You broke it! You broke it!"

Seeking help wasn't safe. I tried to convince myself that I was okay and I didn't need Dr. Emmett's help anymore. When I got the desire to call or self-harming thoughts intruded, I would think, *I can deal with this.* Sometimes I would follow through on the self-harming thoughts, sometimes I didn't. When was it an emergency? I didn't understand when I should handle things by myself and when it was okay to need help.

I felt boxed in by the pledge. If I intentionally injured myself again, it would mean I wasn't paying attention and broke my pledge to Dr. Emmett. If I called Dr. Emmett as I promised, he wasn't going to let me off the telephone until he was sure I wasn't going to harm myself. I felt tricked. I hadn't promised not to self-harm ever again, but the pledge effectively prevented me from ever doing so. I hadn't thought it through before I promised.

Dr. Emmett told me I had free will and could do what I wanted even though I had made a pledge. Although there are times when it is necessary to break a promise, I couldn't imagine a circumstance where it would be okay to break my pledge to him. I freely made the pledge. It would be dishonorable to break it unless he released me from it. He wasn't going to do that.

My calls to Dr. Emmett increased. Sometimes I would leave a message. Sometimes I would just listen to his voice, seeking reassurance he was still there and wasn't going to abandon me.

With difficulty, I distracted myself with work. I took medication to help relieve my anxiety whenever it threatened to incapacitate me. But I wanted a more long-term fix to anxiety than medication provided. I was aware from my professional education and experience that restructuring my thought patterns and learning better ways to cope would almost totally eliminate anxiety and significantly improve my life.

I struggled to alter my self-talk. I would tell myself that harming myself wasn't right. I couldn't do that. It wasn't the way out. It was a blind alley, a dead end. If I injured myself, I would just keep perpetuating my own misery.

I reaffirmed that I was an okay person. I wasn't bad. I was going to be okay. God would take care of me. I needed to forgive myself for not being the daughter my parents wanted me to be, for getting angry with Sue, for letting Uncle Frank touch me.

I needed desperately to talk and reach out but feared people were tired of me. I needed reassurance that I was okay and not a bad person. I needed to convince myself that it wasn't my fault.

I used relaxation exercises to take the edge off. When I didn't have the time, I would take slow, deep breaths. I distracted myself with something positive. I wrote in my journal. Read. Prayed. Anything so I wouldn't think of cutting.

I imagined I was a frightened child that needed nurturing. I tried to take care of her. Stroke her. Love her. Reassure her that everything would be all right.

Lingering in bed, I recalled my visits with my grandmother. In my mind's eye, I saw us sitting at the table on the sun porch. She fed me roasted peppers and apologized for not having more food to give me. She told me stories of how and why our family left Italy for America.

"Everything works out for the best," she often reassured me. "Margherita, keep your faith," she urged.

"I will," I promised her.

Suddenly I knew with certainty there was a God. My entire being radiated with joy. God had always been there for me. In the midst of my worst times, I prayed to God and He eventually helped me. When I sank into that dark space and yielded to those desires to injure myself, I was not with God, even though He was always with me. When I injured myself I became one of the people who abused me. I was yielding to evil. I was not with God. I wanted to be with God always, to live a life full of God.

*I must not go to the white space ever again*, I thought. *I cannot injure myself intentionally. I am worth more than that. I would never mistreat any other living creature that way. When I begin to space out, dissociate, I am not with God. I need to stay with God. God will not allow me to injure myself. I must stay with God.*

With my car in for repairs, Rev. Karen drove me to and from summer Bible study. "It has been difficult for me to believe in God," I confided on the drive home. "God didn't protect me. After Uncle Frank raped me, he desperately begged me not to tell anyone what had just happened. I pitied him."

"Pity? Not fear?" Rev. Karen asked as she pulled into my driveway.

"In a brief moment in between confusion and fear, I felt pity." I released my seatbelt and opened the car door. "There were two people who needed God that day: Uncle Frank and me. Uncle Frank's sins left him more disconnected from God than I was."

Dr. Emmett told me that things happened the way they did whether or not it was what I wanted. I was left to make the best of it. Dr. Robins, my previous therapist, once talked about Job and acceptance. There are just things we can't change. It is part of our lot in life, like death. The neglect and abuse happened. There was nothing I could do to change it. All that remained was for me to stop abusing myself and forgive those who had abused me.

Dr. Emmett also told me that one of his goals for me was to get to the point where my buttons couldn't be pushed, even when someone was way over the line. That wasn't one of my goals for myself. It sounded like emotional over-control to me. What I wanted to achieve was elimination of anxiety and depression. I needed to figure out how I got myself into the mess at FXUU in order to avoid it in the future.

I threw out old papers from FXUU, except for the emails and letters that documented the conflict. I deleted old orders of service, prayers, and so on from my hard drive. Lyndon urged me to press the issue and sue. But I was fearful that course of action would destroy me emotionally. I thought about filing a complaint with the Unitarian Universalist Association, but feared the repercussions.

While Dr. Emmett and I discussed how FXUU treated me, I felt the anger welling up. Instead of acknowledging their own anger, FXUU members focused on my rage and saw malice in all my actions. Unless they were willing to allow for the possibility that their interpretations might be wrong, there was no chance for reconciliation.

I wrote a letter to Rev. Patience that I never sent. I found it unsatisfying. I tried to write another, angrier letter. I ended up scribbling all over the page, writing "hate" in the center. That was equally unsatisfying. I didn't really hate her. I tried writing out a fantasy of beating her. I couldn't do it. I could fantasize beating myself, but not another person. I didn't want to beat her. I just wanted to be vindicated. I wanted someone else at FXUU or the Unitarian Universalist Association to say what Rev. Patience did was terribly wrong.

I prayed for Rev. Patience and the others. I asked God to forgive them. I asked God to help me forgive them and help them build a church that was full of justice, acceptance and caring.

Too long I had been silenced by people's abusive behavior, by people telling me I didn't fit in, I didn't belong. I was different and defective. But I did belong. An essay in the *Christian Science Monitor* was right: God had a special place for me that could not be taken away. Not by Rev. Patience, or anyone else.

I couldn't let Rev. Patience defeat me. I needed to continue on, needed to find another church community. I needed to continue working as well. My clients and my family depended on me. I would hurt all of them if I hurt myself.

What I wanted was at odds with what people at FXUU wanted. I wanted more than "a little spirituality" from church. I wanted a church full of God, full of spirituality, full of community, full of love and caring and full of commitment. If there weren't a coffee hour, I wouldn't have missed it.

I wasn't sure such a community existed. Perhaps my hopes and aspirations were too high. People frequently betrayed one another. Even if they meant well, they still lied and deceived and gossiped and harshly judged people who were different from themselves.

# Seeking

On Friday night, November 5, 1999, Rev. Karen and I drove to Sudbury to hear Marcus Borg speak. While driving home we discussed the Nicene Creed, the Virgin Mary and tradition. "The belief in a virgin birth is a patriarchal myth that oppresses women by denigrating their sexuality," I told her.

"Lutheran doctrine differs from Catholic on the subject of Mary," she replied. "Mary needed Jesus' salvation as much as everyone else. I didn't find anything objectionable about Marcus Borg," she went on. "You should be able to find a religious home among mainline Christian churches."

Encouraged by Rev. Karen, I suppressed my fear of being hurt again and began attending various area churches, looking for one that was a better fit than FXUU. First I tried Central Congregational Church. Arriving ten minutes early, I parked the car behind the church. Unable to see who was entering the church, I moved the car to where I could see the front steps and watched people enter the sanctuary. When no one was in sight, I got out of my car and climbed the stairs. I entered the vestibule, slipped past a family that was chatting with the official greeters, and took an order of service from a back table. Turning toward the front of the sanctuary I paused, looking for an inconspicuous place to sit. An usher approached me and asked if I had a seating preference. I told him no. After he seated me toward the front I looked over the order of service, which was almost identical to the one used by Unitarian Universalists except all the readings were from the Bible.

At the start of the service, Rev. Carol had a member of the congregation choose a hymn. A teenager chose "Angels We Have Heard on High."

"That was quite courageous of you," Rev. Carol congratulated the youth. "It is quite liturgically correct. Martin Luther said any hymn could be sung at any time."

I left immediately after the service, not staying for coffee hour for fear I would be asked too many questions, or worse, no one would talk to me. After I arrived home, I called Rev. Dorothy.

"Is your cold any better?" I asked.

"Yes, I am doing better. How are you?"

"Getting by," I answered. "Struggling—" Tears choked off my voice. "Do you think what happened to me was fair?"

"Lots of things in life aren't fair," she replied.

"Yes, but we need to be aware of injustice so we can work toward a better world."

"Sue was only responding to what you said. There was no reason to get so upset."

"You minimize what Sue said and exaggerate what I did at the meeting. You weren't even there."

Rev. Dorothy listened but didn't say much more. "Have you been going to church?"

"No, I— You must promise not to tell them anything about me, where I am, what I'm doing."

"All ... right."

"I went to church at Central Congregational this morning."

"How was that?"

"Okay." I didn't trust her.

"I will be officially joining FXUU next Sunday," she said.

"Oh," I said. "Congratulations."

I returned to Central Congregational a few weeks later. I chose to sit by myself in a pew toward the front. The sermon's focus on Jesus' divinity left me with little to connect to. But the congregation sang hymns that I knew and it was a pleasant building to be in.

As I was exiting, I ran into a colleague. Several years before, we both sat on the ethics committee at the state school where we both worked. She invited me to coffee hour, but I slipped out without saying goodbye.

I called Rev. Dorothy to wish her a safe trip to Colorado. She was going to visit her daughter and granddaughter. Unable to restrain my curiosity, I asked her how breakfast and Membership Sunday went. FXUU had five new members, including Rev. Dorothy. I felt a surge of grief. I worked so hard for that growth. I deserved to be there.

I continued to manage my anxiety by writing in my journal, reading and remembering my grandmother's voice. Every morning, I started the day in prayer. I used a quote from St. Augustine as a mantra: "And always You were with me." I reflected on how to make my life full of God. In what way would I respond differently to the events at FXUU if my life were full of God? Would I have set limits sooner with Sue? Would I have raised my voice? In what way was I lacking?

Despite my best efforts, I failed to prevent my expulsion from FXUU. If I had handled it differently, perhaps there would have been a better, less painful outcome for me. I was only trying to set a limit with Sue. Did that limit really need to be set? Perhaps with time, the behavior would have disappeared. But what if it hadn't? The explosion would have occurred at a different time and place. Dr. Emmett believed I had done my best and that was okay. No more could be expected of me.

After considerable self-reflection, I found nothing seriously flawed in my behavior at FXUU. I worked hard, did my share, and encouraged others, particularly Sue, to pursue their own religious beliefs while I pursued mine. I didn't deserve the way they treated me. I committed no sin so severe that I needed to be kicked out of the church and have my attempts to find a more suitable religious community sabotaged.

During a phone call, I told Rev. Karen, "I find evangelical churches' emphasis on The Last Judgment disturbing and destructive. I prefer to focus on God's grace."

"Lutherans believe there is nothing we can do to earn salvation. It is a gift from God."

"But they still believe in hell."

"Yes, some will be saved and some not. Only God knows who. We don't know how many will be saved."

"Well, if there is no Lutheran doctrine on the number, I am free to believe everyone will be saved. I don't believe a loving father would ever condemn any of his children to eternal damnation."

"You are always free to believe what you will. No doctrinal demands are placed on individuals who want to become a Lutheran," she replied.

On December 12, 1999, I attended a Sunday service at Second Congregational, a large church with an excellent choir. During the first part of the service, the choir stood in the front and sang. I felt like I was attending a concert and didn't feel spiritually connected. The excellent sermon focused on the homeless, and places where God appears more present than others. As I was exiting, the minister realized I was a visitor. Embarrassed, I shook his hand, said nothing and quickly left.

I stifled tears while I drove home, feeling tremendous grief I thought was worse than the grief I felt when Dr. Howard died. I knew it took time to recover and needed to be patient, but sometimes it felt like I was never going to get over it.

That afternoon while doing the bills, I again became weepy. I stopped and went looking for my husband, who was watching the football game. I laid down, placing my head in his lap, and wept. I was immobilized by my grief for at least an hour, maybe longer. Orion called, and I cried when he asked me how I was. When the tears finally subsided and I was able to laugh, I went back into my study to finish the bills.

I spoke privately to Rev. Karen about Dr. Howard's death. I thought at first it would have been better if I had died and not Dr. Howard, since at the time I was alone and no one would have missed me. Then I realized that wasn't true. Dr. Howard and my sister Rita would have missed me. It would have been better if Dr. Howard and I had both survived. It didn't make things better if I allowed myself to space out and self-injure. Living my life well was what made things better.

"It frightens me to let go of my defenses and make myself vulnerable," I told Rev. Karen. "I need you to be honest with me."

"I will be," she said, making a promise she would later break. "I will warn you of any situation at Immanuel that might be harmful to you. Why don't you take time to thank God?"

"I used to write down the things I'm grateful for before going to bed, but I stopped when I was pushed out of FXUU."

"FXUU has nothing to do with your family and your home. You should be grateful for those things."

"Please pray for me, Pastor."

"I already am."

Before leaving to attend Sunday services at Central Congregational Church for the third time, I took anti-anxiety medication. While I waited for the service to begin, I breathed slowly and deeply while taking in the church's simple beauty. The white walls were adorned with bright stained-glass windows, including a rosette window over the altar. I was comforted by the sunlight streaming through the windows and bouncing off the white walls.

After the service, I went downstairs to coffee hour. Jane, who had been on the Council of Churches Committee with me, greeted me and asked about FXUU.

"I've left," I told her.

"It is such a difficult choice to leave a church," she said. "I was a member of a smaller, struggling congregation. I tried to make it work for me. I finally had to leave."

When the church was nearly empty, I approached Rev. Carol. I had only intended to speak with her briefly. While I was talking to her, I burst into tears. She took me into the nursery and closed the door. Among the brightly colored toys strewn about the floor, we each took a seat in a rocking chair. She listened empathetically and didn't pass judgment. I felt supported.

The following day I was worried I had shared too much too soon with Rev. Carol. Did she believe me? Rev. Karen reassured me that Rev. Carol had an excellent reputation around the area and could be trusted. Rev. Karen thought it was good that I finally went to coffee hour.

I called Rev. Dorothy. She sounded pleased when she realized it was me. But I wasn't sure about her. I wasn't sure about anyone. I didn't know who was really my friend and who wasn't. I didn't know who would or would not misuse personal information. Rev. Dick didn't misuse his personal knowledge of me until two years later. The same was true for Sue. But Dr. Howard taught me you have to take a risk and trust people sometime. Perhaps all I could do was cross someone off when and if they broke confidences.

Rev. Dorothy asked me out to lunch. Did she really want to see me, or did she just pity me? Desperately wanting to salvage the connection with her, I met her at a restaurant near her home. While we ate, she asked after my husband and children but never asked how I was. I didn't tell her that Dr. Emmett said hello. I didn't want her to know I was still in therapy.

I read her the last email I received from Rev. Patience. Silence. What did that mean? Was Rev. Dorothy shocked by it? Did she agree with it?

At some point Rev. Dorothy stopped listening, started judging and gave unasked-for advice. I didn't know how to bridge the gulf between us without reopening wounds. The more we talked, the more emotionally overwhelmed I became. I ended the visit.

On Christmas Eve, a friend of my husband's dropped by. Standing in my foyer, he asked how I was.

"It's been rough—"

He stepped forward and hugged me, pressing my face into his chest. I tried to pull away. He tightened his grip. "I don't want to know," he said.

After he released me, I kept my distance while I showed him into the kitchen. I offered him some juice while he waited for Lyndon to return home from shopping. He asked how I had been doing since I last saw him.

"It has been a difficult year."

"Besides that, how have you been?" he asked.

"It has been a difficult year," I repeated.

"How have you been?" he asked again.

"It has been a difficult year," I said again.

"How is your health?" he asked.

I took a slow, deep breath. "My physical health has been fine."

"How's work?"

"Fine." I changed the subject to his family, and how much Christmas was costing him. I suggested I call Lyndon and let him know he was visiting.

"That's not necessary," he said.

To my relief, Lyndon arrived home shortly after. As soon as he came in, I got up and started mending some clothes. Lyndon's friend asked what I was doing. I gave him short, curt answers.

Lyndon and his friend sat at the kitchen table, talking about plans for the holidays and for our wedding anniversary. I was sitting at the sewing machine, and started telling the friend that many of the theatres here are closed on our wedding anniversary, unlike New York.

"Let it go," he said to me.

When I tried to say something else, he interrupted. "Let it go."

Angry, I told him, "You don't know anything about me and don't want to know anything about me, so don't tell me to let it go!"

I withdrew and continued my mending. He left shortly after that. I explained to Lyndon what was going on, but he wouldn't listen. We quarreled.

Upset, I telephoned Rev. Dorothy. "He's intrusive," she said. "But why did he upset you?"

*Why doesn't she understand*, I thought. Why was it so hard? Why did she expect me to just tolerate other people's intrusions? Didn't I have a right to set boundaries?

I mentioned the argument with Sue. "Can't you let that go?" Rev. Dorothy asked. "You haven't seen her again have you?"

"No," I said.

"I don't understand why you did what you did," Rev. Dorothy said.

After I hung up, I wondered what she thought I did. I wished I had asked her why she felt so uncomfortable talking about the argument with me. I was sure she talked about it with Sue and the others. It was distressing how quickly Rev. Dorothy abandoned me and joined the others in comforting Sue when she cried. My tears weren't even acknowledged.

I have known for a long time that I have difficulty with people who provoke and bully. I knew that had to do with being a target of my father and classmates' emotional abuse. Like a deer who has gotten caught in a car's headlights, I freeze and don't respond to provocative statements at the time they occur. I let the offensive behavior continue without taking any effective action. Confused and scared, I can't think what to do or say. Fearing social disapproval and rejection, I often say nothing.

Each time Sue made a rude comment about Christianity, I should have told her how I felt about it. I had made some attempts to do so but didn't persist, partly because I was unaware how much it bothered me.

However, before the September meeting, I had thought it through. At the meeting, I said exactly what I had planned and wanted to say to her. I failed to anticipate her response. I didn't expect her to say what she did about my brother. But despite that, I didn't respond by attacking her character. I just told her not to speak for me. When she continued, I yelled at her to stop.

On January 9, 2000, I again went to church at Central Congregational Church. I enjoyed the service but disliked the coffee hour. No one spoke to me. I stood watching. The same groups talked with each other. There was little, if any, mixing. I left when tears began welling up in my eyes.

A couple of weeks later, I received a letter from Central Congregational Church inviting me to become a member. It came too soon. I wasn't ready to join a church. I didn't feel safe there yet. I felt safe at Immanuel, but couldn't see how I could honestly buy into their theology. I didn't know what to do.

I telephoned Rev. Karen. We talked about Unitarian Universalism. I shared with her a conversation I had with a Unitarian Universalist woman at the Marcus Borg lecture about the stages of faith.

"Unitarians Universalists are stuck in the critical phase of faith," I explained. "Like adolescents, they question and doubt much of what they once believed and accepted as literal fact. They haven't yet found the metaphorical truth in the Bible, and often confuse Christianity with fundamentalism. Sue at FXUU is just like that. As a pagan she—"

"There are Unitarian Universalist pagans?" Rev. Karen asked, incredulous.

"Yes," I replied.

"You have more in common with Lutherans than with Unitarian Universalist pagans," she pointed out.

"I don't feel like I belong."

"You have never really entered in. You need to focus on one church, one theology, and suspend disbelief if you want to belong."

"Maybe I should take communion," I said.

"Yes, that would be good," she encouraged me.

As we spoke, it occurred to me that Unitarian Universalists lacked commitment to one faith stance. If something doesn't feel good, they immediately discard it. They don't stick with it.

Saturday night, I took time to meditate and pray. For the past few months, I had been teetering on the edge of a cliff about to fall to my death. There were people offering their hands, but I didn't know which ones, if any, could be trusted not to let me go. Who is to say they wouldn't eventually betray me? Then I thought, *God is there, too. God will catch me if I am betrayed.* I felt calm. I prepared myself mentally and emotionally to take communion at Immanuel Lutheran. By doing so, I moved further away from FXUU and Unitarian Universalism and closer to mainline Christianity.

On Sunday, as I knelt at the altar rail, my eyes met Rev. Karen's. I was as jubilant as a Boston fan when the Red Sox defeated the Yankees. Stifling the urge to cheer, I smiled as Rev. Karen placed the piece of bread in my hand. I was the prodigal child returning home and finding there was still a place for her there. Just as Hosea kept taking back his faithless wife, God had taken me back. God had always been with me, even if I had not always been with God.

"I haven't changed. I did listen to you," Rev. Dorothy insisted at our next lunch date. We were now meeting once a month. "Back in the fall, you were trying to persuade me to agree with you."

"I don't feel you listened," I replied. "I wasn't trying to persuade you. I was just trying to get you to listen."

"I don't believe that."

"You don't know what was in my mind and heart except for what I choose to tell you," I told her. She didn't appear to believe that either.

"Our October fourth conversation was very hurtful," I told her. "You caused me to doubt my own memories of my years at Stony Brook. That drove me to go home after nine years. I should have gone earlier. Your lack of support, and my visit home, moved me to leave FXUU. The cruel reaction to my decision to leave confirmed I'd made the right decision. It was only by leaving FXUU could I heal."

"Are you doing better?" she asked.

"Yes."

"Why did you need to leave FXUU to heal?"

"FXUU was a dysfunctional, abusive church. Rev. Patience promoted and encouraged that dysfunction." As I replied, I felt all my anger and rage beneath my hurt and pain. "The cruel emails to me revealed just how angry Rev. Patience and the others were."

"Aren't you angry, too?" Rev. Dorothy demanded.

"Of course I was angry," I replied. "But I never personally attacked anyone. The worst thing I did was yell at Sue to stop speaking for me."

"You're unaware of your behavior and its effects on others," she admonished me.

I hesitated. Should I ask her to tell me what effect my behavior had that day, or should I ask her if she was aware the effect the others had on me? I feared her answers, and assumed I would have the opportunity to ask other questions at another time. "You presume to know more than you do," I said. "You weren't at the September meeting."

Our eyes filled with tears. "What do you want from me?" she asked.

"I don't know, but we were 'attached' once." I was also grateful for all she had done for me, and I couldn't just walk away from her.

"What can I do to help you move away from the anger?"

"Nothing can be done. You can't help me. It will just take time."

As I moved closer to joining Immanuel Lutheran, I was overwhelmed with fear. I had to fight the desire not to curl up on the couch and sink into the white space. I craved the relief that burning myself would bring. My promise to Dr. Emmett that I would call him whenever I felt an uncontrollable urge to self-harm prevented me from acting on those urges.

I was terrified that if I let my guard down, I would offend someone at Immanuel. I feared the more someone got to know me, the less likely they would approve of me.

I had lunch with Rev. Karen. She reassured me everything was okay, and told me I had found myself a particularly nice group at Immanuel.

At our next lunch date, Rev. Dorothy informed me she had just preached at FXUU, since they were without a minister again. Anticipating that she wouldn't be fellowshipped in the Unitarian Universalist

Association, Rev. Patience had resigned in mid-February, effective immediately although she told the board she would continue until June if they wanted her to. The board voted to immediately accept her resignation. Rev. Patience had been unable to get along with anyone in the church, and there was always a lot of tension when she was around.

Rev. Patience had received a poor evaluation from every church she ever served, I learned. While Rev. Dorothy was district executive, Rev. Patience was minister to a congregation on Cape Cod. She had agreed to do a union ceremony for a lesbian couple. This couple had invited all their family and friends, and had a big reception planned. On the day of the ceremony, Rev. Patience called them and told them it was too far for her to drive. She didn't feel like doing it. They didn't really need her. They could go ahead without her.

I didn't know how to react to the news that was bittersweet to me now. I wanted to cry but I couldn't.

The following morning I woke up feeling angry. A ministerial candidate for fellowship who had failed twice to be accepted should never have been allowed to be the minister at FXUU. As a condition of getting her fellowship, Rev. Patience should have been required to serve in a church where she could be supervised more closely. At the very least, FXUU should have been informed of Rev. Patience's probationary status. Instead, she was allowed to take a position and inflict more harm.

The Unitarian Universalist Association owed me and all the others Rev. Patience harmed an apology. The Unitarian Universalist Association should be responsible for my therapy costs. But getting an institution to take responsibility and make reparations would be close to impossible. However, at the very least, I wanted an opportunity to talk to the fellowship committee and the ethics committee. I wanted an opportunity to tell my story and share my opinion of what was wrong with the way things were handled.

When I saw Dr. Emmett, he suggested I contact the president of the Unitarian Universalist Association. I decided to make the call, but became overwhelmed with anxiety and fear. I curled up on the couch and went to sleep. After my nap, I got up and obtained the phone number off the Internet, pocketed the number and went to work.

Two days later, on March 16, I mustered up the courage to call the Unitarian Universalist Association. I spoke to the president's secretary. "I would like to talk to President John, please."

"What is this in reference to?"

"I want to talk to him regarding some ethical violations by three Unitarian Universalist ministers. I don't want to discuss the details on the phone. Although many of the specific issues have been worked out, I want to talk to Rev. John about the systemic issues that created the environment in which the violations occurred."

"Are you aware such concerns are usually directed to the Department of Ministry?"

"Yes, but I have been advised by a Unitarian Universalist minister to speak directly with President John."

"I will speak to him and get back to you."

She called back the next day. "President John cannot get involved with issues concerning individual ministers. You should call Rev. Diane, Director of Ministry."

It was just as I predicted. Disappointed, I wrote down Rev. Diane's name and number, thinking, *We'll see who this Rev. Diane refers me to. I expect nothing. I don't belong to the minister's club. Why would they help me? The motherfucking, cock-sucking bastards don't care about anything but themselves.* I hated them for what they allowed to happen to me. That included Rev. Dorothy too.

The next day, Lyndon and I attended a seminar on family injustice. Cloe Madanes presented her treatment protocol for treating incest. In her approach, the perpetrator is required to get on their knees and apologize to the victim for what they have done.

I was very pensive after the seminar. No one ever apologized to me for the sexual abuse, the verbal abuse, the neglect or the shunning. No one ever said they were sorry for having harmed me. No one.

Madanes also spoke about how the victim is often excluded from the family. Members of FXUU displaced their anger on me and excluded me even though I hadn't done anything wrong. I appropriately expressed my anger to Sue for harassing me and breaking a confidence. I didn't explode at everybody else. I just yelled at Sue. You would think I had raped, tortured and murdered somebody. All I did was express my anger.

I owed myself an apology for all the times I intentionally injured myself. I was sorry for abusing myself. It was the wrong thing to do. I was innocent but blamed myself. I was sorry I did that. I needed to find a way to make it up to myself and to my family. I hurt them, too. They worried about me and felt they had to monitor where I was and what I was doing. I was sorry I had frightened them.

I called Rev. Karen that night and asked her to hear my confession. We scheduled it for the next day after Sunday service. We talked briefly about how we are all part of God's creation, and when I injured myself intentionally, I was destroying part of that creation.

Fearful that I would be overwhelmed with anxiety, I wrote out what I wanted to say before making my confession to Rev. Karen. Once everybody had left the church, she and I went into the sanctuary. She put on her stole and we knelt by the altar. Using the Lutheran order of service for private confessions, we prayed together, and I read what I had prepared. I confessed how I had turned away from God. How I hadn't always been with God even though God had always been with me. I confessed how I allowed myself to space out and burn, hit, scratch and cut myself. I confessed how I had tried to kill myself when I was younger. I asked forgiveness for not being able to forgive members of my family of origin.

After I made my confession, Rev. Karen laid her hands on my head. She then gave me a big, warm hug. I left the church without saying much of anything. While driving home, I had this sense I had done the right thing even though it wasn't a very Unitarian Universalist thing to do. I was a little embarrassed by it. It wasn't the rational thing to do. But I was glad I made my confession. My life was taking a different turn, and maybe that was one of the good things to come out of all this. I smiled as I heard my Italian grandmother's voice in my mind's ear. I could hear the slight Yiddish accent she picked up working side by side with East European Jews in New York City's garment factories.

"Everything always works out for the best," she said.

I smiled as I parked the car in the garage. *They certainly do.*

# Endings and a Beginning

The day after making my confession, I called Rev. Miller at the Unitarian Universalist Association. Instead of brushing me off as I expected, Rev. Miller's secretary gave me an appointment for Thursday. The anticipation of actually getting to speak to someone at the UUA triggered a bout of anxiety. I didn't get as much work done that day as I wanted.

After my last client left, I went upstairs to my bedroom to change for Bible study. The phone rang. A strange woman asked to speak with me. It was Rev. Miller.

"I need to know more before I can see you," she told me.

After I summarized what had happened at FXUU, she said, "I work twelve hours per day and am the head of a continental department."

I felt unimportant.

"I'm the wrong person for you to see," she said. "I really can't provide pastoral counseling."

"I'm not looking for counseling," I replied. "I want to make you aware of what happened and what I think went wrong and why."

"You need to speak to Rev. William," she said, passing it off. "I'll send him a memo."

Tearful, I left for Bible study. When I arrived at Immanuel I glossed over my distress, telling everyone I had had a really nice day except for one phone call. I chose not to go into details.

I found the Bible study discussion of Psalms peaceful. God would take me in even when I messed up and when others didn't love me. God would live forever. God was eternal. I wasn't God, but a created being who would be here for a limited time. In the scheme of things, I was fairly insignificant.

Unitarian Universalists took themselves too seriously. A little humility wouldn't hurt them.

*God*, I prayed, *please teach me how to live each day fully so that I and all those I come in contact with may prosper.*

The next morning I received an email from Beverly. She asked how I was. It distressed her to see me so upset at Bible study the previous night. I wrote back a brief synopsis of my phone conversation with Rev. Miller. I also shared with her how well I was doing. She didn't reply. This was the third time I had shared something personal with her and she failed to respond. I felt angry and resentful. Beverly shouldn't have asked if she couldn't handle the answer.

On Thursday I called Rev. William from the Unitarian Universalist Association. He was polite and respectful, allowing me to tell my story. He said he would check into things. I followed up our conversation with an email. I felt tremendous relief afterward. I also emailed Rev. Dorothy about my conversation with Rev. William. Neither one of them ever replied.

With my efforts to be heard thwarted, I felt apprehensive. I considered filing a formal complaint and/or suing, but that could expose Rev. Dorothy's breach of confidentiality. I didn't want to do that. I was grateful for all the help she had given me and didn't want to hurt her. I decided to let it go. I was now in a healthy church. It was unlikely, I reasoned, that anything like the conflict at FXUU could happen to me again.

Several members of Immanuel's Bible study urged me to join the chimes choir. Immanuel's minister of music had started the choir because it was a way to involve people with little or no music experience in Sunday services. Although I had played the viola in my high school's orchestra, I was never very good. But I could read music, and all I had to do was flick the chime at the right time. I enjoyed making music and being a part of a group that was contributing to the larger church community.

On April 3, I played with the chimes choir for the first time. I chose a seat in the back of the sanctuary to make it easier to get up to play. I was surprised when the other members of the chimes choir took their usual seats toward the front without inviting me to sit with them. At the end of the service, Ivonne told me, "You can join us. There is no reason for you to sit alone."

Tears welled up in my eyes. No one noticed. I still felt like an outsider, an intruder. I feared that once they got to know me they would reject me.

Rev. Dorothy and I continued to have lunch together once per month. Our conversations were tense and distant. I no longer felt as much love and respect for her as I once did. She had betrayed me. She had been disloyal siding with my enemies. She expressed disappointment in me and stopped listening. I felt indebted to her for the help she gave me while I was in crisis. I maintained contact with her mostly for that reason. At times I missed the relationship we once had.

On April 29, she met me at a Chinese restaurant convenient to her home and the group homes where I provided psychological services. After filling our plates at the buffet table, she and I returned to our table by the window.

"I'm attending church on Sunday," I said. I didn't tell her which church. I didn't want her to know. I feared she would tell the members of FXUU's board and they would spread gossip, sabotaging my acceptance into a new church community. Then I said, "Did the UUA contact you?"

"No. Why?" she asked.

I told her about my conversation with Rev. William. Rev. Dorothy tightened her lips. "I've checked the list of ministerial candidates." She put down her teacup. "I'm sure Rev. Patience is no longer seeking fellowship."

I took a long, deep breath. "That's good." There was an uneasy silence.

"I was talking to Don, and think he might like to hear from you."

I stopped eating. Did Don miss our friendship? *Don't get your hopes up,* I told myself. *This might be more Rev. Dorothy's idea than Don's.*

"I haven't moved," I replied. "I haven't changed my phone number or my email. It wasn't me who stopped talking, it was them. I would talk to him if he called."

"Do you want that to happen?" she asked.

My muscles tightened. I spoke slowly. "I'm not sure. If we talk and it goes well, that would bring closure. If it goes badly, I would be hurt again."

I said goodbye to her in the restaurant's parking lot, and took the back road past farms and stables toward my home. *Why didn't Don call me if he wanted to hear from me? Does he think I'm owed an apology? Probably not.* I was sure he had justified everything. He was never terribly committed to our friendship. To what extent did he collude with Rev. Patience, and why?

*Men. Men are never really friends. Except Lyndon. And Vance. Vance was a friend. Why didn't I keep in touch with him?* I wondered where he was now. *I don't recognize who are truly my friends. I should have stayed in touch. My life is filled with so many losses.*

I didn't know if I wanted or expected too much from relationships or if I expected too little, or if I failed to set limits and tolerated things I shouldn't have. I wasn't sure if I was looking at my friendships as if the glass was half-empty when it was really half-full. Or were my perceptions about my relationships really accurate?

No one called unless I called them. Perhaps I *was* too needy. There had been plenty of people who admired what I had accomplished, but few people who wanted to be friends. What was I doing wrong? What was the matter with me? Rev. Dorothy's general explanations didn't ring true. Nor did they point to a solution. I remained puzzled.

When I arrived home, I picked up the mail and brought it into the kitchen. Spotting the American Psychological Association's *Monitor* among the bills and junk mail, I grabbed it and went into my study to read. Sitting in my recliner, I skimmed the magazine until a brief article caught my eye. Social psychologists had found that the more minorities and women didn't fit the cultural stereotype for their group, the less liked s/he was and the more likely s/he would be mistreated.

*That's it!* I thought. I had broken gender rules for my generation by earning a doctorate and going into business for myself. Rev. Dick had minimized my doctorate by calling it "'cute.'" Angelina and Sue were offended when I referred to a ministerial candidate with a doctorate as a peer. Don objected when I asked that when I was addressed by my last name, he use the correct honorific: Dr. Jones, not Mrs. Jones.

I wondered to what extent race also contributed to my social problems. Lyndon and I were seldom invited into white *or* black homes. The few invitations we received were almost always from other biracial couples. I tore out the article to share with Dr. Emmett. That evening, when I discussed the article with Lyndon, he said, "It is just another thing they use to judge you negatively."

The next morning Lyndon got up before me. I laid in bed between sleep and wakefulness. My mind drifted. I doubted I would ever have the close, supportive circle of friends I dreamed of and hoped for. I hadn't found it in a church community. If I was honest and open about my sexual victimization, people became overwhelmed. It was more than they could handle. If I hid my past and the weak and vulnerable side, they were then overwhelmed by my competence. In either case they ended up avoiding me or outright rejecting me. I was caught in a maze and couldn't find my way out.

It was hard to get others to see both sides of me. If they saw the weakness first, they were blinded to my strengths. If they saw the strength, they expected me always to be strong. They became angry when I was weak, as if I had betrayed them somehow. The people who loved me best were the ones who saw both sides and accepted me for who I was.

Lyndon came over to the bed and kissed me on the forehead. He was on his way out to run errands. I got up and went into the bathroom. *Life is full of its betrayals,* I thought, *big and small.* I stepped into the shower and turned on the water. As the water fell against my face I remembered the times Lyndon had betrayed me and let me down. Despite everything we hung in there, and worked things out better than either one of us dared hope for.

My FXUU "friends" lacked commitment and loyalty. If Sue and the others had discussed the argument with me, we could have checked each other's perceptions and come to an understanding. Things could have been worked out. Instead she called me "toxic" and discarded me as if I had no value.

I sobbed as the shower rained on my head. I wept violently. My whole body filled with pain. There was a hurt deep within my soul that I couldn't even begin to express in words. It ravaged me, taking away any joy I had in living my life. I lost so much when I had so little to begin with. Relationship after relationship ended in abandonment or betrayal, or both.

While I went about my daily routine, I stepped back and tried to figure out what good had come out of all the conflict and pain. Rev. Karen thought my turning to God a really good thing. But would my life have been poorer if I hadn't gone through the FXUU conflict? I thought not. I didn't know what to make of it all. It was so hard. Too hard.

During one of our sessions, Dr. Emmett said the past year was mostly about surviving. He saw the insights I had gained as something that would improve my life. I didn't think I was better off for having gone through this. I went through hell, only to end up in the same place minus the people I thought were my friends. Like Rip Van Wrinkle, I fell asleep. After a horrendous nightmare, I awoke to find myself in a different church community feeling a little lost and bewildered.

Dr. Emmett encouraged me to focus more on what I had and not on what I had lost. He said the past year was about survival. Yes, but it was also about faith. Believing in a God who did not protect me was hard. Yet when I was in touch with God, I felt at peace. I grew spiritually. God rescued me through the kindness of Rev. Karen and the members of Immanuel. God would always be with me. All I had to do was take His hand.

By mid-April, I decided Dr. Emmett was right. It was time to stop focusing on the losses and focus on what I had: a good husband, healthy children, and a sister who loved and cared for me. I was doing well except for a fleeting thought here and there of self-injury. There was no anxiety.

During Holy Week, I attended the noontime services at Immanuel sponsored by the Council of Churches. Sitting though the services, I became more aware of the differences between my own religious beliefs and those of the Christians with which I was attending church. They believed that Jesus was divine and had literally risen from the dead. I didn't. I felt like a fraud and thought I couldn't possibly become a Lutheran.

I decided not to attend church on Good Friday or Easter. Instead, I stayed home with Lyndon. While I stood at the stove flipping pancakes for our Easter breakfast, I thought about therapy. I was better at calling Dr. Emmett when I needed to. My urge to self-harm had decreased. I wanted to forget the past and move on. But that meant saying goodbye to Dr. Emmett. I felt sad. I would miss him.

*Too bad Dr. Emmett and I can't be friends*, I thought. I shook my head. *Don't be foolish. You know better. Therapy doesn't work that way. Dr. Emmett is your headshrinker. What if you need him again?*

I sighed. I was so sick and tired of having a headshrinker. I wasted too much time feeling bad. *Move on*, I ordered. *Put things behind you.*

"I want to terminate in June," I told him at my next session.

He straightened up. "Okay," he said. "I suppose there is always something to talk about."

"Since we aren't terminating until June, we don't need to talk about it now," I told him.

After telling him I was ending therapy, I had an intense bout of anxiety when I turned in for the night. I was feeling terrified, cut adrift. Reminding myself that he would still be around and I could call him if

I really needed to didn't help much. I thought of calling him, but it was close to one in the morning.

When Lyndon came to bed, I told him how I was feeling. My fear subsided. My ankle was aching. I had twisted it during Orion's last track meet. Lyndon went into the bathroom and got some ibuprofen and some Icy Hot. After he massaged my ankle, he fell asleep.

I laid awake, thinking about Dr. Emmett. How did I feel about him? I loved Dr. Howard and cared about Dr. Robins. Dr. Howard was obese. Dr. Robins was old enough to be my father. I wasn't terribly attracted to either one. Dr. Emmett was different. He was younger than my husband and he was handsome. He ran in the morning. No fat. No love handles. His clothes must be covering a sleek, muscular body.

I cared for Dr. Emmett. He did his job well. In a gentle kind of way, he didn't let me minimize the self-injury and the abuse. He didn't let me off the hook. He got me to do the things I needed to do for myself. So of course I cared about him. If I wasn't afraid, I would hug him and thank him.

Once, Dr. Emmett touched me on the shoulder as I was leaving his office. I could see in his eyes he just wanted to comfort me because I was so filled with grief. There was nothing sexual about it. I stiffened up. I didn't know how to respond. I felt my fear had put this wall between us. I didn't want the wall to be there.

The next morning, Lyndon and I laid in bed talking about our marriage. Years ago, he told me he wished I was as beautiful as a female friend of his. I felt threatened and asked him to end his friendship.

"I'm sorry, Maggie," Lyndon said while he wrapped his arms around me. "I only said it because I wanted you to pay more attention to your appearance."

During May as I faced the loss of my relationship with Dr. Emmett, I felt anger and resentment. It was another loss following a period of substantial loss. I had lost my friends, my church, and my denomination. I had lost a certain amount of innocence about the safety of church communities after I was dechurched from Murray and FXUU. There were fewer and fewer safe places I could go to. No wonder I felt terrified.

During my Tuesday session with Dr. Emmett, he loaned me a tape of Jill Harkaway's lecture on women who self-injure. After dinner, I went into the living room and put the tape into the tape deck and pushed play.

I settled into the black leather recliner and listened. It made it clearer what was wrong with my family. My mother was the center. Only what she felt was important. Everything revolved around protecting her. She could get angry. Throw things at you. Spank you with a hairbrush or wire hanger. But don't you get angry or scared. You get a spanking for that.

I was a timid child. Frightened by yelling, I would start to cry. "You're a crybaby," my father scolded. "You're spoiled." When I was older, he told me I was selfish and insensitive and lacked a sense of humor.

Even when I was in the hospital, the focus was on what my hospitalization was doing to my mother. Very little attention was paid to how I was feeling. There was no concern expressed for my welfare. It was all about preserving the family no matter what its cost to me. That was the same message Sharon expressed to me. FXUU was more important than any individual, and she saw my needs as being in conflict with FXUU's needs. It was an either/or, not a both/and. Sharon was angry with me for asserting my needs, my rights.

I took some deep breaths and rewound the tape. Maybe things weren't so bad, I thought. Maybe I was making too much of my parents' mistakes. All parents make mistakes. But when I tried to remember times when I was nurtured and cared for, I couldn't. Maybe that was because the bad experiences overshadowed them. Maybe they were really there and I was blind to them. Maybe I wasn't being fair. But I couldn't remember being nurtured by my mother. I didn't know where she was in my memories.

I went upstairs to bed and fell into an uneasy sleep. While my husband's arms were wrapped around me, I dreamed about having sex with Dr. Emmett. My fear woke me up. Lying still so as not to waken Lyndon, my thoughts ran wild. I wanted to ask Dr. Emmett to help me cut my arms.

*That's really crazy*, I thought. *I'm fucked up. Better to have died thirty years ago.* I wasn't wanted anyway. I was a troublemaker. Whore. Cunt. The day my father stripped my sister Trish down to her underwear and beat her with a belt: there was something sexual about it. Uncle Frank fucked my sister. He would have fucked me if I had stayed in my bedroom. Did he fuck Trish or me when he came in the bed with us? Where were my parents? Where was Aunt Adele? Didn't she wonder where her husband was? Maybe she knew, and was glad it wasn't her. Desperate to be loved and wanted, there were times when I wished Uncle

Frank had fucked me, made love to me. He would have if I had let him. *Sometimes I think I am a whore. Then I want to cut or burn or shove a bottle up my cunt–*

Sensing my unease, Lyndon tightened his arms around me, keeping me safe. The next morning, after he left for work, I called Dr. Emmett. "It's hard to deal with my feelings about you and men," I said. "I'm afraid of being sexually assaulted by you or somebody else." Or maybe it was my wish? When I tried to think this stuff through, everything got muddled and confusing. I couldn't find my way out of the abyss.

"Let's talk about this when I have more time. Can you call me later at twelve?"

At noon, I called from my study. We spoke for forty-five minutes. "I want you to feel safe in therapy," he said. "Why has this issue come up now?"

"I'm uncomfortable because you are a man and close to my age." I was puzzled by his concern and by the question. I had always felt a bit threatened, but had always known it had to do with me and nothing to do with Dr. Emmett. Several months ago during a session, I curled up and he asked what was going on.

"I'm trying to get as far away from you as I can," I told him. Dr. Emmett had always known I have been afraid of his touching me. It was not new news. So why was I more clearly naming the fear now?

How did all of this get going anyway? We started talking about termination. I panicked even though I wanted to terminate, and then all this sexual stuff came up. I listened to the tape, and it stirred things up further. Wednesday night, I had watched a television show on which there was a rape-murder. The night before I woke up at 4 a.m., anxious and fearful of sexual assault. I couldn't believe I shared this with Dr. Emmett. It wasn't very nice stuff.

Dr. Emmett said I had regressed since we started talking about termination. He said I wasn't really ready to end therapy. I didn't want that to be so, and wanted to shout at him to go stuff it. But I contained it because I knew it was so.

He talked about a long termination. I didn't know what he meant by "long." I thought two months was long enough, since I hadn't intended to be in therapy for more than eight weeks. I wanted to get on with my life and put FXUU behind me. I also didn't want to be back two weeks later. I wasn't sure how to go about deciding when it was time to leave.

After the phone call, I drove over to one of the group homes. How did I get myself into this mess? I didn't see any way out in the near future. Despite my best efforts, I was still stuck in therapy. I tried to think of an appropriate metaphor. First I thought of being on a merry-go-round with the brass ring just out of my reach. Then I thought of being locked in a cage with the key just out of my reach. Then I saw Dr. Emmett giving me the key. I thought maybe it 'wasn't Dr. Emmett. *Maybe it's God, or it's God sending Dr. Emmett.*

I drove a couple more blocks. As I passed the Baptist church, I read the wayside pulpit. It said, "In quiet and trust shall be your strength." It was as if the wayside pulpit was there for me. As if God was speaking to me, telling me to let go, stop fighting, stop resisting and trust. Suddenly I felt better, at peace. It was okay. *Trust Dr. Emmett. Trust God.*

In contrast to my internal struggle during the week, my weekends were nearly perfect. I felt happy and safe when I was with my family. The Sunday after Mother's Day, my children and husband came with me to church. It was a long service because there were three baptisms. I was so happy to have my family there. Melissa didn't mind the service at all. After the service Orion went for a run; Lyndon, Melissa and I stayed for the brunch hosted by the confirmation class. Perhaps the Lutheran church was where God wanted me to be.

Unitarian Universalists had it wrong. Morality wasn't relative. There are things that are definitely right and definitely wrong. What people did to me was wrong, cruel and abusive. I suspected that the people who had been cruel to me as adults were the same kind of people who were cruel to me as a child. The majority of people had been cruel to me. Very few people had ever really been kind to me.

I went to FXUU seeking a religious community. Reflecting on the emotional abuse, I had this image of lying curled up on the floor while my former friends kicked and beat me. No one noticed I was crying. They left me to die. Dr. Emmett, Rev. Karen and my family found me wandering around dazed and confused. Like a Good Samaritan, Rev. Karen nurtured and care for me, giving me a place in her church community. Dr. Emmett kept me from bleeding out. My family, loving me well, rocked and comforted me.

It was time for me to move on. When you believe in God, you accept life as it is without despair and know it will work out in the end. I prayed for God to bless me and all those who I loved and all those who had hurt me. In the end we would all be reconciled to God, victim and perpetrator alike.

At the end of May, Dr. Emmett said I needed to start thinking what it would be like not seeing him. While I welcomed not having the expense and not having to get up early on Tuesdays, I continued to dread the loss of not having someone to talk to.

I was finding termination very difficult. I left his office feeling very good and ready to leave. But by the afternoon I was weepy. Maybe it was too soon. *Not now. Later. Get through the summer. Wait until you've mustered up the courage to join Immanuel. Wait until you have lunch with Rev. Dorothy. Wait forever. Go slower. Go every other week. Just drop out. Never go or call again. Send Dr. Emmett a card saying goodbye with a final check. Cut all ties completely. There must be fifty ways to leave–*

No. Dr. Emmett promised to sign my book. Once he did that, I would leave and not look back. No regrets. Have a good cry. Life sucks. Betrayal after betrayal. The ones who said they were sorry weren't the ones who owed me an apology. They didn't do anything. The ones who hurt me didn't care, were oblivious to my pain and discounted it. They thought it was my fault. That's what they would say. They behaved like a mob. No second chances. No discussion. *You're a bitch, church wrecker. Get rid of you and then we will have a nice church.*

But they didn't have a nice church. They were still struggling. How much of that did they blame on me? I was the church wrecker. But now I was in a loving church. I was where people cared about me. Evidently, I only wrecked UU churches. I must have been a closet Christian all along. And you know how dangerous and subversive Christians are. They're intolerant. *Get rid of them. We have no place for them. We are good people, incapable of sin.*

But the joke was on them. They continued to suffer while I made a safe home at Immanuel. I had come out on top.

It was time to move on and say goodbye to Dr. Emmett. Join Immanuel. Find a way to forgive people at FXUU.

I continued to vacillate between wanting to terminate therapy and wanting to stay. Increasingly, I felt fine. I felt I had my old life back. But I didn't really. The friends and connections I had at FXUU were gone. I thought I belonged. Life was good. I had my work, my family and my church friends. When therapy ended, I would have work and my family. No more friends. Not even Dr. Emmett.

Yet I didn't want to terminate. I felt trapped, unable to move forward or back. It was the ending to another relationship. If I could alter the circumstances, I would make it so Dr. Emmett and I could still be friends. If we were friends, if he wasn't my therapist, I would never be expected to say goodbye to him.

People from healthy families get to have their parents' help and support until their parents die. Lyndon and I have had to do so much on our own. We've done okay, but it would have been easier if we had had more support from our families.

It didn't seem so terribly fair. Three of the most significant relationships in my life had been with therapists I had to say goodbye to once I was better. You meet a therapist. You struggle to trust him. You get better. It's over. If I could— If I had more friends, it wouldn't be so hard.

Feeling angry and bitter, I sat in my study rereading the dedications written by my former friends at FXUU in my copy of *The Courage to Heal Workbook*. Don had written that I had the capacity to heal and enjoy my life, and urged me not to give up. Didn't he see the clear, non-abusive expression of anger as part of that capacity to heal? Sharon wrote that I was a courageous woman. A few months later, she viewed me as a threat to FXUU and expendable. She offered her support, which turned out to be very little. Joe, Sue's husband, also wrote about my courage and strength. He actually was the kindest to me after my argument with his wife. Rev. Dorothy wrote that I was valuable and precious, but she didn't have the courage to stand up for me, even privately. Angelina wrote that I could forever count on her. 'Forever' didn't last very long.

The FXUU board members who wronged me were oblivious to my pain and discounted it. They believe it was my fault because I raised my voice and refused to apologize to Sue. They united with one another, shutting me out. There was no second chance. No discussion. Rev. Patience spoke for them when she accused me of destroying the church. There was no way I could defend myself.

Rev. Patience's emails to me made it unlikely I would ever return to FXUU. I understood the FXUU board's silence as tacit approval of her actions. It was clear to me that they believed they could build a healthy and thriving church community by getting rid of me and anyone else whose emotions made them uncomfortable.

At the beginning of June, Dr. Emmett and I discussed when I should contact him again and under what circumstances. I was not to let things go so long. He expected me to be conservative. When in doubt, call. It would be better for me to call when it wasn't really needed than not to call when it was.

I promised to call whenever I felt the desire to hurt myself or whenever I stop wanting to take care of myself. I told myself I would call whenever I broke down and wept, like I did during the meeting with Rev. Terry, or whenever I was being scapegoated. I would call whenever I felt the need to talk because the desire to talk is the healthy side of me, not the weak side.

On June 27, 2000, during my last session with Dr. Emmett, I handed him my copy of *The Courage to Heal Workbook*, saying, "You said you would write a dedication."

"Yes." He grabbed a pen off his desk. "Hmmm." He paused. He turned to the last page in the book, wrote quickly, and then handed the book back to me with the page opened.

In blue ink, he had printed in uneven letters that slanted up from left to right,

Maggie—

You are possessed of a survivor's spirit, a good & loving heart, and a keen intellect and formidable faith. It has been a distinct honor & privilege to share in your journey these past difficult but, hopefully, rewarding months.

May God bless you.

Steve

"Thanks." Other than this, I wasn't sure how to respond. His compliments made me uneasy. I don't recall if we discussed what he wrote.

I handed him a neatly wrapped package. He tore off the wrapping paper to reveal two paperback books by Marcus Borg: *Meeting Jesus Again for the First Time* and *The God We Never Knew*. "Oh, this is a risky book to be giving a Unitarian," he said.

I shifted in my chair. I hadn't meant to make him uncomfortable. I wasn't trying to convert him. I just wanted to give him a piece of myself. I watched while he read the inscription I wrote on the title page.

> Something to remember me by. A final sharing. These books have been part of my journey back to God and health. Thanks for walking with me. Through you, God has been with me. Farewell. Stay safe. I will remember you and yours in my prayers.

He looked up. "My wife and I will enjoy reading them and talking about them."

I relaxed. It was okay.

As the session ended, I asked him if I could give him a hug, just as I had asked Dr. Howard almost thirty years before. In contrast to Dr. Howard, who was as short as I was, Dr. Emmett was over six feet tall. In the preceding months, I was so preoccupied with escape I hadn't noticed how tall he was. While we hugged, the top of my head barely reached his chest.

After I left his office, I hurried down the winding back stairs of the nineteenth- century house and out the back door, thinking I was never going to see him again. Taking the interstate, I drove directly from Providence to Taunton to have lunch with Rev. Dorothy. We met at a Mexican restaurant right off Route 24.

"How are things going at FXUU?" I asked while we took our seats at a booth with dark wooden benches.

"We now have eighteen members, and a new part-time minister starts in September."

"I'll be joining Immanuel Lutheran Church," I informed her. "I just came from Dr. Emmett's office. I've seen him for the last time."

"Are you comfortable with the Lutheran theology?" she asked.

"Yes," I answered.

"Oh," she said, falling into an uncomfortable silence.

"Marcus Borg is an Episcopalian, and you should really read his books," I said. "Mainline Christianity isn't what you think it is."

Rev. Dorothy didn't reply. We discussed other things. She then said, "You could always go back into therapy."

I stared at her. I hadn't expressed any ambivalence about terminating therapy. Why was she throwing ice water on my success? Did she harbor a secret hope that I would repent and return to the Unitarian Universalist fold?

After paying our bill, we left the restaurant together. We paused at my car. There were tears in her eyes. Her body trembled. Why was she so distressed? I was doing well.

Now that I was less tearful and anxious, I had more energy to focus on my work. A few months before, Lyndon and I had expanded our business by purchasing a practice from a colleague I used to work for. The office space needed to be cleaned and reorganized, computers bought and new staff hired.

Since my health insurance hadn't covered Dr. Emmett's entire bill, I had an outstanding balance. Once per month, I sent him a check with a note. I missed him. I hoped to see him again from time to time. However, I wanted to try to cope without his help. I wanted to get through a couple of weeks without calling.

I remained conflicted about reaching out and talking to others. Even though I continued talking to Rev. Karen almost weekly and occasionally to other church members, I was fearful I was scaring them away and giving them the wrong impression of me. Sharon, during her last phone call to me, had told me I was wrong to seek so much support from others at FXUU. Her comment confirmed that I had been right when I told Dr. Emmett that people would eventually reject me if I sought their help. Although I tried not to be a pest, somehow I ended up offending. I tried not to share too much too soon, but then people thought I was closed and distant. I didn't know how to achieve a balance so someone would want to remain friends with me.

Two-and-a-half weeks after my last session with Dr. Emmett, I thought about Rev. Dorothy. I missed both of them. I considered confronting her about her betrayal and abandonment. Other times I just wanted to say, *"Can't we just be happy for each other? You have your church and I have mine."*

A phone call would probably only turn out badly. It would put Rev. Dorothy in the role of rescuer and me as victim, one up and one down. She never shared what she really thought and felt, making an honest and authentic relationship impossible. I doubted an equal relationship had a chance. I didn't think she would allow a friendship. But then, did I really know for sure?

Rev. Karen suggested that part of the problem was that the nature of my relationship with Rev. Dorothy wasn't clear. It had gotten muddled when Rev. Dorothy resigned as minister and became a member of FXUU. She suggested I attempt to establish a relationship with Rev. Dorothy separate from church and find some other common ground.

I called Rev. Dorothy and spoke to her for about twenty minutes. "I thought you were saying goodbye," she said, referring to our last lunch together.

"I didn't say that," I replied. "I was only trying to figure out what was left of our relationship, and if there was a possibility of a friendship or not. Do you want to be friends?"

She hesitated. During the silence I could sense her weighing her answer, trying to decide what to say. I held my breath. Tears filled my eyes.

"Yes," she said at last.

I wasn't sure I believed her. Did she have the courage to tell me the truth? Was she just being nice? In my mind's eye, I saw her saying goodbye to me in the parking lot with tears in her own eyes. Perhaps she was sincere. There was some room for hope. We made plans to get together for lunch.

Experiencing the cruelty at FXUU left my life tinged with sorrow. I felt less safe than I did before I had become a member there. My sleep was often fitful and filled with unpleasant dreams. Once, I dreamed the toilet was clogged with feces. I couldn't get it clean. I didn't have enough time to do it and I was tempted just to leave it. I woke up in a panic. I tried deep breathing and telling myself I was safe, that Lyndon was right next to me. I tossed and turned the rest of the night.

Lyndon and I slept late and made love the next morning. I chased my demons away by imagining God blessing us. Sex was God's gift. God had surely joined Lyndon and me. Making love was a blessing from God.

The occasionally sleepless nights and bouts of anxiety made me wonder if I would ever recover completely. Whenever I was stressed and tired, thoughts of self-harm continued to intrude. Images of slashing my inner thigh or my forearm flashed through my head. Imagining the blood dripping fascinated me.

My thoughts turned to Dr. Emmett. At times I felt confident that I had made the right decision when I terminated treatment. Other times I desperately wanted to hold onto our relationship. It was safe in Dr. Emmett's office. Although the sessions were frequently painful, I knew he wouldn't harm me. It was hard to know if I really needed to see him or if contacting him would, at this point, be running away from my life. Hearing his voice would be soothing. It would help me feel safe and less frightened.

I called him when I knew he wasn't around and listened to his outgoing message, just to reassure myself he was still there. It was silly. Of course he was still there. He cashed the check I sent him, didn't he?

Although I visited other churches, I felt safe at Rev. Karen's church. It was familiar and close to home. I knew people from Bible study. Immanuel provided me with what I wanted. Theologically I might have been an odd Lutheran, but I felt accepted and welcomed there. They didn't demonize me for not believing as they did.

Nevertheless, I was cautious about joining Rev. Karen's church. Lutherans, Rev. Karen assured me, dealt with conflict well. If a conflict arose, a mediator would be called in. Each side to the conflict would be given an advocate to assist them. She said something about persistent troublemakers. I knew I wasn't a troublemaker so I didn't ask her what she meant.

In late July at the beginning of a service, Rev. Karen announced that a person was needed to assemble the newsletter once a month. Wanting to contribute more to my new church family, I spoke to her as I exited the sanctuary. She appeared puzzled, but then said Beverly was going to do that. I thought it odd that she had just announced she needed someone when she didn't. I didn't say anything at the time, but now wonder if she was purposely limiting my participation at Immanuel. Perhaps this was the first warning of the trouble to come.

Rev. Karen then said she had this other project she would like me to do for her. She asked me to come to her office. I did, and she handed me materials on the Safe Haven for Children program. She wanted me to read through them and make recommendations. I did as she asked. Rev. Karen listened to my suggestions. Although at least one of my suggestions was implemented, she never asked for any further assistance.

August 6 was a nearly perfect day. I rose early for church. Carefully selecting my clothes, I put on my light-green dress with the floral print and the wide, white collar with the crocheted edge. I buckled the back straps of my matching white shoes. Looking through my jewelry box, I found the sterling silver cross my grandmother gave me for my college graduation and placed it around my neck for the first time in many years.

Nervously, I searched through my office for my baptismal papers. Instead I found my First Communion certificate. That would have to do, I thought as I placed it in my bag. I walked to Immanuel. It had been about ten months since I had been kicked out of FXUU. I remembered Rev. Dorothy telling me shortly after my argument with Sue that I was no more spiritual than anyone else. Taken aback, I didn't reply. Why did she say that? I had wondered. I never claimed to be more spiritual.

Within the last year my faith had deepened, and I was clearer about what I believed about God. Did that make me more spiritual? I never thought about it until Rev. Dorothy mentioned it. I was reading more books on Christianity than anyone else at FXUU. Did that make me more spiritual? I was attending more religious events. Did that make me more spiritual? I didn't know how to measure spirituality. I wasn't concerned if I was more "spiritual" than the others. I was just exploring my own spirituality.

Sitting on the black couch in Rev. Karen's office, I filled out membership forms while she copied my documents. The membership chair came in. "Maggie, I would like to take your picture to put up on the bulletin board so other church members can get to know new members."

"Okay," I said, stepped outside and stood against the brick wall while she adjusted her camera.

"Where's your family?" she asked.

"Home. They'll be here later."

"They could have had their picture taken with you."

"They have no interest in being affiliated with Immanuel or any other church." Lyndon was quite cynical about churches, believing they were only interested in your money. My mistreatment at Murray and FXUU only reinforced that view. Melissa also wanted nothing to do with an organization she saw as hurting me. Only by pleading was I able to get them to agree to come to the membership service.

Lyndon and Melissa arrived just as the service started. We sat with Ivonne, my sponsor. I was accepted into membership, along with seven others, by acclamation. During coffee hour, I hugged all my new friends. I felt life could be joyous, and I had been blessed many times over. We were the last to leave.

In the afternoon I worked in my garden, weeding, staking up plants and planting seed. I picked my first zucchini of the season. Lyndon spent the day helping our neighbor put in his new brick walk. They worked past sunset and got the job done. It delayed dinner. I burned the zucchini, the only imperfection in a perfect day.

The next morning I was awakened by the construction crew for the sewer project. The city was taking an easement straight down our driveway to lay some sewer pipe. The huge excavation machines were like monsters engaged in a fierce battle in my yard, tearing up bushes and trees and disrupting the tranquility of my home. So I wouldn't be cornered, I left my car in Immanuel's parking lot. If I needed to escape I could walk through the woods and drive away.

I had some passing thoughts of self-harm. I argued with myself about calling Dr. Emmett. Then I realized it was time. I needed to know he was there, and was still willing to talk to me. I called and set up an appointment for a telephone session at 9 p.m.

After Monday night Bible study, I didn't linger to talk to Rev. Karen and went straight home. Dr. Emmett and I talked for forty-five minutes. He asked if I had any urge to self-harm. I gasped. I hadn't anticipated his question. I don't know why. Dr. Emmett would have been remiss if he hadn't asked. I quickly answered, brushing it off as best I could. I started talking to him about some intrusive gynecological tests I had just undergone that had caused severe pain.

"I'd rather skip all these tests and suffer the consequences."

"Is there some latent suicidality?" he asked.

I was silent. I was imprisoned within this life of mine. Dr. Emmett was blocking my means of escape. Before FXUU, I felt good about myself, happy to be alive. Now, even though there were many things that gave me pleasure, I wouldn't mind dying.

"The time between two eternities is short, why would you want to make it shorter?" he asked.

I knew life could be joyous. I had been blessed many times over. But experiencing the cruelty at FXUU left my life tinged with sorrow. Once, I wondered if I could ever let go of the rage against Uncle Frank. Years later, I realized it was gone. I don't know how it happened. Now I wondered if I could ever get past the sorrow. I knew too much about the cruelty of life.

We discussed my feelings about having things put into my vagina. "Medical procedures are different from Uncle Frank putting his fingers in you. You need to remind yourself of that."

My current distress was internally generated. I hadn't been mistreated. In fact, I was treated with kindness and respect.

"You're trading physical safety for emotional safety when you avoid needed medical care," he said.

"I know I can't allow myself to die. I need to seek medical treatment for my family's sake."

"It's an act of love for you to do that."

"I'm the one most likely to hurt me."

"How do you feel about that?" he asked.

Silence. I couldn't bear to feel it.

"When something goes wrong," he said, "you look and look, trying to figure out what you did wrong. When you can't find anything, you conclude you are inherently bad and unfixable."

I didn't know how to get past that. I didn't know if I would ever get past it. It was as if I internalized all the abuse from others and continued dumping it on myself. I had become them. My vulnerability incited others to bully me. Although Dr. Emmett lacked the power to protect me from others, he protected me from my self-destructive urges. He kept me from harming myself.

"I'm backsliding," I told him.

"Not at all. You called me like you were supposed to. You are taking care of yourself. Even though you're afraid, you're making all of your doctor's appointments."

Reflecting on therapy, I thought of the therapists in my life as God's agents on earth. They protected me by providing me with a safe place to go to and teaching me how to protect myself. It isn't so different with God. God was always there to talk to. His sanctuary had always been a safe place. FXUU wasn't a safe place because people had forgotten it was God's house.

In late August, I had lunch with Rev. Dorothy at the Asian restaurant near my office. I asked after her family and her recent visit with her daughter.

"Are you still going to church at Immanuel?" she asked, changing the subject.

"I attend services every Sunday," I guardedly replied. I didn't want to discuss the issues that divided us. "I go to Bible study on Monday nights, and I'm a member of the chimes choir."

"Sue retrieved a message off FXUU's answering machine," she said. She gave me the name of the caller. I didn't know the name. "They were looking for a Unitarian Universalist minister to do a funeral. Since all the Unitarian Universalist ministers were out of town for the summer, I did it."

Why was Rev. Dorothy telling me this? Did she think I knew the deceased and his family?

"It must be hard to do a funeral for a young person," I said, careful to say nothing about Sue.

Rev. Dorothy had been dishonest with me in several ways. At times I would think she was never attached to me, but then I would remember the tears in her eyes. She always denied them. I think she was crushed when I joined Immanuel. Perhaps she hoped I would apologize to Sue and return to FXUU or some other Unitarian Universalist congregation. I don't think she fully understood what happened. I suspect others lied to her and distorted what had happened, or both. It wasn't possible to find out, because she admitted to nothing. What was she told? Did the group get together and plan a strategy to handle me? Did they think I was splitting, manipulative, or so on, and without my consent, chose Rev. Dorothy to be the only one to talk with me? Were they playing amateur psychologists? What were they thinking?

"Helen had a breast removed." Rev. Dorothy's voice broke into my thoughts.

I bit my tongue, thinking, *I don't care about her.* I wished Rev. Dorothy would apologize. I wished she would say, *"I'm sorry we treated you so badly."*

I fantasized that the new minister at FXUU would call and come talk to me. That she would tell me that people were sorry and that they missed me. But they weren't sorry, and they probably weren't even thinking of me. The people who felt sorry about it were not the ones who harmed me. The guilty parties were silent.

When I had first told Don I was leaving FXUU, I told him I intended to write a letter, but never did. Originally I was going to thank him and the others. Now, a year later, I sat down in front of my computer screen and began composing a very different letter than the one originally promised.

While I typed, I remembered Smedes writing in *The Art of Forgiving* that you only forgive those who you blame. Without blame and the conception of sin, there can be no forgiveness. I think that's why asking abuse survivors to forgive is a mistake. They first need to blame their perpetrators and not themselves. Then, maybe, they will be able to forgive.

I blamed Sue, Don, Sharon, Angelina and Rev. Patience for hurting me, for being emotionally abusive and for their betrayals. I blamed Rev. Dorothy for lying to me, for breaking confidences and for deceiving Dr. Emmett. I blamed all of them. Without clearly blaming them, there was no hope of salvaging our relationship.

I delayed mailing the letter. I wanted to complete the chapter on confrontations in *The Courage to Heal*. I planned to send the letter so it would reach them on September 19, exactly one year after I received the abusive emails.

When I discussed the letter with Rev. Karen, she asked me what response I expected to get. I told her I thought they would look at the letter as proof that I was crazy and not respond to me at all. The only way to get them to talk to me was for me to apologize for raising my voice. I would not say "sorry" for something I didn't regret. I would not lie.

I just wanted a voice, to have my say. When I was denied a voice, I got the urge to self-injure. I wanted FXUU to know how emotionally abusive I regarded their behavior, and how much it devastated me. I also wanted them to know how strong I was, that I had passed through the storm and survived. Rev. Patience had silenced me, but I wouldn't remain silent forever. Writing the letter empowered me.

I rewrote the letter to FXUU. I asked Lyndon to read it. Refusing, he stated, "This is why things keep happening in Bosnia. People aren't willing to let things go."

"I am letting go," I replied. "This is how I'm doing it."

I considered calling Rev. Dorothy and having a frank conversation with her. She used to be there for me. I still needed and wanted her in my life. Now that I was strong, she no longer called. I needed her to be honest and forthright with me. I needed her to be honest about her feelings. No more lies. If we were to have a friendship, she needed to be authentic.

I telephoned her to let her know I had mailed the letter. I left her a message inviting her to call me. She never returned my call, leaving me to wonder if she was ever really my friend. I didn't understand why we couldn't talk about mutual interests. Why we couldn't have lively conversations about religion. Why she was never really honest with me. Did she tell me all sorts of lies to be polite? Was I misjudging her? Why didn't she call?

As time went on, I realized that while I was at FXUU I had lost sense of who I was, and allowed others to define me by demonizing me. But I wasn't a demon. I was a pretty decent human being who valued honesty in all her relationships. What FXUU had to say simply wasn't true. I was a constructive force there, not a destructive one.

I finally wrote a letter to Rev. Dorothy. It was just as I wanted it, short and to the point. I didn't expect her to respond and she didn't. That hurt, but it was time to move on. I resolved not to initiate contact with her again. I was confused about her motives and expectations. At times I felt hate for her. I didn't want to feel that way. I didn't want to demonize her. I wanted to forgive her and let it go.

Rev. Dorothy had played an important role in my life. It would have been fine if she had said she wasn't up to being a friend and she could no longer take my phone calls. When she announced she wasn't going to continue as FXUU's interim minister, she should have ended her pastoral relationship with me. Instead she tried to assuage my distress by meeting with me and telling me everything would remain the same and she would always have time for me.

In July 1999, the day after she admitted to me she had lied about breaking confidentiality, she revealed her resentment and anger when she told me I was "too much." I had inadvertently intruded and needed more than she was willing to give. She never desired my friendship. She liked being needed by me, but wasn't prepared for what that meant. She expected me to heal quicker than was reasonable.

Rev. Dorothy's impatience and intolerance delayed my recovery. My encounter with her became more damaging than the events that originally triggered the relapse. She lacked true compassion and understanding. She forgot it was her responsibility to clearly define the nature of our relationship. She then blamed me for her failure to be honest and set limits.

Sending her the letter left me feeling anxious. I was fearful she would respond in a vengeful, hurtful way, rejecting and abandoning me further. If she ever had any affection for me, it was highly conditional. Although she was there for me, she abandoned and rejected me when I showed some strength. She didn't like it. She didn't like it when I

checked into who was lying to me. It spoiled her image. Rev. Dorothy
very much liked to keep up appearances.

Due to my experience with Rev. Dorothy and FXUU, I feared I
wasn't connecting with Rev. Karen very well. I feared sharing my deepest
secrets with someone would ultimately push them away, leaving nothing
on which to base a relationship. At times I wished I could stay home with
Lyndon and give up church. At least with my husband, I knew I was
loved and accepted. The most important thing Rev. Karen could do for
me was accept me and never turn me out.

I spoke with Rev. Karen about Rev. Dorothy. I told her I needed to
hate Rev. Dorothy for now. During my morning meditation, an image of
Rev. Dorothy as a burning witch had flashed through my mind. How
absurd and cruel and evil it was to terminate a relationship because I
joined a Christian church.

Rev. Karen told me that, in Rev. Dorothy's eyes, I sold out. Rev.
Dorothy wasn't happy for me. She didn't really understand or know what
I believed about Jesus and God. I didn't even know. It was evolving. It
wasn't fixed. I was a Unitarian Universalist in exile at the Lutheran
church.

A couple came in to see me for marital counseling. Their religious
differences were causing conflict. The husband was agnostic, his wife was
Protestant, and his ex-wife, the mother of his child, was Catholic. While I
spoke to them, I realized some good had come out of the last two years
after all. Having been at one time or another agnostic, Catholic and
Protestant enabled me to understand each person's perspective. I was
better able to bridge the gaps between them and assist them in resolving
their conflicts.

I wrote a note to Dr. Emmett and sent it with a payment. I informed
him I wasn't going to initiate contact with Rev. Dorothy again. It was
over. Nothing remained of FXUU except the grief and pain. I was going
to do my best to move on and become a good Lutheran.

# Passing it Forward

The Catholic nuns and priests had taught me that Sunday was a Holy Day of Obligation. It didn't matter if you were vacationing or backpacking, on Sunday you went to mass, even if it meant hiking down a mountain to get there. That lesson was so well learned that unless I was sick or away, I attended services at Immanuel Lutheran every Sunday. I went to the nine-thirty service and sat with my friends from Bible study.

At the end of each service, I would step out into the center aisle and take my place on the line that slowly moved forward as each congregant greeted Rev. Karen and shook her hand. I chatted with the other congregants while we waited. After wishing her good morning, I moved to the right, toward the breezeway, while others exited the church through the front door. A folding table was set up along the back of the last pew. On it were several letters printed on the church's ivory stationery, addressed to the people who were sick or grieving and telling them they were in our prayers. I lined up to sign them.

In June 2000, two months before becoming a member at Immanuel, while I was signing the last prayer letter, a flyer from Lutheran Social Services caught my eye. I put down my pen and placed my hand on the white sheet of paper. Foster parents were needed for teens who had survived the Sudanese civil war and who were currently living in Kenyan refugee camps.

*Oh, I can't do that,* I thought, straightening up and taking one step to the left. My children were grown. We were done with childrearing. But our spare bedroom hadn't been used for several years.

I shifted my weight onto my right foot and turned back to the table. Picking up the flyer, I moved to the side of the table where I could read it carefully without holding up the line.

*Hmm,* I thought. *It isn't hard to love a child.* Holding the paper with my left hand, I held my chin with my right while I studied the flyer. I smiled as I remembered cradling Orion in my arms while I rocked him to sleep in our bedroom.

"Maybe we should have another one," I had said to Lyndon while he changed his clothes.

"No," he said. "We can't afford it. We agreed to two."

217

I did the arithmetic. The daycare costs would eat up my salary. If we had a third child, I would have to give up my career. I sighed as I laid Orion in his crib and pulled up the rail.

The years I spent raising our son and daughter were the happiest and most gratifying years of my life. They had turned out well.

I moved my right hand away from my chin and grasped the paper with both hands. Lutheran Social Services wasn't looking for homes for small children. They wanted to place teens. *We won't need babysitters,* I thought. Folding the flyer in half, I put it in my handbag.

When I walked into the house, I found Lyndon in the kitchen and spoke to him. He was reluctant. He was looking forward to having fewer parenting responsibilities. I replied that, at most, it would be a four-year commitment. A foster son would be leaving home just as our own children were completing college. It wouldn't add all that many years to parenting.

I went upstairs and spoke to Melissa, who was sitting on her bed studying. I sat down next to her and handed her the flyer. "I didn't get along with Pernille," she said, referring to a Danish exchange student who lived with us for a few months.

"But you did fine with the other exchange students. You really loved Uta and you got along fine with Naul."

"Maybe if we get a boy it would work better. I get along with Orion."

"Okay. We don't have to make a final decision today. I'll get more information."

I left her to her studying and went downstairs to my study to call Orion. After explaining I was considering taking in a Sudanese foster son, he replied without hesitation, "Mom, we have the room." I was proud of his generosity.

On Monday, I called Lutheran Social Services and spoke with Jeanne, the director of the program. I questioned her carefully about the Sudanese boys. She called them unaccompanied minors.

"Given all the trauma these children have suffered, aren't there attachment and behavioral problems?" I asked.

"The boys have been carefully screened by the State Department," Jeanne reassured me. "Any child with antisocial tendencies has been screened out. Only those teens who are highly motivated to obtain an education are allowed to enter the United States."

"They're coming from a patriarchal society. Any boy moving into our home would have to accept my status and that of my daughter."

"This won't be a problem," Jeanne assured me. "The boys have to go through an orientation program, and once they're here, you will be provided with a Sudanese caseworker who has successfully made the transition to America. They will help the boys adjust."

Satisfied with Jeanne's answers Lyndon and I initiated the application process. Jeanne toured our home. I took her upstairs and showed her the middle bedroom that would become our foster son's.

"Who uses these other rooms?" Jeanne looked into the two bedrooms at the end of the hall.

"My kids."

"Where are they?"

"My son is at the Coast Guard Academy. My daughter lives at home and commutes to school."

"You have a lot of space here. Would you consider taking more than one?"

I wanted to do the right thing. I knew we had the space. "I—"

"The State Department has recommended that the boys be housed in small groups."

"My husband would never consent to taking more than one. I work several evenings per week. I only have so much time to give a child in my home."

Jeanne didn't press the issue. Finding people to take even one child was difficult. She would have to accept what she could get. A few days later, she interviewed each one of us separately. Rev. Karen provided a letter of recommendation.

Excited, I went to Bible study. Because Immanuel had no air conditioning, we were meeting at Ivonne's house for the summer. I sat in one of the chairs that had been taken from the dining room and placed across from the sofa. After everyone had gotten settled, I announced to the group that Lyndon and I had decided to take in a Sudanese refugee.

"Wow!"

"That's wonderful."

"This won't be easy.," I said. "We'll need all the help and support you can give us."

"Sure."

"We'll do whatever we can."

A few weeks later, Lyndon and I flew down to Charlotte, North Carolina to visit my sister Rita. Sitting in her living room, we discussed our plans to foster a Sudanese boy. Rita, a licensed social worker, had extensive experience with foster children.

"I'm worried LSS will reject us as foster parents because of my history of post-traumatic stress disorder," I said.

"The trend in foster care and adoption is to assist all families who are willing to be parents," she replied. "Your history is a strength. You've been in therapy and have resolved so much of your childhood trauma."

When we returned home from North Carolina, we heard from Jeanne. We had been accepted as foster parents. We would be getting a Sudanese teen sometime in the fall.

Like expectant parents, we began preparing for our foster son's arrival. We looked at what we already owned and adapted it. There was an old green corduroy comforter in the linen closet that used to be Orion's. Melissa painted the middle room a pale green to match it. Lyndon built a twin platform bed and put the spare futon mattress on it. I spent a Sunday afternoon arranging the furniture, making up the bed and hanging the curtains.

On a bright Wednesday afternoon, I drove to the beauty parlor to get a haircut. The sidewalk from the parking lot to the beauty parlor's door ran past a daycare center and their play yard filled with red and blue plastic play equipment. I was disappointed that the children were inside and not to be seen.

While my hairstylist was cutting my hair, we chatted happily away about our families and future plans. Our daughters had gone to high school together.

"How's Melissa doing?" she said.

"Fine. She's going to school in Massachusetts now."

"Happy to have her home?"

"Yes."

"They grow up so fast."

"Yes." There was a pause while we remembered our childrearing years. "I'm expecting a son," I blurted out.

"What?" In the mirror, I saw her eyes open wide with astonishment as she stepped back with her scissors in her right hand and a comb in the other. "At your age?"

"I haven't hit menopause yet," I said, leading her on.

"I thought you were done with having children."

"I was." I giggled. "We're taking in a foster son from the Sudan."

"Oh! You had me going. I couldn't believe you would be having another child at your age."

"I loved being pregnant, but I'm not up for that."

"Congratulations. How nice of you to do this."

"Thank you." After she cut my hair, I got up and paid my bill. I left the salon beaming with pride.

Jeanne scheduled a training session with other prospective foster parents for Monday night, October 30, 2000. After comparing the directions I obtained online against my book of street maps, Lyndon, Melissa and I drove thirty miles to a Lutheran church located in a decaying neighborhood of a small city.

As we walked through the church's side door, we were greeted by a Sudanese man with manhood initiation scars on his forehead. Each tribe had their own unique marks. I immediately recognized him as Tere, our caseworker, whom Lyndon and I met a few weeks before when Jeanne toured our home.

"We're meeting down the hall," Tere said as he shook our hands.

"Tere," I said, stepping aside so he could see Melissa, who was behind me, "I would like to introduce you to my daughter, Melissa."

Tere shifted his gaze from Lyndon and me toward Melissa. His eyes sparkled, and he immediately moved closer to Melissa and started talking to her. Jeanne walked up with several other people and began introducing the other foster parents to Lyndon and me. She then escorted all of us down the hallway toward a Sunday school classroom. At the classroom's doorway, I noticed that Tere was still talking to Melissa. Their conversation was interrupted when Jeanne asked Tere to help set up some chairs. Melissa rejoined us as we took our seats at a folding table. Next to us sat a heavyset woman who had fostered unaccompanied minors before.

"The Vietnamese were the easiest. They were the least damaged by the war. The Haitians were the worst," the woman informed us.

Before I could respond and ask her more questions, Jeanne moved to the head of the table and started the meeting.

"There are no good guys in the Sudan," Jeanne said. "The government is run by the Arabs in the north. When most of the teens were only four or five, government soldiers attacked the black villages in the south while the men were out tending their cattle. When the slaughter started, the villagers ran. The boys, separated from their families, wandered together through the jungle trying to avoid lions and other predators. They crossed the river into Ethiopia, where they were allowed to stay only for a brief while. When the Ethiopian government tired of their presence, they drove them out, back across the crocodile-infested river. Boys were either shot, drowned or eaten. The survivors continued to wander through the jungles of Sudan and were often conscripted into the rebel army."

"What about the girls?" someone asked.

"It was even worse for the girls. Fewer of them have survived. Many of them have been raped. And it's harder for them to come to the US."

"Why?"

"It isn't important to the rebels that the girls be educated. They are allowing the boys to come because they want them to get an education and come back to help establish an independent southern Sudan."

"Back?" I said. "How can they go back? I'm not taking in a boy for him to return to the Sudan to be killed."

At the end of the meeting, Jeanne informed us that our foster son would be sixteen-year-old James. She knew very little about him, except he had been picked up by the United Nations and taken to a refugee camp in Kenya when he was ten years old. When the UN searched for his parents, they learned that his mother probably died from cholera. His father was also presumed to have died during the fighting. Jeanne only had an approximate date of arrival. Once James and the other boys reached Nairobi, she would call us with more specific flight information.

The date of James' arrival kept changing. With only a day or two's notice, we were finally told James would be arriving in Boston on Monday night, November 6. I quickly cancelled all my appointments for the next five days.

Monday evening, Lyndon and I drove to Logan Airport. We met Tere at Budget Rental and rode the shuttle bus to the terminal, joining other Lutheran Social Services staff and other foster parents at the gate.

"There's a delay," Jeanne told us. "They've gone through customs in New York and are on their way."

We took a seat and waited, passing the time talking to LSS staff and the other parents. I kept looking at my watch and out the plate glass window onto the tarmac.

"That's the plane!" someone said.

We all stood and watched the plane taxi to the gate. Standing along the glass wall, we watched for the boys.

"There they are!" an LSS staff member said. "They're the ones carrying the plastic bags. They don't have any luggage."

I didn't see them until they were almost directly under our second-story window. The small group of thin, tall, dark-skinned boys, poorly dressed in light cotton slacks and T-shirts, stood out among the well-dressed Americans in their winter overcoats. When the boys disappeared from our view, we turned to the gate and watched passengers make their way up the ramp.

Tere and the other Sudanese staff stepped forward when the boys walked into the waiting area. They walked right past us. Tere called to them in one of the tribal languages. The boys kept walking.

"Wait! Wait!" we called and chased after them.

Tere tried a different language, and the boys finally stopped and gathered around him. Lyndon and I stood with the other parents while Tere sorted out who was who and what language they spoke.

"They were told not to talk strangers," I heard someone say. "That's why they kept walking."

Tere began introducing each boy to his new parents. *Which boy is ours?* I wondered. I took a deep breath to slow my heartbeat. *Where is he? Where is he?* I restrained any outward show of excitement and impatience. Finally, Tere introduced us to a startlingly handsome boy. Unlike Tere and the other boys, there were no scars on his forehead.

*He was never initiated into manhood,* I thought. *He appears to be in better shape than we were told to expect.* His teeth appeared healthy. Most of the other boys were missing teeth and had unfilled cavities.

Lyndon gave James his old green winter coat to put on. Although it was way too big it would keep him warm until I could buy him another in the morning.

Tall and lanky, the boys raced through the terminal toward the shuttle. Unaccustomed to the stairs, they stumbled taking two or three steps at a time. I gasped when one of the boys almost lost his balance when his canvas sneaker fell off his foot. Barely slowing down, he bent over and slipped his foot back into the shoe that was a couple of sizes too big. Fearful they would fall, I started to call out to them, but stopped when I realized they wouldn't understand me. I turned to Tere, who was already calling to the boys in their tribal tongue. The boys slowed down and waited for us to reach the bottom of the stairs. Together, we boarded the shuttle.

On the ride back to our car, James sat facing us, on the opposite side of the aisle. I slid my right arm around Lyndon's forearm, linking my slender, pale fingers with his thick brown ones. The contrasting shades of our skin looked like the white and chocolate swirls in a marble cake. Leaning my head against his shoulder, I peered furtively at James, who was looking at us from the corner of his eyes. I wondered what James thought of a black man married to a white woman.

When we arrived home, we introduced James to his sister, Melissa, and showed him his room. Needing to determine his clothing size, I asked him to step on the bathroom scale. He surprised me when he removed his thin cotton slacks, revealing gray sweatpants and a second pair of cotton slacks underneath. Not having any winter coats in Kenya, the boys were instructed to layer the few clothes they had to keep them warm.

With Melissa's help I weighed and measured his thin, emaciated body. There was a large, ugly scar on his leg caused by an infection he got while living in the Kenyan refugee camp. After we were sure his immediate needs had been met, we said goodnight and retired to our bedrooms. In the middle of the night we heard loud, thumping sounds coming from James' room. Lyndon got up and checked.

"He's fine," Lyndon said as he got back into bed.

In the morning James admitted to having difficulty sleeping on such a soft mattress. He awoke in the night and thought he had fallen out of a tree onto the remains of other boys eaten by lions.

Lyndon smiled. "There are no lions here."

James chuckled nervously.

After Lyndon and Melissa had left for the day, I drove James over to the church to meet Rev. Karen. Laurie, the church secretary, was standing at the door as we ambled up the covered walkway. While James was speaking to Rev. Karen, she whispered to me how handsome he was. I felt like a new parent who has just been told how beautiful her baby is.

After speaking briefly with Rev. Karen, I took James up to Memorial Park to give him a panoramic view of Attleboro and North Attleboro. We walked down the path to the outcropping, and I pointed to the water tower and other landmarks in the distance. The perfection of that autumn day embraced us. As I breathed in the fresh, warm air, I felt my heart fill with love for my new son whom God had entrusted to my care.

"See those hills?" I said, unsure how much English he understood. "'Massachusetts' is an Indian word for 'land of hills.'"

After leaving the park, I drove him to a department store, and I started with the absolute necessities: sneakers, socks, a couple of packages of white cotton briefs and crewneck undershirts. At the coat rack, I had him try on a winter jacket. Unable to get him to state a preference, I tried to gauge what he liked from his facial expression, but he didn't smile. Years of struggling to survive in the African bush where adults were as much of a threat as the wild animals had taught him to be cautious. I found myself looking for the faintest of clues: a twinkle in his eyes, a twitch at the corner of his mouth, a grunt.

Moving on to the blue jean department, I used the measurements I had taken the night before to select some slacks that might fit him. I took him to the men's fitting room.

"Go in there and try these on." I handed him a few pairs of jeans. "Come out and let me see."

He went into the fitting room while I waited. When he came back out, the pants appeared tight. I checked the waist. James had put the jeans on over his cotton slacks.

"No. Go back in," I said. "Take off those slacks. Try the jeans on over your underwear."

"These are good, Mom," he insisted. In Africa, necessity had forced him to wear whatever clothes he found or were given him whether they fitted or not.

"No, it is important that they fit right," I said. James appeared stressed. I sighed. I, too, was emotionally drained from all the excitement. But the winter was coming. He needed clothes. This wasn't Africa. "Go back in and try these on. We will get some lunch as soon as you do."

Obediently, he returned to the dressing room. After establishing his size, I selected a couple pairs of jeans and went to the cashier. Using money donated by Immanuel Lutheran and some of our own funds, I paid for them. Later, when the clothing allowance arrived from Massachusetts Department of Social Services, I would buy him some more clothes.

The next day I took him to the local high school. It had been several years since I had been inside. There was a new principal. Standing at the counter, I said, "I'm here to register my foster son."

The secretary looked up from her desk. "I don't know if they will take him."

"What do you mean? By law you have to."

"I don't think so."

"Call the State Department. You have no choice."

"We can't do it today. Come back next week."

"I can't. I took the time off this week. He can't sit home alone. He needs to be in school."

"I can't help you today."

"May I speak to the principal?"

"She's busy."

"I want to speak to the principal. I'm not leaving until I do."

"You don't have to be so rude about it."

"I'm not rude. He has a right to go to school here."

Reluctantly, the secretary went inside the principal's office and came back out. "She will talk to you at 2 p.m."

"Thank you. I'll be back then."

When I met with the principal, she examined the documents I had brought with me. "Where's his birth certificate? We can't admit him without a birth certificate."

"He doesn't have one. He was born in a small village in the Sudan. Even if they issued birth certificates, all records would have been destroyed when the government troops burned his village to the ground."

"How do you know how old he is?"

"The UN has figured out his age."

"He doesn't look sixteen."

"I agree. He looks a little younger. But his immigration papers say he is sixteen."

"I think he would be better placed in the middle school."

"That's okay," I said. "I've been told to get him into the lowest grade possible. I didn't think the middle school would take him because of his age."

"I think we can get away with putting him into eighth grade."

"Thank you."

The next day I met with the middle school principal, who was more welcoming. He gave us a tour of the school and introduced James to his teachers. James was scheduled to start school after the weekend.

Orion came home for the weekend to meet his new brother. The boys spent some time together in Orion's bedroom. Coming downstairs, Orion said he started to answer James' questions about his computer when he realized James didn't understand even basic science. Finding simple ways to explain how things work was challenging, and made more difficult by James' poor English.

James came into our world amazed by what we took for granted: central heating, radios, food. His simple pleasure brought joy to our lives. Prior to his arrival, I often felt it would have been a kindness if God had taken me. But James' presence made it easy to focus on what I had, and not on what I had lost. I began focusing on the present and the future. I now had James to raise. God sent him to me. He was a gift and a blessing. He was worth more than a thousand FXUUs.

On Sunday morning I took James to church with me. During coffee hour, he withdrew from the crowd and stood in the corner, watching, like a frightened animal.

"Come, James. Confirmation class is starting." I walked him down the hall to the classroom. He pulled back, refusing to go in.

"There are kids your own age in there," I said.

"I stay with you," he replied, and pulled back farther.

"I will be right here waiting for you." With that, I gently pushed him toward the door, knowing he was scared but that he wouldn't get over it until he joined his age peers. I wanted him to make friends.

With some more coaxing, he walked into the classroom. He glanced back at me.

"I will be right here," I said.

"Come, sit down, James." It was Rev. Karen. James took a seat. I waited by the classroom door, peeking in occasionally, trying to see how he was doing. My stomach churned. I knew this wasn't easy for him.

After class, he walked into the hallway smiling. "It was good," he said.

I smiled back, relieved. "I told you so."

After dinner that night, he and I returned to the church for youth group, and I signed him up for the winter retreat scheduled for February.

Monday morning after Orion returned to the Coast Guard Academy, I discovered James wearing Orion's silver chain. "Where did you get this?" I asked.

"Orion gave it to me."

"Orion gave it to you? Are you sure?"

"Yes! Yes! He gave it to me."

I called Orion, who explained he had shown the chain to James but hadn't given it to him. "You misunderstood, James," I told him. "You will have to return it to Orion. Someday you will have your own chain."

Monday night, I went to chimes choir rehearsal and Bible study. I passed pictures I had taken of James around the room.

"It's really wonderful of you to take him," someone said.

I felt uneasy, but said only, "We have the room."

"How long will he stay with you?"

"For as long as he wants. Until he's grown. I want him to be part of my family. I would never turn out a family member. It wouldn't be right."

"I would never take a stranger into my home."

Nancy, who was sitting next to me, had said this. The others were looking at the pictures. I turned toward her. "Why not?"

"I'm not comfortable with it. I don't even like to have guests over. It's such an intrusion."

How odd, I thought. "I like having guests. I want my home to be warm and welcoming."

"It's such a large responsibility," someone said from across the room.

"No bigger than raising my own two children," I replied. *Harder in some ways and easier in others*, I thought. Taking James in was simply the right thing to do. We had so much. He had so little. He didn't even have enough food. By fostering James, I was repaying a debt to Dr. Howard and several other people who had helped me after my psychiatric hospitalization. I could never repay them directly. But I could help someone else.

The next morning I spoke to Dr. Emmett on the telephone. We discussed James and people's reactions to us taking him in. "It makes me uneasy," I told him. "I'm not that good of a person."

"It's as if you're more comfortable when people criticize you than when they praise you," he said. "You see criticism as more sincere and authentic."

"I believe people are being sincere, but they're mistaken about me. Once they get to know me they won't like me or want me around anymore."

"You're always waiting for the other shoe to drop. I understand it's hard to have confidence in yourself when your parents mistreated you and rejected you."

"But still, Dr. Emmett, they're putting me on a pedestal. What happens when I fall off?"

"You are overly apprehensive. You will be fine."

Wanting to believe him, I foolishly ignored my own perceptions.

James quickly became the center of attention among the people I associated with at Immanuel. They often commented on how handsome he was. They mistook his childlike reactions to our technological society for innocence. They weren't fully aware that James had witnessed mass murder and might have participated in torture executions. James wasn't a saint who had miraculously survived genocide without blood on his hands. I was sure there were things he had done to survive that would have turned the stomachs of middle-class Americans.

James was barely reading at a third grade level, and his writing was worse. You don't learn to read and write wandering in the jungle with other boys. The schools in the refugee camps lacked books and supplies. How much could a child learn when he's hungry? The food ration was just enough to keep them alive.

I needed help tutoring James. I approached Beverly and Ruth at Bible study. "Ruth," I said, smiling, "how would you like to be a grandmother?"

"I can't be a grandmother," she replied. "I don't have any children."

"James' surrogate grandmother," I explained. "He needs a family."

James was immature for his age. He was an eight-year-old in a sixteen-year-old body. Coming from a communal society, he also wasn't used to being alone, so I made sure he always had adult supervision and someone to talk to. I arranged for Ruth and Beverly to tutor James at our house on the nights I was working.

James didn't always appreciate being tutored. He insisted he could read and write. He didn't think he needed any help. He avoided his schoolwork and looked for ways to get out of it. On a Sunday afternoon, I assigned him a page of simple arithmetic. I left him at the dining room table to complete it while I cooked dinner. In less then five minutes, he came into the kitchen with the page completed.

"That was fast," I said, taking the workbook from him. They were all correct. I thumbed through the workbook. There was an answer key in the back. "Did you copy the answers, James?"

"No."

"My children do not lie to me." I tore out the answer key. "Next time you lie, you will be punished."

When I called Ruth to thank her for helping James, she told me that last Christmas Eve she had been recently widowed, and getting a hug from me as we exited the church meant a lot to her. She told me she

loved me and I believed her. I felt so happy and grateful to have her and
the rest of the Bible study group for friends. I had a place where I
belonged at long last.

James reacted to the American Christmas with the wonder and
excitement of a small child. He delighted in simple things. Christmas
Eve, Rev. Karen joined us for a simple meal of stew that I had cooked in
the crock-pot. For dessert I served tapioca pudding with tropical fruit.
She and I were engaged in a lively conversation when we noticed James
enthusiastically scraping out the last bit of pudding from his bowl. Rev.
Karen laughed, saying, "Why don't you just lick out the bowl?"

Smiling, I said, "I guess I'll have to serve tapioca more often." I had
never seen anyone enjoy a meal so much.

My family wanted James to have as much as the average child in our
community. Lyndon, I and our adult children purchased several gifts
including a sterling silver chain, a stereo, a soccer ball and basketball. On
Christmas morning, James tore off the wrapping paper from his presents.
Delighted, he went outside with Orion to shoot some hoops while I
prepared Christmas dinner.

Lutheran Social Services hosted several social and training events at
the Lutheran church in Arlington for the boys and their foster families.
During one of these events, an LSS staff member let slip that it was
common for problems to develop with unaccompanied minors around
the sixth month of their placement. I wondered why this wasn't being
openly discussed and the foster families prepared on how to deal with it.
Instead, we were taught some things about Sudanese culture that in the
end wouldn't be very helpful. We learned that the culture was extremely
patriarchal, and that men purchased their wives with cows. Women were
expected to obey their fathers, then their husbands, and then their sons
when they came of age. After women prepared a meal, they would bring
it to their husbands on their knees. They wouldn't eat until the men had
finished.

How was I supposed to respect James' culture? Men and women were
equal in my home, and that was unchangeable. He would have to adjust.
Other than allowing him to call the other Sudanese boys each day and
cooking an occasional Sudanese dish, there was little I could do. I could
teach him what I knew, not what I didn't know. I could teach him how to

be a good American because I was an American. But I couldn't teach him how to be Sudanese.

When assigning chores, I gave him the responsibility of feeding and caring for the dog. In his culture men herd cows while women tend the vegetable gardens. Taking care of Sheba was the closest chore I had to that. In addition to feeding her, it was his responsibility to bring her into the house in the morning and put her out at night.

On a bright, sunny morning when I was making breakfast, James came downstairs barefooted.

"Where's your slippers?" I asked.

He ignored me and moved to the glass door to go outside to get the dog.

"James, you're not going outside like that, are you?"

"Sun shining."

"So? The ground is frozen. Put on your slippers."

He scowled.

"James, you—" I stopped. There was no need to argue this one. I turned back to the stove and poured some pancake batter onto the griddle. James went outside barefooted and without a coat to get the dog. When he came back in his shoulders were hunched and he was shivering.

"Will you ever do that again?" I asked.

"No."

I smiled. "Pancakes will be ready shortly." I flipped one over.

"Mom." He moved next to me.

"Yes, James?" I placed a pancake on a platter.

"Why it cold? Sun shinning."

"You just did some homework on the seasons. Don't you remember? It has to do with the position of the earth and the direction of the sun's rays."

I knew he didn't understand. Having grown up in a completely different climate, each of us attended to different cues. A sunny day always meant it was hot to James. If he had noticed the frost on the grass, he didn't understand that it was as cold as the ice in the freezer.

Melissa had some intense conflicts with James. They didn't understand how they should relate to each other. Melissa was only-two-and-a-half years older than her brother, Orion. They were more or less equal. I expected them to take care of each other.

I pulled her aside. "Listen, Melissa, you're ten years older than James. My eldest brother is ten years older than me. When my parents weren't around, I was expected to listen to him."

Clarifying Melissa's role eased some of the tension. I also tried to explain it to James, but he continued to think of himself as a man. Women were supposed to obey him and take care of his needs.

James was like a small child, unable to entertain himself. When I was too busy with my chores to spend time with him, he sought out Melissa, and would interrupt her even if she were studying.

Once, James told me that Melissa had threatened to hit him.

"Why?" I asked. "What were you doing?" Melissa wouldn't have made such a threat without provocation. I knew my daughter.

Unable to get a clear answer from him, I spoke to Melissa. She had discovered shaving cream on her towel in the bathroom. Since Orion hadn't been home, she knew James, who wasn't yet growing a beard, must have been playing with it. She confronted him. He denied it. She insisted he clean it up. He thought she, a woman, should clean it up. He raised his fist and moved closer to her.

"If you touch me," she warned him. "I'll whip your ass!"

Concerned that James threatened to attack her, I went and spoke to him. "You can't threaten to beat people. You are not to hit your sister."

Although James was capable of working hard within a group, he avoided chores he had to do by himself. He was supposed to put the dog out by 10 p.m. Instead of taking her out, he began going to bed early, around 9 p.m. When I peeked into his room the first time it happened, he was in his bed with the comforter pulled over his head. At first I thought he was tired and needed rest. So I put the dog out. The next morning, I reminded him he needed to put the dog out before he went to bed.

The next night, he still didn't put her out. After a few nights like this, I realized he was only pretending to be asleep. The next time he went to bed without putting the dog out, I went up to his room and pulled his comforter off. He was awake and fully dressed. I stood over him until he got up and put out the dog. After a few times of doing this, he began putting out the dog without being reminded.

On Monday, February 12, 2001, he didn't get up to go to school. Lyndon and Melissa had left for the day. I checked on him. "Are you feeling okay?" I said.

He didn't answer.

I placed my hand on his forehead. It wasn't hot.

"You're not running a fever. Get up and go to school." I left the room and went downstairs.

After eating my breakfast, I went back upstairs and opened the door to his room. He was hiding under his comforter.

"James, get up," I said. "You have school."

He partly sat up, leaning on his right arm. He contracted his brows. His eyes were filled with unbridled rage. I felt frightened. I didn't know what he was capable of. Fearing he would physically attack me, I backed off. He spent the day in his room.

When Lyndon got home from work, we called James downstairs into our office. We confronted him about his avoidance and deceitful behaviors. "You are never to skip school again," we told him. "You need to apologize."

"I'm sorry," he said.

"You must promise never to do it again."

"I won't do it again." He appeared contrite.

"When you get home from school, you are to call me and let me know you have arrived safely," Lyndon said. "Then you are to call your mother."

"After you get a snack, you are to do all your assigned schoolwork," I said. "Only then can you go to the YMCA." We had upgraded Lyndon's membership to include James so he could play basketball with other boys his age.

On February 19, I helped him pack for the church ski trip. He had no understanding of the weather conditions and what he needed to stay warm and dry. He wanted to wear his thermal undershirt over his T-shirt.

"James, it's supposed to be worn under your shirt. It will keep you warmer that way."

The problem was, he had no understanding how thermal shirts worked. "No, I'll wear this way."

"No, James. You don't understand, it's cold up there. You must stay warm. People die in the cold."

Before sunrise the next morning, I went downstairs to see him off. Covering his duffle and sleeping bag was the big, black felt sombrero loaned to him by Beverly's husband a few days before.

"James, you can't take that with you."

"It's mine. I'll take it."

"It's not yours. Paul just loaned it to you. You can't take it with you. It will get ruined in the snow."

I left him by the front door to wait for Ruth while I went back upstairs to get something. I heard the front door open, and Ruth's voice. As I was coming back down the stairs, I overheard Ruth telling him, "No, you can't take the sombrero. We're going skiing."

"James!" I said, angry. "Don't ask another adult for permission when I have already told you no!"

Turning to Ruth, I said, "I'm sorry. I had just told him that. By the way, could you make sure he wears his thermal shirt under his other shirt? I'm worried he won't dress warm enough."

"Okay."

When he returned home, I discovered he had disobeyed me regarding the thermal undershirt. I scolded him while sitting with him in the dining room.

"I want to leave," he said. "Eleven years I'm fine. No parents. I don't need parents."

"Yes you do. You're only a boy." My heart started beating rapidly. My breaths were short and shallow. My son didn't want to be with me. Was I being too hard?

"I'm a man."

"In the Sudan. Not here. If I am caught in the African bush, I am following you," I told him. "You know how to survive there. But I know how to survive here in the States. You need to listen to me."

"I go live with someone else. It will be better."

"You'll have the same problems elsewhere." Was he right? Would he be better off living with other Sudanese boys? How would he survive in America if he didn't learn our ways?

On Sunday, he and I attended church. During coffee hour, I overheard some of the adults who had gone on the ski trip talking about James. Unaware of the danger, James had wandered off inadequately dressed. As it was getting dark, one of the adults had to go looking for him and bring him back down the mountain in deep snow.

"I'm sorry he did that," I interrupted. I had been right to be concerned about the thermal shirt.

"No. It was all right."

"No, it wasn't." James had put himself and the adult who fetched him at risk. James' naiveté could have ended in tragedy. The adults didn't understand how much supervision he needed. They didn't live with him.

After coffee hour James had his confirmation class, so I walked home from church alone. I ate my lunch and wrote in my journal. At 12:30 p.m. he still wasn't home. I wondered if he had stayed to talk to Rev. Karen. She and I spoke a day or two later.

"I told him," she said, "he was being foolish. That if he left, he would be giving up a lot."

"I appreciate your support."

James called Tere, who then spoke with me. Tere wanted to set up an appointment with Lyndon and me.

"I won't meet with you if it's to tell us you'll be moving James," I said. I couldn't bear the thought of him leaving. If the decision had already been made, they should do it quickly. It would be less painful that way.

"That's not going to happen," Tere assured me.

Relief. He understood. I was going to keep my son after all.

On Wednesday, February 28, I spoke with Dr. Emmett on the telephone. We talked about the effect being abused had had on my relationships. We talked about the beating my father gave me when he called me a whore. My parents didn't love me. They wanted a daughter who was obedient, pretty and popular. I could never be what they wanted. Disappointed, they unleashed their anger on me.

When the phone call ended, I felt panicked. Abandoned. Never welcomed. Never wanted. Frequently rejected. So few real friends. Just Lyndon. Was I to lose my son, too? My stomach churned. It was difficult to focus on work.

On Friday, March 2, Jeanne, the director of the LSS program, called. "It's not James' choice where he lives," she told me. "James needs to listen to you. I appreciate what you're trying to do for him."

James wasn't going anywhere. I relaxed under her reassurance.

Saturday night I dreamed I was driving my car, with Rev. Karen sitting in the front passenger seat. She was rejecting, saying angry things, abandoning me. I woke up shaking. I turned over onto my back.

Forgotten. Unloved. Unwanted. I took some deep breaths and tried to focus on the relationships I had. Thinking of them helped a little. Thinking of God didn't help as much. I needed lots of holding and rocking.

Lyndon moved closer to me. I felt safer lying next to him, skin to skin, with his muscular arms around me. I had nothing to fear. Lyndon loved me.

I continued to need Dr. Emmett. I needed to know and be reassured that he was out there for me. I needed his support even though it felt foolish. I spoke to him on Wednesday, March 14, and talked to him about Immanuel. Then I called Rev. Karen.

"I still fear people at Immanuel will reject me. I don't believe Lutheran theology the way they do."

"People enter through the church door at various levels of belief. The Lutheran Church puts no doctrinal demands on them."

I was surprised at this, since I thought Unitarian Universalism was the only church that made no doctrinal demands.

"The only requirement is for members to be baptized," she continued. "Only those who are baptized are allowed to take communion."

I felt accepted. The Lutheran Church appeared to me to be a more loving church than Unitarian Universalist congregations. When I awoke the next morning after a good night's sleep, my whole body radiated with joy. I had a family that loved me, a church to nurture and sustain me. I was safe. God would always be with me.

On Saturday, March 24, I took James to an art party hosted by Khalid Kodi, a Nuba Sudanese artist, in his Jamaica Plain studio. After finding a parking space along a dead-end street, we entered a building with a heavy steel door and climbed a stairway to the second floor, where we walked along a long, narrow hallway cluttered with art supplies. The hallway ended at a room that spanned the width of the building. Tall windows on both sides provided ample light.

There was a large movie screen in the room. In front of it were a couple of long wooden objects. There were a few rows of chairs for an audience to sit. James joined the other Sudanese boys who had arrived before us. I found a seat next to another foster mother. After Mr. Kodi introduced himself, he explained that the long wooden tubes were didjeridus, traditional Australian aborigine wind instruments. Australian musicians played them for us. We were then invited to participate in a variety of art and music projects. James chose to write a song with his friends; I chose to do some painting.

After I completed my project, I chatted with the Lutheran minister from Arlington while his children completed their projects.

"How long have you been a member at Immanuel?" he asked.

"I joined in August."

"Where were you before you joined?"

"I was raised Catholic, and then was a Unitarian Universalist for fifteen years."

"Why did you leave?"

"There was a nasty church conflict."

"Have you gone to synod assembly?"

"No. I don't want to get involved with church politics."

"Synod politics are healthy. It would be good for you to experience that."

Before I could reply, we were called to join the main group in front of the movie screen. Professor Ambrose Beny, a Southern Sudanese American, had arrived to speak about his transition to America. He took a seat in front of the screen, and the boys gathered around him. He urged the boys, "Don't worry about your family and friends in the Sudan. You can't help them now. After you get an education and become American citizens, then you will be able to help them."

I looked across the room to where James was sitting. He was talking to his friends. He didn't appear to be listening.

"Listen to your foster parents. They will help you. Don't be afraid to be alone. It is a different kind of journey."

Turning to the girls, Professor Beny said, "Speak up for yourselves. You don't have to obey the men. You can have a life of your own."

"Grandfather," one of the boys asked respectfully. "Don't you want cows for your daughters?"

"The love I receive from my daughters is more valuable than cows," Professor Beny replied. "Why would you want a wife you have bought with cows instead of one that loves you?"

The next day Melissa, James and I attended a Cambodian dance performance held in the sanctuary of Murray Unitarian Universalist Church, the church where I had been shunned when I asked for dialogue and openness about selecting a minister who was gay. There was a reception in the fellowship hall afterward. I felt uneasy as I entered the room and looked around. Gretchen wasn't there. A couple of people greeted me and asked after my family and me. The chair of the music committee approached me and told me, "We're going to have a special women's choir at next Sunday's service. You would really enjoy it."

I shifted from one foot to another. She hadn't asked me what I had been doing. She was so busy trying to entice me to come back to Murray, she never thought to find out if I was a member of a church anywhere else. It had been almost seven years since I left Murray. So much had happened. Her efforts were too little, too late.

The following Sunday, I helped the confirmation class complete some crafts. As we were leaving, I told James we had an errand to run.

"I don't want to go, Mom. I want to go home and watch the basketball game." He aspired to be a professional basketball player.

"I have a surprise for you. You must come with me. Trust me."

"No, I don't want to go."

"You'll see."

He walked slowly toward the car. I drove him over to a church member's house. "Come on, James," I said as I opened the car door. He followed me up the driveway, where the owner of the house greeted us. He pointed to bicycles that were parked along the wall. "Which one of these do you want?" I asked James.

Delighted and happy, he thanked me repeatedly on our way home.

"I am on your side, James. You need to trust me more."

On Maundy Thursday, I was hurrying home from my Stoughton office. I needed to get to Immanuel early. The chimes choir was playing in the service that night. Traffic was backed up on Interstate 95, so I decided to cut through Foxboro and not get on the highway. This brought me past FXUU. Their wayside pulpit announced an Easter renewal service. Were they moving back toward Christianity now that I was gone? A tear rolled down my cheek.

The next day I attended the Council of Churches' Good Friday service at the Methodist church, which was located at the top of the hill overlooking Route 1. The Methodist minister, a large towering figure, walked down the center aisle while he delivered his homily in a thundering style. I shifted in my pew, away from the aisle. I felt unsafe near him. Beverly, who was with me, noticed and commented on my discomfort.

"I find him intrusive," I told her.

After the service, while showing me her new car, she whispered, "I wonder if this is the sin I should focus on tonight."

"What are you talking about?" I asked.

She explained to me how at the end of the Good Friday evening service, everyone writes on a piece a paper what sin they want to overcome.

"Why shouldn't you enjoy your new car?" I asked.

"You don't think it's too materialistic?"

"No."

"You know Rev. Karen looks at what we write," she said. "She often figures out from the handwriting who wrote what."

"That isn't right." I opened the door to my car. "I will see you tonight."

James and I attended the evening service at Immanuel together. As we entered the sanctuary, we were given a piece of paper to write what sin we were concerned about. Mindful of what Beverly told me, I debated what to write. I considered leaving the paper blank. Finally, I wrote "anger," even though I didn't consider any emotion including anger sinful. But it was general enough, and I couldn't think what else to write.

At the end of the service, the wooden cross was carried down the center aisle. James and I stepped out of our pew and slowly followed the other worshipers out of the church. When I walked through the sanctuary's doors, I saw the wooden cross resting against one of the posts that supported the covered walkway. I waited while the person before me nailed his paper to the cross. He then handed the small hammer to me. After I nailed my paper, I turned to hand the hammer to James, but he wasn't there. Confused, I gave the hammer to someone else and walked down the sidewalk toward my car, thinking that somehow James had gotten ahead of me.

As I approached my car, I saw my friends from chimes choir and Bible study standing under the streetlight talking. "Have you seen James?" I called to them.

"He's behind you," Ivonne said.

I glanced over my shoulder and saw him walking down the sidewalk. "James is always disappearing and reappearing," I said, and laughed, feeling foolish.

My friends neither laughed nor smiled, but moved off as if they were going to their cars. Then they stopped to talk among themselves. I was left standing alone. Matt, another member of chimes choir, joined the group. I felt like I was being shunned, rejected, and abandoned under that streetlight. Was it my imagination? It felt surreal. It was like I had been there before. Just like high school, Murray and FXUU.

Feeling tears rising, I got into my car and picked James up at the end of the sidewalk. As I drove by, my friends were still talking among themselves.

I pulled out of the church's driveway and drove home. James went to bed. I found Melissa sitting at the computer desk in Orion's room. "How was the service?" she asked.

"It was moving. Matt sang 'O Sacred Head.'" My lips quivered.

"Mom, what's wrong?"

I sank down to the floor and rested my back against the wall. I told her what had happened in the parking lot. "I felt ostracized. It's like losing FXUU all over again." I began weeping.

Melissa tried to reassure me. We talked for an hour. The phone rang. I got up and walked down the hall to the master bedroom to pick it up. It was Ruth. How odd, I thought. She had never initiated a call to me before.

"Hi, Maggie," she said. "I just wanted you to know why I didn't wait to speak to you after the service."

"I didn't even know you were at the service," I replied.

"I arrived late and sat in the back. I had locked myself out of my car. And my cell phone was locked inside, too."

"Oh, no!"

"I barely made it to the service. I hadn't eaten, so I rushed home. I didn't want you to think I was avoiding you."

Did she know what had happened with the others? "I didn't think that," I said. "I didn't even see you."

There was an uneasy silence. Then I said, "I'm feeling hurt and rejected. I don't believe Ivonne and the others like me." I suspected Ivonne took a dislike to me shortly after I returned from my niece's wedding. Ivonne was concerned and worried about her daughter. I was distressed over my brother-in-law's behavior. She took offense at something I said and withdrew. She stopped returning my phone calls.

"Of course they like you," Ruth reassured me.

"Then why didn't they include me when they went out after chimes practice two weeks ago?" I asked.

A few weeks back, while we were putting the chimes into their boxes, a member of the chimes choir asked another member, "Where are we meeting for dinner?"

"Morin's," came the reply.

I shifted uneasily from my left foot to my right. I hadn't been told of any plans for the choir to go out. Was I invited? The group continued to discuss their plans, but said nothing to me. Should I ask? I hadn't walked with my wallet. I looked at Ruth. She didn't say anything. I walked home alone while the others climbed into their cars to go out to dinner together.

"That was my fault," Ruth said, assuming blame for the others. "I forgot to tell you about it. You will always have my friendship and a place at Immanuel."

Although Ruth's call cheered me up, I remained uncertain about Ivonne's feelings. I tried not to be overly concerned. There were plenty of people at church who liked me.

On April 17, the schools were closed for Patriot's Day, which commemorates the start of the Revolutionary War. Ruth and I took James to Concord and walked the Battle Road together. The weather was overcast and a bit raw. There weren't many other tourists. In the evening James was quite chatty, with an overabundance of questions. "Where was Joseph when Jesus was crucified? Who wrote the Bible? How do they make so many books?" he asked, awed by American technology.

The following weekend, he wanted to go to a Sudanese party an hour away from our house.

"Sunday I was going to prepare the garden for spring," I said with a sigh. In truth, I also needed a break from the Sudanese events.

Saturday, while we were at Orion's track meet in Connecticut, James tried to persuade me to take him to the Sudanese party. "I think we will skip this event," I said. "We have gone to all the others. I need some rest."

"I want to go," he said.

"It's an hour away from home. I'm tired."

"But I am needed."

"I need your help getting the vegetable garden ready for spring planting. We will go next time."

As soon as we arrived home from the track meet, I began preparing veal cutlets for dinner. James called his caseworker, Tere, to tell him of our decision not to go to the Sudanese party. Tere asked to speak to me.

"I can't speak to you right now," I told Tere as I put a breaded cutlet into the frying pan. "I'm cooking."

Tere kept talking. "We have prepared something special for the party and we need James."

"I need to get some rest, and I need James to help me in the garden."

"But we need James," Tere pleaded.

"Look, I can't talk right now. I'm trying to get dinner on the table—"

Tere continued speaking.

"Tere, I am going to hang up." Annoyed, I put the phone back on the hook.

James also called Rev. Karen and Ruth in an attempt to pressure me into saying yes. I detested being pressured. His efforts moved me to a solid and immoveable "no."

At the dinner table, he continued to plead his case. "I need your help in my garden," I told him.

"That's just a stupid garden," he said.

Melissa glared at him. "That's Mom's garden! It's important to her. After all she does for you! The least you can do is to help her tomorrow."

"Listen," Lyndon said, "you need to be more respectful. You will help your mother in the garden tomorrow."

Sunday morning, Tere called at 8 a.m. "We need James. You should bring him."

"Why are you calling me so early? I already told you no." I hung up. Tere wasn't any better than James. He wasn't respecting my parental authority. I needed some rest. My life had been consumed with Sudanese activities. I just wanted a break. There were only a few weekends when I could start the garden. If I put the seeds in late, the plants wouldn't have enough time to grow. There would be no harvest before the fall frost.

I told James to turn the compost pile while I turned the soil in the planting beds. Angry that he couldn't go to the party, he pouted and worked slowly. I looked up from the planting bed. "That's not the way to get what you want."

# Theft

The week after refusing to take James to the Sudanese party, Orion and Melissa received invitations to their cousin Stephen's wedding. At first I assumed Lyndon's and my invitations were delayed in the mail and we would get them in a day or two. When that didn't happen I telephoned my sister Rita, Stephen's mother. She was out so I asked her partner, Eileen, if she knew what was going on.

"Roy and Pinky," Eileen said, "are very racist."

"Roy and Pinky?"

"Robert's in-laws." Robert was Rita's eldest son.

"What do they have to do with it?" I asked.

"The wedding is being held at their ranch."

"Oh, I didn't know that."

"Stephen spends a lot of time over there visiting his brother."

"How do you know they're racist?"

"They say things. Make jokes."

I vaguely remembered seeing a Confederate flag magnet on their refrigerator when I was there for Robert's, Stephen's older brother's, wedding. Were we being excluded because Lyndon and James were black? That didn't sound like my nephew. Had he compromised his principles to have the wedding at Roy and Pinky's ranch?

Rita called later that day and told me she had spoken to her son, Stephen. "They divided the chore of sending out the invitations among some friends. They all didn't go out at the same time. Mom didn't get hers either. You'll be receiving yours soon."

"So there is no problem with bringing James?"

"Of course not, Maggie. I raised my sons better than that."

The anxiety created by the confusion and fanned by Eileen's comments subsided. My own son, after hearing about the commotion, said, "It wouldn't be Stephen's wedding if it was well organized."

I laughed. I remembered how Stephen frustrated his mother when he was growing up. He frequently lost things. His room was in constant disarray. Orion was right. The problem with the invitations had nothing to do with race.

When I got off the phone, James approached me. "I'll stay here. Not go."

"Here? By yourself? I won't leave you home alone. Besides, it was all a misunderstanding. All of us are invited. You are part of the family. You're coming."

A few weeks later, my sister Rita and her partner came up for Melissa's college graduation. They brought Eileen's eighteen-month-old grandchild with them. To celebrate we took a ride down to Newport's Cliff Walk. James had never been there before.

Liberated from the confinement of winter, James played on the rocks as the waves splashed against them. With boyish delight, he raced ahead. When we rounded a corner and he was nowhere to be seen, I became concerned. I called to him. Then I heard him laughing. I looked up. He was sitting on a branch of an old gnarled tree bordering the walk. After I snapped a picture of him, he jumped down and joined us.

He stooped down to talk to and caress the baby. He then took a turn pushing the stroller. I walked beside him while Lyndon and the others walked ahead of us. James asked me about my sister's relationship with her partner. I took a deep breath. I wasn't sure how to explain it. "They are gay, James."

He grimaced. "Why, Mom?"

"I don't really know. People disagree about that," I replied. I wasn't sure how to explain homosexuality to him.

"In Sudan they killed. Not good."

"They make each other happy." I wanted to keep my explanations simple.

"I like them. They nice to me. It okay."

Relieved, I smiled. James was choosing to accept my sister just as she was.

On June 2, I took Lyndon, Melissa and James out to celebrate Lyndon's fifty-fifth birthday at the Memphis Barbecue. While waiting for a table, we sat on the porch in rocking chairs, enjoying the evening air. Melissa and James sat together on the steps, laughing and giggling as if they had always been brother and sister. I rested my head against the back of the chair while I rocked, marveling how on one day Melissa and James could have these intense arguments, while on others, they thoroughly enjoyed each other's company. Pleased that they were learning to like and care for each other, I was hopeful that James would always be a cherished member of our family.

Mid-June, on a Friday night, Lyndon, Melissa, James and I drove to Richmond. We spent the night at my niece Rebecca's house, twenty minutes away from the Baptist church where the wedding and reception were being held. My sister Rita was staying at a hotel with Eileen and Eileen's teenage son. On Saturday morning Rita called.

"Eileen's son is bored here alone at the hotel. Wouldn't James like to come over and swim in the hotel's pool?"

"That's a great idea. Hold on." I covered the mouthpiece of the phone and turned to James, who was eating his breakfast at the dining room table. "Would you like to go swimming at Aunt Rita's hotel?"

James' eyes lit up. "Yes."

I uncovered the mouthpiece. "Okay, Ree. He wants to go. When will you pick him up?"

"I'll come right now. It will take no more than twenty minutes. We'll take James to the wedding, so have him bring his dress clothes."

After James left, we spent the morning chatting with Rebecca and her husband. After lunch, we dressed for the wedding but were delayed when Rebecca, who was pregnant, had a bout of nausea. When we finally arrived at the white clapboard church, the bridal party were lining up in the vestibule. We rushed past them into the sanctuary, and were surprised to find James sitting alone in the back pew.

"Why are you sitting here?" I asked.

"They told me," James replied.

"I don't understand it. You should be up in the front with our family." What was going on? I knew we were late but why hadn't Rita kept James with her?

I looked around. What the hell were we doing in a white Southern Baptist church?

The music for the bridal procession started.

"Maggie," Lyndon said, "it would be better to stay here."

"What's going on?" I whispered loudly to Lyndon. "James and the rest of us should be seated in the front with Rita and her family."

"Shssh!" Lyndon replied. Annoyed, I joined my family in the back pew.

After the service, Lyndon and I gathered with my brothers in front of the church. "You missed the drama," my brother Rich said. "Eileen was upset she wasn't escorted by the ushers to the front with Rita."

"How did James end up in the back of the church?"

"Ree had her hands full. She was trying to calm Eileen down. She sent James to the back to wait for you."

"Oh." It hadn't been about James. It was about Eileen's position in the family.

Rich chuckled. "The family paranoia was in full swing."

At the wedding reception, I introduced James to the rest of my family. My mother, wanting to get to know her new grandchild, sat with him. As she did with her other grandchildren, she asked him questions about his interests and school. While I listened to their conversation, I was reminded of my maternal grandmother's emphasis on hospitality. "Where there is the breaking of bread, there are no enemies," my grandmother repeatedly told me.

Years before, while I was still an undergraduate student, I made the long ferry and subway trip to my grandmother's apartment in Queens. Sitting in her living room, I told her about Lyndon.

"Is he a good man?" she asked. Although she was an Italian immigrant, she had learned English working side by side with East European Jews in New York City's garment factories. She spoke with a Yiddish accent.

"Yes, Grandma."

"Is he Italian?" she asked.

I smiled. I knew where this was going. "No."

"That's nice," she replied. I knew she would prefer him to be Italian. After a brief pause she asked, "Is he Catholic?"

"He was raised Catholic." I didn't tell her he no longer went to church.

"Aah! That's nice."

"Grandma," I summoned up my courage. "He's black."

She moved back into her chair. "That's not right." Before I could reply, she thought better of it. "Is he from a good family?"

"Yes, Grandma." I didn't elaborate.

She paused again. "Does he make you happy? Does he treat you well?"

"Yes, Grandma."

"Then God must want it!" She rose out of her chair. I stood up with her. She embraced me. After Melissa was born, Grandma placed the photo of Lyndon, Melissa and me on her table with all the other family pictures. It was one of the first things visitors would see when they entered her home.

My mother and I were true to what Grandma had taught us about hospitality. "For you were a stranger in a strange land." That's what the Bible said. And Joseph, she would say, didn't he take in Jesus and raise him as his own? In my family, our love wasn't limited by bloodlines.

James spent the rest of the afternoon running around with the other teens behind the church. As the wedding reception ended, he approached me with his tie loose and his shirt only partially tucked in. "Mom, can I go back with Aunt Rita?"

"You really enjoy swimming, don't you?"

"Yes. Africa we swim." He moved his arms as if he was swimming.

I smiled. "I'm glad you're having such a good time. Of course you can go with Aunt Rita to the hotel."

Lyndon, Melissa and I returned to my niece's house. Late in the evening, Rita brought James over. While the adults talked, James took his belongings downstairs to the guest room, and then rejoined the family. After a brief visit, Rita and her family returned to their hotel.

The next morning while I was carrying my suitcase out to the car, I noticed James go downstairs to the family room where he had slept. I thought he must have forgotten something. As I walked back into the house, I saw Rebecca and him standing by the stairway. Rebecca had something in her hands.

"Thanks, James," she said.

"James, we have to go. Do you have everything?" I asked.

He walked toward me, and we both went outside. While he held back, Lyndon, Melissa and I kissed and hugged Rebecca and her husband before we took our seats in the car. As Lyndon drove north on Interstate 95, Melissa and James sat in the back, laughing and talking with each other like they had always been siblings. I rested my head against the back of the passenger seat and listened, closed my eyes and smiled. It was such a pleasure to see my children getting along with each other.

Ten hours later when we arrived home, I called Rita to let her know we had arrived safely. James lurked in the kitchen while I left a message on her answering machine. Hanging up the phone, I took my book and went into the living room. James followed and sat next to me.

"You believe in God?" he asked.

I put my book down. I looked at him suspiciously. Why was he bringing this up now? "Yes."

"Dad doesn't."

"I wouldn't say that. He just isn't sure." I wondered how James had correctly deduced that Lyndon and Melissa weren't believers. I was certain both of them had been careful not to undermine James' Christian education. Had he overheard some of my conversations with Lyndon?

"He doesn't go to church," James said.

"He gets bored. What do you believe?" I asked.

"Maybe there is no God."

I looked at him. What was he up to? Was he trying to get out of going to church?

The phone rang. I got up and walked backed into the kitchen to answer it.

"Hi, Maggie." It was Rita. "How was your drive home?"

"Not too bad. How was yours?"

"We left later than planned. We ended up going over to Rebecca's before leaving."

"Oh. Did you have a good visit?"

"Is Lyndon around? I want to speak to both of you."

"Lyn!" I called downstairs to his office. "Pick up! Rita's on the phone!"

"What's up?" I asked my sister.

"I debated whether I should tell you this or not," she said.

"Hi, Rita." Lyndon had picked up the extension on his desk.

"I was just telling Maggie I wasn't sure if I should tell you this or not. But I decided you should know."

"Know what?" I asked.

"While the boys were in the hotel's pool, I noticed my jewelry wasn't where I left it. I searched the room, including our entire luggage. As a last resort, I checked the plastic bag James had brought with him. The jewelry was in this bag with James' clothes on top. I thought maybe he picked it up by mistake."

The muscles in my back tightened. My stomach churned.

"This morning I couldn't find my camera."

"Oh."

"I called Rebecca and asked if she had seen it. James had given it to her just before you left."

"So he found it?"

"No. I think he took it."

"Are you sure?" My breathing increased. My speech became pressured. "Maybe you left it at her house when you dropped off James last night."

"We didn't use the camera after the wedding. We left it at the hotel when we drove James back to Rebecca's."

"No, that can't be!" My heart sunk. Just like someone who had just been told someone they loved had died, I denied it because I didn't want to believe it.

"I'm sorry to have to tell you this, Maggie."

"Thanks, Rita," Lyndon said. "I'm sorry James took it."

We hung up the phone. I went downstairs to Lyndon's office immediately. "You can't believe he took it?"

"James!" Lyndon called up the stairs.

James, who had been lurking while we were on the phone, came into Lyndon's office, and Lyndon said, "Sit down."

James took a seat on the green leather sectional closest to the door by the stairway. I sat on the opposite end. Lyndon sat in his gray desk chair. Lyndon, who had been trained by the army to investigate crimes, began questioning James. "Did you take Aunt Rita's camera?"

"No."

"How did you get it?"

"I found it in my bag. I gave to Rebecca."

"How did it get into your bag?"

"Maybe he picked it up by accident?" I interrupted.

"No. I didn't pick up."

"Then how did you get it?" Lyndon kept his eyes on James.

"Maybe Eileen's son put it there," I interrupted again.

"Maggie! Let me handle this!"

"I found it," James said. "I gave to Rebecca."

James continued to deny he took the camera. We sent him to bed.

"Why would he take it, Lyndon? He has his own camera."

"I don't know. But he is lying," Lyndon said.

"I don't believe it."

Lyndon and I quarreled. We went to bed angry with each other. The next morning while Lyndon got ready for work, I laid in bed thinking about it. How *did* the camera end up in James' possession? Either James or someone else put it there. Cameras don't walk by themselves. I could come up with no plausible explanation of how the camera "accidentally" came into his possession. I was puzzled about James' motives. We had given James his own camera when he went on the ski trip. He had had some difficulty using it, and often insisted it was broken when it wasn't. Ruth, contrary to our wishes, often loaned him her camera, so James never learned how to use his with confidence and ease. He didn't need Rita's camera. He just needed to learn to use his. Perhaps he took it out of habit. While living in the bush without adult protection, the boys scavenged whatever they could to meet their needs.

As Lyndon was leaving the bedroom, he leaned over and kissed me. "Maggie, think about it. Who else could have put the camera in James' bag?"

I got up, showered and dressed. By the time I went downstairs Lyndon had left for work. James and Melissa left for school. I called my sister. "Tell me again what happened, Rita. Start from the beginning."

"After we got back to the hotel the boys went swimming in the hotel pool. When they got too rambunctious Eileen scolded them. I might have let some of it go. But Eileen didn't. When the boys mouthed off to her, Eileen ordered them out of the pool. They whined and complained all the way up the elevator."

"How do you know it was James that took the camera and not Eileen's boy?"

"As we were leaving the hotel James said he had forgotten his bag. We were in the lobby. I gave him the room key. We waited while James went up to the room to get his things. He was the only one who was alone in the room."

"Are you sure?"

"Yes. In the morning when I couldn't find my camera, Eileen and I searched the room. Because I had found my jewelry in James' bag, I called Rebecca. But you had already left. When I told her about the camera, Rebecca said James had found it in their downstairs guestroom. Since he was the only person to go downstairs, he had to have taken it."

"Thanks, Rita. I'm sorry I didn't believe you last night."

"It's hard. I understand. No parent wants to believe their child has stolen."

"I know you have lots of experience working with foster kids."

"I debated whether I should tell you or not. But I thought you needed to know so you could do something about it."

"Thanks. We can't allow this. What if he had stolen from another guest at the hotel and the police picked him up? A black boy in the South. Poor English. Think about what could happen. We'll ground him. He can't steal again."

I called Lyndon. We decided to restrict James to his room for the week before he was to go to Confirmation Camp, a Lutheran-sponsored youth retreat. I called Ruth and told her James was on restriction for stealing my sister's camera. On Tuesday while I was at work, Ruth came over to tutor James as usual. James called me after she had left. "Mom, Ruth said I go to school dance Thursday."

"What? You're on restriction."

When I got home Melissa told me Ruth had taken James out for a drive. I called Ruth.

"I thought since it was a school event you would let him go."

"He's on restriction. He stole a camera."

"He says he didn't."

"He's lying."

Wednesday night while I was sitting at my desk paying bills, James came into my study and took a seat in my brown corduroy recliner. "Mom, I go dance?"

"You are on restriction." I continued writing checks.

"Mom, if I had taken the camera home that would have been a big mistake."

I put the pen down and turned toward him. "Yes, James, that would have been worse. Did you take Aunt Rita's camera?" I held my breath. If he told me the truth I could reward his honesty by allowing him to go to the dance.

James looked down at his feet. He appeared to be thinking.

"Well, James, did you take the camera?" I prodded.

James looked up. "No! I no steal!"

"You cannot go to the dance."

"Ruth said I could."

"It isn't Ruth's decision."

Late Thursday afternoon as I gathered up my briefcase, I hesitated in front of his room. *Maybe I should take his shoes and dress clothes. No, he will do as he's been told.* I picked up my car keys and left for work.

Thirty minutes later, after I had arrived at my office, Melissa called. "Mom, I told James he was grounded and he left anyway."

"Do you know where he went?"

"He headed up the hill toward the church."

I called Rev. Karen. James was with her and telling her he wanted to become a Lutheran. Should I tell her James was just buttering her up? Just three nights before, he told me he didn't believe in God. I held my tongue. She told me she would be sending him home. I relaxed. I was sure she was telling him to obey us, just as she had done after the ski trip.

When I arrived home from work around 9:30 p.m., James wasn't home and the school dance had ended. Lyndon was on the phone with Jeanne from Lutheran Social Services. He was telling her James could no longer stay with us.

"What's going on?" I said.

"Mom," Melissa said, entering the room, "James didn't come home for almost an hour. He went upstairs and changed into his good clothes."

"Just after I parked my car, he entered the garage from the house," Lyndon added as he put the phone down. "I asked him where he was going. He wanted me to drive him to the dance. I told him to get back into the house. He squared off. I wasn't going to fight him."

Lyndon shook his head. "When James moved toward the bicycle, I told him he wasn't taking it. I told him if he leaves, don't think he can come back."

*No!* I thought. *He's just a boy! You can't possibly mean that! You lost your temper. You didn't think. You should have talked to me first.*

"Where is he now?" I asked.

"I don't know." Lyndon was still angry.

Imagining James wandering around in the dark, afraid to come home, easy prey for thieves and pedophiles, I frantically called Ruth, Rev. Karen and James' teacher, looking for him. No one knew where he was. I tried to reassure myself. *James will come home. He survived the jungle. He will be okay.*

When he still wasn't home by 11 p.m., I called the police and explained the situation. Immediately after I hung up the phone, James called. He was at a party at a schoolmate's house. He would be walking home.

"No, I'll come get you. It's late. Where are you?"

"At house by school."

"Put your friend's mother on the line."

"Hello."

"Hi," I said, taking a deep breath. I didn't want to scream. "I'm James' mother. Did you know he was on restriction? We didn't know where he was."

"Oh, I'm sorry. I thought he had your permission. You must have been worried."

"Yes. Terrified." My heart was pounding. "Where do you live? I'm coming for him."

The woman gave me directions.

"Yes, I know where that is." I hung up and immediately drove over to her house. *How could James be so disobedient? Doesn't he realize what this could mean?* What was I going to do? How could I convince Lyndon to let James stay?

I was at the house in less than ten minutes. It was lighted up with the music blaring. James was outside running around, with his good clothes disheveled and saturated with sweat. When he saw me, he got into the car.

My heart was pounding. My breathing fast and shallow.

"Hi, Mom!" He didn't appear to be aware of what he had done.

"You fucking idiot!" I screamed. "You stupid, stupid boy! What the fuck do you think you are doing? You've blown everything!"

He didn't respond. *Oh, no!* I thought. *Now I've made it worse.* Did he understand what I just said? What was he going to tell Rev. Karen and the others? Would they understand?

As we pulled into the garage I said, "Look, James, I'm sorry I swore at you. Go to bed and we'll sort this out tomorrow."

I found Lyndon in the study. "You should have talked to me before talking to Jeanne."

He looked directly at me. He thought for a moment. "Yes. You're right. I'm sorry."

"I'm exhausted. I'm going to bed."

The next morning I spoke to James. "You need to tell your father you're sorry. You need to make this right. If you tell him you're sorry, he'll let you stay. I know him."

After James left for school, I called Ruth and told her where he had gone the previous night. "Tempers are running high," I told Ruth. "Can you pick James up after school and keep him for the night so I can work things out with Lyndon? And please urge him to apologize for his behavior. Lyndon will never allow him to continue to live with us if he doesn't show some remorse. He needs to demonstrate some respect for our authority."

In the late afternoon when I was sure James had gotten home from school, I called him from my office. At first I got a busy signal. I tried again, and he picked up. "Ruth will be picking you up," I said.

"Ruth isn't home, Mom."

"How do you know that?"

"I called her. She didn't answer."

"You shouldn't be making calls. You're on restriction. Never mind, Ruth will be there shortly."

I spoke to Jeanne from my office that evening. James was making wild accusations, claiming grounding him was abusive. We agreed that he would spend the night at Ruth's. I called Ruth. She informed me she and James were having a great day. She had taken him out to the store and bought him things. She was cooking him a special meal.

Ruth wasn't getting it. We were going to lose James if we didn't get him to apologize to Lyndon. No way was my husband going to allow a teen, one we had no parental control over, to remain in the house. Ruth, on the other hand, wasn't going to risk losing James' affection by admonishing him. Months before, concerned by James' growing sense of entitlement, Lyndon and I had asked people not to buy him gifts except on his birthday and Christmas. Ruth never fully respected our wishes. She allowed James to use her camera when we told her we wanted him to use his. She bought him small gifts such as pencils even though we had asked her not to give him anything. Now, when it was critical to do so, Ruth was totally disregarding our parental authority. Didn't she understand how much I loved James? I would risk everything for him to grow up into a man we could all be proud of.

"What are you doing?" I asked Ruth. "You're rewarding James for bad behavior! He needs to apologize for what he's done."

I had made a mistake. I should never have allowed James to go to Ruth's. "Please let me speak to James."

"Hi, Mom."

"James, I'll be picking you up later tonight after work."

"I stay here."

"No, James, I'm coming for you."

"You obey me and then I come home."

"No, James, you need to obey both your father and me. You must apologize to your father and accept your punishment if you are to continue to live with us."

"No, you obey me."

"This isn't the Sudan," I replied.

"I came to America to have fun."

"No, you came to get an education."

"Jeanne said I could stay at Ruth's."

I called Jeanne again. She apologized for inadvertently undercutting Lyndon's and my authority. I considered calling the police to remove James from Ruth's. What if he resisted? In my mind's eye, I saw the police dragging James out of Ruth's house, Ruth and I both crying. No, I would have to deal with this in the morning. I reluctantly agreed to let him stay the night.

The next morning was Saturday. While Lyndon and I sat in the kitchen eating breakfast, I pleaded with him to allow James to remain in our home. "But I love him," I said. "Don't do this."

"It's not safe, Maggie. Melissa is stronger than he is, but you're not. We don't know what he'll do."

I remembered James' hostile glare the day he refused to go to school. He also had threatened to beat Melissa. Thursday night he squared off, expecting to fight Lyndon, who was a hundred pounds heavier. I knew what Lyndon was talking about. My heart tried to deny it. But James had shown no signs of remorse, and he didn't appear to have formed any emotional bonds with any member of our family. He favored Ruth because she gave him what he wanted. James didn't love me as I loved him. He understood power, not love.

I looked directly at Lyndon, preparing to argue that I was willing to take the risk. Then I saw his pain. In a moment of clarity and anguish, I realized I was placing Lyndon in an untenable position. He was torn between what he saw as his duty to protect me from physical harm and not wanting to break my heart. No matter how much I pleaded, he would never agree to something that put me at risk. Out of love for my husband and my children including James, I gave up my desperate struggle to keep him in our home. Heartbroken, I wept.

I went into my study and called Jeanne. I told her we could no longer provide James with a home. He would stay at Ruth's until Sunday. Then he would spend the week at Confirmation Camp as previously planned. That would give her a full week to find another placement for him.

"Do you have adequate support?" Jeanne asked.

"Yes."

"You seem to have a good relationship with your pastor."

"Yes, I do," I replied.

Jeanne then assured me James would not be placed in Attleboro, and wouldn't be allowed to disrupt our lives any further.

I called Ruth and told her James could stay at her house until Sunday. This would give her time to say goodbye to him. I would pack what he needed for Confirmation Camp. He could pick it up later. Ruth agreed.

Shortly after I got off the phone, Beverly called and told me she and her husband were going over to Ruth's. Jason, the youth director and his wife, Jessica, were already over there. They were all giving him gifts. Beverly was going to give James her father's watch.

"What?" I shouted. "He steals a camera and you give him gifts!"

Certain that Rev. Karen would understand and support me; I took the shortcut across our property, up over the hill and through the woods to Immanuel. I found Rev. Karen in her office getting ready to leave. Before sitting down with me she made a phone call to explain her delay to whoever was waiting for her. Turning to me, she said Lyndon and I were "too strict."

*What? Two weeks' restriction for stealing a camera is too strict? I should protest. Ask her what she means by that.*

But I didn't. The beating of my heart became so loud, I couldn't hear myself think. My head spun. She was out there, and I was in here.

"I'll have to find James a home with someone else in the church," she said.

My heart rate increased. I concealed my panic. I couldn't have him near us. It would further disrupt our lives. That wouldn't be fair. It would be too painful to see him every week. I could never bear it. Whose side was she on any way? I was her parishioner, not James. And she had provided me with pastoral counseling. Wasn't she supposed to be on my side?

"Jeanne told me he wouldn't be placed in our town," I said.

Rev. Karen scowled, but said nothing more about finding another home for James. Besides, it wasn't her responsibility. James wasn't the church's ward. Then suddenly, her voice softened. "I'll keep James away from you during tomorrow's service."

"Thank you." I could feel my shoulders drop and my muscles relax. *It's going to be okay*, I told myself. *She understands. I can trust her.* Later, I would learn that after I left her office, she joined Beverly and other church members at Ruth's. She hadn't understood at all.

When I returned home I received a call from Nancy, from Bible study. "Are you okay?" she asked. "If you couldn't manage James with all your education and training, no one else could." Referring to the other church members she said, "They need a scapegoat. It will blow over."

"I don't want to be anyone's scapegoat," I replied. I hung up the phone, thinking, *Maybe with Nancy's support it will all work out.*

While James was at Confirmation Camp, no one called. The loneliness was crushing. What was I supposed to do? James was only a boy. I had welcomed him into our family and into my heart. Was it right to turn him out? No one acknowledged, not even Lyndon, what a difficult choice I had to make. Giving up a son! How could I do that?

What to do? Too many people at church had gotten involved. Too many people with opinions based on what they wanted to believe, not the facts. What if I got them to back off? Maybe I didn't have to give James up. If I could get Rev. Karen and the others to acknowledge our parental authority and not interfere, I could convince Lyndon to give James another chance. Then everyone would win. We could turn it around. With renewed hope, I called Rev. Karen at camp and tried to explain it to her.

"I don't take calls from parishioners while at camp," she said.

I felt confused. Until LSS found another placement for James, he was still my responsibility. This was a crisis. Didn't I have a right to know how my son was doing at camp?

Later that week I received an inexplicable call from Laurie, the church secretary. She left a voicemail message saying Rev. Karen realized I was right about James having a severe attachment disorder.

What prompted that call? I wondered. And what did it mean?

I called Ruth.

"I called and spoke to Pastor," she told me.

"Oh." *Rev. Karen spoke to Ruth, but wasn't willing to speak to me?*

"If James is to live with us, I need you to stop interfering," I said.

"James didn't steal that camera!"

"How do you know that? Were you there?" I said. She was totally beguiled by James' charm, I realized. I was never going to get her and the others to stop interfering. For James' sake and for ours, he needed to go to another home, where he wouldn't be able to manipulate the adults. I wanted James to grow up to be a fine young man with integrity.

I called Jeanne, who assured me Tere would be picking James up when he returned from Confirmation Camp. "I'll leave his things at the church where he can get them."

I packed up James' belongings, the clothes we had bought him, his compact discs and his books. Lyndon and I left the bags in the portico to the church's rear door along with his bicycle. The next day, I telephoned Laurie and informed her where we had left James' things. She told me Ruth planned on keeping James for the weekend.

"Absolutely not! Tere will be picking James up. It is time for him to go to his new foster home."

While I drove past the church on the way to my office, I considered turning around. *Maybe I should stay to meet the bus and make sure James gets off all right. No, that would be too painful for everyone. Better to let Tere handle it.*

The next day I called LSS and confirmed that James had been picked up and Ruth hadn't been allowed to take him home for another visit. James had been taken to a home in Boston. I had met the foster father at one of the events sponsored by LSS. He was a single man, an English teacher I thought. He had three other Sudanese boys living with him. There were no women or girls in the house. Maybe that would be better for James.

A few days later, on July 2, I telephoned Dr. Emmett and told him everything that happened with James. He supported my decision to terminate James' placement with us, but urged me not to leave the church. While he understood my desire to run away, it was his opinion I would be throwing "the proverbial baby out with the bathwater."

Encouraged by Dr. Emmett, I resolved to salvage my place at Immanuel. I believed the way to do that was through honest dialogue. The next day, sitting at my computer, I typed the following letter.

Dear Rev. Karen,

I am hurt and disappointed by several things you have said and done. During the recent crisis with James you aligned yourself with him, undermining my attempts to save his placement with my family. If Lyndon and I couldn't keep him, what did you think was going to happen to him? If we didn't address his stealing and he stole outside the family and was caught and arrested, what do you think the INS was going to do with him?

White Americans didn't think of these things. They figured that so long as they are law-abiding, the police are on their side. They didn't fear their children would be beaten and mistreated. I continued typing.

> When I last talked with you in your office, you didn't understand my anger and you said when I began to cry that that made more sense. But both the anger and the grief made equal sense. I will not have you negate and ignore the anger.

There was the anger thing again. Just like Rev. Patience at FXUU, Rev. Karen wanted to focus on the hurt and deny the anger. I wanted to be allowed to feel both.

As I typed, things became clearer and I felt empowered.

> James rejected all that my family offered him and betrayed us by stealing from my sister who had warmly welcomed him into the family, and by then lying about it afterwards and by lying about how he was treated. Of course I was and am angry. I am also filled with grief and sadness. I lost my son. It is as if he died. Sending him away was one of the most difficult things I have ever had to do in my life. Whether you like it or not, I need to talk about it. It is unfair of you to try to silence my pain.

I stopped typing and reached for a tissue. After blowing my nose I continued.

> While James was at camp, it is my understanding you allowed him to call Ruth on your cell phone. So when you told me you didn't want to be in the middle of a triangle, you already put yourself there. You could put yourself in the role of mediator, but instead you have chosen to align yourself with James and Ruth. This is not in the best interest of any of us.

Just like the Unitarian Universalist clergy, Rev. Karen said she didn't want to become triangulated. She was using family systems theory as an excuse not to talk to me. Although when I was a student I had watched Salvador Minuchin, a well-known family systems therapist, demonstrate his approach to family therapy, I had never thoroughly studied it. I felt confused. I didn't think Rev. Karen understood it right. But I didn't understand it well enough myself to refute her.

I stretched and rubbed my back, then kept typing.

> I suspect from my telephone conversations with you that you harbor a bias against me. I believe your statement that you didn't want this to continue for six months to be an innuendo about the FXUU conflict and my struggle to recover from post-traumatic stress disorder. I also believe your knowledge about my childhood history also unfairly colors your judgments about me. I am an excellent parent. I was an excellent parent to James, and so was my husband. I have a reputation within my field of being tough but fair.

Which clinician had said that to me? Was it when I was the clinical director at the Aftercare Clinic, or was it when I was the director of the psychology department at the state school?

> My psychiatric problems in no way impaired my ability to parent. In some ways it has made me a better parent. You shouldn't decide who to align yourself with on your notions of who is psychologically healthy, because they are flawed and incorrect. We all have our psychological strengths and vulnerabilities. That includes Ruth and Beverly and yourself.

The stigma of mental illness: People commonly lumped all emotional and psychological problems together, seeing therapy clients as more disordered then they really were. One of the benefits of my psychiatric hospitalization was that I knew I wasn't any different from anyone else. We all were vulnerable.

> Finally, James lived in my home. My family knows him better than anyone else in the church. Because of our professions, we also are in a better position to recognize any psychiatric disturbance. I am sorry it angered you, but James has a serious attachment disorder. James' charm is a symptom of that. Don't let your attachment to him blind you to his problems. It will not help him. James is only able to maintain superficial relationships. He feels entitled, and is easily angered when thwarted. He tells cover-up lies. He lacked remorse over his misbehavior. He was unconcerned

about the pain he caused Ruth and my family. As he told me, he came to America to have fun. I stood in the way of his fun. He also belligerently told me I needed to obey him. He threatened to beat Melissa. He challenged Lyndon to a fight. James is not the innocent angel you think he is. Don't presume you know everything that went on.

Despite what I suspected and knew about James, I loved him. His rejection of all that my family had to offer him broke my heart. I grieve the loss of my son and I am angry with you, Ruth and other members of the church who intruded and tried to rescue him from us. Your response to me has made things more painful. Accepting James into my family was a risky endeavor and it failed. James failed. Let's hope he will do better in his next placement.

Finishing the letter, I wept. Would anyone at Immanuel ever understand my grief? I printed the letter and signed it. I put it in the mailbox hopeful that Rev. Karen would listen and we would work out our differences. She should have it by Thursday, July 5.

On Independence Day, I sat in my recliner with my journal in my lap. I picked up my pen to record the events of the last few days. I lost track of what I was writing and in what section I was in. I had a fantasy that James would be waiting for me at the church to speak with me. He would tell me how sorry he was and ask if he could come home. I put down my pen and began weeping. There would be no fixing this.

Dr. Emmett had been pleased that I wasn't anxious and hadn't been thinking of harming myself. But the night after our phone call I couldn't sleep. Thoughts of self-harm resurfaced. While lying in bed, I kept ruminating. I wanted to go back to the time where I could space out, where I could go back to the white space where it was soft and safe. No one bothered me there. There were no sounds. Nothing to see. No pain. Numb. There was a whole different set of rules there. All reason was turned upside down.

In the white space, I could let all the pain out by cutting or burning myself. I could cut my wrists and watch the blood run out. Be cleansed and live. But Dr. Emmett, Rev. Karen and Lyndon were standing in the way. I couldn't get past them. I couldn't will myself there. I lost the way. It was harder this way. No running away. No curling up in a corner with matches or knife. Injuring myself was more personal than sex. It was like having an orgasm, a tremendous release. But I was also dimly aware it was like the Sirens of Greek mythology, whose irresistible charm would lure mariners to their deaths on the rocks. If I kept returning to the white space, I would lose my life.

Besides, Dr. Emmett and my family would never let it go that far. They would hospitalize me before they allowed me to go through that door. I would rather die than be hospitalized again. But I wasn't even close to that. I wasn't going to space out. I was determined to live my life until its natural end, until God finally took me and let me be at peace.

I didn't really want to self-harm. I just wanted happiness, strength and acceptance. I never wanted to be beaten down again by the backbiting and jealousy of others. I wanted to be able to walk into that church. Sit where I wanted. Participate to the degree that I wanted. Not worry about making friends or being popular. Be my own person. I wanted to be proud and free and just and generous and forgiving. I would walk through those church doors on Sunday and God would be with me.

# Drowning in Grief

**W**hen Rev. Karen didn't reply to my letter, I became fearful I was being rejected and abandoned. I feared she wouldn't talk to me, just like everyone at FXUU. Just like Rev. Dorothy.

I telephoned Rev. Karen on Friday.

"I've been away," she said. "I have been having some personal problems."

"I'm sorry to hear that. Is everything okay?"

"Yes. I haven't had the chance to read your letter yet. Is it okay if I read it next week?"

"I'm fine with that." I just needed to know she would talk to me about it.

"Will we be seeing you at church on Sunday?"

That was one of the most healing things she could have asked me. "I'm taking it day by day. I'll decide on Sunday morning."

The thought of walking through the church doors on Sunday was terrifying. What was everyone thinking of me? What would they say? Would they welcome me?

What about my feelings? The problem was Ruth. I couldn't set aside my anger toward her so easily. She seriously disrespected me and my family. It was clear to me she didn't trust me or respect who I was. I was an obstacle in her way. She wanted to be the parent. I had been in competition with her for my son. Trying to talk to her about it had made things worse. So I needed to keep my distance.

I didn't want to sit with her anymore. During the services, she frequently talked. When the choir sang Vivaldi, she treated it like elevator music and chattered. When Anna, who was sitting behind us, joked, "We'll have to separate all of you," instead of apologizing, Ruth became indignant. She continued talking.

Ruth did what she wanted to do. It made her happy to have James over, but she didn't care what message she was sending him. It made me so angry. I loved James. I wanted him to grow up into a man we could all be proud of. That foolish little woman with her head in the sand! How much did she really care about him? Ruth wasn't willing to make him angry with her for his sake. She bought his affection. *It won't last long. Soon she will no longer hear from him.*

On Sunday, despite my fear, I walked to church and took a seat on the other side of the sanctuary, away from Ruth. She glared at me. During coffee hour, members of the Bible study gathered around her and didn't speak to me. Standing alone in the fellowship room, I watched church members socialize with each other. No one approached me. I was being excluded. I choked back the tears.

The shunning made it clear. They were blaming me for James' departure from my home. People who did less condemned me for not having done more. I knew that out of my hearing they were demonizing, blaming and judging me. They thought I had more power than I had. They refused to see that James had some responsibility for what happened. He stole. He defied his father and me. He refused to make amends. I was being held accountable for things that were beyond my control. I felt shamed all over again.

I tried everything to help James, to find a way he could stay in my home. But I had to consider the welfare of my entire family, and whether I could reasonably expect his behavior to improve. I did my best to influence him to make better choices. All the love and caring in my heart wasn't enough. In the end, it was James who chose not to obey our rules and to move out of our home. I had no power to stop him.

When I got home I called my sister. "You're responsible, Maggie, for the effort, not the outcome," she said.

"They're blaming me for the outcome." I feared there was only a place for me at Immanuel if I succeeded, or if I subjugated myself to their will.

Reassured I had done nothing wrong, I decided to go to Bible study and potluck dinner on Monday night, even though it was being held at Ruth's. When I arrived, the side door was open and someone called to me to come on in. As I entered Ruth's kitchen, people were talking while they loaded their plates with food. I had barely put my covered dish down when Ruth, who had spotted me from across the kitchen, reached me. She gave me a hug and said, "I'm glad you came. It took courage for you to come."

Was that sincere, or just for show? What had changed from the day before when she glared at me? Had Rev. Karen spoken to her? "Thank you," I mumbled.

With renewed hope, I engaged in light conversation with the other members while I ate my dinner. After everyone had finished eating, we went into Ruth's small living room. I took a seat across from the bay window that looked out onto the front lawn. As I was sitting down, Rev. Karen and Ruth were chatting about how when they had phoned each other, they discovered they were on the same exact page of the book the group was reading. It was clear Ruth and Rev. Karen had been talking to each other more frequently than either had been talking to me.

For the summer we were reading James A. Michener's *The Source.* During the discussion, one of the men disparaged a point I made. Everyone except me laughed. *They dislike me,* I thought. *They don't really accept me. They're just tolerating me. They aren't taking me seriously. My emotions overwhelm them. I don't really have a place here.* I was being kept on the periphery. I pulled my face tight and suppressed my tears.

On Tuesday evening, during a break between clients, I called Rev. Karen from my office to speak to her about my letter. She made some excuse for not calling me.

"People are coming to my office about you," she scolded.

"Who?" I asked.

"It doesn't matter who," she said.

"I don't know what you're talking about. Who has come to you?"

"Laurie after Sunday's service. You were insensitive to her."

"How?" I said. "On my way out, I told her I was sorry to hear she had breast cancer."

"That's not all you said," Rev. Karen replied. "You got angry with her when she urged you to get a mammogram."

"Laurie started insisting I get a mammogram. I told her that was an issue I didn't want to discuss with her. It was between me and my doctor. I wasn't angry."

"You should have been more sensitive to her," Rev. Karen replied.

"I don't know what you expect from me."

"I'm not your friend," she said.

I pressed the phone to my ear. I wasn't looking for her to be my friend. I just wanted her to be my pastor. "I know," I replied as I hung up the phone.

The next morning I called Dr. Emmett. We discussed Rev. Karen's response to my letter. I also tried to explain how I missed spacing out. Dr. Emmett was empathetic. I told him I wished he would release me from my promise.

"What would that get you?" he asked. "How do you feel after you harm yourself?"

"Better."

"That's immediately after. How do you feel an hour later?"

"Ashamed," I whispered. I knew he would never remove the constraint imposed by the promise.

When I arrived home later that same day, I listened to a message left by a worker from Lutheran Social Services. What did she want? Maybe James was now sorry and willing to admit to what he had done. Then we could forgive him, and he could come home. But all she probably wanted was for us to take another child. Lyndon wouldn't even discuss it. He wanted an empty nest, time to ourselves, less stress and more fun. He didn't want me hurt and crying again. He worried about my mental health. I didn't think there would be any way I could convince him.

A few days later on July 16, LSS called again just as I was entering the kitchen. It was a woman who said she knew Lyndon from Long Island. She was now working for Lutheran Social Services here in Massachusetts. She asked me to take another child. I wanted to do it. I wanted another child. I wanted a chance to prove we were good parents. But it was hopeless. I knew Lyndon would never consent. When I got off the phone, I went into my study and wept.

Regaining my composure, I listened to the phone messages. One was from Beverly! Someone from church was calling me! I hadn't been forgotten. I listened further. She was looking for her Bible atlas she had loaned James. My stomach tightened and I felt a little nauseous. She wasn't calling to see how I was. She just wanted something from me. No one from the church called. None of them could be counted on as friends.

Later that night I looked for the Bible atlas. I found it sitting on the corner table in the living room. I telephoned Beverly from my study. "I have the atlas. Didn't you give this to James?"

"No, I just loaned it to him. That's an expensive book."

I sighed. "James doesn't understand the difference between a gift and a loan."

"I don't want to hear what James did wrong. I'm willing to be supportive, but I don't want to talk about James."

"There's no way you can be supportive without talking about him." My voice quivered as I choked back tears.

"Members of the church believe you threw James out and forced him on Ruth."

"James could no longer return home because of his open defiance and the potential risk that he would be violent toward me," I told her. "James refused to come home and Ruth wanted him there."

"I was told it was all over by the time I returned home from our cruise," Beverly said. "That's why I didn't call you."

All over? James was gone but I was still here. Didn't she consider how I might be feeling? Beverly must have been told by Ruth and the others that I had been coldhearted and unforgiving and didn't need or merit support. It was easier to believe rumors that confirmed her bias than call me.

After hanging up the phone, my stomach felt queasy. My muscles tightened and twitched. The pain was unbearable. I needed relief. There would be peace if I died. Peace for everyone. My life wouldn't be much to relinquish. It had been so wretched. Even when I tried to do my very best, I failed. It wasn't good enough. People who said they were friends rejected me. They chose James, a boy they knew for only a few months, over me, who they had known for a few years. Some sense of Christian duty was probably the only reason they tolerated me. I wasn't really accepted.

I covered my ears to muffle the Sirens' call. There must be a better way. Something I could do. *I know! I'll write Ruth a letter. If I get her to listen, Beverly and the others will follow. That's what I'll do! I need her to know how I feel. I'll write Rev. Karen, too. It's the only way I know how to fix this. Just keep communicating. Maybe someone will listen.*

The next two days I focused on my work and forgot about writing those letters. Saturday, July 21, Lyndon and I drove down to Cape Cod to attend a weeklong conference on couples therapy. We stayed in a studio apartment with a beautiful view of the salt marsh and Cape Cod Bay.

After we put our luggage in the apartment, we took a late afternoon walk along the beach. We ran into a neighbor who questioned who we were. We had inadvertently strayed onto her property when we followed what appeared to be a right-of-way. She mistook us for a family who lived down the street. When she realized her mistake, she chuckled and said she had made an assumption, since there were probably only three black families on the Cape.

When we returned to the apartment, we ordered pizza and spent the evening sitting on the balcony watching the sunset over the salt marsh. I wrote in my journal. I wondered how much my having a doctorate and being married to a black man had gotten in the way of forming friendships. It set me apart. Very few white or black families had ever invited us into their homes. It had mostly been other interracial couples. On top of that, many people are intimidated by well-educated women. When you narrowed it down to those who were comfortable socializing with a well-educated biracial couple, there was really a very small pool of possible friends.

I liked Beverly and Ruth. I enjoyed their company even though they only had a high school education. That never bothered me. I had grown up in a working-class family and community. I regarded Beverly and Ruth as my friends. But maybe they had found it difficult to be with me. Maybe the differences between us led them to misinterpret the things I said and did.

The following day, the temperature rose above ninety degrees. Despite growing up in the tropics, Lyndon had difficulty coping with the heat. When I mentioned James, he got angry. "You're always talking about him."

"I need to talk. I am grieving," I said.

"James isn't dead," Lyndon said, cutting me off. But I was never going to see James again. He would never be a part of my life. It was over. I had lost him.

I needed to talk about James. No one was willing to listen except Dr. Emmett. My husband, Rev. Karen and people at Immanuel responded to me with anger. I was shut off and in excruciating pain. I needed to release the pain. I thought about cutting but there was no way to do it. Lyndon was with me all the time. I thought about calling Dr. Emmett.

I needed to talk about James without worrying someone would get angry with me and abandon me. Rev. Karen and people at Immanuel had put blinders on and rushed to judgment. They were refusing to talk to me. I didn't know what to do. I was stuck. I was drowning. I couldn't even weep. There was no safe place or time to do that. I desperately needed to be held and rocked. I didn't know what to do. I didn't know how to fix things. I hurt so badly.

Lyndon and I spent a week on the Cape and returned home on Saturday afternoon. On Sunday, I went to church at Immanuel. Since greeting and socializing with my former "friends" was uncomfortable, I chose a seat several pews behind their usual seats and presumably out of their sight. However, they took seats farther back than usual. Jason and Jessica were sitting on the opposite end of the pew from me. Ruth,

Ivonne and Irene, a member of chimes choir, were sitting behind them.
During the service I began weeping. Jessica came over and put her arm
around me, triggering more tears.

"Would it be better if I move back to my seat?" she asked.

Unable to speak, I nodded yes. She respected my wishes and slid
back to her original seat. During the Peace, when everyone shakes hands
with the people near them, Ivonne, who hadn't been returning my phone
calls, insisted on hugging me. Confused, I acquiesced.

Later that day while I was reading, Lyndon came down from James'
bedroom where he was setting up the double bed. He had found a
letter written to James in December 2000 by his biological father, who
was supposed to be dead. I called Lutheran Social Services on Monday
and spoke with Jeanne.

"I thought the boys were orphans. I thought they had to be to come
to the US."

"People are willing to do almost anything to get out of the refugee
camp."

"James at times said his father was alive. I thought he was confused."

"Could you please send me the original letter?"

"Yes, of course." I thought it odd that she emphasized 'original.'
What did she think I was going to do? Send her a copy?

I called Dr. Emmett. We talked about the grief I was experiencing. I
missed spacing out. I wished he would release me from my promise.

"I will not," he said. "It is your choice to keep it or not."

"You know I won't break it. You tricked me."

"With time, you will resent it less."

*No I won't*, I thought. *I will always resent it whenever I'm anxious.*


On Tuesday, during the downtime in between appointments, I felt
anxious and depressed. The twelve years in Attleboro, Massachusetts had
turned into such a disaster. I would never be accepted here. Maybe it
would be good to move midway between Lyndon's job and my office.
That would cut down on Lyndon's travel time. We could move into a
smaller house, or maybe a condo with recreational facilities. I want to get
away from all the people who had betrayed me and abandoned me. I
wanted to escape to someplace where I wouldn't be ostracized.

At my request, Rev. Karen scheduled a time when we could meet
and talk. She sounded more upbeat than she had in the recent past. I
wasn't sure how much she really wanted to talk to me. I didn't know

what I really wanted to say to her. Should I share the latest information I had about James? How could I focus on the now and move forward in a positive way?

When we finally met in her office, Rev. Karen was angry. "Jessica said you rebuffed her on Sunday."

Rebuffed? Jessica felt rebuffed? I was grateful when Jessica asked if it would be better for me if she left me alone. I thought she understood my need for some space to regain my composure and dignity. Did Rev. Karen expect me to accept all offers of help whether they were good for me or not? Why was she putting their needs before mine?

"I'll call Jessica and straighten it out," I said.

"Good," Rev. Karen replied.

I got up to leave.

"You should return to Bible study," Rev. Karen said.

"I'll think about it."

Staying home was safer. I enjoyed coming home Monday nights and eating dinner with my husband and daughter. Until Melissa left for AmeriCorps, I wouldn't even consider going back to Bible study.

On Saturday, August 4, I telephoned Jessica to thank her for the concern she showed me during church.

"Would you like to get together and talk?" Jessica asked.

"Yes!" My hopes rose. I imagined sitting out on her deck, talking and working things out on a warm summer evening. "How about tonight?" I said.

"No. Jason and I are going out."

We tried to find a time during the week, but our schedules didn't match. She was working when I had time, and I was working when she had time.

"We'll have to wait until I get back from vacation," she said.

"Okay." I was disappointed, but excited that someone from church was finally going to sit down and talk to me.

The next day, following the church's outdoor service at the local Catholic shrine, I walked over to the cafeteria where coffee and refreshments were being served. While I stood outside under the covered walkway, drinking lemonade and eating a brownie, Jessica approached me and said, "I really want to get together with you."

"Thanks. I do, too." I smiled.

"I'll call when I get back from New Hampshire."

"Okay." As Jessica was walking away, I noticed Rev. Karen standing a few feet off to the side.

At the end of each day, I checked my answering machine. There were no messages. Would Jessica really get together with me when she returned from vacation? Those who called themselves my friends had abandoned me for a sixteen-year-old boy who lied and stole. They sided with James because they liked him, not because he was right. As in high school, it was popularity, not truth, people were interested in. And I was never the popular one. When they sided with James and shunned me, they exposed their dislike for me. I was supposed to forget their betrayal and go back to the way things were as if nothing ever happened. But something did happen. It altered all my church relationships. It ended the illusion that they were my friends.

I yearned to jump back into the abyss and allow myself to space out and self-harm. There was something alluring about it. It felt so safe in the white space. When I was there people cared for me, were interested in me, and called. Now, even though I was hurting, they didn't call. They seemed unaware of the effect this had on me. It didn't occur to them I was hurting. If I cut, then they would know I was hurting. They would see my pain and understand how serious this was, and that I needed their help.

I didn't understand why people rejected and abandoned me. I was a good, loyal friend. I had a generous heart. But they preferred James and Ruth to me. They couldn't figure out how to give all of us support. *Perhaps I should move on and give up trying to live a religious life,* I thought. I was successful at home and in my practice. I was a miserable failure at church.

I couldn't confide in Rev. Karen anymore. Her anger leaked out whenever I tried to speak to her. She engaged in sniper attacks. It was becoming difficult to predict how she was going to treat me. At times she was supportive and understanding, while other times she was stern and critical.

Rev. Karen suggested we go out to lunch. Become friendly again. But she said over and over we weren't friends. She stopped providing me with pastoral care, never asking what impact these events were having on my faith. She had forgotten her promise to shield me from church conflict. I wondered if she realized that Immanuel was no longer a safe place for me.

My family and I were proud we took a risk when we opened our hearts and our home to James. We did a good job taking care of him. We were an excellent foster family. I didn't know why God hadn't blessed our efforts with success. Perhaps James was too far gone to reclaim. Perhaps the rest of the church was too jealous.

I needed God to help me. But where was God? He allowed so much evil to take place. I needed to be vindicated somehow, some way. It was hard to wait for time to pass and for people to reconsider their behavior. I had to hold fast to what I knew was the truth: We offered James a beautiful gift of a home and a family. He took it and then trampled on it.

At the end of August, Melissa moved out to take a position with Habitat for Humanity in New Jersey. On Sunday, August 19, I added her name to the prayer list to ask for God's blessing. Rev. Karen, for the first time since James left, initiated a call to me a few days later.

"Maggie, how are you doing?"

"Fine." I was cautious. Would this be the kind and supportive pastor or the angry and mean one?

"You must be upset over Melissa's leaving."

"No, I'm fine." I was dumbfounded. When I desperately needed her help and support, she didn't call. Now, when I didn't need her help, she did.

"I know it's hard adjusting to an empty nest," she said.

What was she doing? Why was she assuming I was having difficulty with Melissa leaving? So I could be sad about Melissa but not about James? She didn't get that. Or maybe she did? Maybe this was her way for making up for not being there when James left. Maybe she was trying to breach the divide. I clenched my teeth and did my best to be civil, but I'm sure the anger leaked through.

"I'm fine with it," I said. "It doesn't bother me in the least. We're looking forward to being empty nesters." Lyndon and I were starting to plan our retirement. We talked about going home to New York City. How I wanted to leave this place and correct the mistake we made twelve years before. Move back to New York. Find an apartment. Never return to New England. Simplify our lives. Work less. Play more.

Rev. Karen paused. "You know, I didn't have any trouble with my daughters leaving either."

Relieved by her honesty, I replied, "I have other things to occupy my time."

"So did I."

The next day while sitting in the fellowship hall, I saw Ivonne walk into the room with Rev. Karen. Ivonne approached me while Rev. Karen went toward her office. She took a seat next to me. "How can you not be upset over your daughter leaving?"

How did she know that? Rev. Karen must have told Ivonne about our telephone conversation. She had no right to do that. Don't ministers understand anything about confidentiality?

"It was expected, and part of the natural order of things," I said.

"It bothered me when my daughter left," Ivonne replied.

"I'm sorry the transition was hard for you, Ivonne. But this is the beginning of Melissa's career. It's a good thing. Lyndon and I are proud of her."

"Don't you miss her?"

"She calls. In some ways, I get to talk to her more now that she's gone than when she was home. Her father and I are happy for her. It's what she's been planning for a long time."

Ivonne looked at me, an odd expression on her face. What was she thinking? Was this confirmation for her that I was a cold-hearted bitch who didn't love or care for her children? That it was easy for me to send James away?

*It was such a hard decision! Why can't they see that? I'm so weary. How much more pain can I take?* I had been too naïve when I took James into my heart. I shouldn't have been so generous. But I never expected to be rejected because he failed to adjust to our home. I never expected to be blamed for his mistakes and foolishness. Rev. Karen's and the others' refusal to talk about it was making it worse. Like Jesus in the Garden of Gethsemane, no one would sit with me. I was alone.

Over the next several weeks, my moods swung between utter despair and rage. I would look at the abyss from the edge; I considered returning there. *People become more interested in me when I'm in the white space. They appear to like the sick me better than the healthy me.* My family, however, loved all of me. It was better to live healthy with my family even if abandoned by friends and acquaintances. I wasn't going to allow myself to sink into the abyss to be rescued and cared for by others.

Determined not to surrender to self- destruction, I looked for a way to value my life. I wanted to leave the self-harming behind. I didn't like how the self-harming consumed my life, leaving little time or energy for productive pursuits. It added to my pain and left me worse off than before. I didn't like me when I was like that. I could be so much healthier and happier than that. I wanted to learn to value myself enough that harming myself would be as unthinkable as harming another person. I wanted to feel I was good enough, and that I was not this bad person who deserved all the harm others inflicted on her.

On August 31, I put on my college and high school rings. I wanted to be reminded of my accomplishments, how I outclassed almost everyone at Bible study. *I am better educated and more cultured, and have more integrity.* It was hard for me to say that because it wasn't humble. But when I lost sight of that, it became easier for them to hurt and devalue me. Then I devalued myself and wanted to self-injure.

I had lost respect for Rev. Karen, Ruth and the others when they aligned themselves with James and against me. I despised them for abandoning and rejecting me. I hated them even more each time they refused to discuss it with me. They knew if they talked to me, they would have to face the truth. An illiterate sixteen-year-old had deceived them.

# Apologies

Labor Day weekend Lyndon and I drove down to New Jersey to visit with Melissa. She was living in a small brick row house renovated by Habitat for Humanity. We ate lunch at an Asian restaurant whose carpets were faded and worn. Melissa sat to her father's left in our booth, I across from them.

"I have an appointment on Wednesday with Rev. Karen," I told her after the waitress took our orders.

"For what?" she asked.

"To plan our renewal of vows." I emptied two packets of sugar into my tea and began stirring. Five years before, while I was still a member at FXUU, Lyndon and I agreed we would renew our vows for our silver wedding anniversary. When we married, Lyndon and I didn't have the money to pay for a wedding, and no one else was going to help us out. During our years together we earned our college degrees, more than tripling our income while we raised two children. I put my spoon down and picked up my teacup, and smiled with pride as I glanced over at my daughter, thinking that she had grown into a fine young lady. A public celebration of Lyndon's and my marriage was past due and well deserved.

"Dad," Melissa's voice penetrated my daydreaming, "I know you mean to support Mom, but when you act that way she feels you're angry with her."

I turned my attention back to them. They were talking about Immanuel Lutheran.

"She lets them hurt her," Lyndon said in reply.

*Let them hurt me? How can he say that?* When I first met Rev. Karen she was kind and supportive. How was I to know how cruel she would become? "I–"

"They treated Mom badly," Melissa replied. "Because they didn't see her as one of them."

*Yes, that's right, Melissa. You see it.* I waited for Lyndon's reply, but he just scowled. The waitress delivered our food, and we began eating. The conversation shifted to the work Melissa was doing for Habitat for Humanity. While Lyndon and she talked about gutting and tiling a bathroom, I thought about Rev. Karen.

Right after I left FXUU and joined Immanuel, Rev. Karen encouraged my desire to renew our vows. She showed me *The Lutheran Book of Worship's* service for it. But when James left, she had asked while we sat in her office, "You don't still plan to renew your vows, do you?"

I was taken aback. Why would I cancel something I had been planning for close to five years? Why shouldn't Lyndon and I have a public celebration of our marriage? Twenty-five years ago, he and I avoided our families' objections to our biracial marriage by marrying quietly at Staten Island Borough Hall with only two friends present. Racism had cheated us out of a wedding. A public celebration of our marriage was overdue. "I most certainly do," I had replied.

The week before we left for New Jersey, I telephoned Rev. Karen from my office. "When can I meet with you to plan the renewal ceremony?"

"You're not going to talk about James are you?"

I felt a sharp pain in my side as if Rev. Karen had just jabbed me. "No, this isn't about James."

*She doesn't want me to do it,* I thought. *I'm not welcomed at Immanuel. She doesn't want to do anything for me. I'm not good enough.*

After hanging up the phone, I searched my office for something sharp to cut myself. I found a pair of scissors in my secretary's desk drawer, but they looked too dull to slice my thigh. I considered stabbing myself, but that would do more harm than I wanted. I heard the office door open and close. I dropped the scissors back into the drawer and shut it just as my client entered the waiting room.

Saying, "Good evening, I'll be right with you," I locked the drawer and escorted him to my consultation room. After he settled into his chair, I asked how his week went.

"Pretty bad. While driving home last night I thought about driving my car into a tree or something."

"What would that get you?" I forced my own desire to self-harm out of my consciousness and focused on my client.

"I don't know."

"We all are going to die sooner or later," I told him. "I hope later. Life is short enough. Why hasten it?"

I knew, of course. He wanted to escape his pain just as I did. If I took my own life, what would happen to him? Wouldn't that encourage him to do the same?

A few days after Lyndon and I returned home from New Jersey, I walked over to the church for my meeting with Rev. Karen. I didn't want anything that Rev. Karen said or didn't say to trigger self-harming thoughts. I repeated over and over while I walked, "I am a reflection of God. I have a place in this world that no one can take away from me."

During my meeting with her, I focused on the ceremony. If she asked about my family, I just said they were fine and didn't give any details. As I had learned to do with my parents and my classmates, I put on a poker face and avoided telling her how I was feeling. She gave me a copy of the Lutheran renewal ceremony to take home to look at, along with some suggested readings for the service. I thanked her and left.

When I reached home, I called Melissa. As we spoke, it became clear to me. I could tell Ruth and Rev. Karen that if they wanted a friendship with me, they would have to be willing to discuss James. The intensity of my grief and anger made me unable to associate with them until our differences were resolved.

That night I saw two television segments on adolescent offenders. The first was sympathetic to the offender, pointing out how troubled he was. Once he realized his parents cared about him, he began to improve. Maybe, I thought, we didn't show James how much we loved him. But how could I? James maintained his distance. Would he have allowed me to hug him? Even after the boy on television understood how much his parents loved him, he still kidnapped someone and acted out violently. His parents' love hadn't been enough.

The second television segment was about a teenage boy who had stolen a car. During the police chase, several cars were damaged and a riot started. The boy's mother collapsed and was taken to the hospital. James' behavior had created havoc in our lives. Just like the adolescent offenders, he needed to be loved unconditionally and to be held responsible for his actions.

During a commercial, I called Ruth and left her a message. She called me back within the hour. I invited her to dinner for Monday night, September 10.

"I'm still in contact with James," she said.

"I know that." A wave of hate surged through me and then dissipated. Like a bad divorce, Ruth alienated my son from me by giving him the material things I denied him and rescuing him from the consequences of his own misbehavior. Forgiving her would be hard, especially if she remained unrepentant.

Monday night while Lyndon was seeing clients downstairs, I cooked dinner for Ruth and me. We ate in the kitchen and talked about insignificant, mundane things. After we finished our meal and I put our dirty dishes in the dishwasher, I showed her into my living room. She chose a seat at the end of the black leather sofa with her back to the bay window. I sat at a right angle to her on the other sofa. A corner table separated us. I told her how distressed I was over what happened with James.

"No one stopped to think how you were feeling," Ruth said. "There were things I shouldn't have done."

"No one has initiated any calls to me since James left."

Her eyes opened wide. "I didn't know that. During the July cleanup of the parsonage's yard, Jessica and I were talking about you and James. Rev. Karen stepped out and told us not to talk about it with you or anyone else."

I wasn't surprised. Ruth had just confirmed my suspicions. At a time when I was in desperate need of support from my faith community, Rev. Karen was encouraging everyone to shun me.

"Jessica told me I was wrong to send James away," I said.

Ruth frowned. "You did your very best to give James a good home."

At the end of the evening, I escorted her to the front door. We hugged, and I watched as she walked down the front steps to her car. It was a good start toward reconciliation. I was sure she would talk to the others and encourage them to talk to me.

The next morning, as was my routine, I called the group home where I consulted around 10 a.m. to let them know I was leaving to pick up my client.

"How is he doing?" I asked.

"He's pretty upset since the attacks."

"What attacks? Has someone assaulted him?"

"No, haven't you heard? We're under attack."

"Who's under attack?" I asked.

"We're under attack." The staff member sounded as if she was crying. "They've closed all the federal offices in Boston."

"I don't know what you're talking about."

"Planes flew into the World Trade Center and into the Pentagon. We're at war! Turn on your television."

I dropped the phone. "Lyndon! Lyndon!"

He came running up from his office. "What's the matter?"

"Turn on the TV!"

"In the middle of the day? Why?"

"Turn it on! Turn it on! We've been attacked!"

He turned on the television set in the family room just in time to see the South Tower fall. I blurted, "Oh, my God!"

We stood watching, transfixed. The North Tower fell close to 10:30 a.m. Lyndon said nothing.

"Oh, my God! How could that happen? There will be thousands dead," I said. He put his arm around me. "My city, my beloved city! What are we doing here? We belong there!" I cried.

I took some deep breaths and gathered up my briefcase. "I need to see my client. He'll be pretty upset by this."

"I need to go to work, too," Lyndon said.

We said goodbye to each other and drove our cars out of our driveway. To my surprise, my paranoid schizophrenic client was calmer than I expected. Perhaps he didn't fully understand what had happened. As I drove to my New Bedford office, my own conflict with Immanuel appeared insignificant compared to the attacks on our nation. We were now at war. My son was in the military. Would he be safe? Would any of us be safe?

The next day I received a phone call from someone I used to work with. "Maggie," she asked, "is your family okay?"

"My husband's family called and they're safe. Only my brother Rich works in Manhattan. He works uptown from there. I'm sure he's safe." I hadn't heard from him but I was sure it was due to the phone service being down.

After I hung up the phone, I walked out to get the mail. There was a letter from Ruth. She hadn't realized how deeply wounded I had been. She was sorry for her part in it. I was overjoyed, and certain Ruth would speak to the others and the shunning would stop.

Later that evening my joy was overshadowed by my apprehension about my brother's safety and whereabouts. A couple I was seeing came into my office. They were relieved. The phones were finally working. Their family called from New York. They were safe. Suddenly I felt tears rising up. Where was my brother? Why hadn't he called? I frantically tried to visualize the New York subway map in my head. What train would he take to work? What if he had visited friends in Brooklyn and was riding into work on the IRT? *Oh, my God, the train runs right under the World Trade Center.*

When I arrived home from work I noticed the local newspaper sitting on the kitchen table. On the front page was a picture of a young woman who had been on the plane that hit the North Tower. She looked familiar. The phone rang. It was my sister Rita.

"I just want to let you know Rich is okay. He was just exiting the subway near Lincoln Center at the time of the attack. He was with his boss. Her husband works across from the World Trade Center. She started walking down Broadway searching for her husband. Rich felt he had to go with her. They finally found him at Union Square."

"Did he call you?" I slipped off my coat.

"No, Trish did. She was at the New York Foundling Hospital when the planes hit."

"I thought she was in Vermont."

"She's still doing some work for the hospital."

"Oh. Why didn't Rich call?" I asked.

"He was exhausted. He had to walk most of the way home because the subways were closed. He just shut himself up in his apartment and didn't call anyone."

"Thanks for letting me know." I hung up the phone and put my coat in the closet. The phone rang again. This time it was Melissa. She was crying.

"Honey, what's wrong?"

"Mom, Donna called. Lynn Goodchild is dead."

"Lynn Goodchild?"

"You remember her. She was Donna's best friend from grade school. She was the manager of the track team."

"Oh!" Melissa and her friend, Donna, had been the best runners on the high school track team. I walked over to the kitchen table and picked up the newspaper. I looked at the picture again. I vaguely remembered meeting Lynn at Donna's going-away party.

"I'm coming home," Melissa said.

"Can you get past New York? All the bridges are closed."

"I think I can cross at the Tappan Zee."

"Okay. Drive safely."

After getting off the phone, I caught up with Lyndon and let him know what was happening. I then checked over my schedule for the next day. I had a breakfast date with Rev. Karen. A week ago I had called her and scheduled it, trying to salvage what was left of our relationship. Drained, I considered canceling it. I worried it wouldn't go well. But it was after 10 p.m. It was too late to cancel. I would have to go. With a sense of foreboding, I went to bed.

The next morning I met her at a diner in the industrial park behind the hospital. Sitting at a small table across from the counter, she asked, "How are you doing?"

There was a little too much concern in her voice. It was as if she was asking about me after I had been seriously ill. I knew she believed me to be mentally unstable. I felt she was prying. I wasn't going to tell her I was speaking to Dr. Emmett. I picked up my napkin and put it on my lap. "How are you?" I asked.

"I'm fine." She picked up her menu. "How is your family?"

"Well." I could see she was frustrated by my short answer.

"How is work?"

Good! A safe question. "Several clients are stressed by 9-11."

She and I talked about the September 11$^{th}$ attack and what kind of response from the United States would be morally responsible. We both agreed that solely seeking to inflict pain and suffering on our enemies would be morally reprehensible. However, taking military action to prevent further terrorists attacks would be justified.

"How are you doing?" she asked again.

"I invited Ruth over for dinner last Monday," I said, ignoring her question. "She sent me a letter of apology."

"You will get no apology from me," Rev. Karen stated coldly as she sat straight up.

I hadn't asked her for an apology.

"James was better off out of your household," she said. "You were too strict."

"My husband and I are good parents," I replied. "Restricting a teen for two weeks was appropriate. We needed to discipline our son so he would never lie or steal again."

"Your husband, Melissa and Orion were cruel to James," she insisted.

"Is that what James told you?" I asked her. It didn't appear Rev. Karen ever doubted anything James said.

"There were other church members in your home who saw it," she said.

My eyes opened wide. Ruth and Beverly had been spying on us when they came over to tutor James! Rev. Karen was contemptuous. She never really saw or respected me for who I was. She treated me as if the post-traumatic stress disorder was the real me. She didn't see or acknowledge the healthy me, the strong me. That is why a sixteen-year-old refugee was given more credibility than I was. I now knew Rev. Karen had betrayed me, and she knew that I knew.

"That's not possible," I told her. "Orion was away at school and wasn't even in the house when they came over to tutor. James lies."

"I know," she replied.

"Do you?" I placed my napkin on the table and stood. "See you in church."

President Bush declared Friday a national day of mourning. Since I was consulting to a day program in Taunton, I attended a noonday service at St. Anne's. The priest gave us a chance to name those for whom we grieved.

"Shawn Nassaney," a young woman said.

I was among strangers. I mustered up some courage. "Lynn Goodchild."

Startled, the young woman turned and looked at me. From her eyes, I knew she knew Lynn. It was too painful to ask her. I felt I had intruded. Who was I? I wasn't kin. I wasn't even a friend. I hurried out of the chapel at the end of the service and returned to my car, where I cried alone. Later I would learn that Shawn was Lynn's boyfriend. They were flying to Hawaii when their plane was hijacked.

Grief-stricken over the death of her friend, Melissa drove home from New Jersey. Over the weekend Lyndon, Melissa and I attended Lynn's wake. A long line snaked around the funeral home. A collage of Lynn's childhood stood at the corner of the building. Soldiers in dress uniform stood at attention by the door. Melissa stopped in one of the parlors to speak with her friend Donna. We filed past the Goodchilds shaking their hands. At first they didn't know us. Melissa reminded them she ran track the four years Lynn was the team's manager.

Monday morning I accompanied Melissa to the memorial service. The Catholic church was crowded. Several priests from the Cape had come up to help serve communion. A picture of Lynn was placed in front of the altar. There was no body. My daughter's face was numb. At times she rested her head on my shoulder. *How hard*, I thought, *to lose a friend at such a young age. And savagely murdered!*

"Lynn was probably sleeping," Melissa said. "She always slept on the bus when we went to track meets. She probably didn't know anything was going on."

I looked at her, sure that wasn't true. But if it made Melissa feel better to believe her friend died unaware, I wasn't going to shatter that illusion. For myself, I was glad she hadn't died alone. I imagined Shawn holding her as the plane crashed into the North Tower.

Seeking the company of friends, I went to Bible study that night. No one asked if my family in New York was safe. I didn't share my connection to Lynn. I didn't share my grief. I felt like I was standing at a window looking in on a party I hadn't been invited to. It was raining. My tears mixed with the rain. No one knew I was crying.

I realized I had been relegated to the margins. That was unacceptable. I would rather not belong than be marginalized. But I wasn't anxious, and there had been no desire to self-injure. I kept reminding myself that I was a child of God and I deserved to be treated better.

While our country's forces prepared for war in the Persian Gulf and we mourned thousands ruthlessly murdered, I struggled to sort out what had happened to me. What to make of it? Other than my husband and children, no one initiated contact with me. What friends did I have? Why did people not recognize and see my need and respond to it?

Resigned to having no friends except close family members, I retreated to the safety of my home. I would not to return to Bible study. Instead I would use the time to read.

On Thursday morning, September 27, while I was cleaning up after breakfast, a phone call from Dr. Emmett startled me, "Hello, Maggie. Thank you for the letter. I have a scheduling conflict on Monday. Can we talk at 7:30, or do you want to move it to the following Monday?"

My breathing became shallow. My heart rate increased. I couldn't wait a whole week to talk to him. "7:30."

I hung up the phone and went into the living room. I sat down and wrote in my journal,

> Maybe Dr. Emmett didn't want to speak to me this Monday. Maybe he was tired of talking to me. Maybe he doesn't like me at all and is too professional to say so. Like Rev. Karen. But when the chips are down his real loyalties will be exposed. He doesn't like me at all. He despises me. He hates me. How do you find out what your therapist really thinks of you?

Although Dr. Emmett had never betrayed me I believed if we had met at a party, at church, or at a seminar, he would have never bothered with me. He would be like everyone else. He would no more be interested in friendship with me than the others.

I had no friends. I was disliked and disrespected. No one cared enough to call. Rev. Karen said she asked them to call but they didn't. They believed the conflict over James was over. But I was left with the pain. Having been easily discarded, I realized I never fully belonged to the group.

As I picked up the pieces of my life, our country did the same. Facing the uncertain future with much fear, I resolved to shake the dust off my feet and move on. I would find a place for myself and achieve some contentment. Those who chose not to offer friendship and who broke promises lost what I had to offer them.

I decided to reach out to Ruth one more time. If our friendship were to survive, she would have to reciprocate and initiate calls to me. It couldn't be one-way. I would tell her that. I expected more. I wanted more.

I spoke to Dr. Emmett on October 1. I found the session unsatisfying. There was so much more that I wanted to say. I wanted to move away from talking about the self-harm and the hurt feelings to finding a solution. At that point I believed the solution wasn't in finding another church; it lay somewhere in staying and getting the others to listen to me. They needed to hear how they excluded me and look at why they did that. Shunning me was undermining the very Christian community they said they wanted and believed in. Hadn't Rev. Karen preached on community and working through conflicts? Were those just empty words?

I had so much to offer them. All I wanted in return was their friendship and acceptance. I wanted to be invited out. I wanted them to initiate phone calls. I wanted to be included. Couldn't we find some common ground and be in community together?

The day after I spoke to Dr. Emmett, I interviewed a woman who was applying for disability. While obtaining her childhood history she informed me she had been a "geek" in high school. The other students teased her and regarded her as a "goody-two-shoes." During a French test, while the teacher was out of the room, they asked her for the answers. She allowed them to look at her paper. After that, although they never invited her to be part of their social group, they left her alone.

Like my client, when I was in school I had often been approached by other students to help them cheat. Unlike my client, I made a different choice and refused to share my answers. I suspected they were trying to use me and give me little in return. I chose not to give up my integrity. What would I have left if I did?

Perhaps I was too good for the people at Immanuel, too well educated, too competent, too generous, and too honest. I refused to participate in gossip that appeared at times to be some kind of bonding ritual. I offered them friendship and they rejected the gift. It broke my heart but I wasn't going to sink to their level. The challenge for me was not to succumb to anger, bitterness and despair.

Lyndon and I spent Columbus Day weekend in New York City. We stayed at a hotel on 55th Street a block from City Center and just north of the theatre district. We went to the planetarium and the new Rose Center on Saturday. We called my brother Rich, and together we visited the Empire State Building on Sunday. Although I had walked past the building countless times I had never been inside.

We took our places on the tourist line that wound around the building and moved slowly toward the front doors and into the Art Deco lobby. After taking the elevator to the top, we huddled in the wind and looked south to Ground Zero. It was still smoldering. A tear made its way down my cheek as I remembered Lynn Goodchild and James. Both of them had been victims of war.

The following weekend, I sat in my study reading a review of research on bullying. Researchers have concluded that victims are despised and bullies admired. Besides the bully and the victim, there are witnesses who either directly or indirectly assist the bully. Alone, without social support, the victim is powerless to protect himself.

I looked up from my book and rested my head against the back of the recliner. All it would have taken to make things better for me, I thought, was for someone at Immanuel to accept my offer of friendship. Ruth started to, but she didn't initiate contact and she never invited me anywhere. I wasn't sure if she was a bystander or the bully leading the pack against me.

Although the bullying research was referring to teens, I realized my experiences at Murray, FXUU and Immanuel were examples of adult bullying. People accepted rumor-mongering as normal and acceptable. My efforts to resolve the church conflicts and find a place in a religious community had failed. I simply hadn't been able to do it alone.

Late October, I sent out invitations to our silver wedding anniversary party. Lyndon didn't want me to invite anyone from Immanuel. They weren't my friends, he said. I, on the other hand, hoped inviting them would be the beginning of reconciliation, and they would see what good and decent people I and my family were. Maybe then they would be more willing to talk to me about James.

I didn't have all the addresses I needed. I emailed Beverly for them, but she never responded. I believe she was avoiding me. I had to call Rev. Karen for them. She called back when she knew I wouldn't be at home and left the information on my voicemail. I was hurt that she no longer wanted to speak directly to me. I missed the times before James left, when she initiated calls to me and was willing to talk. Oh, well, I thought, at least it was better than the others, who didn't respond at all.

I kept trying to detach from the behavior and attitudes of my former friends at Immanuel. I told myself they were ignorant about foster care and the difficulty of caring for a child that wasn't your own. They passed judgment on me in ignorance. But I still couldn't socialize with them and pretend nothing had happened. I had seen how little they valued our "friendship." I knew our relationship with each other would never be the same again.

Lyndon told me that one of his friends saw James volunteering at the local soup kitchen with other members of Immanuel. Ruth obviously brought him. There was little reason to hope that our relationship could be healed. So long as Ruth and other members of the church kept bringing James back, I could never hope to be a part of the church. It would be unbearably painful to sit in the sanctuary while James sat with them and not me. I needed all my ties to him severed.

My mood fluctuated from deep, intense grief to rage. I was drowning in the silence. I wanted to weep. And then I would be filled with so much rage, I was afraid of what I might say and do. I hated all of them. I wanted to shake them. Wake them up. Everything I did, they interpreted negatively. I couldn't win. They didn't care enough to call. I was powerless to change that.

I needed to try to explain it to Rev. Karen. At least I would be upfront and honest. I couldn't continue with things as they were. I needed her to consider the possibility that her judgment about my family and me was wrong.

Desperate, I called her on Tuesday evening, October 30, while she was still at the church. I asked her to meet with me. She reluctantly agreed to meet briefly at 9 p.m. She was a bit distant and cold. She denied telling James he didn't have to listen to us. She denied talking about me with the others. She denied breaching confidentiality. I was sure I hadn't misinterpreted events. Her denials indicated she knew her actions had been wrong.

"You need people to agree with you," she insisted.

"No. I just need to be heard."

"You were a good foster mother," she acknowledged. "You did enough. But Lyndon and Melissa were mean to James."

"Melissa and James argued, but I also found them sitting together at the kitchen table laughing with each other. When James had questions about girls and sex he went to Melissa, not me."

"Lyndon neglected James."

"Lyndon was at the YMCA with James three times per week."

She backed off, saying, "I didn't know that."

There was a lot Rev. Karen didn't know. How could she? She didn't live with us. I felt good about asserting myself. She now had a more balanced view of things. Deluded that the conflict was on its way to being resolved, I hugged her as I walked out of her office.

The next day, Halloween, Sheba, our beloved family dog, died. She had been wasting away for the last week, refusing food and water. We set up her pen and placed her on some old blankets, making her as comfortable as possible. When I arrived home at 10 p.m., Lyndon told me she had died. He had moved her body off the deck and placed her by her doghouse.

Uncertain of the best way to dispose of her body, I called the pound the next morning. No one answered. I left a message. I felt guilty I hadn't done enough to save her. But she was old. Wasn't it kinder to let someone die when their time is near? There had been so many losses in the last few years. Tearful, I called Ruth, who told me she had buried her dog in the backyard. The pound finally called back and told me how deep I needed to dig.

Lyndon was recovering from shoulder surgery, so I didn't want him to bury her. I considered calling a church member who owned a landscaping business for help. But given my strained relationships at church, I thought better of it. I cancelled all my morning appointments and got a shovel from the garage.

The day was unusually warm and sunny, with the temperature reaching seventy degrees. Alone and lonely, I walked up the hill and looked around. I knew the hill wasn't much more than a large rock pile dropped by a glacier thousands of years ago. I surveyed the area and decided to take advantage of the hole Sheba had dug across the path to her doghouse.

According to the city pound, the hole had to be deeper. I struggled to dig out the numerous rocks and make the grave deep enough. Breaking a nail, I winced in pain and sat down in the dirt. What was I going to do? A wave of despair and sorrow flowed over me, and I reconsidered my decision not to call anyone from church.

No, I needed to do this myself. If I didn't bury Sheba, Lyndon would, and that wouldn't be good for his shoulder. I forced myself to get up and began separating the rocks from the dirt. When I was too exhausted to dig anymore, I wrapped Sheba's body in her old blanket and placed her in her grave. I then threw what little soil there was over her body and piled the rocks on top. I further obscured the grave by throwing leaves and fallen branches over it. I was pretty sure it would not be disturbed by any animal.

I missed Sheba more than I expected. Feeding her, letting her out, caring for her had been a part of the rhythm of my life for more than a decade. She kept me company during the day.

I spoke with Dr. Emmett about Sheba's death, Lyndon's recovery, and the church. I cried that I wanted to return home to New York and get away from New England. I wasn't happy living here. Dr. Emmett said something about people not being able to handle the open expression of anger. Anger was taboo here. Rev. Karen and other church members misperceived who I was. They didn't value me. I wondered when they had begun to dislike me. I didn't understand how I could be so intensely loved by my family and so unwanted by everyone else.

Encouraged by my conversation with Rev. Karen on Tuesday night, I attended a church luncheon on Sunday and went to Bible study on Monday night. I sat quietly and didn't offer any opinions that were contrary to accepted doctrine and that would further alienate me from the group. This made it boring. I felt my spiritual growth was being stifled by the other group members' conventionality.

I had just finished reading Fowler's *Stages of Faith*. I concluded my former friends at Immanuel were at the conventional or loyalist stage. Although contradictions in the Bible and Lutheran doctrine were often recognized, the approval of significant others was more important. They often failed to critically examine the beliefs and opinions of selected authorities such as clergy. I, on the other hand, was less influenced by authorities. I was willing to examine my own experience and what was true in my personal life. I was more willing to learn from the experiences and beliefs of other religions. I had a stronger respect for diversity.

On Wednesday, I called Rev. Karen and left a message that I would not be attending Bible study anymore. The group no longer met my needs for fellowship and spirituality. I would move on and find another way to get my spiritual needs met, perhaps through private study.

I also telephoned Jessica and Jason. I left a message that I was pleased they had accepted our invitation to our silver wedding anniversary. They would be welcomed despite the present tension between us.

I also left a message on Ruth's voicemail. She returned my call Thursday morning. We talked a little about how James was doing.

"I understand why you no longer attend Bible study or sit with us," she said. "They never considered how you were feeling."

I wasn't surprised. I wasn't sure Ruth understood that was what made things so very painful for me.

While I couldn't force others to be friends in the way I wanted them to be, I could choose how I responded. I preferred staying home with my family where I was fully welcomed rather than accept marginalization.

The Sunday before Thanksgiving, the chimes choir played at Rehoboth Congregational Church. Mallory from Immanuel came to listen. We talked afterward. She was excited and pleased that we invited her to our twenty-fifth wedding anniversary celebration. She said she admired Lyndon and me for making a success out of our marriage. She also mentioned James, and told me she understood why it ended the way it did. She had gotten to know James quite well. She also told me she wanted us to be friends. She sounded sincere, but she was twenty years younger than I. She admired me too much. This made me uneasy. What would she do when I didn't live up to her expectations? Would she shove me off that pedestal she was putting me on and betray me like all the others? I much preferred friends who knew I was imperfect.

I was thinking about how my situation was like Jesus. Jesus was this good man who didn't live up to other people's expectations. He openly expressed anger in the temple and they crucified him. They couldn't handle what he was trying to tell them. I was betrayed just as he had been.

I used the long Thanksgiving weekend to clean out my files. I found Nickman and Lewis' 1994 article on adoptive families. Dr. Nickman had given it to me while I was working for an agency in New Bedford. I had filed it for possible future use without ever having read it.

I took the reprint and sat in my recliner. It said it can take up to two years for a foster child to be fully integrated into their new family. James had only been with us for nine months. As I continued reading, I strongly identified with Nickman and Lewis' discussion of the failure of professionals to recognize and support existing bonds at times of family stress and inappropriate intrusions into the foster family's life. The article described that, after a honeymoon period, it was not unusual for a foster child to begin testing limits severely. The bond between James and our family, as with most foster families, was less-than-optimal. Rev. Karen and other church members' intolerance of that imperfect bond stigmatized us and deemed us inferior parents. Their active interventions without our consent to "save" James from our attempts to discipline him undermined our parental authority. They didn't recognize James' "traumatically based tendency to lie or misrepresent."

James saw our refusal to physically discipline him as weak. He understood power and hate. He did not understand the loving bonds of an intact family. What Rev. Karen saw as an "overly strict management style" was, in fact, our attempt to creatively deal with James' many problems. Finally, Lutheran Social Services failed to provide adequate support, and never suggested respite. What we needed from Rev. Karen and the other church members was an emphasis on the positive aspects of our family life, rather than their questioning of James' placement with us.

*This is it!* I thought. *I'll use this to open up a dialogue about the issues with James.*

I went downstairs and made several copies of the article. I sent it with a personalized note to Rev. Karen and several other church members.

On Tuesday, November 27, I finished work early and took the back roads through Rehoboth toward Attleboro. The route took me past Jessica's neighborhood. It had been four months since she promised to sit down with me and talk. While I drove, I thought about calling her and reminding her of her promise. When I reached a strip mall at Brigg's Corner, I pulled in and parked and used my cell phone to call her.

"Jessica, this is Maggie. I'm at Brigg's Corner. Can you meet with me tonight?"

"I'm not comfortable with that," Jessica responded.

I was surprised by her cold response. She had been so much warmer and supportive when I spoke to her last July. "Why not? Last summer, you said you would."

"I'm just not comfortable with that. That article with your note offended me. I'm an adult, and don't need to be told how to think and feel."

I stopped breathing, confused. How had I done that? I had just shared an article. I took a deep breath. I weighed and enunciated each word, being careful not to blame or accuse Jessica of breaking her promise, even though that was what she did.

"Do you want to know why I sent it?" I asked.

There was silence. I waited, hopeful she would change her mind.

"I want to move on," she said. "The whole thing upsets me."

I took another deep breath, consciously controlling my anguish, and replied, "I lost a son."

"You didn't lose a son. You gave up one."

I felt the sting of her implied condemnation. She thought I had abandoned him, an unforgivable sin for a woman. I remembered my sister Rita telling me how the young unmarried women she works with are condemned no matter which of the three available choices they make: keep the baby, abort the baby or put it up for adoption.

"It is James who wouldn't come home," I said.

The phone went dead. "Hello?" I said. No answer. Thinking, *Oh, no, a dropped call*, I started to press redial, but paused to look at the screen. The connection hadn't been lost. Jessica had hung up on me. I rested my head against the steering wheel and sucked in air. *I will not cry.* I turned on my car's ignition. *I'll go talk to Ruth. Maybe she will help me.*

I drove across town and pulled into Ruth's driveway. I walked up to the side door and peered through the screen door into the breezeway. My heart was beating rapidly and my breathing was shallow. I wasn't sure Ruth would welcome me dropping in without calling first. I rang the bell and waited. After a few seconds, I heard her footsteps approaching the door.

"Maggie!" She flung open the door. Her eyes were open wide and she was smiling. "Come in."

I entered the breezeway and took a seat on a loveseat that was placed against the garage wall. It was the kind that was meant for patios, with vinyl cushions with bright blue and pink flowers against a white background. She didn't invite me into her house.

After I told her about my phone conversation with Jessica, she said, "I don't understand what's wrong with them. They're difficult people to work with. You're the victim."

I began crying; finally someone understood. She placed her arm around my shoulders. "I'm worried about you. You need to go on and forget about them. Jessica will never be your friend."

She handed me a tissue. I wiped my face and blew my nose and said, "I know that now." I felt grateful that Ruth was taking the time out to speak to me. I was done with trying to talk to Jessica.

Thursday morning while I was sitting at my desk, I received a call from Rev. Karen, who said, "I'm very disturbed."

My back stiffened. I braced myself. What was wrong now?

"Beverly and Jessica both came to me about that article you sent everyone."

*So they are going to her. Rev. Karen could stop that if she wanted to.*

"What's wrong with sharing an article?" I said.

"It was offensive." Rev. Karen sounded like a vice principal scolding a child who had sent a threatening note around the class.

"I sent one to you, too." I replied. "Were you offended?"

"Well, no," she said, softening a little. "But you didn't write anything on it."

"I know Beverly doesn't like to read, so I highlighted the parts I thought were relevant."

How could they be angry because I shared an article with them? I only wanted to get them to understand and see that it wasn't just me, that I wasn't crazy or unreasonable. *And it wasn't just them either. Lots of people make similar mistakes. We could all learn from it and the next time we encounter a foster–*

"She was very offended." Rev. Karen's stern voice broke through.

I never expected this reaction. In my world, sharing articles was a good thing. "Did you see what I wrote?" I said, thinking, *Man, why didn't I make a copy?*

"No," she replied.

"You should ask to see it." I was pleased I was asserting myself.

"Jessica said you drove near her house and yelled at her."

Her tone was strident. Were they going to accuse me of stalking? *Are they going to call the police? Then what?* I felt panic rising up inside me like a tsunami wave. I took slow, deep breaths until the wave lost its power.

"I always take the route near Jessica's home," I said, and sat straight up in my chair. "I never raised my voice when speaking to her. I spoke to Jessica just the way I'm speaking to you now."

"I don't feel yelled at," Rev. Karen said, lowering her voice. Maybe she was starting to believe me. Then she flipped again, "Things have been going on for six months."

"That's because nothing has been resolved. I don't gossip about people, and do my best not to rush to judgment. Jessica's behavior toward me wasn't just."

"Jessica wants to be kind to you, but doesn't want to talk about James."

Kind? Was I someone who was weak and pathetic? I didn't need or want anyone's pity or Christian kindness. Besides, I was done with Jessica two nights ago.

"That's good enough for me, so long as Jessica doesn't invite me to sit with them at church again."

"I'll relay the message."

"Thank you." But that was the problem. Rev. Karen was in the middle, controlling and directing communication. We were never going to resolve things this way.

"You don't want them to come to the renewal, do you?" Rev. Karen asked.

Rescind an invitation? How crass. "I invited everyone I had anything to do with at church. The invitation was sincere, and everyone will be treated well."

"That's mature," she said.

We ended the conversation on that slightly positive note. On Sunday, not wanting to appear guilty about Jessica, I reluctantly went to church. The black-wire globe that held thirty or more candles had been set up in the far corner away from the pulpit. Today's service would focus on prayers for the sick and for the healing of hurts, emotional as well as physical.

I took a seat on the pulpit side of the church, away from my former friends. In a kind gesture, Ruth came over to talk before the service began. I started crying. She tried to distract me with small talk. I raised my head and wiped my tears with the back of my hand. Without being told, Ruth understood I preferred to sit alone. She went to sit with her other friends on the other side of the church.

During the service, I just kept reminding myself that just as Ruth had said, I was the victim here. When Jessica complained to Rev. Karen instead of speaking to me, Jessica was bullying and persecuting me. I just needed to hang on, take whatever benefit I could from the church, throw away the rest, and move on. The tension in my body began to dissipate. I felt better.

Rev. Karen invited people to come up, light a candle and have their heads anointed with oil. As people were filing past my pew, I prayed to have the strength to bear the rejection and abandonment, and for Jessica and Beverly to open their eyes and see how unjust they had been to me.

At the end of the service, Beverly came over to talk to me. Expecting trouble, I grabbed the back of the pew in front of me and braced myself.

"Maggie, I am so sorry for hurting you. Is there any way to fix this?"

Wordless, I just hugged her as the happy tears ran down my cheeks. Just like the candles in the globe, my hope for reconciliation was rekindled.

"I was praying for God to help me fix some relationships at work when I saw you," Beverly continued. "I realized then God wanted me to mend my relationship with you."

"I'm so glad," I replied.

"James is different from the other boys. If we had gotten one of the other boys, it would have worked."

Perhaps, I thought. There was at least one Sudanese boy who wanted to go to med school. *If we had gotten someone like that–*

I caught a glimpse of Rev. Karen watching us from the back of the church. What was she thinking? Why was she always watching?

"I'll call you later," Beverly told me.

"Yes, do. I really want to talk to you."

Later that day, Beverly and I continued our conversation over the telephone. "Rev. Karen told me you had complained about me," I informed her.

"I didn't go to her to complain about you. I needed advice on how to respond. I didn't understand what you wanted."

I had repeatedly told Rev. Karen that I wanted people to talk to me, but apparently she never suggested to Beverly that she speak to me. "Why didn't you call me directly?" I asked.

"I don't know, but I will call in the future."

"I appreciate that."

We talked about Jessica's refusal to speak with me. "Jessica likes to talk about people behind their backs," Beverly said. "She gossips at work and bullied another coworker." Beverly and Jessica worked for the same employer.

"At times Jessica publicly befriends me and offers to talk," I explained to Beverly. "But then she complains about me and gossips."

"Jessica wavers. She's ambivalent. That's why she acts like that."

Two days later, I called Dr. Emmett. I was feeling overwhelmed and spent. We discussed my conversations with Jessica, Ruth, Rev. Karen and Beverly. He started talking about my inner child, and my trusting others. I saw it differently. I was proud of how I handled things for the past six months. For me it wasn't about my inner child, but about learning to stand up for myself. I made it clear I wouldn't tolerate being gossiped about, and that people should speak directly to me if they had an issue with me. I wouldn't pretend James was never part of my life and that my acquaintances at church were true friends. They betrayed and abandoned me. Each person had his or her own reason for doing so. People outside my family were not to be completely trusted, largely because they handled conflict by gossiping rather than directly confronting me.

I wrote in my journal almost every day, trying to write through all my pain and disappointment. I was overwhelmed with anger and grief. I had done nothing wrong, but was treated like I had committed a mortal sin. People attempted to blame my "irrational behavior" on my having post-traumatic stress disorder. But my anger was just. I was unfairly judged about how I parented James, and not given a chance to defend myself. That was abusive. I hated my former friends for their behavior. They shot the messenger and were self-righteous about it. They had no compassion for me. They were thoughtless, and trampled all over my emotions. They never even stopped to consider how I was feeling. They didn't care. I was unimportant to them. I was nothing.

While demonizing me, they canonized James. He was everything: the angel, the faultless one, the one without sin. Except he was never innocent. He wasn't the victim. I was.

People hate victims. They'd rather be the bully's assistant. Rev. Karen and the others were James' assistants. They taught him it was okay to steal, lie and trample all the people who love you, to use and throw away people.

They didn't love him enough to discipline him. I did. I risked losing him to teach him to be an honest man with integrity, courage and humility. They risked nothing.

During the past three years, I had lost myself. I felt numb and battle worn. I wished I could say I was grateful for my life and happy to be alive, but I felt more like a prisoner serving her time, waiting for death to relieve her pain. I felt something dead in me, a disillusionment, a loss of innocence. When I graduated from high school, I thought I was leaving the bullying, the ridicule and the rejection behind. I thought I would finally find acceptance in college. But then I was so depressed and miserable, I made no lasting friends there. I searched for a place in one church after the other. I thought I finally found a place for myself at Immanuel, only to be rejected and abandoned there, too.

As the year came to an end, I asked God to guide me as I tried to rediscover and reclaim my identity. I had lost so much of myself the last five or more years. Where was the educated, cultured Margaret who enjoyed discussing politics, religion and new ideas? Who had enjoyed classical music and dance? By becoming over involved with churches, I had forgotten who I was and where I belonged. I didn't fit in with people who valued form over content and viewed any expression of anger as sinful. In the coming year, I hoped to read more and focus my energy on my family and my work.

I decided to attend church at Immanuel until the end of 2001. After our silver wedding anniversary party and our trip to Florida, I would decide if I wanted to continue going or stay home with my husband. It depended on how painful going continued to be, and whether I could get anything positive out of it. I hoped our anniversary party would give people a chance to meet my extended family and see that we weren't villains. I hoped the apologies from Ruth and Beverly would be the beginning of my being fully accepted by the other church members.

# Matthew 18: 15-17

On Friday, December 28, I received a phone call from my niece Rebecca. She would not be coming to our twenty-fifth wedding anniversary. She had a sinus and ear infection. She was also eight months pregnant. She needed to rest so she could deliver her baby without any problems. I was crushed. I had counted on her. To make it worse, Rebecca, a trained singer, was supposed to sing at the ceremony. I had to scramble. Rev. Karen urged me to use Ivonne. I was reluctant, but had little choice. So I asked her. She agreed.

I knew I should be grateful but I wasn't. Ivonne had been avoiding me for months. She hadn't initiated phone calls or returned them. She was no friend of mine. If I couldn't have someone who cared about my family and me, I would have preferred to have a total stranger. But there was no time to find and hire someone else.

I sent over the music Rebecca and I had chosen to Ivonne and the organist. Later that evening, the organist called me and suggested alternate pieces for Ivonne to sing. She didn't say it, but I understood Ivonne lacked the musical skill to sing the selected pieces. Another disappointment. There was this cloud that kept blowing over our renewal service. I had to keep pushing it back.

Saturday, the night before our twenty-fifth wedding anniversary, I invited Rev. Karen and our out-of-town guests to our house. I had repeatedly asked Lyndon if his family was coming over, but he never gave me a clear answer. That night we had our siblings and mothers at the house.

I had focused so much time and energy on planning the renewal ceremony and reception, I hadn't adequately planned Saturday night's dinner. I blew it. I, who usually cook an abundance of food, cooked too little. I didn't handle it with grace and poise. Instead, I fretted. "I don't think we have enough food," I said to Lyndon. I am sure my guests heard it. I apologized. I felt so embarrassed. I don't know why I didn't send him out to get some pizza. I don't know why it never occurred to me. Why no one else suggested it.

I had hoped after Rev. Karen met my siblings and mother, she would realize that despite whatever mistakes they might have made in their lives, they weren't villains and they weren't racist. But Rev. Karen wandered from the family room into the kitchen into the dining room, barely speaking to anyone. She hardly smiled, and she stood upright, as stiff as a board. This wasn't the warm and poised Rev. Karen I had seen at countless church functions. I don't know if it was my unease about the quantity of the food, or if she felt uncomfortable around so many black people, or around people she believed had mistreated James. As soon as she could politely do so, she left.

Sunday afternoon, Lyndon and I dressed for the renewal service. I had purchased a silver gown and had a matching hat made for the ceremony. We drove with our children to the church. As we pulled into the parking lot I saw Marie, a member of the congregation, scurrying up the sidewalk. She was dressed casually in jeans and a sports jacket. I was surprised to see her. We hadn't had much contact with each other. Her clothes and haste suggested she made a last-minute decision to come. Was this a sincere gesture of friendship? Since she never called me or spoke to me during coffee hour, I didn't know what to make of it.

My children, Lyndon and I entered the church through the classroom wing. Melissa and Orion walked down the aisle before us. Lyndon and I followed arm in arm. The ceremony went smoothly, except that people didn't sing the hymns. After renewing our vows, Lyndon and I exited the church with our children and drove to the Norton Country Club.

It was a gray winter day but it wasn't snowing or sleeting, so I was glad about that. We waited in the clubhouse lobby for our guests to arrive, and shook their hands as they entered. The mood was cheerful. I began to relax. This was going to be fun. This was going to work.

After our guests had found their seats, Lyndon and I entered the hall together and sat at a table with Rev. Karen and our elder sisters. My sister Rita later told me that Rev. Karen asked her about her work with North Carolina's Department of Social Services. Rita placed children with foster families. Rev. Karen said she was adopted, and had never had a desire to find her birthparents. Rita was surprised. Her work had nothing to do with reuniting adopted children with their birthparents.

After we ate dinner Lyndon and I made the rounds, talking to all the guests. Several of my church guests asked me when I was going to be returning from our vacation. It was odd that they never asked where we were going. Rev. Karen moved her seat to be with the other guests from

Immanuel. I didn't mind this. I understood that people would mingle with their friends and acquaintances.

The DJ I hired did his best to get people up and dancing. Slowly, people were getting on the dance floor. I urged everyone who was able to get up and have fun. The party was beginning to rock, and I was starting to have a great time. Then suddenly, our guests from Immanuel approached me and said they were sorry to leave early but they had work the next morning. It was only seven o'clock. We had the hall until nine p.m. Once one group left, then the guests with young children said they had to leave and get back to their kids. The waitstaff began cleaning off the tables including the water glasses. I stopped them and insisted they leave some water for the guests to drink.

At eight p.m., I found myself standing in the middle of the dance floor with only my children and husband around me. Disappointed, I had to push back the tears. Not even my siblings stayed. Melissa and Orion tried to comfort me. New Englanders, they told me, don't know how to party. They roll up the sidewalks at eight.

Most of the guests, I realized, had come to the ceremony and reception out of obligation. Very few of them sincerely wished Lyndon and me well. I guess I wanted people to finally accept and be happy about our biracial marriage. The only ones who truly appreciated the reception were a few of Lyndon's friends. One said the reception had been a needed reprieve after the September 11th attacks.

I went home that night with Lyndon and my children regretting the expense, the time and energy spent. Going forward with the renewal ceremony had been a mistake. I should have postponed it until our thirtieth anniversary and only invited the people who truly cared about us.

The Tuesday morning after our anniversary reception, Lyndon and I flew to Florida. We spent the first two nights at a bed-and-breakfast in St. Augustine, and then drove down to Disney World for the remainder of the week. We returned home on Tuesday the eighth. While our plane was landing in Providence, I leaned my head against the window and closed my eyes, remembering the time I flew into LaGuardia in New York City on a clear spring evening, dazzled by the lights of the Big Apple's skyline. As our plane touched down in Providence, I regretted our return. Massachusetts would never be home the way New York was. We had no friends, no family in New England.

On Sunday January 13, 2002, I entered Immanuel's sanctuary. It was lighted with candles. A snowstorm the night before had left the area without electricity. I paused at the entrance and looked around while I unzipped my coat. My eyes met Rev. Karen's. She was standing near the prayer book, dressed in her liturgical robes. Seeing me, her eyes widened, but she hastily covered up her surprise by walking toward me as she extended her hand. I realized in that instant that she hadn't expected me to return to Immanuel after our renewal ceremony.

Very few people were in the church. Ruth, Beverly, Jason and Jessica weren't there. I sat with Dorrie, a friend of Ruth's. After the service, I left immediately and didn't speak to anyone.

At home, I waited for people from church to call and welcome us back. The phone never rang. On January 20, twelve days after we returned home, I telephoned Beverly. She was sick.

"Oh, I'm sorry. I'll call back when you're feeling better," I said.

"No, I'm glad to hear from you," she said. She began to chatter about her work, her husband and the church, apparently unaware of my reactions to her rambling.

"You don't dance as well as the rest of your family," Beverly said to me. "They have more rhythm."

That sounded like a racist remark. What did she mean by that?

"Your anniversary party gave Paul and me a chance to talk to Ivonne and Tony over some drinks."

*Drinks? We didn't serve any alcohol at the party.*

Beverly said something about the Union Station Restaurant.

*Is that why they left the reception early? To go drink? Did I hear her right?*

"We've decided to take a vacation together to Nashville."

I felt a pang. I swallowed and took a deep breath. "That's nice," I said, hearing the false smile in my voice. "I'm glad you guys had a good time. I'll let you get some rest now."

I hung up the phone and immediately called my sister Rita, to congratulate her on the birth of her granddaughter, Olivia, two days before. While Rita and I were talking, I began to weep. It was then I realized Beverly's chatter about her friendships at church left me feeling excluded. She never extended an invitation to me to go anywhere or to do anything. This seemed to prove that I was never truly welcomed at Immanuel. No one ever called me except for my husband, children and niece, and occasionally Rita. Every day I came home and was disappointed that my email and voicemail were empty.

I tried to distract myself by staying busy, focusing on work and on reading. I considered finding a discussion group more intellectually stimulating than Immanuel's Bible study group. I wanted to find friends who were as well educated as I was and who understood and tolerated my emotionality. I investigated a few groups, and considered networking with other professional women. It was hard because so many people felt no need to let new people in.

The last week in January was tumultuous. I discovered that Ruth brought James to church while we were in Florida. A confirmation prayer attributed to James was published in the church's newsletter. He couldn't have written it. His written language skills weren't that good.

Upset, I pushed the fast-dial button to call Ruth but hit Beverly's number by mistake.

"I'm not feeling well," Beverly said. "My blood sugar is high."

"I can call back at a better time," I suggested.

"No, no, it is fine for us to talk."

After sharing my distress over the newsletter entry, Beverly became angry and hostile. "Why don't you just let it go!"

"It's not that easy," I told her. "James was my son. I loved him."

"If you had adopted James, then your reaction would be understandable," she responded. "You should have never taken him in. You weren't fit to parent him. You were never home."

Beverly's words rained down on my head like the fists of a schoolyard bully. I winced as I curled into a fetal position and covered my head. My hand gripped the phone so tight, my palm dripped with sweat. *How do I get out of this? I didn't mean to call her.*

"I don't understand you," she continued. "You need to see someone. You're sick. Let it go."

I was seeing Dr. Emmett, but I would never tell her that. "Bev," I tried to interrupt her, desperate to hang up and end her verbal barrage.

"I am going to hang up now," she said. "You need to let me hang up."

"'*Let*'" *you hang up?* I thought. *I have been trying to hang up. I want you to hang up. I need you to stop your verbal assault.*

With a final, "Don't call me back," she hung up the phone.

Shaken and tearful, I called Ruth. "We need a better solution. I don't know what to do. I am crying every day. I am on the verge of leaving the church. I want to find a win-win solution. Perhaps we could go talk to Rev. Karen. There must be a way to fix things."

"I don't think we should go to Rev. Karen," Ruth cautioned. "She's been very negative. I'm disturbed that you're thinking of leaving the church. I feel bad that you're so upset. Why don't we get together and talk? I'll do anything to help. I'm worried about you."

I had no solution to the situation. I didn't believe there would ever be a place for me at any church in Attleboro. The church made their choice. They made it before James left. I was tolerated but not wanted. Marginalized. Never really belonging. I wasn't willing to settle for that.

Several days after my phone conversations with Beverly and Ruth, another foster parent who had taken in two Sudanese boys called. Gwynne wanted me to come see the house she had just purchased. In the couple of years I knew Ruth and the others at church, I had never been invited to their home.

"It will take years before the James episode passes in the church," Gwynne said. "You shouldn't have to go to church with a scarlet letter sewn on your dress."

Gwynne was right about that, but since she didn't go to church, she didn't understand my need to belong to a community of faith.

I began distancing myself from my acquaintances at Immanuel while I considered my options. Not sure if there was a place for me beyond my home and work, I couldn't force myself to fit in where I didn't. I was who I was. I needed to find a group where I truly belonged, to find people who loved books and the free expression of ideas as much as I did. Maybe Gwynne was one of those people.

Although I was still willing to be friendly with people from Immanuel, I no longer hoped they would provide me with the companionship and loyalty I wanted from friends. If I joined another church, would Rev. Karen sabotage my membership there? I remembered her telling me it was common practice for clergy to call each other to warn them about problem parishioners. I wondered if she would do that to me. Would she tell them I was a church wrecker, spoiling any chance of my being accepted elsewhere? What would she do? How could I avoid that? Confront her directly, or just quietly slip away?

Over the next two weeks, I struggled with bouts of depression. My estrangement from Immanuel intensified my need for a spiritual connection with a faith community. On February 13 I attended Ash Wednesday services not at Immanuel, but at the local Episcopal church.

At lunchtime, I drove the mile to the fieldstone church occupying the opposite corner from the Catholic church. As I walked up the steps to its red doors, I looked around to see if anyone I knew was watching. Seeing no one, I slipped into the church and found myself in a vestibule with steps going up on the left and a long hallway in front of me. I hesitated until I noticed the massive wood doors at the top of the steps. I walked up the steps and found myself in the back of an aging sanctuary that needed some paint and a new carpet.

Seeing no one, I again paused until I heard voices coming from behind the columns on the far side of the sanctuary. I walked across the church and found people sitting in the side pews that formed a small chapel area. I chose a seat that was away from everyone else. There was a man in one of the pews, on his knees praying. Uncertain whether I was expected to kneel first before taking my seat, I sat half-kneeling and half-sitting and watched while other people entered the church, greeted each other and took their seats. Although I was relieved that everyone ignored my presence, I also felt alone and out of place.

At twelve noon, the priest and an assistant entered from the front of the church. I picked up The Book of Common Prayer and did my best to follow along. Although the Episcopalian service was similar to Lutheran and Catholic masses, they weren't identical. I wanted to be sure to stand and kneel at the right times. I didn't want to make a mistake and draw attention to myself.

After the opening prayers, a member of the congregation stood and read from Joel, "Blow the trumpet in Zion, sound the alarm ... a day of darkness and gloom ..."

I lifted my head and listened, and suppressed tears as I contemplated leaving Immanuel. I felt overwhelmed and hopeless.

"Return to the Lord, your God, for he is gracious and merciful...."

*I am here, Lord,* I prayed. *Look at me. Tell me what I should do. Tell me who is right and who is wrong. If I have sinned help me see it and repent. I want to make it right. I never wanted to hurt anyone.*

After the readings the priest delivered a homily. Although I remember being moved by it, I cannot tell you what he said. After the sermon, we were invited to come up and receive ashes. I was careful not to be the first or last person stepping out into the aisle. As I approached the altar, I paid attention to how each person before me behaved as they knelt before the priest. When it was my turn, I bowed my head and closed my eyes. I felt the priest make the sign of the cross on my forehead after he had dipped his right thumb into the ashes.

"Remember, you are dust and to dust you will return."

After the imposition of ashes, the Great Thanksgiving was recited and I again walked up to the altar rail to receive communion. After the service ended, the priest walked down the aisle and stood by the exit.

*What do I do now? What do I tell this minister? How do I hide my three failed attempts at belonging to a church since I moved to Massachusetts?*

People gathered around the priest. During my childhood, I had learned how to make myself invisible. I quietly walked past the priest, using the other worshipers as a blind. I don't think anyone noticed. If they did, I was quickly forgotten.

That evening, as I was on my way up to bed, I checked my email. I found a post from Rev. Karen. She had sent it at 10 p.m., after Immanuel's Ash Wednesday service. She wanted to give me "a heads-up" and warn me that James would be at the 9:30 service on Sunday.

Angered by what I saw as a betrayal by Ruth, who had told me she would never bring James to church when I was going to be there, I paced around the house. I decided to email her and Ruth. Lyndon urged me to wait a night before replying, but I didn't think it really mattered what I said or when I sent it. Rev. Karen was going to judge me negatively, or not hear it, or deny it had any validity anyway. At least by replying, I got to vent my rage.

First I emailed Ruth.

> Rev. Karen gave me the heads-up that James will be at the church on Sunday. I assume you are the one bringing him. Something to do with the ski trip. I am asking you, Ruth, to stop bringing James to the church and allow both of us to go our separate ways. I am a member of the church, not James. He lied and stole. Not me. It is time you stop thinking about yourself and truly think this through and stop hurting me so much.

I clicked send and off it went. Next, I replied to Rev. Karen's email.

> I don't know whether to thank you or curse you for the heads-up. Did you do that for me, or because you fear a scene at the church? I think if it was for me, you would have called and told me directly. I am a member of Immanuel,

not James. Why not just let him go? He has a new home
and church.

The last I had heard, James was going to a black church down
the street from his new home. Something I supported. Rev. Karen didn't
like it very much because it wasn't a Lutheran church. The message
continued:

> Why must I be pushed further and further out of the
> church? How would you feel if the church chose your
> husband over you? When will you stop judging and start
> trying to understand? When James left, my family should
> have been thanked by you publicly for taking him in and
> taking him as far as we could. Instead we were gossiped
> about and vilified. When will you minister to me as well as
> to James and the others?

The next morning I sat in my living room with the loose-leaf binder
that contained my journal. I had decided to work through my thoughts
and feelings by writing. I took out a blank piece of paper and wrote across
the top of the page, My Complaint against Rev. Karen, Ruth, Jessica, Ivonne
and Beverly. I then began a summary of what had happened with James. I
got as far as James going to the school dance without our permission
when the arrival of my first client forced me to set it aside.

In the evening around dinnertime I received Rev. Karen's reply to
my last email. She took exception to my remark about her husband.
I winced. She was probably right about that. She didn't see it as a matter
of choosing. Church services, she wrote, were open to anyone. She
couldn't tell anyone to stay away unless they created a disruption. She
had been told I wanted to know if James was coming to services.

Who had told her that? Beverly? Ruth? I hadn't. What I wanted was
for them to stop driving forty miles into Boston and bringing James back
to Immanuel. That is what I wanted.

Rev. Karen explained she was going to be away for this year's ski trip
and would be back in her office on March 5. She would seek "some
outside advice (outside of Immanuel, that is) on this issue" on how to
handle it in the future.

I emailed Rev. Karen the following day.

> The remark about your husband was my effort to get you to
> understand this from my point of view. No offense was

intended. What offended me about your email was your
failure to speak directly to me about a very painful issue. It
appears to me you are avoiding talking to me but have no
trouble talking about me with others. We can pick this up
when you get back in March.

Instead of going to church on Sunday, I chose to stay home and
write in my journal. I was trying to process all that had happened at the
church. Should I stay or go? I was trying to be heard and respected. The
more I tried, the more church members became emotionally abusive
toward me. They were feeding off my distress and kicking me when I was
down.

I was slowly coming to accept that they were never going to listen to
me. Seeing and indulging James satisfied their own needs. They were
venting their anger and rage on me. Perhaps they were getting even for
some slight they never told me about. If that assessment was right, the
thing to do would be to ignore them.

I picked up where I had left off on my written complaint. As I wrote,
what I wanted and needed became clearer.

Our desire to have James out of our lives needs to be
honored. James is now living in Boston in an all-male
household. He has a church there he can attend. If people
want to see him they can visit him there. There is no need
to bring him to Attleboro. His presence disrupts my life,
doesn't give us the time and space to heal; it just keeps
opening up the wounds. Church has become unsafe for me.
I never know when I will be accused of saying or doing the
wrong thing. If I cry, no one wants to take the time to
understand how and why I feel the way I do.

I sat back and looked at what I had just written. I wanted to remain
a member of Immanuel, but needed to work things out with Rev. Karen
in some way. I no longer hoped I would find and make friends at the
church. But I wanted to go to mass to worship God undisturbed.

I remembered Mallory's kind words to me around Thanksgiving.
I had noticed in the last newsletter that she was the current vice president
of the Church Council. I decided to call her. Maybe she would be willing
to help me find a way to remain at Immanuel. I hoped a neutral third
party could help us resolve the conflict and find a win-win solution.

Mallory asked me for a written summary of my complaint. On February 21, I edited the complaint I had written in my journal and emailed her a typed copy.

On February 24 I went to the early morning service, wanting to avoid my adversaries who usually attended the 9:30 mass. When I entered the sanctuary, I was surprised to find Ivonne and several of the people I was trying to avoid there. Reading over the order of service, I saw that Ivonne was singing the anthem. Since she and her friends were sitting in the back near the organ, I decided to sit on the pulpit side of the church toward the front. I was as far away from them as I could possibly be.

During the Peace, Ivonne and Irene crossed the aisle and approached me from behind and to the side. Before I could extend my hand, they hugged me. I wasn't able to push them away.

I didn't want to be hugged by them because they weren't returning my phone calls. They weren't my friends. They were just pretending to be good Christians. I found their behavior to be emotionally abusive. It made me feel dirty.

After church I rushed home and took a shower, trying to scrub their hugs off. They had ignored and disrespected my needs and invaded by personal space, just like Mr. Stahl and Uncle Frank had when I was a child. I was being denied the right to choose who, when and how I was to be touched. Feeling violated, I took several extra showers throughout the week, trying to rid myself of the feel of their touch. All I wanted was to go to church and worship quietly and not be bothered by anyone. I just wanted to be left alone.

I found myself wishing I could go back to that place I used to go, that white space that belonged just to me. Even though I cut and burned myself in that space, it belonged to me. I controlled it. The pain was wholly and exquisitely mine, a friend that never abandoned me.

I wished I could will myself back to the white space, but I had lost the ability to go there. Besides, I had promised to call Dr. Emmett whenever I felt like hurting myself. I wasn't going to break a promise. The promise kept me safe.

A funny thing, though, was that when I was unhealthy and not taking care of myself, not reaching out to others, there were more people beyond my family who emailed me, who returned calls, who behaved as if they were my friends. Now that I was healthier, not going to the white space, not pretending, no one called, not even to say goodbye.

Dr. Emmett pointed out the pattern of my being singled out and scapegoated within my family of origin and within the church. But I didn't know how to stop it from happening. What was it that I was doing or failing to do? How could I change it?

Lyndon and Melissa believed I was too nice about things, that I didn't fight back effectively, didn't defend myself very well. I was easily intimidated. My former therapist used to say I needed to learn to engage in some verbal fencing. In many ways, they were right. I caved in and withdrew too easily.

Sending my complaint to Mallory made be feel I had more control over my life. As my mood improved, I felt life was moving forward. Following Mallory's advice, I didn't discuss my complaint with anyone, including Rev. Karen. Mallory then asked me to provide her with a list of names of anyone who had or had not been helpful. I told her it wasn't that simple, and divided the list of names into those who were initially supportive and then withdrew, those who had been unsupportive and hostile, and bystanders.

At the end of February, Mallory put me in touch with Sarah, the chair of the Staff Support Committee who handled relations with Immanuel's minister. Sarah first wanted the committee to meet with Rev. Karen and me separately. Sarah regretted that she wouldn't be able to get her committee together until after Easter. I was unhappy about the delay, but had no choice but to accept it.

Following Mallory's suggestion, I sent for and received from the Evangelical Lutheran Church's national office two copies of their ethical standards for ministers and church leaders, and copies of a document entitled, "Visions and Expectations." I gave Mallory a copy.

On March 7, Rev. Karen called to set up a meeting. I believed she hadn't been told about my complaint yet, and that she was merely responding to the email I had sent just prior to President's Day. On Saturday afternoon, I walked through the woods to church to speak with her. When I arrived, she behaved very oddly. Instead of sitting in her rocking chair as she usually did, she took a seat behind her desk. I took my usual seat on the black couch. This placed her in a higher position than me.

Instead of inviting discussion of my concerns, she took on a stern tone as she said, "James is a member of Immanuel, and you will have to accept it."

*She's doing the one up, one down thing,* I thought. *She isn't going to listen to me.*

I stared directly at her and said, "James is brought. He doesn't come by himself."

"And as for Mallory ... I have dealt with her."

I felt panic. *My one ally–* I rose up. I didn't have to take this. I wasn't going to be reprimanded by Rev. Karen. She wasn't my superior. I wasn't going to be treated like a disobedient child.

"Sit down," she ordered.

"No, I am leaving." I gave weight to each word while I moved toward the door.

Her eyes widened and she straightened in her chair. She hadn't expected my open defiance. "I am the pastor to other members of this church, too."

I stopped in front of her 30 by 60 desk piled high with papers. "That's right," I said, raising my voice. "But you are supposed to be my pastor, too." It was then I noticed my hands were clenched tightly in a fist. Had Rev. Karen noticed? I didn't want Rev. Karen to think she had anything to fear from me. I was angry but I would never attack her. I lowered and opened my hands, pressing my sweaty palms against my thighs. I took a step toward the door.

"You can call Rev. Rachael if you want," Rev. Karen taunted. "She won't help you."

I hesitated. *Who is Rev. Rachael? Better not to ask. I'll figure it out later. She must be someone in the bishop's office.* "I will," I said, and walked out the door, slamming it behind me.

I almost ran across the church's back lawn and up the hill into the woods. Three minutes later when I arrived home, I was out of breath and crying. I immediately called Mallory and left a message. "I just met with Rev. Karen," I panted. "I'm worried I have put you in a bad position. I never meant to make trouble for you."

I fretted the rest of the day and despaired when I didn't hear from Mallory. While I was undressing for bed the phone rang. It was Mallory.

"What did you tell her?" she whispered.

I explained what happened when I met with Rev. Karen.

"I'm not supposed to be talking to you. Rev. Karen met with me with someone else present. I'm on the church council. It's a conflict of interest."

"I don't understand. How is it a conflict of interest?"

"You'll need my vote later. I can't be involved now. Contact the bishop's office."

Mallory was cutting me loose. I could no longer depend on her. Instead of making things better for me, her advice had only made things worse. When I hung up the phone I climbed into my bed, too numb to cry.

The next morning I went to the healing service at Immanuel. My stomach was queasy and my heart was racing when I walked up to the altar rail to have my head anointed. Rev. Karen's hands shook as she placed them on my head. I was surprised. Her hands had always been firm and sure. *She's afraid of me*, I thought. My open defiance the day before had unnerved her.

I followed Mallory's advice and called the bishop's office. I spoke with Rev. Ronald, a bishop's associate. He advised me I needed to make a formal written complaint before any action would be taken. He also told me I should read Immanuel's constitution before I did so. He had a secretary email me a copy of the Evangelical Lutheran Church of America's constitution.

The logical person to ask for Immanuel's constitution was from Laurie, the church's secretary. But she was closely allied with Rev. Karen, so I decided to try to get it from another church member. I made several calls. No one had a copy. Desperate, I called Christopher, a board member. I was close to tears when I said, "I don't want to get you involved."

"Thank you for that. I don't have a copy of the church's constitution. Laurie may have it."

After I got off the phone with Christopher, I reluctantly dialed the church and left a message.

A few days later on Friday, I received a call from Sarah. "I and the Staff Support Committee want to meet with you tomorrow."

I glanced at my desk calendar. It was March 15. "I thought we were going to meet after Easter."

"Something has come up," she answered. "Rev. Karen will be present."

"I thought you wanted to meet with each of us separately first."

"It needs to be this way," Sarah insisted.

*Something's not right,* I thought. *Maybe I should tell her I can't make it.* Saturday was Melissa birthday. It really wasn't a convenient time. "It is rather short notice."

"Why don't we schedule the meeting for another time?"

Sarah's voice had changed. Did she really want to meet? "I'm not sure—"

"We can wait until after Easter," Sarah said.

"I might have plans for tomorrow."

"Why don't you wait until after Easter?"

Was she trying to warn me? *Beware the Ides of March. Don't be silly. This isn't a Shakespearean play.* "No," I said, "it's okay. Can I bring someone with me?" An ally might help.

"Yes," Sarah said.

"By the way, I still haven't gotten a copy of the constitution."

"You will have it by the end of the day."

The mail arrived around noon. I quickly picked out the 12 by 10 envelope from Immanuel and tore it open. Immanuel's constitution had been typed and printed out on standard white copy paper. I went into my study and sat down in my recliner to read it. I searched for the section that covered complaints against the minister and how to initiate mediation. It wasn't there. There was only a section describing how a minister could bring disciplinary action against a lay member of the congregation:

> C15.01 Denial of the Christian faith as described in this constitution, conduct grossly unbecoming a member of the Church of Christ, or persistent trouble making in this congregation are sufficient cause for discipline of a member. Prior to disciplinary action, reconciliation will be attempted following Matthew 18:15-17, proceeding through these successive steps: a) private admonition by the pastor, b) admonition by the pastor in the presence of two or three witnesses, and c) citation to appear before the congregation council.

I stood up and began to pace. I reread the section. That was why Rev. Karen behaved the way she had at our last meeting. It was meant as "a private admonition by the pastor," and the proposed meeting with the committee was to be "an admonition by the pastor in the presence of two or three witnesses." Rev. Karen's ultimate goal was to suspend or exclude me from membership in Immanuel.

With my heart racing, I dropped the constitution on my chair and walked into the living room, picked up the Bible from the glass end table and turned it over to the back. Resting the book on my left forearm, I opened it. The header said "Romans." I thumbed through the pages. *Damn ... I passed it.* I slowed down and turned the pages back more carefully. *Okay, Matthew. What chapter?*

I walked back into my study and picked up the constitution. My eyes scanned the section. Matthew 18. I turned back to the Bible on my forearm. *Here it is.* "At the time the disciples came to Jesus ..." *Wait, what verse am I looking for?* I glanced back at the constitution. Verses 15 to 17. My fingers moved down the page while my eyes scanned the numbers. *Here it is:*

> If another member of the church sins against you, go and point out the fault when the two of you are alone. If the member listens to you, you have regained that one. But if you are not listened to, take one or two others along with you, so that every word may be confirmed by the evidence of two or three witnesses. If the member refuses to listen to them, tell it to the church; and if the offender refuses to listen even to the church, let such a one be to you as a Gentile and a tax collector.

Matthew 18 presumed a person was guilty. There was no provision for the accused to be represented by an advocate, nor was there any provision for a fair hearing before impartial judges. I reread Immanuel's constitution, looking for a definition of persistent troublemaking. There was none. Apparently, it was anything the minister said it was.

In contrast, a minister could only be removed for physical or mental incapacity that was supported by competent medical testimony, or when the pastor had been disciplined by the bishop. I pulled out my copy of the 1994 "Definitions and Guidelines for Discipline" I had received from the national office. It was very clear. A minister could only be sanctioned for "preaching or teaching in conflict with the faith confessed by this church," and adultery, promiscuity and sexual abuse of another.

After putting my Bible away, I called Sarah back. "Is the purpose of the meeting to discipline me?"

"Yes," she replied.

"Why didn't you tell me?" I asked.

"It wasn't for me to tell you."

"Do you think this is right?"

Sarah didn't answer.

"All I want is to discuss it and find a win-win solution to the conflict."

"That is the way Rev. Karen wanted it."

"Rev. Karen is a fucking bitch! She is abusing her power as minister."

Sarah became hostile. "I can't help you. I don't know who can. Why don't you take some time away from church?"

*Time away from the church?* That was a euphemism. What she meant was leave the church and never come back. I was no longer welcomed there. If I left, I would save them all the trouble of a formal disciplinary hearing. Tomorrow's meeting would be nothing more than a kangaroo court.

"I will not be coming to the meeting," I said, and hung up the phone. Rev. Karen had played hardball and had successfully trumped me. I was completely spent. To preserve my own mental health, I stopped attending Sunday services at Immanuel.

On Sunday March 17, Lyndon and I took Melissa to a high-end restaurant for her birthday. An old childhood friend from New York who was now living nearby came with us. It was so pleasant to sit and talk about old times. We laughed as we shared stories about the girls' childhoods. We had something good and special on Long Island. Moving to New England had been a social disaster. The good life was right where we were, and we left it all behind for what? Money? Professional advancement? In the end, it wasn't worth it.

The next day while browsing through my junk mail, an advertisement for Mary Hammond's *The Church and the Dechurched* caught my eye. I immediately logged onto the Internet and ordered the book.

On Thursday, March 21, I wrote and sent a letter to the bishop's associate making a formal complaint against Rev. Karen. I requested an impartial investigation into the events following the termination of James' placement with our family.

...Rev. Karen has not been in right relationship with my family and me. She usurped my husband's and my authority over our foster son and inappropriately intruded on our family life. She has not been empathetic, has denied my pain and has misused and continues to misuse personal information she has about me. Rev. Karen has repeatedly tried to silence me for reasons I do not fully understand. Rev. Karen also served as a conduit for gossip. Much of what I said and did has been taken out of context, making church a very unsafe place emotionally for me.

...I am not seeking to have Rev. Karen removed as minister nor do I want her censored. I merely want to be heard and have our conflict mediated and resolved in a constructive way. In order for that to happen there needs to be an impartial investigation and mediation of the conflict. I respectfully ask you for your assistance in arranging that. I am willing to provide you with any information or documentation that you require.

I felt good right after I mailed the letter. My mood changed during lunch, after I read an article in the newspaper about the Catholic Church sex scandal. Over the years it had been difficult to prosecute any clergy, regardless of denomination, for sexual abuse. Clergy were presumed to be good. In Florida, they convicted and sentenced a priest to life in prison for raping children. After serving only two years, the governor granted him clemency. From the day of his arrest he told police and the district attorney he had friends in high places.

Reading the article put me in a dark mood. I felt irritable. If you can't make an obvious, blatant crime stick, how impossible it would be for anyone beyond my family to understand how emotionally abusive Rev. Karen became, and how seriously she violated boundaries.

Friday evening, Lyndon was tired and wanted to be left alone. Feeling rejected and abandoned, I quarreled with him. Unable to get him to give me the attention I craved and needed, I went upstairs and curled up under the covers. I vented my rage by impulsively scratching my leg, breaking the skin in several places.

Feeling better immediately afterward, I was glad I had done it. I didn't feel any regret until the following afternoon. I thought of telling

Dr. Emmett. Then I thought I would just tell Dr. Emmett to shove it and that I would do what I wanted. But that wasn't the way to handle the rage. It wasn't right. I should have called Dr. Emmett Friday afternoon when I started getting into the funk, but it was his day off. I was worried if I called too much, eventually he wouldn't want anything to do with me. I expected he would eventually betray me in some way.

The book I ordered arrived at the start of Holy Week. After setting the box on the kitchen table, I tore it open and removed the book from its shrink-wrapping. After examining the book's steel-blue cover with the shattered red cross on the front, I turned it over and read the back cover.

"Dechurched people are those who have lost a faith they valued or left a faith community because of a bad experience."

My heart pounded. My breathing quickened. *This book,* I thought, *is speaking to me.* I carried it into my study and curled up in my recliner. After reading the introduction I turned to the first chapter, "Stories of the Dechurched." I wasn't the only one. My experiences at Murray, FXUU and Immanuel were not unusual. There even was a woman who had been dechurched multiple times just as I had.

Mary Hammond, an American Baptist minister, wrote that churches often operate like dysfunctional families, enforcing *don't talk, don't feel, don't think,* and *don't trust* rules. *Yes, yes,* I thought, *that is what happened.* As a child I was often yelled at or made fun of for crying by my parents and classmates. In both my FXUU and Immanuel experiences, my anger was treated as inappropriate, especially when I directed it at clergy and the church leadership. I wasn't supposed to feel. My legitimate anger about Rev. Dorothy's deceit and Rev. Karen's undermining of our parental authority was repressed. Rev. Dorothy and Rev. Karen encouraged me to respond with silence and "shallow acts of forgiveness," as the *Dechurched* book described it. When I didn't, I was punished with shunning and threatened with disciplinary action.

The don't trust rule, I read, discourages members from sharing their personal struggles with mental illness, sexual abuse, addiction, marital distress and other problems. I had unwittingly broken this rule when I disclosed my history of sexual abuse to Rev. Karen and told my friends at Bible study about the conflict at FXUU. Instead of being a refuge where "weary, brokenhearted individuals could speak the truth of their lives and discover unconditional love," Immanuel was a place where I was expected "to don guarded masks and wear them constantly." When I broke the don't trust rule, just as Rev. Hammond wrote, instead of receiving support, I was rebuked, lectured and stigmatized.

On Holy Thursday, I attended the noonday service hosted by the Council of Churches at Central Congregational Church. Worried about what Rev. Carol and the other ministers had been told about me, I took a seat away from the other worshipers. At the end of the service I was the first to leave the sanctuary and go downstairs to the fellowship hall. I passed Rev. Karen, who had just arrived on the landing. Our eyes met. My heart started racing. I looked away and continued on my way without speaking to her.

The following morning, inspired by Mary Hammond's book, I wrote an affirmation in my journal.

> This morning with the sun shining through the front window, I am fierce with life. I am rediscovering, reinventing myself. I am taking the pain of the last three years and I am integrating it and using it to become more completely me. No more using my creative energies to try to please others. Instead I am going to use my life energy to write and study and understand what my life has been about. I am going to use it to help others, to stop the pain, the evil that infects us. I am going to integrate my knowledge of psychology, religion, my personal experiences of being bullied, my personal trauma, and use it to help others, to advance our knowledge of the human condition.

On April 1, the day after Easter, I made an early morning call to Dr. Emmett for our scheduled phone session. During the call, he focused on the March 22 self-harming incident. "I don't care," I insisted. "I'm glad I did it. It makes me feel better."

Dr. Emmett switched to talking about Immanuel, then he tried to talk about the self-harm again. By the end of the session, I felt overwhelmed. Anxious, I shut down for several hours. I couldn't let go of the self-harming behavior. I wanted it. It was under my control. It was more dependable than a friend. It was always there when I needed it.

Mid-morning, I walked out to the mailbox and found a letter from Rev. Ronald. He thanked me for my letter and informed me he had spoken to Rev. Rachael, the bishop's associate for the region Immanuel was in. He also gave her my letter. He didn't say if, when and how she would be contacting me.

Once back inside the house, I went into my study and logged onto the Internet. I found Rev. Rachael's contact information on the synod's website and immediately emailed her. I provided her with my contact information. Mid-afternoon, I checked my email. Rev. Rachael had replied that although she had spoken to Rev. Ronald on the telephone, she hadn't received my letter yet. She suggested that I email her the nature and details of my complaint to her. I responded by sending her a copy of my letter.

Forty-five minutes later, I wrote in my journal,

> Churches are dysfunctional. Don't talk. Don't feel. Don't think. Pretend things are good, that you believe, that we are all saved. Saved from what? Not evil. Evil exists. Bad things happen to good people. No place is safe. Ministers are despots in their own private kingdoms. Stay away from them. Danger. Beware!

I took my pen and slammed it into the paper scribbling all over the page. Just below the scribble, I vented my rage.

Fuck.     Shit.      Bastards.
Cut. Burn. Feel better.
I    did    nothing    wrong.

I panted as if I had just flipped over some table and chairs. I waited for my breathing and heart rate to slow down. Then I wrote,

> Then why am I hurting myself? Haven't I been punished enough for speaking out, for feeling? What church would want a three-time loser? Perhaps I should go into Providence and enjoy the music and serenity of the Episcopal service there. Perhaps I should go to the Episcopal church in town. Should I trust again? Take another risk? Another blow could be even more devastating. At times I am tempted to return to Immanuel, make my presence felt. Make them deal with me. Let them be uncomfortable sitting in the sanctuary with me. I hold on too long. Once they betrayed me back in June I should have left.

When Rev. Rachael didn't confirm that she had received my letter, I worried she hadn't gotten it or had had difficulty opening the letter. But she should have received the original from Rev. Ronald. So why wasn't she responding? Unable to wait any longer, I emailed Rev. Rachael on April 8 at eight in the morning.

> Please advise me on how you plan to proceed. I don't know what to reasonably expect. Please pardon me if I appear impatient. This unfortunate situation has caused me and others considerable emotional distress. I am anxious to get it resolved.

Four hours later Rev. Rachael responded. She received Rev. Ronald's letter but was out of the office for a few days. The tension in my shoulders eased. She wasn't ignoring my complaint, but why hadn't she told me she would be out? When she asked for the email, I assumed she would be handling it right away. Otherwise she could have just waited for the letter. I continued reading.

> You needn't apologize for appearing impatient ... It is evident that you are in considerable pain related to your relationship with Pastor Karen and Immanuel Lutheran Church.

*Good, she sees that.* Hope rose in my heart.

> Please be assured that you are still in my prayers, in hope that the strain on these relationships may be resolved. It is certainly true, as St. Paul writes, that when one member of the Body is injured, all suffer.

Like a wave, my hope for reconciliation swelled.

> It is not clear from your letter whether any of Pastor Karen's alleged offenses rises to the level requiring intervention by the Office of the Bishop. If that is not the case, and you have tried unsuccessfully to address the issues with her directly, the next step would be to ask to meet with her in the presence of a couple of council members—

I moaned. *But I already did that. Rev. Karen turned it into an ambush.* Rev. Rachael ended her email with, "May the Peace of the Risen Christ empower and sustain you." *I could use a little less God talk and more action,* I thought as I closed the email. Picking up my journal, I moved to my recliner. I touched the tip of my pen to a blank page. Nothing. I couldn't write. What was the point?

Over the next three days, I mulled over Rev. Rachael's letter. I wasn't going to subject myself to Immanuel's kangaroo court. Like a boxer who has been knocked down but not out, I rose to my feet. I emailed Rev. Rachael on April 11.

> I believe the conflict between myself and Rev. Karen has risen to the level requiring intervention by the Office of the Bishop. What information do you need me to provide you in order to clarify this?

Remembering Rev. Karen telling me Rev. Rachael was not going to help me I asked,

> Have you or anyone else in the Office of the Bishop communicated in any way with Rev. Karen regarding me and/or my complaint either before or after I sent the letter to Rev. Ronald? If not, at what point would you do that? If you have communicated with her regarding this matter, what was Rev. Karen's response?

I was fairly certain Rev. Rachael had discussed me with Rev. Karen. If Rev. Karen had been shown my letter, it would only be fair for them to tell me what, if any, were her charges against me.

Several hours later, Rev. Rachael responded to my email. "Let me reiterate," she wrote, "my empathy for you as you struggle through this conflict with Rev. Karen."

*Here we go,* I thought. *This is the part where she tells me how much she understands but she can't do anything to help.*

Rev. Rachael denied communicating with Rev. Karen about my complaint, but was "certain that it must be a source of anguish for her as well."

*Yes, of course it is. I know that. So let's sit down and work this out. There must be a win-win solution.*

Rev. Rachael went on to explain, "Like the discipline of any member, the basis for a parishioner's complaint against a pastor is found in Matthew 18, beginning with a face-to-face conversation, and aiming always toward reconciliation."

Matthew 18? I was being bludgeoned with the Bible and told to do what I had already tried. Reconciliation? How I longed for that. That's why I approached Mallory. I needed a neutral third party to mediate my conflict with Rev. Karen.

If one-on-one efforts failed, Rev. Rachael advised me to speak with the mutual ministry committee or congregation council. If the dispute remained unresolved, it was then up to the council to request help from the bishop's office. Without such a request, the bishop's authority to discipline a pastor was limited to matters of gross misconduct.

Rev. Rachael's advice was to go in front of a committee that had already tried to ambush me. I wasn't going to subject myself to any more emotional abuse. The wave carrying my hope for reconciliation crashed upon the rocks.

# Labyrinth Walk

Following my failure to get the bishop's office to help me, my childhood feelings of abandonment, rejection and worthlessness resurfaced and intensified. Sinking down into my recliner at the end of a busy day I was flooded with traumatic memories and feelings.

Once, when I was walking home alone from high school with my books resting in the crook of my right arm, an obese boy from my class called out from behind me, "Hey, look at the square!"

I straightened my back and tightened my grasp around the handle on my viola case. Looking straight ahead, I climbed the railroad embankment and crossed the tracks. As I reached Long Island Avenue the boy caught up with me.

"Hey, Margaret, what music do you like?"

"Classical," I answered, hoping he would leave me alone.

He started laughing. "That's your problem. You're queer."

I sucked in my tears and quickened my pace. The boy ran up beside me. "You're really ugly."

"Leave me alone!" Tears rolled down my cheeks despite my best efforts to stop them.

"What a baby." He sneered while his eyes glistened with satisfaction.

I wiped my tears, sucked in my stomach and straightened my back. I looked straight ahead and walked toward home. The boy moved closer and sniffed. "What's that smell?" He pinched his nose. "BO."

I turned my head toward him and stared. It didn't make sense. I had showered, brushed my teeth and put on clean clothes that morning. How could I possibly smell? I took a deep breath, trying to muffle the sob rising from the core of my being. The boy, seeing my distress, laughed more. Shamed, I turned my face away.

Nothing I did or said was acceptable. My own father told me nobody would ever want me. I began sobbing. My very being was wrong. My birth was wrong. Satisfied, the boy ran off toward his home.

When I graduated from high school, I thought I was leaving the bullying behind. My teachers had often told me it would be better in college. I would be with other kids like me who would accept me as I was. But it didn't work out that way. I was so depressed and miserable I made no lasting friends in college either. After I graduated from college and married, I searched for a place where I would be welcomed in one church after another. I was drawn into Immanuel by Rev. Karen's kindness. Finally, I thought I had a community where I belonged. I didn't understand how conditional that acceptance would be.

Like an abandoned child longing for her mother, I wanted someone from Immanuel to reach out to me, ask me what had happened, and help right the wrong done to me. On April 17 I telephoned Ruth and Mallory, leaving messages for them to call if they wanted to be friends. In between clients, I checked my home voicemail for messages. They didn't call.

As I reset the answering machine, I saw in my mind's eye Rev. Karen and the Bible study group running away from me while I stood alone. *Wait, please wait*, I called. Ruth and Mallory stopped and looked back. As they started to take a step toward me, Rev. Karen stepped between them and me. Rev. Karen said something. I couldn't hear it. Ruth and Mallory turned away. I fell to my knees and wept as they joined the stampede away from me. They never really were my friends.

On April 16, I had visited Mary Hammond's church's webpage and sent her an email. Rev. Mary responded almost immediately and informed me that working with individuals who had been mistreated by congregations was "a unique ministry" for her church. She felt privileged to walk along with me while I tried to work through my thoughts, concerns and experiences with abuse in churches.

Two days later I emailed her back.

> Thank you for replying to my email. Until I get to know you better and feel safe I am not going to provide you with any details about what has happened. My recent experiences have made me wary of ministers.

> My current plans are to do some reading and research, maybe write an article or two. I have been thinking long and hard about how and why this happened. I am trying to make some coherent sense of it all. One way you could help is share with me just what kind of training you received in clergy ethics. I am a psychologist and as part of my training had to take an ethics course and learn the American Psychological Association's ethics code inside and out. I have reviewed my denomination's ethics code for ministers

and am appalled by what is not covered in it. Psychology's ethics code is far more explicit and stringent. It appears psychologists are held to a higher standard than clergy are.

Rev. Mary responded with a two-and-a-half-page email explaining that she didn't have a class on clergy ethics "but had to sign a Code of Ethics about pastoral conduct." She believed that all denominations required "a class on Denominational History and Polity, and that the Code of Ethics is covered in there." Rev. Mary further wrote,

> Another part of the Code of Ethics is related to how pastors comport themselves with other clergy and respecting of boundaries of their ministries (I think that has been related to churches trying to woo parishioners from other congregations). I know sexual ethics are included in the Code of Ethics. Also included are how pastors "leave" churches, without staying entangled with members in ways that undercut the following pastor's authority.

That was the part Rev. Dorothy had been so concerned about and why she insisted on telling Rev. Patience about my personal problems. I continued reading.

> Many denominations also have types of "watch care" programs for their seminarians as they work with mentor pastors... So, there are various checks and balances in place, particularly as one prepares for ministry and begins the work of ministry. After one has been in ministry for awhile, that accountability may be weaker.

Like the blue line of police officers, I thought. Once someone became a minister, their fellow clergy uncritically jumped to their defense and prevented others from holding them accountable for ethics breaches.

Rev. Mary continued:

> The other reality I have found is that, in a dysfunctional church, dealing functionally with conflict is a misnomer. If there are other signs of dysfunction and denial in the congregational life, then dealing with conflict badly often just goes along with this. Many church members don't deal well with conflict in their own lives, either...

Both Rev. Dorothy and Rev. Karen had failed in their marriages. So they certainly had had difficulty handling conflict with their significant others. I wondered how that affected their leadership roles in their congregations. Avoiding or suppressing conflict appeared to be preferred over open and honest discussion. At FXUU, Rev. Terry advised us to no longer discuss the conflict with Rev. Dick. Rev. Karen had also squashed discussion about James. Their actions prevented any true resolution, in the end leading to more conflict.

Rev. Mary and I continued to correspond with each other over the next couple of years. I eventually told her what happened with James. Every time I sent her an email, I would wait fearfully for her to reply. I feared that the more she knew me the less she would want to associate with me. I feared she too would view me as a toxic antagonist or persistent troublemaker. Her quick and long responses to my emails proved that she was more reliable and honest than that.

During the months following my dechurching from Immanuel, my mood swung between rage and inconsolable grief. It was difficult to drive past the church and not feel the sting of rejection.

I needed to talk the way someone who has almost drowned gulps for air. I needed to talk, even though talking was extremely painful. I feared Dr. Emmett would grow tired of my crying and neediness. I feared he would tell me I was "too much," just as Rev. Dorothy had. Rev. Karen told me she had more important things to deal with. She didn't recognize my grief as legitimate. She insisted it was only an issue for me and no one else, implying that my feelings and concerns weren't valid. Even though the religious perspective insists that every single human being has value, I was not valued.

I longed for the relief cutting or burning my arms would give me. I imagined stabbing my armpit and ripping all the way down to my wrist and just letting all the pain run out. If I did that, I thought, I would be in the white space beyond all pain.

Frightened, I called Dr. Emmett on April 29. I apologized for breaking my promise at the end of March and recommitted to calling him prior to any self-harming behavior. Dr. Emmett pointed out that most of my emotional distress was over how I was neglected and abused at home, school and church. I was distressed that I wasn't cared for or nurtured.

"I hope," he said, "you will at least take care of yourself. You would at least be able to count on yourself."

I hadn't considered that. I had spent my adult life caring for my clients and my children. I had never learned to nurture myself. In response to all the emotional and verbal abuse, it was I who was cutting and burning my arms. I had joined my tormenters in harming me. Internalizing all the taunts and putdowns, I erroneously concluded something was inherently defective in my character. No matter how hard I tried, I couldn't correct it. The only solution I could see was to destroy myself.

Over the years, I kept trying to live up to the standards of abusive systems. Like the miller in Aesop's fable, "The Miller, His Son, and Their Ass," I responded to people's criticism by redoubling my efforts to be a more sensitive and caring person. But no matter how much I tried, I couldn't gain their acceptance. I failed to recognize they were projecting their own fears onto me. It hadn't occurred to me that what my tormentors said about me was wrong, and it was they who needed to repent and correct their behavior.

Judith Herman's *Trauma and Recovery* makes it clear that survivors' emotional distress and rage has more to do with their perpetrators' betrayal and very little to do with the survivor's personality. If someone had struck my knee with a baseball bat, no one would be surprised that the blow had shattered my kneecap. No one would whisper that the injury was due to my defective character. If enough stress is applied, all of us would eventually break.

I hungered for the spiritual solace attending church gave me. Although I found the Episcopal service to be stodgier than the Catholic mass of my youth, during March and April I visited several Episcopal churches in the area. I didn't attend any of the other Lutheran churches because I feared Rev. Karen had spread malicious rumors among all the Lutheran ministers and I wouldn't be welcomed in their churches.

Terrified, I drove into Providence and attended services at the Episcopal church, where there was little chance anyone would know me. As if I had a scarlet letter sewn to my dress, I furtively took a seat away from the other worshipers. Speaking to no one, I sought God's protective embrace.

During the service, a woman who had been raised in the church and who raised all her children in the same church spoke about the love and care she had received from her religious community. Like a starving child looking through a window while people feasted and who would never be invited to stay, I envied her. Tears filled my eyes. Where and when would I find a spiritual home? Exiled, I had become a spiritual nomad, taking up residence for a season and moving on when I was no longer welcomed.

Feeling the sorrow and fear rise within me, I bowed my head and closed my eyes. If anyone noticed they would think I was praying. I purposely breathed slow and deeply. I leaned forward, placing my elbows on my knees while resting my head in my hands. In my mind's eye I saw Jesus walking close to me. I touched his robe and God blessed me. I belonged to Him.

I was voraciously reading anything having to do with clergy misconduct and ethics. I wanted to understand what happened to me and what to do to prevent it from happening again. In May I read Candace Benyei's book, *Understanding Clergy Misconduct in Religious Systems: Scapegoating, Family Secrets and the Abuse of Power.*

On May 30, I attempted to integrate my personal experience with what I had been reading about churches and about bullying in schools by writing an intellectual analysis of what went wrong at Murray, FXUU and Immanuel. I tried to explain why I was victimized.

Just like the churches Dr. Benyei wrote about, when conflict occurred at Murray, FXUU and Immanuel, knowledge about it was suppressed and/or its severity minimized. Church members who wanted to maintain peace and order outwardly conformed to the ideas and opinions of clergy and church leadership. If their genuine thoughts differed, they never shared them. This impeded direct action by me and by anyone else who might have been dissatisfied. This also prevented examination by the entire church community.

Instead of accepting responsibility for their own actions, my former friends made me into a scapegoat because I was independent and refused to remain silent. Uniting against me, they mythologized, demonized and turned me into a thing. During her visit to my home on September 10, 2001, Ruth said no one had considered how I was feeling. There was little or no awareness or respect for my feelings. By sacrificing me, my former friends avoided acknowledging their own guilt.

Although I was aware there was a clique among the leadership at Immanuel, I didn't comprehend the danger. Barbara Coloroso in *The Bully, the Bullied, and the Bystander* explains how exclusion by peers during childhood denies victims like me important learning experiences. I had never learned to critically evaluate groups. I failed to recognize that many church groups thrive on having a scapegoat and welcome someone to play that part. I never asked, "Can I be good and true to myself here?"

Some individuals with whom I have shared these events have concluded that I must have been partly responsible for what happened. Wanting to be fair, they say, "Most times when there is an argument both sides are wrong." In fact this is only one possibility. It is also possible for one side to be the innocent victim of the other. Similar to victims of abuse, bystanders might not want to accept that I was vulnerable and powerless during the conflicts at Murray, FXUU and Immanuel. If they accepted my vulnerability, they would have to admit their own culpability or that they too can be unfairly victimized.

As I came to understand and accept that my detractors' behavior was abusive and I wasn't responsible, my mental health improved.

Gaining strength from Rev. Mary's compassionate support, I took the risk of attending services at St. Matthew-Trinity Lutheran Church. St. Matt's location in a bordering town across the state line made it less likely that I would run into people I knew from Immanuel.

The first time I attended services at St. Matt's, I refused to sign the guest book and only gave them my first name. The greeter respected my anonymity and didn't pry. I quietly took a seat in a vacant pew toward the front. After the service, I avoided the minister by walking up the side aisle in silence and slipping out the front door while most people were entering the fellowship hall on the opposite side of the sanctuary.

After several weeks I gained the courage to exit up the center aisle.

"Good morning," Rev. Rick said, and extended his hand.

I shook his hand and awkwardly returned the greeting.

"What is your name?"

"Margaret," I replied, hiding behind the formality of my proper name.

"Where are you from?" he asked.

"Around here," I replied.

Rev. Rick looked startled. Before he could ask any more questions, I walked off toward the little-used front door.

Over the next few months, Rev. Rick built trust by respecting my privacy. He didn't speak to me unless I spoke to him and he didn't ask any more questions. After church on August 4, I realized I would never become a member of St. Matt's community if I continued to hide. I sent the following note to Rev. Rick at St. Matthew-Trinity:

> I have been attending your church for a few months but have declined to give you or anybody else my full name or address. While this protects me, it is awkward. I have considered talking to you after the service but have chosen to write instead. It feels safer. There is this deep well overflowing with hurt inside me that may never dry up. I would welcome a response from you. You may hand me a note or email me. I trust you will keep my contacts with you confidential.

Rev. Rick responded via email the day he received my note. He had noticed my presence at St. Matthew's and my reluctance to share personal information. He stressed his ordination obligated him to maintain confidentiality and he considered it a sacred duty.

By using a different email alias, I continued to conceal my identity while exchanging posts with Rev. Rick. Although it was hard for me to withhold information, I asked him not to ask any questions regarding my identity. His assurance that he wouldn't pry helped increased my sense of safety and security.

I also sent a letter to Candace Benyei about her book, *Understanding Clergy Misconduct in Religious Systems*. She responded by email.

Dear Margaret,

> Apparently you have become aware how difficult it is to be "churched" and discover that the church does not walk its talk nor want to address its glaring problems. Welcome to the club.

> Unfortunately churches do not deal with conflict well, and most want to sweep it under the carpet—as well as get rid of the folks that suggest they have a problem. It is part of the reason the church is dying. One would think that it might want some help or a little therapy, but I am afraid that for the most part churches are highly defended systems that cannot tolerate outside aid and instead employ massive denial.

I wrote back a one-and-a-half-page summary of what happened with James. Candace responded later the same day, quoting the Episcopal bishop, Shelby Spong, and explaining that she was a liberation theologian. She further wrote,

> I have a colleague that adopted two children similar to James. He and his wife have had many trying times with both because these kids develop lots of dysfunctional behaviors in the service of survival. They have to lie, steal, manipulate, etc. simply to stay alive in their countries of origin. And since the behaviors are old bad habits, they hang on to them maybe for the rest of their lives.
>
> Unfortunately the goodie goodies in your church—including the minister—were not only naïve, but extremely intrusive, and I sense the congregation is not healthy. I imagine that eventually they will discover the hard truth about James if they continue to court him. I also doubt they will ever apologize to you...

While apologies would be healing, I knew they could be empty. Ruth had apologized last September, but never changed her behavior; she continued to disregard my feelings. What I really wanted was for my former friends at Immanuel to sit down with me and listen to my pain. I wanted them to learn from this so they could do a better job of supporting families who were trying to raise adopted or foster children.

I was now sending and receiving emails from Rev. Mary, Candace and Rev. Rick. A lot of it was sharing of backgrounds and just getting to know each other. Whenever anyone, usually Rev. Mary, suggested I read a book, I went out immediately and bought it.

Mid-August, as Rev. Mary suggested, I was reading Joyce Rupp's *Praying Our Goodbyes*, which talked about Jesus' pain when people refused to "wake up to the truth of the kingdom." It reminded me of my own pain when James rejected our own gift of a secure, happy family. All that was left was for me to bear witness as well as I could. I needed to speak my truth to power and develop inner resources to withstand the storm that speaking that truth would generate.

I sent a letter to Dr. Emmett, telling him it was time for me to give up any yearning I had to lay down and die. I committed myself to living my life out to its natural end, not just because of the promise I made to him, but because God expects us to be good stewards of our own bodies and not reject the gift of life He has given us.

On the first anniversary of the September 11th attacks, I poignantly remembered the intertwining of my personal pain over the loss of my foster son and the shared grief over the death of 3,000 Americans including my daughter's high school friend. It felt like the very fabric of existence had been torn apart and there was a big, gaping, unfillable hole.

I walked the two miles from my home to the town common for the remembrance service. As I passed the local Episcopal church, I hesitated. The doors were wide open, welcoming all passersby. I considered entering. I was sure I wouldn't meet any of my former friends there, and it was a half-mile closer than the common. But then I remembered my visit there the previous Easter. Although some people stared at me, no one had greeted me. I continued walking.

I turned left onto Park Street and walked one block. I found myself walking behind Beverly. She appeared unaware that I was there. I dropped back and tried to disappear in the crowd converging on the common. When I reached the grass, I saw several of my former friends from Immanuel scattered throughout the crowd. I tried to stand away from them but failed to notice Mallory standing in front of me. She turned around, saw me, and like Judas in the Garden of Gethsemane she greeted me with a peck on the cheek. Caught off guard, I mumbled hello and stepped back. Feeling violated, I tried to wipe its memory from my face.

After some speeches and music, I joined the procession that was walking to the Congregational church. I positioned myself not to be near my enemies. As I walked up the steps to the church, I saw Rev. Karen standing near the entrance greeting people as they entered. Fearfully, I looked straight ahead and walked past her while she was speaking to someone else. I took a seat toward the front. My former friends were across the aisles on either side of me.

Taking several slow, deep breaths, I prayed for God to hold me and protect me in the shadow of His wings. *Love me. Cherish me. Give me strength to confront those who persecuted me.*

Gaining courage, I sat up straight. There was no scarlet letter on my chest. I hadn't sinned. God would protect and shelter me. I had nothing to fear.

When Rev. Karen walked up to the pulpit to deliver her homily, I looked at her hard. She looked away and her voice quivered. Had she seen me? I wasn't sure. Perhaps she knew I regarded her as a hypocrite. She could talk the talk but couldn't walk the walk.

A few days after the service, I wrote a brief letter to Mallory.

> On September 11 we bumped into each other at the Remembrance Service and you kissed me on the cheek. I am sure you meant well. However, if you are sincerely concerned about me I ask that you telephone, email or write me and get to know me better. In time we may become friends. If you are not interested in doing this and we should bump into each other again I kindly ask you never to touch or hug or kiss me. I reserve physical expressions of love and friendship for my family and my true friends.

Mallory never responded. I was disappointed but not surprised.

Since I had never formally withdrawn my membership from Immanuel, I continued to receive the newsletter. The October issue arrived on the second. Rev. Karen was leaving to marry a Lutheran minister from Bridgeport, Connecticut. There would be a luncheon held at Immanuel in her honor on October 20.

*That was quick,* I thought. *When did her divorce go through? Wasn't she still married to her daughter's father back in March? Hmm, her fiancée is from Connecticut. Is that the friend she visited on her days off?*

The divorce was expected. She was estranged from her husband for the last ten years. I was just surprised she had found someone else so quickly.

As Rev. Karen's last Sunday at Immanuel approached, I struggled with grief. I did my best to avoid driving by Immanuel, but the church was between my home and the interstate. A few days before Rev. Karen's goodbye luncheon, I sat down at my desk and took out a handmade note card I had purchased at Immanuel's last craft fair. On its cover was a picture of the tapestry that hung over the altar. Even if Rev. Karen weren't going to say goodbye to me, I would say goodbye to her.

I opened the card and picked up my black pen. *Hmmm, how should I start?* Perhaps it was best to keep it formal. I took a deep breath and wrote,

Dear Rev. Karen:

You are leaving. Despite your final unjust demonization
of me, I remember you were once kind and generous to me.
May you find happiness and peace.

Dr. M. Jones

I didn't expect a reply but my heart still hoped and longed for some rapprochement. While I sealed the envelope, I recalled the short essay at the beginning of *Praying Our Goodbyes*: All is on loan to us. The present moment is to be treasured and enjoyed, because it is precious and fleeting. My place at Immanuel was a temporary resting place where I healed from the wounds inflicted at the Unitarian Universalist church. It was the place where I realized Frank Flynn, who molested me, needed God just as much as I did, and I moved closer to forgiving him.

Following Rev. Mary's advice, I devised a goodbye ritual. On Friday, October 18, after my morning prayers, I gathered together all the photos, all the things I had ever been given by people at Immanuel, and placed them on the bottom of our gas grill on the patio. I turned on the gas and lit it. I watched the photos curl and burn. When they were completely turned to ash, I opened the bottle of holy water I had been given during a service at Immanuel. As I poured the water on the hot ashes, I watched the steam rise and listened to the sizzle.

I carried the empty jar down to the garage and rolled it up in a towel. I took Lyndon's rubber mallet off the wall and smashed the jar, breaking it into many small pieces. That was especially gratifying.

Returning to the living room, I lit a candle. Using some prayers from *Praying Our Goodbyes*, I prayed as if sitting shivah. They were dead to me. I would act as if I never knew them. All that was left was for me to bear witness as well as I could, and as Anita Hill did during the Justice Thomas hearings, speak my truth to power. I would develop the inner resources needed to withstand the storm that speaking the truth would generate.

The next day while I ran my errands, I noticed several cars going in and out of Immanuel's parking lot. *They must be preparing for Rev. Karen's luncheon,* I thought. *At least after she leaves I will no longer have to worry about the bad things she might say about me.* Her departure might give me a better chance of being accepted into a church community.

But as I witnessed all the activity at Immanuel, tears caressed my face. In the privacy of my home, I wept. She really was going to leave without calling to say goodbye. I meant so little to her. I would never see her again. It was so hard living so close to Immanuel. Every time I drove by there, every time I heard the bell toll, I was reminded of my rejection and loss.

In the evening just before dinner, I emailed Rev. Mary and Candace about Rev. Karen's departure and attached the article about her that appeared in the local paper. Candace wrote back later that night, asking me if I planned on returning to the Lutheran Church.

I replied,

> I will not return to Immanuel even though Pastor Karen is leaving and the church is directly behind our property. I have other enemies there and they still bring my former foster son there on occasion. They are, in my opinion, enmeshed with him. They have never held him accountable for what he did to my family and have never acknowledged what my family did for him. They simply cast us as demons never wanting to be bothered with the facts. I have since learned by speaking with others who have fostered children that this is not uncommon. Even though I know my family acted generously and with integrity, it is hard not to regret taking James in. If anyone ever asks me if they should foster a child I will tell them no. My mother-in-law attempted to warn us when she asked if we were sure we wanted to take in a Sudanese boy. She told us that no matter what we did it would never be regarded as enough.

Candace replied the next morning.

> As I am sure you are well aware, this issue is far from done for you, especially as you cannot feel comfortable making yourself part of another community. Why not try the Episcopal church, which is equally liturgical and doesn't have the "disciplinary" stuff that you discovered in the Lutheran church? Then you can attend without

fear. I have a shrinky sense that this issue hooked some of your old, unfinished, childhood business somehow. Something about an issue in which you were unjustly accused, punished, and powerless to do anything about it. Your inner child seems to be hanging around the Lutheran church to try to finish the work, not allowing you to kick the dust off your sandals at a house that did not welcome you, and move on to the next. I would ask yourself about the possibility of mother-transference regarding Rev. Karen, and an inner-child hope that she might forgive you. Personally, I would have no interest in having anything more to do with the bitch, who, aside from the article, is dangerously unaware and has very poor boundaries.

Unsure how to respond to her psychoanalysis, I waited several days before I replied.

...First of all I want to thank you for your support. As you said, the issue with Immanuel Lutheran is certainly not completely resolved. However, the concept of the inner child or other psychodynamic conceptualizations have never fully resonated with me. All of us have past experiences that make us who we are and that frame how we respond to events in our life. I find it more helpful to look at Immanuel as grieving a major loss. I am only six months past the time when I was pushed out. I assume it might take another six months to a year to fully recover and go on. ...

The next several weeks, Candace and I exchanged emails about our experiences with churches. On November 13, I asked,

I was curious about how you came to write a book on clergy misconduct. Most people are blissfully unaware of the cruelty that can happen in a church and cling to the myth that their church is the perfect society. Would you mind sharing?

Candace replied five days later.

I was in a congregation where I watched it happen, and had clients who had also been abused by clergy. I also had clients who were After Pastors [ministers serving in congregations where a former religious leader engaged in unethical conduct]. I now do a lot of work for the Lutheran Church as it is the only denomination that has a really good program to help After Pastors and victims. Ironic, yes?

I gasped. I felt the tears forming in my eyes. Laying my head down on my desk, I wept. The next morning I replied,

... Prior to joining Immanuel Pastor Karen had told me such a process was available in the Lutheran Church. When I approached the vice president of Immanuel's board I was trying to access that process. But Pastor Karen thwarted those efforts. She had gone to the board and the bishop probably weeks before I did. I was condemned as a persistent troublemaker, church antagonist before I even got out of the gate and was never afforded an opportunity to prove otherwise. In order to initiate that process I would have had to go through the Matthew 18 thing, and then there were no promises that the board would ask the bishop to bring in a mediator, someone to help. I wasn't willing or able to subject myself to a process that I was experiencing as abusive.

In my fantasies and desire for justice I was finally given an opportunity to correct misperceptions, I was finally listened to and heard. That was all I ever really wanted. I wasn't trying to hurt anyone, including James and Rev. Karen.

An hour later Candace wrote back, suggesting I contact Rev. Larraine, who was in charge of the national Lutheran Church's department for the prevention of clergy sexual misconduct. I hesitated. I didn't know this woman. She was a Lutheran minister. Maybe Rev. Karen knew her. When I sought help from Mallory, it backfired. Mallory abandoned me and allowed me to be pushed out of Immanuel. I asked Candace for more information. She reassured me. She knew Rev. Larraine. They were writing a book together.

Late that same day, I emailed Rev. Larraine and introduced myself. Before I would speak with her, I asked her about her education and training and how the process would work. I didn't want to be victimized again. I had burned everything from Immanuel, doing my best to move on, but here the wound was being reopened. Would I bleed to death or would the infection be purged?

While waiting for Rev. Larraine to respond, my fears grew. Perhaps Rev. Karen had contacted Rev. Larraine months ago, just as she had the bishop's office. The bishop's office then judged me without ever speaking to me or informing me what Rev. Karen had told them. It was hard if not impossible to fight shadows.

Four days after emailing Rev. Larraine I wrote Candace.

> Have you considered the risk to me if this doesn't work out? If Larraine is the person you believe she is, then it could be healing, but there is also a serious risk that my hopes will be raised only to be dashed again.
>
> What have you told Larraine about me? What did she already know? Is it possible she already has had some contact with Rev. Karen? I recall the name from somewhere. Maybe your book or maybe from Rev. Karen. Memory does play tricks on you. I have become so jaded and suspicious since all this happened.
>
> Please bear with me.

Candace replied eight hours later.

> I think you are being a bit paranoid. I only told Larraine that you had been abused by the church (I didn't specify or say more than that) and that you really wanted to remain a Lutheran, and that I had given you her phone number and email address.
>
> I think it would be good for you, at this juncture, to reenter psychotherapy (I'm assuming that before you entered clinical practice you did do your own work) so that you can metabolize the trauma. My sense is that the experience you had with the church has really pushed your buttons.

An hour later I replied,

> ... I have been and continue to be in treatment since the start of this mess. I am well aware what my mental health

needs are at this point. My asking you questions about Larraine, although they sound paranoid to you, are perfectly logical given some of the things Rev. Karen said and did. I believe in your book you called it murder in the guise of caring.

We all have our psychological vulnerabilities. What has happened to me at the UU church and at Immanuel would traumatize even the healthiest individual. It is the healthy side of me that has written you and asks you questions and that seeks win-win solutions. It is when I stop communicating that I get ill. In many ways I am the healthiest that I have ever been. I also suspect I am far more healthy than Rev. Karen and the rest of the Immanuel gang. The episode with James clearly pushed their buttons and caused them to be quite cruel to me.

Candace continued to reassure me. Finally on December 3, Rev. Larraine emailed me and provided me with information concerning her credentials. She described in detail the process for making a sexual abuse complaint. Uncertain whether she could help me, I sent her an email the next morning. I explained I was not making a sexual abuse allegation, but had been emotionally abused, scapegoated and driven out of my church. I informed her that part of the bullying included unwelcome and very public hugs by people with whom I was in conflict. Rev. Karen chided me for not wanting to be hugged by these people. I also told her that Rev. Karen engaged in gossip with these same people and, through innuendos, breached confidentiality.

Rev. Larraine replied late that same night that she would welcome an opportunity to speak with me. She provided me with some times that she would be available. She also wrote,

> Breaking confidentiality is a violation of Visions and Expectations for the clergy of ELCA. Although the clergyperson would not go through the same process as described in the policy against clergy sexual abuse, I would expect someone on the synod staff to be concerned about that kind of behavior. Usually when a clergyperson crosses a boundary and they are confronted with it, the pastor should have some remorse and stop the behavior.

When a pastor responds differently, it is an indication that they
lack empathy and have poor Christian boundaries of love.

Validation! My heart rate and breathing increased. Here was a chance
to be heard. I shut off my computer monitor. I imagine I am friends with
Candace and Larraine. I have become an expert on bullying in churches. I
train laity and clergy in church community rooms across the country. At
the National Synod Assembly, in front of hundreds of clergy and laity, I
stand on the stage, an advocate for change, no longer a victim.

At noontime on December 9, I spoke with Rev. Larraine on the
telephone. I told her the whole soap opera in between the tears.

"There was a rush to judgment," she said.

"They didn't want to hear my side. I think Rev. Karen was using this
book, *Antagonists in the Church*. It's a terrible book."

"Yes, I know of it," Rev. Larraine said. "That's not one of the books I
recommend to pastors. The focus on you must have been a diversion
from some other issue."

"Rev. Karen got divorced and remarried right away," I offered.

"Perhaps that was the issue," Rev. Larraine replied.

"I'm not sure what was going on. Nobody would tell me." I pulled a
tissue out of the box sitting on my desk.

"There isn't much I can do. If you want me to I'll contact the
bishop's office and speak to her."

"Thanks, that's very good of you."

"I'll get back to you."

I hung up the phone. Placing my elbows on my desk, I rested my
head in my hands and prayed. *God, please open the ears of the bishop and let
my story be heard. I have been cheated out of my son. God, You know what the
truth is. Please help me. Amen.*

Understanding it would take several weeks for Rev. Larraine to get
back to me, I tried not to think too much about Immanuel. In the
mornings I followed my routine of checking and replying to my emails.
Rev. Mary often sent me these wonderful, upbeat letters, as if we were
truly friends, which brightened my day. I hoped Mary and Candace
would become the true friends I had longed for most of my life.

On Thursday morning the twelfth, after Lyndon left for work and I
was alone in our house, I sat on the black leather sofa in my living room
with my legs crossed and my hands resting on my thighs. With my eyes

half-closed, I listened to some sacred music. I saw all the faces of my enemies. Anger and grief rose within me.

    *God*, I prayed, *I don't want empty apologies. I want restitution. I want to be publicly thanked for all that my family did for James. I want James held accountable for the wrong he did to my family. I want a homily urging people who have wronged another to apologize to their victim, make restitution and alter their behavior so it never happens* again. *I want people to be educated about foster and adoptive families. I want a lot,* I thought as I uncrossed my legs, but simple, private apologies would no longer be enough.

As Christmas approached, I did my best to focus on the holidays and not Immanuel or Rev. Larraine. Originally we didn't expect our son Orion to be home for the holidays, but the Coast Guard changed his orders. He flew in on the twenty-third. We spent Christmas quietly at home, exchanging gifts in the morning and enjoying a meal together.

    On the twenty-seventh, I emailed Candace.

> ...Larraine hasn't gotten back to me yet. She said she would after she spoke with the bishop. I worry that I didn't represent myself very well when I spoke to her. I did a lot of crying. I don't think I articulated very well what and why I regard what happened to me as emotionally abusive. Nor did I indicate to her how carefully I have considered the ethical issues, how much reading I have been doing etc.

> Since I have been stonewalled so much, I do not have any confidence that Larraine will get back to me after the holidays. I fear after speaking with the bishop she will take their accusations at face value and not realize that since the bishop has never spoken with me, anything the bishop says about me would be what Pastor Karen fed her. I fear Larraine will believe them because they are ministers and invalidate anything I say. I fear I will not be told what the accusations are and not be given any chance to defend myself. I fear these things because that is what has happened in the recent past.

> Whether Larraine gets back in touch with me or not I intend to find a constructive way to be heard. I have just completed

an article for the "My View" column in *The Lutheran* and intend to send it off after I have proofed it. I am also looking into writing a book. Perhaps you could share with me your experiences in getting published.

Candace replied later that night.

... I think it would be good to try and rein in your abandonment anxiety, and practice patience. Larraine is a VERY busy person, and lives away from her spouse during the week because of her job. I'm sure she is spending the holidays at home. If she said she would speak to the Bishop, I am sure she will. What the Bishop does is of course up to the Bishop and out of her control. Her office is primary concerned with issues of sexual misconduct, and as this is not your complaint, she does not have real jurisdiction. I sent you to her because I felt that she would listen and might know someone who could help you.

I felt chastised. I reined in the impulse to respond immediately. It would be wiser to mull it over before writing back. On Saturday the fourth of January, Lyndon and Melissa went shopping together. I chose to stay home and have the house to myself. While cleaning off my desk, I came across an American Psychological Association newsletter. I quickly skimmed it and was about to throw it away when I noticed a listing of websites. One was for victims of professional misconduct. I clicked on my browser and typed in www.advocateweb.org. I signed up for their email list, HopeTalk, a support group for those abused by professionals.

At the end of the day I responded to Candace's last email.

If I haven't already I want to thank you for trying to help, but as you once told me religious institutions are very well defended. As much as I would welcome sitting down with a neutral third party and working out a win-win solution with my former friends at Immanuel, I don't think that will ever happen. You trust Larraine, and maybe she will follow through and try to speak with the bishop. However, unless she has more power than the bishop, my guess is she will be stonewalled and put off until it becomes more effort than it is worth to her.

As for reining in my abandonment anxiety, I wouldn't characterize my anxiety over Larraine contacting the bishop as abandonment anxiety. I have no emotional connection with Larraine. And I prefer to talk about calming, soothing my fears. One way of doing that is to share those fears with others. Given my recent experiences, I think it quite rational for me to be suspicious and skeptical. As for practicing patience, I have been living with this for a year and half. I need it resolved sooner rather than later.

The events at Immanuel heightened my fears of rejection and abandonment. I didn't trust anyone to stay in a relationship with me. Monday morning the sixth, I woke up anxious. I was convinced since Candace hadn't responded to my last email, she was breaking off our relationship. I feared that once HopeTalk heard my story they would tell me I didn't belong on the list.

Later that morning, I found an email from Candace in my inbox that answered a question I had about her latest book. She also suggested I take a look at the subsidy publisher she was using. I felt reassured. She wasn't rejecting me.

It was going to take time and the steadfastness of family for me to feel secure again. I summoned up my courage and began participating in HopeTalk. Although most of the group had been sexually victimized by therapists, there were also others who were victimized by clergy and physicians. When I shared my story, the group's response was very supportive. Unfortunately, most of the posts were by the women who had affairs with their therapist. Without thinking too much about it, I was using my email account whose signature line clearly identified me as a psychologist. This made many of the list participants suspicious of me. There was almost no talk of abuse by clergy. No talk of emotional abuse.

I wondered if the list realized that emotional abuse often was more damaging than the actual sex part of sexual abuse. Women who had been raped by strangers and whose families supported them often weren't as severely damaged as women who had been abused by a close family member or trusted professional. In the latter cases, the perpetrator usually manipulated and blamed their victim for the abuse. If the women disclosed the abuse and weren't believed, they were damaged even further.

By the end of January, I still hadn't heard from Rev. Larraine. Unable to sleep, I got up at 2 a.m., went downstairs to my study, and sent an email to Candace.

> I can't sleep. A lot is happening. Although most of the emails on AdvocateWeb concern people who have been sexually exploited by their therapists, I have made contact with a couple of people who have been dechurched in similar ways to me....

> Rev. Larraine never got back to me. It makes me wonder what happened. Did she contact the bishop? What was she told? People are being told something to make them not want to talk to me. But I don't know what it is. How can I defend myself if I am never told? Is there no one with the courage to tell me?

> Although I didn't do anything wrong there are people who believe I am some kind of lunatic, that I am evil. I am so nonviolent. They are afraid of me, a mouse. It would be funny if it didn't hurt so much.

> I am going to try to make a difference. But it takes up so much time and energy. It is like Anita Hill. Her life's work became about sexual harassment because of what happened to her. Now my life is becoming about dechurching, shunning and other social cruelty. Sometimes I wish I could just walk away from it. Forget it ever happened. But if I do that it just continues. It will and is happening to someone else right now as I type. I am now absolutely sure what happened to me was not some rare aberration. It is past time that churches become safe places.

Candace replied five hours later.

> It is the ancient and historic reality that churches are not, nor will they ever be, safe places. We would like them to be the safe family we never had, but it is an illusion we cannot create in real-time. All organizations

eventually become about power, and the church is no exception. You need to let go of this one.

Let go? Give up? No! It certainly was true that churches, for centuries, have been unsafe places overly concerned with maintaining the power of the elite. However, I didn't believe it would always be so. God was working through reformers like Abraham Lincoln, Mahatma Gandhi and Martin Luther King Jr. to establish His kingdom here on earth. Armed with a greater understanding of the problem and with psychological science, reform was inevitable. I choose to struggle, with God's help, to do my small part in establishing a more just society in both our secular and religious institutions.

Candace also wrote,

> Please let go your paranoia regarding Larraine. She is in the process of resigning her position at the national office because it is in Chicago, and her husband, who lives in Rochester, was not able to find a job in that area so he could relocate. So, after a three-year very stressful at-a-distance marriage, she is going, or has gone, back to Rochester. She did what she could do. Yours is not a case of sexual abuse, so it was rather out of her area of responsibility, anyway. She did you a favor. What the rest of the hierarchy does, is not in her control.

I appreciated Candace's attempt to help by getting Rev. Larraine involved. I was amazed and grateful when Rev. Larraine offered to contact the bishop on my behalf. I didn't ask her to do that. It was all I had ever hoped for. I didn't know if Rev. Larraine ever made the initial call to the bishop, or not, because she never got back to me. I was unaware of her personal circumstances. It would have been a common courtesy for Rev. Larraine to call or email me explaining briefly why she couldn't do as she originally offered. My hopes were raised, only to be disappointed yet again. She didn't do me any favor except listen to my story for an hour. It would have been kinder if the offer of help had never been made.

I continued reading.

> Certainly your prior pastor was really out of line, but your transference is all over this issue, and you need to do some serious personal work here. Many "mommies" are not safe,

> and this is simply an unfortunate aspect of human life. As a
> psychologist, you should be aware of this. If you can't see it,
> this is a bad thing. You need to ask yourself why you can't
> let this one go and find a more welcoming house—or ask
> God what God is asking you to do.

Candace didn't know me well enough to draw the conclusions about
my "transference" being "all over this issue" and needing "to do some
serious personal work here." I was forced out of my church community
less than a year before. I had been responding as best I could to the
betrayal and rejection, and to the very real threat to my family and myself.
That was not paranoia. I was not and had never suffered from psychotic
delusions of any kind. I read on.

> I suspect that my suggestions will make you angry. It would
> be good if you took a look at that also. Absolute personal
> honesty and acute awareness of our own issues and how
> they affect us on a moment-to-moment basis are what makes
> us good shrinks.

She was right. I was angry. I counted how many times she used "you"
and "your." Thirteen times. *Is this how Candace works with people? Setting
herself up as an expert and telling them how they should think and feel?* She had
no idea what kind of therapist I was. What made her think she was more
skilled than I was?

After talking to Dr. Emmett and Lyndon, I sent Candace an email
that I thought was well written and respectful. I also called her and left a
message thanking her and asking her to call me. On Saturday she emailed
me, terminating our correspondence. That hurt, a sharp pain. It wasn't
unexpected.

I also emailed Rev. Larraine, asking her if she ever contacted the
bishop. Rev. Larraine responded a week later. Her time had been
consumed with a big event and her move back to Rochester. She had
called Rev. Rachael and left her a voicemail briefly stating the
purpose of her call and asking her if she would be willing to discuss
why they chose to discipline me instead of seeking reconciliation. She
never heard back from her. That was no surprise.

Rev. Larraine also brought up the general matter to her unit
committee. They had had several similar cases, and discussed what could
be done from the national office. She wrote further,

...We realize that in the ELCA the bishop is responsible for the care of pastors and the pastors are responsible for the care of parishioners in their congregations.

*Oh, that is very cozy. So who is responsible to ensure pastors behave ethically? Where are the checks and balances?*

It was also noted that if the church-wide office became involved in such matters that we could easily become triangulated without knowing all the facts.

*Triangulated?* There was that word again. I first heard it in reference to church conflicts by the clergy at the Unitarian Universalist Association, and then by Rev. Karen. I had since called Rita, who was familiar with family systems theory, and I also looked it up on the Internet. The term referred to parents who focus on their child's misbehavior to avoid discussing problems in their marriage. If anything, I was the one being triangulated. Rev. Karen held the church together by identifying me as a persistent troublemaker. As the rule enforcer, she did her best to silence me. I was a persistent troublemaker only because I was a teller of truth.

In addition, it was noted that some parishioners are calling the church-wide office because they feel that they have no other recourse.

*There is no other recourse,* I thought. *ELCA's and Immanuel's constitutions have little or no provisions for handling conflicts.* Ironically, secular institutions were more just than religious ones. There were rules and bills of rights that protect citizens. With the separation of church and state, the state provided little oversight in how the church conducts its affairs. Work environments were fairer because employers must comply with labor laws. Unions helped to balance power. There were no such structures within churches to protect individuals from abusive ministers. There was little discussion, if any, about the unequal power and what to do about it. Forgetting that all people sin, parishioners naively believed that if everyone had faith, conflicts wouldn't occur and all would be fair and just. But, as Leonard Swidler wrote in *Toward a Catholic Constitution*, it is due process based on just rules and procedures that protect people from power abuses.

I continued reading Rev. Larraine's email. After discussing reconciliation with her committee, she decided she needed to educate people on how and when to use that model. After apologizing for having nothing to offer me "except to hold up reconciliation as a model of working things through," she suggested I call the bishop's office and ask for someone to meet with me. "Perhaps time," she wrote, "can bring another perspective."

I had already tried to speak to the bishop. If they wouldn't speak to her, did Rev. Larraine really think they were going to talk to me? I clicked on the reply button and tried to compose a response, but stared at the screen for several seconds. "God," I whispered, "Help me clearly and fairly tell my story to all who will listen. I trust in time a just solution will present itself. Amen."

That night I dreamed I was with my mother and my sister Trish, who I hadn't seen in years. Looking at my watch, I gasped and ran down the street toward Dr. Emmett's office. Cars and people blocked my way. No matter how hard I tried I couldn't get to his office. I missed my appointment, and never saw him again. I woke up weeping.

Not sure how to respond to Rev. Larraine or if I should respond, I put the email aside while I continued to network with others abused by churches. At times I was overwhelmed with fear. The more involved I became, the more likely my activities would get back to my enemies. I prayed they would leave me alone and not attack me. All I wanted was to make churches safer places for everyone.

I continued to participate on AdvocateWeb's email lists. I was invited to submit an article for an ebook they hoped to publish. I was flattered and excited about the request. Writing an article would be a good way to integrate my personal experience with my reading on misconduct in churches and bullying in schools.

On February 9 after dinner, I sat down at my computer and began writing. I was limited to fifteen pages double-spaced. Trying to figure out where to start the story and what details to include was challenging. I shared the first draft with my sister Rita and her daughter Rebecca. Rita's response was less than positive. Rebecca and her husband said it clearly showed how extensive the problem of ministerial misconduct was. The following night, I attempted to incorporate their comments into the final paper. Eight days later on President's Day, I submitted the completed article via email to AdvocateWeb.

My anxiety increased. I thought of talking to Dr. Emmett, but he was away on his annual ski vacation. On February 18, I finally sat down and wrote an email to Rev. Larraine. Though she had terminated our correspondence, I also sent a copy to Candace.

Rev. Larraine,

I want to thank you for trying to help me. I was not surprised by the result as I had contacted the bishop's office months before I called you. They insisted I submit to the Matthew 18 process before they would even listen to my side of things. Since I viewed this as an abusive procedure I refused. I know you did the best you could do under the circumstances.

I believe the inter unit committee concern about triangulation is misplaced. Professional ethics committees and licensing boards investigate and review ethics complaints all the time without fearing triangulation. I think it is time for ministers to be held accountable for all their misbehavior, not just their sexual misbehavior. ELCA needs to rewrite their constitution and eliminate the persistent troublemaker clause, which is undefined and demonizes individuals rather than focusing on behavior. I also think there needs to be a way to have a conflict mediated before things escalate out of control. In schools now there are programs where a student can go to a neutral third party when they are having a conflict with another student or teacher that they are unable to resolve by themselves. How successful these programs will be time can only tell.

Since speaking to you, I have come in contact with individuals researching abuse in churches and a group of survivors who are trying to find ways to help and change things.

Thanks again for your help.

The next day Candace surprised me with a reply.

Hi, Margaret,

I think this was a good letter and you have an excellent
point. "Persistent Troublemaker" is a label, and pastors
SHOULD be held accountable for abusive behavior, sexual or
not. Perhaps you could find some folks in the ELCA that
would be willing to work on amending the constitution.

Amend ELCA's constitution? I would have to be part of the denomination's leadership to do that. As much as I wanted change, I didn't
think I possessed the political skills to get elected to the church council.
Besides, the bishop would never let me get close. I doubted I would be
welcomed at the synod assembly.

A list mate from AdvocateWeb wrote about not staying where she
wasn't accepted. *We all need acceptance. But what do we really mean by that?*
I wondered. *If we took a picture of it, what would we be saying and doing?*

I resolved that at the end of each day I would affirm what I had done
right. Whenever I started feeling anxious, I would soothe myself by
reminding myself I am valued by my family, my clients and by God. I
would stroke rather than burn or cut myself. I would not be afraid to be
more of who I was, and whom my family loved and cherished. I decided
to be a better steward of myself: getting yearly physicals, being more open
with my physician; taking more walks; buying stylish clothes; wearing
makeup; reading more. I had courage, integrity and a generous heart
whether people at Immanuel saw it or not.

During this time, I stopped whatever I was doing when a news
report aired on the Catholic Church's sex abuse scandal. I searched
the newspaper for articles on it. Inspired by Voice of the Faithful,
a Catholic lay organization formed to assist survivors of clergy sex
abuse, I was determined to be heard and to do my part to bring justice
and peace to the small part of the universe I inhabited. I wanted to
avoid demonizing others, while focusing on their hurtful behavior. I
acknowledged humanity's primitive, power-hungry, dominance-seeking
behavior, while I sought ways to empower myself and others.

My position frightened an email pal from AdvocateWeb. She saw
anger as all consuming. I wasn't sure if she was aware of the possibility of
harnessing anger's energy to do good. Anger was, like any other emotion,
neither good nor bad. It was what you did with it that mattered.

While I read and responded to posts on the forums on Hopetalk and www.christiansurvivors.com, I read extensively about bullying and spiritual abuse. The patterns of behavior identified by Rachel Simmons in *Odd Girl Out* were similar to the behavior patterns I encountered in churches. Since it was unacceptable at FXUU and Immanuel to express anger directly, my former friends harmed me by shunning me and gossiping about me. Rev. Karen, who probably instigated the aggression, maintained or enhanced her power with a façade of politeness. While ignoring me, she lobbied for support among my friends and built a coalition that left me completely isolated. Since the aggression took place in a group, no one was ever directly responsible for their behavior. This made the aggression harder for me to identify and intensified the psychological damage done to me.

During my weekly therapy sessions, Dr. Emmett wondered if my perceptions created a self-fulfilling prophecy. I disagreed with him. I believed it wasn't the accuracy of my perceptions that created trouble, but my failure to trust my perceptions and take appropriate action. I either failed to notice or ignored warning signs that I was about to be betrayed. My perceptions of being excluded in the parking lot on Good Friday two years before had been accurate. It was one of the early signs that I wasn't really considered a full member of Immanuel.

The bullying at school and at church had very little to do with me. It was easier for my adversaries to say I was sick than to take responsibility for their own behavior. Of course I had problems. Who didn't? Their knowing I was vulnerable didn't excuse their behavior, but made them more culpable. When is it moral to take advantage of another's weakness? My adversaries furthered their own agendas by exploiting my vulnerabilities. They knew I couldn't or wouldn't fight back effectively.

My church experiences reinforced the lesson I learned while growing up. As soon as you cry or display any emotion that makes others uncomfortable, people stop taking you seriously. They stop listening. They don't ask, "Why is she so upset? What happened?" Rather they say, "What is wrong with her? She shouldn't be so upset. Why can't she control herself? She must be crazy."

As I read *Odd Girl Out*, I decided to let go of my concerns about friendship. I tried too hard to be liked by people who weren't worthy of my loyalty and companionship. Although I liked the people I found at FXUU and Immanuel, they didn't like me as much as I liked them, and didn't share the same values as mine. From this point forward, I swore I would choose my friends more carefully instead of accepting pseudo friendship. I wanted to expand my social network and seek friendships with individuals who shared similar interests and values.

As Ash Wednesday approached, I felt spiritually empty and there didn't appear to be anything I could do about it. It had been a little over a year since Rev. Karen had tried using Matthew 18 to have me ousted from church for persistent troublemaking. I wanted to further my own spiritual growth by attending a Lenten study. But where could I go? I felt like I was marked with a scarlet letter on my chest.

Strengthened by my reading and the support of strangers like Rev. Mary and Candace, I decided to attend the Lenten service and lunch at St. Matt's on Wednesday, March 19. When I arrived, I quietly walked down the center aisle. Another worshiper saw me, smiled and said hello. Frightened by her hospitality, I barely nodded while I slipped into my usual seat away from everyone. Sitting in the pew, I watched other worshipers greet and talk to each other. I felt I was intruding. I didn't belong here. I wasn't a member. I worried about saying the wrong thing and being rejected.

After the service, I was one of the first people through the lunch line. I took a seat at an empty table and watched the others. Rev. Rick, in contrast to Rev. Karen, was a gracious host, waiting on members of the congregation. He made a point of sitting with me. We made small talk. I asked him a few questions about himself. He told me he wrote his dissertation on rhetoric. I thought it a peculiar thing for a minister to write about. Feeling safe, I suggested we needed to talk. He agreed.

I met with Rev. Rick the next morning. "What do you make of me?" I asked.

"You are obviously acquainted with Lutheranism," he answered. "Something has happened to make you terrified."

He must have noticed how easily I followed the service in The Lutheran Book of Worship and that I knew the prayers. If he knew anything about my connection with Immanuel, he said nothing. I relaxed and told him my story.

"I certainly hope your experience at St. Matt's will be much better than what you've gone through," he said.

As I stood to leave, he suggested I make a presentation on confidentiality to the Rhode Island Conference of Ministers.

"They will never allow me to speak to them."

He didn't believe anyone would interfere. "Rachael will probably never find out."

"I'll think about it."

When I returned home, I printed out and sent him a copy of the article I had written for AdvocateWeb. While waiting for his comments I became fearful I would be shunned again without explanation. I feared Matthew 18 would be used again to exclude me from church if I made any attempt to defend myself.

Hungry for a positive religious experience, I checked the religion page of the local newspaper. The Council of Churches was hosting a labyrinth walk at a church a little over a mile north of Immanuel. The announcement said labyrinths were different from mazes. They didn't have dead ends to confuse you. Combining the imagery of the circle and the spiral, a labyrinth had only one meandering but purposeful path. Was this some kind of New Age thing? I wondered.

I read further. No, labyrinths were often found in monasteries and the great cathedrals. The labyrinth represented a sacred journey to our own spiritual center and back again out into the world. Perhaps this was what I was looking for.

On Saturday, March 22, I drove a mile past Immanuel to the church where the labyrinth walk was being held. My heart rate increased. This was where I first met Rev. Karen. While I walked up the slate steps past the azaleas, I recalled Rev. Karen sitting at the registration table in the church's lobby while I signed up for a meditation class three or four years ago. I was a Unitarian then. I sighed as I pulled open the church's door.

I walked across the lobby and down the hall toward the community room. What if someone from Immanuel was here? What would I do? How many other people had heard the rumors about me?

As I walked through the double doors into the community room, the canvas labyrinth was being spread out on the floor by four women. I stopped and watched.

"Maggie, how are you?"

I turned toward the voice. At first I didn't recognize her. As she began talking, I remembered she had served with me on a Council of Churches committee. *What if she asks about Immanuel? What do I tell her? Maybe she already knows I was expelled from Immanuel? But then why is she talking to me? Breathe in slowly.* I smiled while the acid in my stomach churned.

"I'm fine," I said. If she didn't know what happened I wasn't going to enlighten her. "How have you been?"

We talked long enough to be polite. I then found a seat in a circle of chairs across from where some women I didn't know were sitting. I sat alone. Everyone else was with somebody. I felt conspicuous and lonely.

At 2 p.m. sharp, the owners of the canvas labyrinth passed out some papers on the history of labyrinths and ways to use them as meditation aids. After the brief presentation was over we were invited to walk the labyrinth. *Wait*, I told myself. *You don't want to be the first one up. You don't want to look impatient, too enthusiastic. What would people think of you? Probably nothing. They wouldn't even notice me.*

It was like I was invisible. I was nothing to them. I waited until some other women stood.

Following the instructions given to us, I removed my shoes. I leaned over and struck the ringing bowl placed on the floor by the entrance to the Chartres labyrinth. I stepped onto the canvas. Nervous, I started out too fast. I caught myself. *It is not a race.*

I shortened my steps, carefully placing one foot in front of the other. Soon my pace was slow, steady and rhythmic. I followed the path in toward the center and then out again. I watched another woman pick up one of the scarves that had been placed along the outside edge of the labyrinth and stretch it over her head as if dancing. I considered doing the same. Seeing a sheer red scarf in front of me, I bent over and picked it up. *What do I do with it now?* I draped it over my shoulders and continued walking.

Taking a slow deep breath before each step, I became poignantly aware of my loneliness as I paradoxically sought solitude. I pulled the red scarf up over my head and allowed it to fall in front of my face. Veiled, I was separated from the rest of the group while still being present. As I made the walk, I became more comfortable with my aloneness and felt at peace with it even though there were people all around me.

I was halfway to the center of the labyrinth when I saw Opal, a member of Immanuel's Bible study group, strike the ringing bowl and enter the labyrinth. My back stiffened. *What should I do? Leave?* Was it possible to cut across the labyrinth and slip out the back door without being noticed?

My heart raced and I walked faster, trying to increase the distance between Opal and me. Had she seen me? I tried to keep track of her.

Where did she go? I rounded a curve near the center and there she was, on the path next to me. I looked down and away. Had she recognized me behind my red veil?

I didn't want to pass her again. *I have to slow down. I have to time it so she's on the outer edge while I'm near the center.*

The path turned to the right. I had reached my destination. I was standing in the center with some other women, all strangers to me. *What do I do now? Is anyone else aware of what was going on?*

My heart was pounding, my breathing shallow. I sat down and crossed my legs. I took slow deep breaths. I peered between the legs of the other women, searching for Opal. There she was, walking along the outer edge of the labyrinth. I pulled the red veil tightly around my body while I considered what to do. *I need to calm down.* I took more deep breaths.

As my heart rate slowed, my thinking became clearer. Opal hadn't played an active part in my dechurching, but she wasn't an innocent bystander either. She colluded with Rev. Karen and the others by remaining silent. Bystanders were as much to blame as the active participants. I didn't forgive any of them. Was I wrong for that? Wasn't I supposed to forgive?

The center was becoming crowded as each woman arrived. There was no escaping. Opal would soon catch up with me. I didn't want to meet her there. I would have to pass her again, but it would be on my terms: on the path, not the center.

When I regained control of my heart rate and breathing, I stood up and started down the path. I walked slowly, stopping here and there, timing it so I would pass Opal again. This time we were on the same path. Without acknowledging her, I turned my back to her as I stepped past, our bodies almost touching. It was then that I knew God didn't expect me to forgive my enemies at Immanuel who continued to deny any wrongdoing. I vowed I would not forgive them until they asked for my forgiveness, made restitution and altered their behavior toward me and my family.

The third and last time I passed Opal, I looked her straight in the eye. She said something. I said nothing. When I exited the labyrinth, I felt exhilarated.

After I arrived home, I sat at my computer and shared my experience in a post to AdvocateWeb's HopeTalk, sparking a discussion about forgiveness. I considered the divergent religious views expressed in Simon

Wiesenthal's *The Sunflower*. The Jewish position resonated with me. When you have sinned, you need to make things right with the person you harmed by apologizing and making restitution. Then you need to reform your behavior. Only after this can you go to God for his forgiveness. You cannot be in right relation with God if you are not in right relation with your fellow human beings.

Jesus demonstrated that confession and forgiveness are intrinsically linked by only forgiving those who asked for it. I was only obligated to forgive when a perpetrator sincerely sought my forgiveness and was willing to make restitution. Not before. So long as my enemies refused to discuss what happened and refused to acknowledge the wrong they did me, I owed them nothing.

For some it might be important to feel they can forgive the perpetrator, but for me, healing came from making a conscious choice not to forgive unless my enemies acknowledged their wrongdoing. Having already paid a high price for the sins of others, I was determined that those who robbed me of my son weren't going to blight the rest of my life. Finally standing up for myself, I began to earnestly insist on some small measure of justice.

It had been two weeks since I sent Rev. Rick a copy of my article. I worried he would reject me after reading my story. Dr. Emmett attempted to reassure me. "Your story is very compelling and needs to be told."

"It's hard for me to believe that after reading my story anyone would remain my friend or ally," I replied. "People withdraw without explanation. It's hard to wait patiently."

"Give it time," he said.

How much time, I wondered. It was hard to remain brave, to press on even though I was frightened.

On April 6, I received Rev. Rick's response to my article via email. After reading my article he took time to think it over. "I obviously see why you want me to keep it confidential," he wrote.

I felt a twinge of shame. Did he think I had done something wrong? While reading my paper he wondered if he was being asked to take a side. I never asked him that. I just wanted him to listen.

In order to take a side, he continued, he would have to hear "from each person's side and that course, for many reasons, would not be wise."

Fair enough, but why would it be unwise? What was he saying? I didn't feel validated. I worried he was allied with my enemies. Perhaps he had spoken to them after all. Later, Rev. Rick would say he didn't want to become enmeshed in the situation. It was never his intention to prove who was right and wrong but simply to provide a safe environment for me to worship in. I respected him for that.

Not wanting to overreact, I telephoned my niece Rebecca and her mother Rita. Rebecca also expressed some reservations. Lyndon called Rev. Rick's email placating. Rita, however, viewed it more positively.

Unsure how to respond to Rev. Rick's email, I said nothing to him. I felt anxious to the point where I wished I could handle it in the old way. It frustrated me that the desire to self-harm was so easily triggered. Burning myself would bring quick relief even if it didn't last very long. In some ways it was easier and far more reliable than seeking help from people. People are fickle. You can never be sure they will be there for you no matter how long you have known them or how kind they have been toward you in the past.

Like a refugee, I yearned for the life I had before the conflict at FXUU. But there would be no going back. My dechurching radically altered my view of the world and other people's motives. I clearly saw what my social status was and that groups of people rejected me because I wasn't like them. Since I was unwilling to become like them, I would always be an outsider: at best, ignored and neglected, at worst, rejected.

# Mediation

On April 18, Maundy Thursday, I went to mass at St. Matt's. It was quiet and simple. I wasn't as moved as I had been at the first Maundy Thursday service I attended at Immanuel, but it was done well enough. I left the church feeling at peace.

Ten days later my brother Rich called. Our mother was in the hospital. The circulation in her legs was poor due to uncontrolled diabetes. She wasn't following her diet. There was some talk of amputation. As I hung up the phone I thought about her. Mom had been so paralyzed with anxiety, she had never been able to care for me and my siblings. We paid the price for her dysfunction, and now we would pay again. I wished we would act like a healthy, functional family and pull together. Arrange to sell our mother's house and have her move into an assisted living facility near to her present home.

The next morning I called Dr. Emmett. "Your mother wanted you to be popular," he said, "but she didn't help."

"What do you mean?"

"She didn't make sure you went to school clean and well groomed."

"My mother couldn't take care of herself, let alone take care of us," I replied.

When I was a teen, Mom would go shopping for herself, buy clothes that were inappropriate for herself, and then give them to my sister Trish and me. I hated when she did that. I didn't want the things she picked out. But now I realize she was working around our father, who never wanted to pay for any clothes for his daughters. He got angry when I told my mother I needed new underwear.

And then there were the boots. Winter was coming and my old boots no longer fit. I asked Mom if instead of the rubber boots that went over my shoes, I could have the new winter boots with the warm fleece lining like the other girls in my class. To my surprise, she said yes.

"Really?" I squealed as I hugged her.

That evening, my father and mother drove me to the big-box store to buy the boots. I tried on a brown pair that went up to my calf. "What do you think?"

"They look fine, honey," my mother said.

"They will really keep me warm when I walk to school in the morning."

While my father and I walked over to the cash register, Mom stopped to look at some clothes. After the boots were paid for, my father handed me the bag. "How dare you demand those boots?" he snarled.

The sparkle in my eyes vanished. "But I asked Mom for them."

"You are so selfish."

I dropped my head as I took the bag. Any pleasure I had in owning those boots was gone. I tried as best I could not to ask my parents for anything ever again.

On Sunday, I asked Rev. Rick to include my mother in Sunday prayers. After the service, as I shook Rev. Rick's hand he asked me if I had seen my mother lately.

"No, I don't stay in touch with her."

I walked off before he could ask me any more questions. Later that day I typed an email to him.

> Thank you for including my mother in the prayers today and for the interest you expressed as I was leaving the church. I fear I was abrupt when you asked if I had seen my mother recently. I wish I had simply said I last saw her at the end of December 2001 during the celebration of my twenty-fifth wedding anniversary.
>
> I do not want you to have the wrong impression of me. Unfortunately, we have met at the end of a difficult time in my life. There is a whole lot more to me than the anger, fear and pain that you have seen. Prior to my dechurching, I was really quite happy and content, having recovered from my childhood of neglect and abuse. People used to comment on how often I smiled and laughed.
>
> I haven't responded to your comments on my paper because I needed time to think about it and discuss it with my family. I remain uncertain of the best way to respond.
>
> On the issue of confidentiality—thank you for respecting my privacy. It is my story to tell and no one should tell it

without my permission. However, I want it to be clear that I am not ashamed of anything I said or did. I firmly believe that I was bullied and victimized. The mistake I made was that I trusted people who were not worthy of my trust.

Since I haven't been able to hide my emotional distress from you I thought it would make things easier if you were told the story of my dechurching, narrowing the gap created by keeping secrets. I was not asking you to take a side, to play detective and investigate the incidents. I am aware you know some of my enemies and have good relationships with them. I do, however, expect you to be on my side, which is different from taking sides. Had my former pastor been on my side she would have followed the advice of Lutheran Social Services, honoring what my family did for our foster son and ministering to everyone's grief and disappointment. If she had done that, reconciliation would have been possible and a win-win solution found.

Another reason I shared my story with you was to educate you about dechurching and spiritual abuse. I am increasingly involved with other victims/survivors and am working to reform our religious institutions. So far my efforts have included financial support to organizations like Voice of the Faithful and AdvocateWeb, attending conferences, sharing my expertise, doing extensive reading on ethics, abuse and bullying, and writing. I hope you will be open-minded enough to hear what I have to say and not hide behind your clerical collar.

On May 7, I received a reply from Rev. Rick.

Greetings and thanks for your message.

I hope this "difficult time" in your life soon transitions to better days. I know there are many unethical and corrupt clergy. It is very unfortunate that certain members of the clergy broke your trust. I have known pastors who are not only unethical and difficult to work with but are also

flaming jackasses. No collar can or should hide such
people....

Broken trust takes time and new trust to heal. I hope that
will happen for you here....

As far as knowing people at your former parish, I know
only a couple by name. I do know Ruth from attending
synod assemblies. I find her to be fun and enjoyable.
Though I know she very much liked your adopted son, I
have never talked with her about you and never intend to. I
also know Rev. Karen. Frankly, from a couple of my
experiences with her, I don't think I would ever want to
enter into a friendship with her or spend much time with
her. Oh well, I'm sure there's people who feel the same way
about me. May this place be a place of peace and healing for
all of us!

Rev. Rick then offered to speak with his conference dean about my
doing a presentation to the conference pastors about the issue of
confidentiality. "It is a very important issue," he wrote, "and from your
personal and professional experience you have a message to be heard."

With my consent, he contacted Rev. Beth about my doing a presentation
on confidentiality. She replied she would be happy to place me on the agenda
at the end of the year. That was fine with me. It would give me more time to
prepare both mentally and emotionally.

Mid-May, Gwynne, one of the other foster mothers, called to set up a
dinner date. My heart rate increased. What did she really want? *Don't be
silly*, I told myself as I took some deep breaths. *She's just offering friendship.
Don't be so suspicious. There probably isn't a hidden agenda here. Calm yourself.
You have never been so afraid of friendship before.*

I knew I should call Dr. Emmett. He would want to process what I
was feeling. I didn't want to. I wanted to be left alone where I was safe.
When I thought of being safe, paradoxically I would then think of
slashing my arms and all the blood washing all the pain away. Relief.

But it wasn't really safe to do that. If I cut the way I imagined I
would die. It would break my family's heart. Cutting didn't really relieve
the pain. Just spread it. I didn't want to do that.

Although I continued to see Dr. Emmett, I was very ambivalent about it. Dr. Emmett didn't totally understand the ambivalence. He saw no way to resolve it. I just wanted the tension to end. Either give in to the need to have him to talk to, stop fighting it and see it as an investment in myself, or walk away from it, never coming back.

The years out of therapy were happy years. *I can't get back to them. Won't I ever feel safe again? It is a terrible thing they did to me. Cruel. They don't see it. Will it always influence my life? It is something I will never forget.*

I wanted to move on. Had this experience so changed me that I was no longer capable of living my life independently without the support and intervention of a therapist?

I didn't want to depend on anyone. Dr. Emmett wouldn't be in my life forever. Someday he would close his practice and retire. Or he would abandon me or reject me for some other reason. Relationships were temporary. They didn't last, at least not for me. Except for Lyndon. He had chosen to stay with me until death.

I didn't want to be viewed as crazy and unstable. Someone that lacked any credibility. Someone in need of pity. I wanted to be viewed as strong and trustworthy and competent.

Competent. How often I had been viewed as not smart, not capable, pitiful. My fifth-grade teacher and my sixth-grade guidance counselor told me I wasn't college material. My skills and abilities were often ignored or overlooked by others. And once people know you have been in a psychiatric hospital or have been in therapy for serious problems, forget it. You will never be taken seriously again.

*So I take care of myself. Deal with my own problems. Pursue my own interests. So long as I do that I am okay. When I get caught up with trying to belong, that is when I lose myself.*

But reaching out to Dr. Emmett: wasn't that taking care of myself? And the people who would put me down and not take me seriously: were they really worth worrying about?

I so wanted to truly accept my vulnerability, but there was this wall of fear inside me. I was having difficulty getting over it. I just couldn't give up the ambivalence, just as I couldn't totally give up hurting myself. It was dependable in a way people were not. But it wasn't right. I had no more right to hurt myself than to hurt others.

Sometimes I thought I should just put therapy in the budget the same way as food and clothing. Just one of those things I needed right now to keep myself safe. Stop fighting it. Call Dr. Emmett when I wanted to. Look at it as something I did because I wanted to, not something I needed to. If I thought of doing it because I needed to I got caught up in trying to figure out if I really needed to, and if I tried harder I could manage on my own. After all, healthy, normal people didn't need therapy. And I so wanted to be healthy and normal. Then maybe I would be accepted, finally. No longer defective.

*I'm defective: too emotional,* I thought. Somehow, if I were a better person, none of the abusive experiences would have happened. But my parents' emotionally and physically abusive behavior had very little to do with me. The bullying at school, at church, had more to do with their jealousy, their issues than mine. They just took advantage of my vulnerability and kicked me when I was down. Being vulnerable: that was what got you rejected and abused. So you had to put on a strong façade. How else did you protect yourself?

Continuing in therapy left me wide open. People would say I had problems. No one would have to take me seriously. When I got emotional, people stopped listening. They didn't ask, *Why is she so upset? How can we help her?* They instead said I shouldn't be upset and I can't control myself? I must be crazy.

I needed and wanted Dr. Emmett's help. Regardless of what we talked about, just sitting in his office felt safe, a brief respite from the world, the way church used to be. Where was the harm in it?

Dr. Emmett was trying to help, but couldn't that become destructive? Look at Rev. Dorothy, I told myself. She supported my healing only to a point. She had different ideas about what needed changing. She probably wanted me to be more like her: unemotional, controlled. She was trying to convert me when she gave me that poorly written book for Christmas on women's spirituality. When I became a Lutheran, she was no longer interested. And Rev. Karen: What was her beef? Jealousy? I wasn't Lutheran enough? What was it?

I searched for ways to declare "This is who I am." In *The Wounded Heart of God,* Andrew Sung Park wrote of negating the self negated by others. I interpreted that to mean rejecting the false judgments of others and accepting my own identity unblemished by other people's projections. Until reading this, the talk of emptying oneself never made any sense to me. Now I understood it.

The last few months, I had been traveling down the wrong path. Withdrawing and avoiding others, including Dr. Emmett, wasn't the answer. Instead I needed to empty myself of other people's false projections that had been motivated by their envy. I needed to accept myself and see myself for who I was. I needed to affirm that I was a kind and generous person who was passionate, intelligent, vulnerable yet strong, educated, and faithful. That was the answer.

By enriching my prayer life, I strove to remain centered. While I prayed in the morning, my mind turned toward seeking justice. I had a client who worked her way up the chain of command at work and eventually received justice. I considered contacting the bishop again and asking her to meet with me. I wanted to be heard. I wanted her to know my side of the story.

In early June, I shared with Rev. Rick my labyrinth experience. On June 10 he sent me an email. As I feared, he focused on forgiveness and missed the point about justice, about holding my enemies accountable. He failed to acknowledge that I had had a deeply moving spiritual insight.

God didn't expect me to excuse what others had done to me. Rather, he expected perpetrators to acknowledge their sin, make restitution and reform their lives. Jesus spoke for the oppressed: the victims, not the perpetrators. God expected me to forgive only after the perpetrator sought my forgiveness and was willing to make restitution. So long as my enemies refused to discuss what happened and refused to acknowledge the wrong they did me, I owed them nothing.

Three days later, I spoke to Dr. Emmett. I had difficulty explaining my objection to Rev. Rick's emails on forgiveness. I don't think Dr. Emmett always understood where I was coming from. Perhaps he couldn't because he had never been victimized the way I had. And he was basically a kind soul who wanted to believe the best of others.

I wanted those who sinned against me to be held responsible. The only way that was going to happen was for me to do it. I would refuse to speak to them until they apologized and made restitution. I would not forget what they did and what they failed to do.

Friday, June 20, after several days of rain, the sun shone through the bay window. I had a lot to be thankful for. The wind was blowing through the trees. The sapling I transplanted the previous fall survived the long, cold winter. Everyone was healthy in my family. I appreciated who I was better. I liked that I was so well educated and could think critically. I loved that I enjoyed discussing serious topics and that I was outspoken. I was proud that I strove to be honest and had little tolerance for keeping up appearances.

I was starting to feel strong and happy again, gaining power from the insights of the past few years. My perceptions of people were accurate. They weren't biased and incorrect. Very few people had the honesty and integrity I expected from myself. Being excluded from the crowd and isolated allowed me to develop a clearer, independent vision of the world, myself and God.

So much was happening. So little was happening. No crisis. Life was returning to a routine, comfortable pace. I continued to read and write to people on the Internet. The intense feelings of rage, betrayal and grief settled down. I was crying less as I sought a way to obtain justice for myself, and others like me.

I was taking pleasure in small accomplishments. My secretary had just gotten off the phone with her sister. Her niece had a bug bite with a strange ring around it. "What is it?" she asked me.

She assumed I would know even though she knew I wasn't a physician. And I did know. "Take the kid immediately to the doctor. It's probably Lyme disease."

I was right. The child was given antibiotics and would be spared a potentially chronic, crippling disease. I helped that child. A child I never met and will probably never meet.

Over the July Fourth weekend I read Catherine Fairbanks' book, *Hiding Behind the Collar*. I was startled by words I could have written. When Catherine Fairbanks was a child, church was a refuge away from her abusive stepfather. After she was dechurched years later, she reacted to the hypocrisy of the wayward pulpits just as I had. I, too, wanted to get out of my car and alter those signs from "All are Welcome" to "Some are Welcome."

After I finished reading Catherine's book, I realized there was a possibility that I could successfully sue for clergy misconduct. I wasn't sure if an attorney would be interested since I didn't sustain any loss in income. Regardless of that, I decided to seek Catherine's advice on how to find an attorney. After obtaining her email address from AdvocateWeb, I wrote her. A week later she wrote back suggesting we speak on the phone. I gave her my phone number and she called me on Sunday.

Catherine explained that after calling twenty or more attorneys, she finally found one who assisted her in filing an insurance claim against her church. She explained that suing involves the courts, while filing an insurance claim was similar to filing a claim following a car accident. Catherine filed a claim for breach of confidentiality, fiduciary responsibility and defamation of character.

Encouraged by Catherine, I called and spoke with a Connecticut attorney I was acquainted with. He was very gracious with his time and listened to my story. He informed me I had a case worth pursuing but needed to find an attorney in Massachusetts.

I then called Stan, a Massachusetts' attorney who was on Advocate-Web's advisory board. My spirits sank as I tried to contact him. I feared it was hopeless. But then he called. He was representing several of the victims of Catholic priests. He was well acquainted with the kind of issues I was dealing with. I felt validated. It wasn't just me this kind of thing happened to. He suggested I call him the following week.

Wednesday, July 23, I called Stan from my Stoughton office after my clerical help had left for the day. Sitting at the counter that spanned the file cabinets I dialed his number. We talked for about ten minutes. He advised me that there simply aren't the laws to sue for most ethical violations. It is even difficult to hold clergy responsible for blatant violations such as sexual abuse. We discussed the possibility of filing an insurance claim. He suggested I write a letter to the bishop asking for compensation for my therapy expenses.

I emailed Catherine and discussed his suggestions. The bishop, she wrote, had nothing to gain by doing anything. I agreed.

On Tuesday, July 29, I drove into Boston to consult with another attorney, who also refused to take my case. He didn't understand church hierarchies. He gave me the name of a Methodist minister-turned-lawyer who mediated church disputes, and the name of another lawyer handling the Catholic Church scandal.

While I drove to my office, the tears streamed down my face, blurring my vision. I wiped them away with the back of my hand. *If I go into mediation,* I thought, *I'll go alone.* I had no advocate. My husband had withdrawn from the issue. Catherine and my sister were far away.

Catherine encouraged me to find an attorney who had some experience with emotional abuse. While I searched for an attorney to represent me, I felt intensely anxious for brief periods. Paradoxically, I

also felt more at peace while remaining determined to correct the wrong
done to my family and me.

Intent on showing my enemies I wasn't defeated, I chose to attend
Immanuel's outdoor service held at the local Catholic shrine on August
tenth. It was a neutral place. They couldn't throw me out, a baptized
Catholic. I wanted to declare by my presence and manner, *Here I am. I am
not insignificant. I cannot simply be discarded. Look at yourselves. Acknowledge
your mistakes. Ask for my forgiveness. Make restitution. Reform your behavior.*

I decided I would arrive five minutes late. Take a seat. Sit proudly. I
would not greet anyone unless spoken to. Perhaps I would simply turn my
back. I didn't forgive them. I held them responsible for the harm they did
me, the harm they did to James and to themselves. I knew I walked with
God.

Prior to attending the outdoor service, I had prepared some
responses to things that might be said, but omitted how to handle
simple, polite greetings. After parking in the large lot, I walked across the
asphalt toward the outdoor chapel. My heart pounded with fear and
anger, interfering with my ability to think. Irene, who I knew from Bible
study and chimes choir, was handing out the order of service at the end
of the wide concrete entrance walk adorned with flowering bushes.

"Maggie, hi." She was surprised to see me. "How are you?"

Without making eye contact, I mumbled, "Okay."

Failing to see a seat in the front, I sat in the last, weatherworn cedar
pew. Marlene came and sat close. She greeted me. Again, I mumbled a
response without making eye contact. I sat up straight and stared at the
back of people's heads.

Ruth sat two pews in front of me. She didn't appear to be aware of
my presence. During the Peace, after I had sat down, she turned around
and extended her hand. "Peace," she said. I limply shook her hand
without making eye contact.

Just before communion, it started raining. We hurried to the pews
under the pavilion. I imagined God weeping for me, healing my anger
and sorrow.

During a hymn, Marlene couldn't find her photocopy of the hymn. I
shared mine with her.

Colleen was serving communion. As I approached the communion
rail, she said, "Maggie." She appeared startled and pleased. I didn't

respond. I took my communion wafer and returned to my seat. I left immediately after the service without speaking to anyone.

A couple of weeks later, I telephoned the Kansas City attorney who had represented Catherine. After listening to my story, this attorney told me I lacked sufficient corroborating evidence even though the pattern of events strongly suggested I was right. Without knowing I had already done so, she advised me to return to Immanuel and make my presence known. It would be empowering, and eventually someone would step forward telling me what they heard. Then, armed with that information, I could file suit.

In an email, Catherine cautioned me,

> Her suggestion is good—only if you have the support to go with the knowledge that things (most likely) will not be as you would like. When I went back to show that I was still standing, it did nothing but make the priest and the community dig their heels in deeper—and to prepare for any future visits I may have made. This reached out into the community level. Don't underestimate what Karen may do.

On September 16 I arrived, as usual, fifteen minutes early for my appointment with Dr. Emmett. He had moved his office to an old Victorian house near Wayland Square. I took a seat by the window in what once was the front parlor. It was early and there were no other clients waiting. Having forgotten to bring a book, I picked up one of the magazines lying on the wicker bench and began reading an article about a September 11th widow. Life, she said, had returned to normal, but normal was now different.

I looked up from my reading and closed my eyes, resting my head against the wall. Things for me were also returning to normal. More days than not, I felt good. I felt happy. I only had brief, intense bouts of anxiety approximately once per week. Usually they were triggered by some reminder of FXUU or Immanuel. Those bouts were getting shorter and less intense as I handled them better.

Looking back, what had I learned? What had changed? I was more fully aware of my social status as an outsider, someone on the margins, never to be fully welcomed and accepted. When things went wrong I was blamed. I was rarely recognized for my contributions or they were minimized. At best I was ignored. A tear made its way down my cheek.

*It's okay,* I told myself. I had my husband and my children. Despite my isolation, I was growing content with my life. I coped with loneliness in the same way I had in high school. I occupied my time reading about clergy misconduct and spiritual abuse. It was becoming my survivor's mission. I wanted to understand what had happened at FXUU and Immanuel so I could prevent it from happening again, not just to me but to others as well.

I sighed when I thought about Kenneth Haugk's book, *Antagonists in the Church.* I had first seen it lying on Rev. Karen's coffee table. My face burned bright red with shame and embarrassment as I recalled Haugk, a psychologist, linking mental illness with church conflict. He offered no empirical evidence for his assertions and appeared quite unaware of the devastating consequences to the person accused of being an antagonist. Just as I had been, Haugk advocated isolating the accused antagonist from the rest of the congregation and not providing them with a fair chance to defend themselves.

I preferred Arthur Boers' book, *Never Call Them Jerks.* Boers, a Mennonite, focused on the religious community as a whole rather than condemning individual personalities. I felt affirmed by the elegant and loving foreword written by David Augsburger. I identified with his description of Boers' troublesome behavior while in seminary: "Arthur Boers has the gifts for being there when conflicts happen, for bringing issues that we consent to leave invisible into the clear, reasonable light, and for joining in the struggle for a new justice." I agreed with Augsburger's statement, quoting Martin Buber, that:

> ...authentic Christian community is not a "community of similarity," a union of like-minded people who have eluded or eliminated all potential detractors. Instead, it is a "community of diversity" that does not exclude the intrinsic and natural variation and divergence that constitutes human groupings.

Further, Augsburger concluded:

> Shooting the messenger, blaming the one who shouts "fire" for being the arsonist, or excluding those who are willing to speak up only buries the injury for the moment and contributes to the creation of later and greater injustices.

"Maggie."

I opened my eyes. Dr. Emmett was standing on the stairway. I picked up my bag and stood. At Murray, FXUU and Immanuel I was the messenger, *not* a self-condemned antagonist. I was excluded for speaking up. Other church members projected their own shortcomings onto me. By expelling me, FXUU and Immanuel deceived themselves that they were innocent.

"Good morning," I said as I walked past Dr. Emmett into his office. *Normal is indeed different*, I thought as I sat down.

When my attempts to find an attorney stalled, Catherine suggested I contact the Mennonite Conciliation Service. I called and spoke with a woman there who, after consulting with a colleague, told me my situation was a good case for mediation. She gave me a number of a mediation service in Massachusetts. On September 25 Kevin Campbell, a Presbyterian elder trained as a Christian mediator, agreed to mediate my dispute with Immanuel. We talked at length on the telephone. He agreed to contact Immanuel's interim minister.

Working with the mediator stirred up fears of rejection and abandonment. How could I be sure that Dr. Emmett wouldn't eventually abandon me just as Rev. Dorothy, Rev. Karen and my parents did for having too many needs? Once, I was frightened by my parents yelling and screaming at each other. I remember sitting on the stairway in my childhood home crying. I must have been about eight years old. My father yelled and told me to stop. When I couldn't hold back the tears he slapped me across the face. I gulped and suppressed the tears as best I could.

While I waited for Immanuel to reply to Kevin's phone call and emails, Kevin asked me,

> ...who specifically do you envision being at a mediation? Please list all of the people whether or not you think they'll come. Make your ideal list (include Rev. Karen if you think that's important) and I will see if the pastor and I can get this thing going. Also, if you could give me one or two specific things you'd like to accomplish by this meeting. They don't need to be profound, they could be things like "to have a chance to tell my story." If you'll give those some

thought and prayer, perhaps we can present them to the pastor when I speak to him.

I wrote back,

I envision inviting everyone who was aware of what was going on to be there, everyone who knew me and who knew James...

From this process I would like to have my family's side of the story be heard and why I blame Rev. Karen and church members for what happened. I want them to hear how devastating it was for me. I want church members to finally share with me what they were told and what they had discussed about my family and me amongst themselves. I want an opportunity to refute accusations made against us.

In my fantasies, I also hope for justice, which would start with the above but would also include apologies and restitution. Restitution would include reimbursing me for my psychotherapy costs incurred as the direct result of Rev. Karen's and church leaders' emotional abuse. I believe their insurance would cover it. It would also include church members educating themselves about the challenges foster parents face and possibly initiating some sort of project to support them in their efforts to care for society's throwaway children. It would also include rewriting the congregation's constitution, eliminating the persistent troublemaker clause and replacing it with conflict resolution procedures that are consistent with best practices in the social sciences. Due process would also be guaranteed. I would also like church members, especially leaders, to be educated about church conflict, spiritual abuse and its impact.

I know the above is hoping for a lot but in my heart of hearts I believe it is just. My family and I were the victims here. Not James...

Following Catherine's attorney's advice, I attended services at Immanuel on October 19 for the first time since I was dechurched.

Wanting to make my presence known, I made sure I was dressed well. I wore my blue khakis with a pink turtleneck. On my feet were pink socks in blue skids. I topped it off with my multicolored striped muffler and my blue newsboy cap. My nails were painted red. I looked smart. I felt empowered.

Unaware that the ministerial candidate was conducting the service, I was surprised by how crowded the sanctuary was. I didn't recognize most of the people there. I took a seat toward the front, on the pulpit side away from Ruth and the others. I spoke to no one. This time I wasn't rattled. I wasn't afraid.

Matt, a member of the chimes choir, served communion. As he poured the wine he acknowledged my presence by using my name, "Maggie, the blood of Christ shed for you."

Was he welcoming me?

I left immediately after the service. I had no interest in taking part in the farce of an election. There was only one candidate, selected by the bishop. I wasn't going to stamp my approval on her choice. Whether I favored the candidate or not would make little difference.

The next day I received an email from Kevin.

Hi Margaret,

I received an email from Rev. David at Immanuel. He spoke with the church council at Immanuel. I got the sense from his email that he is open to hearing what you have to say. The council expressed a different perspective as to why you left. My guess is that many don't know fully what you have told me. Rev. David said in his email that he is committed to conflict resolution and he offered to speak with you. I will be trying to contact him Tuesday to talk more with him. He obviously knows nothing of what happened.

I got the impression from our discussion that you were still on the membership rolls there. From what Rev. David said, the council seems to think you transferred your membership to a church in Pawtucket. Did I get that wrong? Anyway, perhaps you and I could try to speak on the phone Thursday or Friday? Are there times when that might work? Please let me know. Have a great day.

Well it looked like my going to church at Immanuel the previous day stirred things up. I replied to Kevin.

> I am happy to hear Rev. David responded. Thank you for working on this. Regarding my membership status, I have never resigned from Immanuel nor transferred my membership to any other church. I also have never received a letter from Immanuel removing me from membership. I continue to receive Immanuel's newsletter. I have made two contributions of record, one in August, the other yesterday.
>
> The majority of the names I provided you with were/are either on the board during and after the conflict and/or were employed by the church. Most had some role to play in what happened. There are few, if any, innocent parties among the church leadership. Anna, the wife of the current board president, telephoned me last July. Her excuse was that she wanted the book she loaned me returned but I believe it was to act as a scout to see if I was going to church elsewhere. At that time I told her I was not a member of any other church. I do not believe I told her I was attending services in Pawtucket. How would they know that? I shared my anger and distress with her about Rev. Karen and Immanuel.

Four weeks later, Rev. David still hadn't replied to Kevin's phone calls. On November 16, I again attended services at Immanuel. Arriving ten minutes early, I was again surprised to see the parking lot overflowing. When I walked through the doors I was greeted by someone who recognized me but whose name I didn't remember. I took the order of service she handed me. As I was walking toward my seat I saw Colleen, who was busy preparing for the service. I don't believe she saw me as I walked by her without greeting her.

Once again I chose a pew on the pulpit side near the front, and sat down at the far end. I sat straight and proud. Reading through the order of service, I realized it was First Communion Day, and that was why the church was unusually crowded. No one, to my relief, sat next to me.

During the service, I felt inspired and gained courage. I resolved that I wouldn't avoid the minister and would shake his hand on my way out. I sat and memorized what I wanted to say, "I am Margaret Jones. I want to personally urge you to return Kevin Campbell's call." I would avoid further conversation and leave.

Larry, a member of the choir, saw me, and as he walked past my pew whispered to me, "Nice hat." I smiled as I looked away. I wanted to be seen but I didn't want to engage anyone in conversation.

At the end of the service, the choir stood at the back of the church with baskets of freshly baked bread. They handed each person a loaf as they exited the church. The minister had left the sanctuary. Unsure what to do, I stood in one of the back pews. Anna, a member of Bible study, saw me from several feet away and greeted me. I nodded my head but didn't smile.

After most of the people had filed out of the church, I took my place in line. When I reached the back, a choir member handed me a loaf of bread.

"Thank you," I said.

"Maggie."

I looked to my left and saw Colleen standing right next to me.

"I've been concerned about how you were doing," she said.

I took in a deep breath, mustering my courage, then said, "If you were so concerned about me, why haven't you called in the last two years?"

She looked confused. "Who, me?"

"Yes, you," I replied.

"I know," Colleen said as she cast her eyes downward.

"No one in this church cared enough about me to call." As I spoke, I choked back the tears and rage. I had reached my limit. I could no longer bear it. I turned abruptly toward the exit. Pushing open the heavy wood door, I stepped out onto the sidewalk and let the door slam behind me. Some people who were standing on the sidewalk chatting looked toward me. I straightened my shoulders and tightened my facial muscles. Stepping onto the grass, I strode past people strolling toward the parking lot.

When I reached my car, I slid into the driver's seat and turned the keys in the ignition. My heart was pounding. *Better wait*, I thought. *I shouldn't drive when I'm so upset.*

I took a deep breath and rested my head against the back of the seat. Out of the corner of my eye I saw Ruth get into the car next to mine. I waited for her to look in my direction. She didn't. Did she know I was there?

*I better leave before someone stops to talk to me. I would really lose it then. I need some privacy.* I drove a mile up the road to the supermarket and parked, and sat in my car until my heart rate and breathing returned to normal. When I finally entered the store, I focused on choosing the produce I needed for Sunday dinner.

I picked up a Macintosh apple and turned it in my hand, admired its bright red and green skin. Satisfied there were no bruises, I placed it into my basket and picked up another one. I took pleasure in selecting fruits and vegetables for the people in my life who truly loved and cared for me.

On the checkout line, I saw Ellen, Mallory's mother, in the next line. Our eyes met. I was determined not to turn my gaze away. She made small talk about having kids around the house again. I wasn't sure who she was talking about.

"How is Mallory doing?" I asked.

"Oh, she's in Pennsylvania visiting her boyfriend," Ellen replied.

"That's nice." I paid for my groceries and left the market. I wondered if Ellen knew her daughter had caved into Rev. Karen's threats and left me high and dry. Mallory was a wuss. She had no backbone. I would be embarrassed if she was my daughter.

On the drive home, I resolved that I would call the interim minister and say what I had intended to say before I left the church this morning. After I put the groceries away, thinking perhaps she really was concerned about me, I decided to call Colleen first. I looked at the clock. *She might not be home from church yet. I'll leave a message. See what she does with it.*

Her answering machine beeped and I said, "Colleen, this is Maggie Jones. If you're really concerned about me and want to help, give me a call."

I hung up the phone and dialed the church. Colleen picked up. I hadn't expected that. "I just called your house and left a message."

"I'm just finishing counting today's collection," she replied. "I'll be leaving for home shortly."

"May I speak with Rev. David?" I asked.

"I'll go get him." I heard her put the phone down and walk down the hall away from the phone. She came back a short time later. "Rev. David is just sitting down to lunch with the First Communicants. He'll call you back when he's finished."

"Thanks." I hung up the phone. I wondered how I sounded to her. Had I successfully covered up my fear? Would Rev. David, the interim minister, really call me back?

The phone rang. Rev. David was keeping his promise.

"I don't want to take up your time," I said. "I just wanted to ask you to return Kevin Campbell's phone call."

Before I could hang up he asked, "Who is Kevin Campbell? Is he a lawyer or what?"

"No, he's a mediator," I replied. "He's a graduate of a Presbyterian seminary. The Mennonite Conciliation Service referred me to him."

Rev. David started to tell me how my behavior wasn't Biblical. "Luke says that before you go up to communion you should resolve things with your brother."

"I have made many attempts to resolve things," I replied.

"You're no longer a member here," he said.

"I never resigned my membership. I've donated money to Immanuel within the last year. I am still getting Immanuel's newsletter."

"Aren't you now a member of St. Matthew?"

"No," I replied. "Why is that relevant? Whether I attend another church or not doesn't absolve people of the harm they did me." Then I asked, "How do you know I have been attending services at St. Matthew?"

"Rev. Beth told me," he replied.

"Rev. Beth?" I asked, puzzled.

"Rev. Beth presented your proposal to speak to the minister's group. The group discussed it but didn't want to get involved with anything like that."

*Anything like what?* I wondered. "The presentation was Rev. Rick's idea."

"He wasn't even there during the discussion."

"I wasn't surprised by the ministers' decision not to meet with me," I told him. "Ministers have little or no interest in professional ethics."

We then spoke briefly about the difference between the ethical standards of psychologists and Lutheran ministers.

"I don't trust you," I told him.

"Why? Because I sit in the chair once occupied by Rev. Karen?"

"Unfortunately, yes." I felt my jaw tighten.

"Do you want revenge?"

"No, I want justice," I replied.

"Why didn't you speak to anyone at the outdoor service last August?" he asked.

"It was the first time since being pushed out that I attended a service. I didn't feel safe."

"I am concerned," he said, "that the proverbial shit will hit the fan when the new minister starts in two weeks. I don't want to hand over a church to a new minister with this problem still unresolved."

"Yes," I said, "but doesn't your being a lame duck give you an advantage?"

"A meeting had been arranged and you didn't show up."

"Do you want to know what really happened?"

"Yes," he replied.

"I had tried to get assistance from the Staff Support committee. Rev. Karen blocked and subverted it. She turned it into a disciplinary process. I wasn't told about the meeting until the day before. It was an ambush."

We then discussed ELCA's and Immanuel's constitutions. "A person can be expelled from the church for 'persistent troublemaking.' There is no behavioral definition for it," I said. "A persistent troublemaker is anyone the minister has decided is one. There is no way a person can disprove it. Everything the person says or does is taken as proof that they are a troublemaker."

"I'm only an interim minister here. This is my last week. It isn't appropriate for me to deal with Kevin. You should have contacted the bishop."

"I did, and they wouldn't meet with me."

"You should have written a letter."

"I did that, too. I also contacted the national office and spoke with Rev. Larraine." I was now crying. "I'm tired of being told why people can't help. I just want someone to help me."

"What you need to do is get the word out," Rev. David said. He then told the story of someone who hadn't gotten the Nobel Prize because he wasn't as politically connected as the other scientists. This person then took out a full-page ad in the *New York Times*.

*He can't be serious,* I thought. *That would cost a ton of money and get me what? Is he really trying to help or is he just playing me?*

"Of course, if you do something like that you get a reputation," he said.

"I already have a reputation," I replied.

"I'll call Kevin today," he promised. "I'll get back to you on Monday."

Monday morning I received an email from the mediator, Kevin Campbell, informing me he had spoken to Rev. David and would like to call to talk about it. I emailed him back, giving him my home phone number. While I waited, I posted to AdvocateWeb's listserv,

> Anyone out there today? Is there anyone out there willing to wait with me? The interim minister called and spoke to the mediator. The mediator is supposed to call me today as soon as he gets his kid down for a nap. My anxiety is high. I fear this minister has convinced the mediator what a bad person I am and why don't I just let things go etc.
>
> Anyone out there care about what is going on with me?

Other survivors responded and kept me company by emailing me throughout the day. I posted back,

> As I wait and think about yesterday's phone conversation with the interim minister I wonder, Why is it about my refusing to yield to their will and needs and not about understanding my hurt and pain? Why is it okay for my former "friends" to give me unwanted hugs during the Peace and then refuse to speak to me during coffee hour, but it isn't okay for me to go to church services and leave without saying hi to them? Why is it okay for them to talk about me and not to me, but it isn't okay for me to seek an outside mediator? Why?

My list mates responded that clergy regard themselves as special persons and didn't believe the feelings of their victims mattered. One woman cited Jesus' words from *The Message* that warn there are people who make a big show of saying the right thing but who really don't mean it. I replied,

> It isn't just the clergy here. It is the church leadership, the laity that is in charge. They are just as bad. Their values

are so different from mine. Keeping up appearances appears
to be what is most important. There is a disconnect between the way you act in the sanctuary from the way you
act outside. It is religion as performance. Pretend peace.
Pretend harmony. I won't go along so I am the bad one.
They think I am the fraud. And for some reason they are
afraid of me. That was clear yesterday.

Thanks, everyone, for waiting with me. Kevin, the mediator,
is home with a sick child so he is uncertain when he will call
today. Let's pray that it is soon and this agony can end for me.

Needing to get out of the house, I went to St. Matthew-Trinity's
Bible study. Troubled by some of the things Rev. David said about the
Rhode Island Conference's rejection of my presentation, I stopped by
Rev. Rick's office before Bible study started. He was at his desk gathering
up some papers. I started telling him the reason Rev. Beth had given me
for the conference's rejection of my proposal.

"That's not the reason," Rev. Rick interrupted. "I'm sorry, Margaret,
it was like trip wires going off everywhere. Rachael, the bishop's assistant,
became involved. I don't know how she found out about it. I was advised
to call Rev. Karen and speak to her about you. I didn't want to get
involved in that kind of thing."

We agreed to talk after Bible study in his office. Taking a seat on one
of the green upholstered chairs in the corner of his office, he and I talked
for about forty minutes. Weeping, I said, "I can't defend myself against
people who won't tell me what their complaint is. I can't fight shadows. I
trusted all the wrong people. I don't know if I can trust you or not."

Rev. Rick expressed concern for my distress. "I hope I can provide
you with a safe place within my congregation."

I was grateful for his honesty. He confirmed my suspicions about
Rev. Karen blacklisting me. I wasn't paranoid after all. I really did have
something to fear.

I told Lyndon about it while we undressed that night. He said little. I
took my place in our bed, lying on my right side with my back toward
him. I curled up into a fetal position. I felt nauseated. I needed relief
from the intense anxiety I was feeling. I thought about cutting myself.
Lyndon pulled me close to him, wrapping his strong arms around my
body. I could barely move. In this way, he kept me safe through the night.

While I waited for Kevin to call me, I decided I must take action against Rev. Karen and the bishop's office. They were never going to leave me alone. I needed a lawyer. But I didn't really want to take legal action. I prayed for the blacklisting to stop. Unless it stopped, I would never be allowed to become a full participating member of a church community. I also wanted to be compensated for my therapy costs. I thought that was only fair.

Kevin and I finally connected late Thursday afternoon. Parked at a sheltered workshop in Taunton, I spoke to him on my cell phone.

"Rev. David doesn't want to get involved since he's leaving in a few days and the new minister would be starting," Kevin informed me. "Rev. David also thinks you should send a certified letter to the bishop."

"I did that in 2002."

"What do you hope to get out of mediation?" Kevin asked. He sounded like he didn't think I should pursue it further, although he offered to call each member one by one. I declined, believing that the expenditure of energy wouldn't be worth it.

"I will be looking into legal avenues to stop Rev. Karen's blacklisting," I told him. "Thank you for all that you did."

"I didn't do much for you," Kevin said.

"We accomplished more than you realized, even if it wasn't what we had hoped for."

After saying goodbye, I closed my phone and put it into my pocketbook. My perceptions of Immanuel had been validated. It was now clear where I stood with my former friends who claimed they were concerned about me. Freed of the hope for reconciliation, I could move on. I was ready to make a commitment to St. Matt's.

# One Last Try

When I arrived home from work the day I spoke with Kevin, I sat at my computer and posted to AdvocateWeb's listserv.

> I am feeling pretty discouraged tonight. It seems no matter what I do I can't get any justice for myself. I don't want Rev K to get away with what she has done but I feel powerless to prevent it.

My list mates responded with words of support and encouragement. I spent the night sitting in front of my computer screen reading my email. There was one woman with a similar story to mine. I visited her website. As I read about her struggle with her church community, I noted she tried some things that I hadn't and thought, *If only I had* ... But in the end she was still dechurched. I sighed. Unless someone else at Immanuel clearly stood up for me, there was nothing I could do to regain my place there.

Monday, November 24 was a beautiful day. The morning sun shone through the bay window, warming my houseplants. Before going into the kitchen for my breakfast, I went into my study to check my email. There was one from Rev. Mary.

> I'm sorry to hear about the recent things you learned re/Immanuel, but I guess in some ways it's one of those things that is better to have confirmed rather than be in the dark about (even though I know how it stings). It is beyond my imagination how there could have been no attempt by the church to meet you in your desire for mediation and instead simply "write you off." And yet, I've witnessed (and been the brunt) of that experience, not in an organizational sense, but with that friend. And I have seen Ohio churches disfellowship a congregation we were very close to in Southern Ohio, and then the attitude of vast numbers of pastors was, "Good riddance! Glad we got rid of THAT problem" instead of grief and sorrow and a sense of the fracturing of the body of Christ....

Grateful for her support, I turned the computer monitor off. I would reply to her later. After eating breakfast, I walked into the living room and took a seat near the window on the black leather sofa. Through the dining room windows, I could hear heavy construction machinery uprooting and splitting trees apart as they prepared to build houses between my home and Immanuel.

Dressed in my lightweight blue-and-yellow plaid pajama bottom and a green flannel shirt, I crossed my legs and set my hands on my knees, palms up. Closing my eyes, I tried to center myself. I had set aside this time to begin working on writing this book. I asked God to guide me while keeping me safe.

Finishing my meditation, I took out my black clothbound journal and began writing a letter to Dr. Emmett.

> I have a lot of news to share with you tomorrow about church mediation and my being blacklisted. It boggles my mind how people can make up their minds without hearing the other side of things. People want to believe in the boogieman and are willing to believe I am evil, that they need to stay away from me. It is like I am a lightning rod for all their unresolved issues. They can't admit to their anger so they dump it on me.

For Thanksgiving, Lyndon and I drove down to Richmond, Virginia to spend the holiday with my sister Rita's family. Melissa was in Florida with her boyfriend and Orion was out to sea on patrol. My niece told me it was her turn now to cook the feast while Lyndon and I played with our grandniece and nephew.

The time in Richmond passed too quickly. It was hard to leave the warm, protective embrace of my sister's family and return to New England, where we were never really accepted. I could be so much happier, I thought, if we moved closer to my family. But Lyndon wanted to stay in Massachusetts.

"I'm not going to be run out of my home," he said.

The following weekend it snowed, leaving twenty-eight inches on the ground. I didn't go to church because of it. Two days later on Tuesday, December 9, I received a voicemail message from Christopher, who was now the president of Immanuel's board. He wanted me to meet with him and the council's vice president the following evening.

"I hope we can resolve things in an hour," he said.

Why, after Immanuel's leadership refused mediation, was Christopher now asking me to meet with him? Was he repeating Rev. Karen's attempt to ambush me? Were they initiating a disciplinary process aimed at excluding me from the church, or was this a sincere effort to make things right? I was being given less than twenty-four hours' notice. That fact alone made me suspicious.

*I work weekday nights anyway*, I thought. *Surely they knew me well enough to know that.* I immediately emailed Kevin, the mediator, and asked if he was still interested in meeting with Immanuel's leadership. I didn't want to go to a meeting at Immanuel alone. I thought it wise to have someone present who wasn't emotionally involved.

Wednesday morning I returned Christopher's phone call from my study. I expected to leave a message. Instead I got Christopher.

"I can't meet tonight," I told him. "I need more notice."

"Okay, I'll have to see if we can come up with another time."

"What is the purpose of this meeting?" I asked.

"I want us to get together," he said, "to discuss a way for you and other church members to be comfortable at church."

"Is that the only agenda?"

He hesitated.

"Is this the start of a disciplinary process?"

"If the meeting fails," he said, "the bishop's office has advised us to proceed with disciplinary procedures against you."

"Why? What have I done?"

"Other church members have complained that when you attend church services, you have been defensive and abrupt."

"Who told you that?" I asked. "Colleen?"

"I've been told you have been uncivil."

"I guess we have a different definition of civil."

"How do you define it?" he asked.

"I think saying she was concerned but never calling to see how I was doing to be uncivil and unkind," I explained.

"People are saying you have spoiled their worship experience and made them uncomfortable."

"How?" I asked. "I haven't disrupted services. Why isn't it okay for me to quietly take a seat by myself and then leave immediately after? What is wrong with that?"

"People feel uncomfortable," Christopher repeated.

"Why can't I come to church and sit away from them? Do I have to sit with them? We're no longer friends. Why is it okay for them to put on this big display about how much they care about me while in the sanctuary, but then refuse to speak to me during coffee hour or to return my phone calls?"

I took a deep breath and lowered my voice. "Chris, how come you never called me to see how I was doing?"

"I didn't know there was a problem."

"But you did know," I said. "I called you looking for the church's constitution. You knew I was crying."

"Rev. Karen told me it was a deeply personal matter. I didn't want to intrude."

How clever, I thought. Rev. Karen systematically isolated me from the rest of the congregation even though I had repeatedly told her I needed and wanted others to call. She had appealed to the universal desire of bystanders to see, hear and speak no evil. She had also cleverly provided Christopher with a justification for not getting involved. He could always tell himself he was respecting my privacy.

"Rev. Karen was breaching confidentiality when she said that. She should have encouraged you to ask me."

"Maybe it wasn't Rev. Karen," he said. "Maybe someone else told me that."

*He's backpedaling,* I thought. *He isn't stupid. He knows the church might be liable.*

"Are you seeking revenge?" he asked.

"No," I answered. "I want justice, not revenge."

"If you can't be friendlier," Christopher said, "then the conflict is unsolvable. We'll have to take it to the next step."

*What next step?* I wondered. *Disciplinary action? Against me, not them?*

"Why?" I asked. "You and the council are rushing to a problem solution before there has been adequate problem discussion. I think resolution is still possible."

"The events occurred so long ago. I hoped time would bring healing for everyone."

"It wasn't so long ago. Time alone will not resolve this. There needs to be problem discussion."

"I'm not authorized by the board to okay such a meeting. I'll have to speak to the church council and get back to you after the holidays."

"Okay. By the way, since I spoke to Rev. David, I stopped getting newsletters. I'm still a member at Immanuel."

"You are a member," Christopher replied. "They'll have to accept that. I'll make sure you get the newsletter. The post office probably lost it."

"Thank you," I said. *The post office didn't lose it,* I thought. *They're actually pretty reliable. They took me off the mailing list. They don't want me to be part of Immanuel.*

"I'll get back to you after the New Year," Christopher promised.

Immediately after my telephone conversation with Christopher, I felt proud I had asserted myself. Several hours later, the full impact of what he said hit me. My very presence at church made people uncomfortable. I wasn't wanted. I was too defective to be allowed in church. My heart broke. Immanuel's leadership was still trying to silence me. If my former friends had sat down and talked to me rather than about me, this conflict would have been over years ago.

I despaired. All the mean and cruel things said about me became a jumble in my head. I was flooded with memories of my father belittling me and my high school classmates refusing to sit next to me. Fear seized me and I curled up into a fetal position on the black leather sofa. *What if this has more to do with me than with my attackers? What if I'm laughed at, told I'm making it up, told it isn't that bad? Maybe I really am too sensitive. Maybe I am a troublemaker. Maybe, as it says in Haugk's book,* Antagonists in the Church, *I am self-condemned. Then there must be something powerfully evil about me. Just my presence destroyed things.*

But God knew the truth. Whether I was accepted by a church community or not, I still belonged to God. I could worship God outside a church. He would always accept me. *As I struggle, I get stronger and stronger. I expand my knowledge and insights. I am a better person for it. God has blessed me in a peculiar kind of way.*

Late Friday morning, I spoke with Rev. Rick and told him about my conversation with Christopher. He advised me to write a letter to Immanuel's church council reaffirming my desire to meet and work things out.

"What kind of trouble can you get into for providing me with support and advice?" My speech was pressured.

"I don't believe it will cause me any problems."

"I think you might be naïve," I said. I remembered Mallory's attempt to help me. Rev. Karen, using Matthew 18 as justification, threatened her with expulsion from Immanuel. Didn't Rev. Rick have more to lose? Couldn't the bishop threaten his livelihood?

"How much do you trust me?" I asked him.

"I have wondered to what extent you are culpable," he replied. "In my experience, when there's conflict, usually both sides bear some responsibility."

"I used to think that, too," I said. "Until I was dechurched. Now I realize that wholly innocent individuals can be scapegoated, especially if they're meek and not aggressive. I am sure that anger was inappropriately displaced on me."

I never said or did a mean thing to anyone. I had tried hard to resolve things by confronting the conflict and not running away from it. Despite my best efforts to be a good member of the churches I belonged to, those efforts weren't acceptable, and eventually I was scapegoated and rejected. My problems weren't created by a failure on my part to take personal responsibility for my faults. To the contrary, I had tried too hard to fix problems that were not of my making.

As Rev. Rick advised, I wrote a brief letter to Christopher that reiterated my willingness to meet and discuss the issues. While I waited for Immanuel's church officers to respond, my anxiety rose. Driving past Immanuel on Wednesday night, December 17, I wondered if the church council was meeting and what they would decide. I reminded myself that they really couldn't do anything more to hurt me. They had already made Immanuel such an unwelcoming place that for the sake of my mental health I began attending church elsewhere.

If Immanuel's leadership chose to formally expel me, they would only be exposing themselves for who they really were. I hadn't done anything wrong. It was their guilt that motivated them to be so cruel.

"God forgive them," I whispered as I pulled into my garage. "Forgive them for all the hurt they have inflicted on James, my family, themselves and me. May the Holy Spirit move them to be just."

The next morning I anxiously wondered if the council had indeed discussed me. I wondered what was decided. Would it be safe for me to go to church at Immanuel on Christmas Eve? St. Matt's only had an early evening service. I didn't understand why people preferred that time. It interfered with dinner. During my childhood, my parents had followed the Italian tradition and attended midnight mass. Immanuel was the only Lutheran church in the area having a late-night service.

Contact with Immanuel had me in a whirl. My mood fluctuated wildly. I was ambivalent about therapy. Sometimes I thought the best way to get over Immanuel was to just walk away. When that didn't work, I tried to deal with it by seeing Dr. Emmett. When that became overwhelming, I would pull out again. Seesaw. I felt like puking.

Despite my ambivalence, I was desperate to see Dr. Emmett. I made every session. But I had difficulty trusting him. I desperately needed his help but feared he would abandon me. I didn't want him to leave me. I needed him to stay. I feared he wouldn't be there the next time I needed to talk. I feared he would grow tired of me for being too needy.

Therapists and other significant people had come and gone in my life. Dr. Howard died. Dr. Robins retired. Rev. Dorothy had promised to always welcome a call from me. Where was she now? Rev. Karen had once assured me the Lutheran church sought to mediate conflicts in a fair and just manner. Instead, disciplinary action was initiated against me.

When I saw Dr. Emmett on December 23, he asked me how I felt about him. I laid my head on the arm of couch while I pulled my green parka up over my head. I'm not sure I ever answered. I was more focused on the clock and escaping.

*The whole thing is foolish. I shouldn't sweat the small stuff. It is all small stuff. None of this will matter when we are dead and gone. So how do I feel about Dr. Emmett?*

I peeked out at him from under my coat. *What difference does it make? Sooner or later, he and I will part ways, never to see or hear from each other again. We probably won't even know when the other has died. So what difference does it make how I feel about him?*

The flip, hostile answer was that I didn't have any feelings about Dr. Emmett. He was just one more headshrinker. At times I had resented his presence in my life and his interference in the self-harming behaviors. Then there was that period of time when I felt a strong attraction, which was scary and confusing.

*But I know I'm safe in his office. No one is going to berate me, put me down while I'm here with him. He isn't going to let me harm myself while I'm with him.*

"I don't know," I told him, pulling the coat down. "I don't know how I feel about you."

*You have been dependable and kind,* I thought. *You haven't betrayed me. At least, not yet. I suppose I would be upset if anything happened to you. But there is no real connection. I'm just another one of your clients. You mean more to me than I mean to you. It's all phony and contrived. Eventually we'll be going our separate ways and we'll never see or hear from each other again. So I'm not going to allow myself to feel close to you. There's no point in that.*

"I think there's a genuine connection between us," Dr. Emmett said.

"Fuck off and go to hell." I sat up and glared at him.

"You're distancing yourself from me," he replied calmly. "Maybe you do that with others, too."

I didn't really think so. As he said, our relationship was unique. I didn't have these conversations with others. *I'm not thinking clearly. All I can think is that I hate him. I hate him for intruding into my life. Lying to me about how he feels: I don't want him close. I want him out of my life. I want him to go away and leave me alone.*

Time. The session was over. I panicked. I wanted to say, *"No, not yet. I'm not ready to leave. I need to talk."* But I was afraid to.

On the drive home from his office, I started crying.

*Die.* Why couldn't I just die? If God took me in His arms, I would finally be safe. No one to yell at me, telling me how sick and worthless I was. No one to pretend they're friends only to reject and abandon me later. No one to complain that my mere presence "spoils their worship experience."

*I want to be safe,* I thought. If I slashed my arms, all the blood would wash all my pain away. It would bring relief. But only for a few minutes. I wouldn't really be safe if I did that. I would die. My death would spread the pain. It wouldn't really relieve it.

*I am safe with Lyndon and my family. I don't need or want to trust anyone else.*

The next morning I called Dr. Emmett and left a message. "Can I see you next week? I regret distancing myself from you yesterday."

He returned my call and instead of saying hello he said, "No regrets."

Regrets. I had a lot of regrets. I regretted letting Don talk me into staying at FXUU in the spring of 1998 and not returning to Murray. I regretted not defending myself better at FXUU and letting the others silence me; it wasn't good for my mental health. I regretted not seeking help sooner. I regretted forgiving Rev. Dorothy too quickly for lying and not demanding more from her. I regretted not confronting Sue sooner. I regretted taking James into my home and trusting people at Immanuel.

If I had it all to do over again, I would be more assertive and pay more attention to my own perceptions. By disregarding the threat, I left myself unprotected and unable to mount an effective defense. When you are bullied, you have to push back. I hadn't been good at that. Mostly I retreated.

On Christmas Eve, I cooked and ate dinner with my family. After we cleaned up the kitchen we watched some television together. At 10:30 p.m., I kissed my husband goodbye and drove over to Immanuel for the 11 p.m. service. There were fewer cars in the lot than I remembered being there a few years ago. I worried I had gotten the time mixed up.

I pulled open the wooden door and walked into the sanctuary. An usher handed me an order of service. I stood for a moment in the back. There weren't many people there. As I walked to a front pew on the pulpit side I passed Colleen, Irene and Mallory.

Several people glanced at me and then looked away. I was wearing my new red felt hat with feathers along with my red silk blouse, black skirt and black jacket. Almost everyone else was dressed in jeans and pullover sweaters. It wasn't like the midnight mass of my childhood when everyone came decked out in festive clothes. I sighed. Perhaps I should have gone to the midnight mass at the Catholic church up the road.

I took my seat and spoke to no one. During the Peace, Colleen, who was the communion assistant, walked over. In the unkind manner of a teenage girl, she smirked as she extended her hand to me. I feared I looked silly in my hat. A man sitting behind me winked. "Nice hat," he reassured me.

At the end of 2003, I was seeing Dr. Emmett every other week and calling in-between whenever I felt the need to talk, which almost worked out to once per week. Often I thought I should just see him every week and stop fooling myself. But my insurance only covered twenty-six sessions per year, and I knew if Immanuel's board agreed to meet I was really going to need to see him then.

If Immanuel finally took responsibility and filed a professional liability claim on my behalf, then therapy would be paid for. I didn't know if that was ever going to happen. I wasn't even sure Christopher would call me back. I didn't want to get my family further into debt on account of me. So my head just spun and I felt whacked out.

Since the events at Immanuel, I hadn't been able to sustain participation in any group beyond my family. I became reclusive. My experiences with church left me fearful of being abandoned. I couldn't even tolerate friendly acquaintances. The anxiety became more than I could bear. I was terrified of getting close, being friendly, getting involved and making a commitment. How long would it take the next time for people to reject and abandon me?

When Gwynne invited me out to lunch, I struggled not to be panicked by her offer of friendship. I had become frightened of relationships in a way I had never been before. Sitting across from her at the pub, I wondered what the hidden agenda was. I did my best to suppress my suspicion and relax. I fought my desire to retreat and isolate. We talked about our experiences with our Sudanese foster sons. Gwynne had taken in two boys. They had threatened her. For her own safety and sanity, she had them removed from her home. She started seeing a therapist.

Dr. Emmett wanted me to be less guarded and less distant from him and others. He was concerned that I was becoming a recluse. I wanted to keep myself emotionally and physically safe. Dr. Emmett wanted me safe, too, but saw my impulse to self-harm as the bigger threat. In my despair, I saw it as a refuge that I yearned to go to.

It was more than a month since I sent the letter to Christopher asking Immanuel's council to meet with me to discuss our differences. On Friday morning, January 30, 2004, I was on the verge of making a decision to file an insurance claim against Immanuel. This thought increased my fear. There was no telling for sure how nasty it would or wouldn't get. I had a strong desire to isolate and hide from anyone who might harm me. But I knew the only way to conquer my fear was to behave as if I wasn't afraid.

I called Christopher and left a message asking him to call me. I had little hope he would respond. While waiting for his return call I took out the yellow pages and looked up attorneys. I began with the A's and started working my way through the alphabet. I kept getting the same answer. Since I hadn't lost any time from work, I could only sue for my psychotherapy expenses. It wasn't worth an attorney's time and effort. I was about to give up when a female attorney suggested, "You should find an attorney just starting out who has time on their hands and would be willing to take a small case."

"Where do I find a new attorney?" I asked.

"Actually, someone I went to law school with might take your case. His name is Michael Lustig."

After thanking this attorney and hanging up, I immediately dialed the number she had given me. I got Mr. Lustig's answering machine. Disappointed, I left a message. I didn't really expect it to go anywhere.

The next day at noon while I was getting ready to leave for my son's track meet, Mr. Lustig called. I briefly told him my story. Silence. He said nothing. Clutching the phone tightly against my ear, I sunk down to the floor and squatted against the kitchen wall, bracing myself for another disappointment. I was certain he was going to tell me why he couldn't help me. I stifled my tears.

"You've piqued my interest," he said.

"What?" I said in disbelief.

"You've piqued my interest," he repeated.

I slid down until my butt was on the floor. I hugged my knees against my chest. Finally I had someone willing to help me. With tears streaming down my face, I scheduled a meeting with him for Wednesday morning, February 4.

Later that same day after I returned from my son's track meet I received the long overdue phone call from Christopher.

"I'm sorry it has taken me so long to get back to you," he said. "Your letter sat in my mailbox at Immanuel. I haven't checked my box in weeks."

"That's okay," I replied. "I should have sent it to your home."

"After reading your letter, I see no reason why things can't be worked out at Immanuel. The bishop's office was another matter. They remain highly resistive."

"It's okay with me to separate my issues with Immanuel from my issues with the bishop's office and Rev. Karen."

My head was spinning. I felt overwhelmed. I squelched the urge to tell him it was too little, too late. I had just found an attorney. I didn't know what to do.

"Are you willing," he asked, "to speak with our new pastor?"

"The new pastor can call but I need to discuss things with my family," I replied.

Over the next two days, I considered what I wanted. On Monday morning I wrote in my journal that I wanted to ask my former friends why they had refused to meet with me. I wanted to check with them what they really said and did. I wanted each person to recognize what they did, apologize directly to me and state what they did wrong. I didn't want them to just say they were sorry I was hurt. I wanted them to make restitution by writing to the bishop, exonerating me, and by supporting my claim for reimbursement of my psychotherapy expenses. I wanted all that we did for James acknowledged. I didn't want them to approach me and touch me except for a handshake during the Peace. I didn't want them to go out of their way to shake my hand. I wanted the gossip and slander to stop. I wanted the church leadership to set an example about that and not to tolerate it. I wanted people to be educated about conflict resolution. I wanted the church's constitution to be modified, eliminating the persistent troublemaker clause and replacing it with something fairer. I wanted everyone to be educated about ethics. There was so much that I wanted.

Monday morning, I received an email from Christopher introducing me to Rev. Julie. He wrote,

> ...full understanding and healing can take place if all involved parties are able to fully listen and express their feelings and understanding of where each of them is, and work together to resolve hurts, unintentional and otherwise, from the past. I also know that we cannot force anyone to do anything against their will, especially listening with an open heart and mind, and it is possible even after all the perspectives are shared and heard that people may agree to disagree.

> However, to me the worst thing is not attempting and failing, but is not trying at all.

Christopher suggested the next step was for Rev. Julie and I to speak with each other. He hoped,

> ...with Christian love we can heal this wound. It may not be healable, and even if healed there is likely to be a scar that remains, yet we shall work to heal it.

Thank you, Maggie, for having the courage to work toward this healing.

I contacted Rev. Julie and agreed to meet with Christopher and her on President's Day, February 16. Since Christopher himself had separated the congregation issues from Rev. Karen and the bishop's office, I decided to focus on rebuilding a relationship with Immanuel while pursuing an insurance claim against Rev. Karen and the bishop's office. On Wednesday I kept my appointment with Michael Lustig. He agreed to take my case but was willing to wait to see what came of my meeting with Christopher and Rev. Julie.

The next Sunday, February 8, I attended services at Immanuel. As I was leaving the church following the 8:15 am service I ran into Dorrie, a tall, slender woman in her late fifties. She came to church infrequently because she worked as a nurse and usually didn't have Sundays off. I had been friendly with her, especially since she used to sit with Ruth and me whenever she attended the 10:30 a.m. service.

"Hi, how are you, Maggie?" she said.

*Should I give her a perfunctory answer or tell her the truth?* I decided to try the truth. "Not very well."

"You've lost a lot of weight," Dorrie said. "Have you been ill?"

"I've lost the pounds this church put on me." I tossed my head back and peered at her. Was she friend or foe?

Taken aback, she asked as we walked down the sidewalk, "Do you really think this church put the weight on you?"

"All that stress eating," I replied.

"From what?" she asked.

"From when James left and people kept bringing him back here."

"I don't know anything about that," she replied. "I wasn't involved."

*Yeah, right,* I thought. The last time I spoke to Dorrie was in fellowship hall shortly after James left. Ruth and the other Bible study members had gathered on the opposite side of the room, ignoring me.

"Emotions are running high right now, Maggie," Dorrie had said.

I looked at her with tears in my eyes.

"I'll try and talk to them." Dorrie patted my arm and walked over to Ruth. I was grateful for her offer of help. Nothing, however, ever came of it. I hadn't seen or spoken to her in two years. I was sure Dorrie had listened at length to my detractors and not given me equal time. That in itself wasn't neutral. She had taken sides.

I bit my lip. "I don't know what your culpability is or isn't. But what happened at this church shouldn't have happened. They were cruel to me."

"I wasn't involved in that."

"In studies of bullying, it is the bystanders who have the power to stop it." As we continued walking toward the parking lot I thought how bystanders needed to be educated about what they can do. Social psychology research into bystander apathy has indicated that in order for people to offer aid, they first must realize there is a crisis. If they recognize there is a crisis, they then must believe they have the resources and ability to help. All Dorrie had to do to stop the bullying was just say, "This doesn't sound fair to me." That could have made a tremendous difference. In studies of bullying, it just takes one individual to tell the bully to stop.

"I didn't know you were being bullied."

"Whether you call it that or not, it was bullying," I said, annoyed.

"I'm sorry you feel that way."

"It isn't just that I feel that way, that is the way it happened," My jaw muscles tightened.

"I've heard the other side, and now I've heard yours."

"You haven't heard my side," I told her. How could she say that after a one-minute conversation? She didn't want to hear my side.

"They believe you're trying to force them to bend to your will."

"They have never met and discussed things with me. There was never any way for them to check their perceptions or for me to check mine," I said, fully aware of my strength and clarity.

"It is important to talk when there is conflict," Dorrie said. "No one wanted you to leave."

"That isn't true," I replied. "You don't know what went on. This kind of thing is not uncommon in churches."

"Churches have their ways. Shunning and that sort of thing," she replied.

So she did know what was going on. We reached the parking lot. I took a deep breath. "You really look good," I said. "Take care of yourself."

I walked over to my car and got in. I was steamed. Dorrie thought she was virtuous for not getting involved. Wanting to preserve her relationship with Ruth and the others, she never reached out to me. She never listened to my pain. She thought herself innocent but she was not. She knew more of what happened than she cared to admit. She sat with my enemies and heard what they were saying about me. By remaining silent, she tacitly consented to my being abused and mistreated.

Churches, I think, need to do a better job of educating their members about their moral obligation to intervene. I just needed one person to be supportive. Oddly enough, I think Rev. Karen knew that, and was very effective in keeping anyone from offering me help.

Driving home, I worried Dorrie would run to the church hierarchy and the meeting I worked so hard to get scheduled would be cancelled because of what I said. It had been hard to get my former friends to see that what they did was emotionally abusive, that they usurped Lyndon's and my parental authority, resulting in the loss of our foster son. They never understood or accepted how much I loved James. They never understood that for his sake and my family's sake, I had to let him go. They never understood that in order to let him go, I had to close my heart to him. They never got how painful that was, what a sacrifice that was for us. And because they never got that, they didn't understand I was grieving the loss just as much or more than if he had died.

They left me alone with my pain. They claimed to be my friends but they never called. They never inquired how I was doing. They responded to my requests to talk by ignoring them or by becoming hostile. They told me I was sick. When they hugged me without my consent, they told me there was nothing wrong with a hug. Hugs are good things, I was told. My former friends violated my emotional and physical boundaries and proclaimed they had every right to.

*I just want a little piece of justice for myself and my family,* I thought as I pulled into the garage.

Eight days later Lyndon and I drove over to Immanuel to meet with Christopher and Rev. Julie. The office was arranged just as Rev. Karen had it except there was no rocking chair. After Christopher introduced us to Rev. Julie, we took our seats around the coffee table.

"This is only a first step," Rev. Julie said. "Other meetings are going to be necessary."

"Yes, we agree with that," I replied. "First, I want it to be clear I am not seeking counseling by you. That's not what I need from you."

Christopher looked surprised, and looked toward Rev. Julie. He then said, "Yes, I understand. Why don't you tell us your side of the story?"

Tearful, I told them what had happened after James left. Christopher kept framing it as "my perception." I corrected him. "It isn't just a case of perception. These events really happened."

I knew what I said or did. I knew I had behaved well and hadn't been abusive to anyone. I knew I was the injured party. Christopher and Rev. Julie would need to take time to investigate my allegations and try to figure out what was true.

Toward the end of the hour, Christopher asked what I wanted to come out of this. I pulled out a list of talking points that I had prepared for the meeting.

"I want my family's generosity to James acknowledged and an apology for the emotional abuse we suffered," I said. "If James is continuing to attend services here, I want Rev. Julie to speak to him about what he did and the impact it has had on our lives."

"I haven't seen James in a while," Christopher interrupted. "I'm not sure where he is."

"I also want to be reimbursed for my psychotherapy expenses."

"How much is that?" he asked.

"I'm not sure. I haven't added it up," I replied.

"Except for speaking to James, it's all within the realm of possibility," Christopher said.

"The next step," Rev. Julie added, "will be for Chris and I to discuss it. We'll get back to you in a couple of weeks."

"That's okay, so long as a couple of weeks doesn't mean never."

"We will get back in touch with you," she reassured me.

We stood and shook hands. Lyndon and I said goodbye and left.

"Let's go to lunch," Lyndon said as we walked toward our car.

"I don't want to get my hopes up," I told him. "I don't want to get slammed again. But maybe this time it will really work out."

"Maybe," he said, putting his arm around me.

"I hope they don't think I'm crazy and that I imagined it all. That I'm too sensitive and misperceive things. But I know what I said and did. I know I never said or did a mean thing to any of them. I know I tried really hard to resolve things by confronting the conflict, not running away from it."

"That's what got you labeled a persistent troublemaker," he said.

What was I supposed to do? Be quiet and obey?

"Churches are corrupt," he said.

But my heart was breaking. How was I supposed to stop weeping?

A month went by and I hadn't heard from Rev. Julie, so I called her and asked for an update. She informed me there was one person willing to meet with me and possibly a second. I replied that I understood that the process would be slow. I could be patient so long as there was some progress and I was kept informed. Rev. Julie apologized and promised to keep me in the loop.

I began attending church at Immanuel every Sunday while maintaining my connection to St. Matt's by attending their Lenten services on Wednesdays. Ruth came to a service at Immanuel with a Sudanese man who I at first mistook for James. I was sitting on the pulpit side of the sanctuary while she sat a few pews in front of me on the opposite side. It had been close to two-and-a-half years since I last saw James. I seethed with rage equal to what I felt over being raped when I was eleven. Ruth alienated my son from me by giving him gifts and rescuing him from punishment. It isn't like stealing a camera. You can always replace an object. You can't replace a son.

I suppressed my tears and made a point of sitting up tall. I consciously took slow, deep breaths to slow the beating of my heart. I imagined Jesus whispering in my ear. I reminded myself that God knew the truth. Even if my heart needed to be broken a million times, eventually I would triumph. God knew they alienated my son from me. Ruth couldn't hide from her sin forever.

When Rev. Julie failed to keep me in the loop as promised, I called her again. She informed me that the two people who had agreed to meet with me had pulled out. Both stated they had already spoken to me and saw no reason to discuss things again. I began to cry. It felt like another dead end.

"Who told them not to meet with me?" I asked.

"I don't believe they spoke to anyone about it," she replied. I didn't believe her.

"I think about you every day. Things will get resolved," she reassured me. "The congregation isn't used to dealing with conflict directly. I need time to teach them to communicate."

"Is there anything you want me to do or not do?" I asked.

"Just keep coming to worship and do what you feel comfortable with," she advised.

I followed up our conversation with an email. I thanked her for her efforts. I acknowledged it was a difficult situation and that people had become entrenched and polarized. I also informed her that when I didn't hear from her or Christopher, I had no way of knowing if she was working on the dispute or if they had abandoned it.

I told her that I understood that dealing with the conflict added stress, and that it would be easier for her and Christopher to avoid dealing with it. In contrast, I was motivated by the desire to end the pain caused by the emotional abuse. Avoidance and delays were only prolonging my pain. I again requested that she or Christopher keep me updated at least once per week. I also offered to help in any way I could.

Shortly after sending the email on March 28, I again attended services at Immanuel. Moved by the service, I considered attending the Sunday Bible study on homosexuality. I quickly rejected the idea, but decided to study the materials on my own.

As I exited the church, I asked Rev. Julie for a copy of the study guide. She directed me to a box at the far side of the fellowship hall. Seeing all the people I would have to walk past, I hesitated. Apparently believing I didn't understand her, Rev. Julie repeated they were in a box on the chair and for me to go and get a copy. She further said she would make sure I had found it when she came into the hall.

With trepidation, I proceeded down the breezeway, grabbed a pastry from the coffee table, and approached the box with the study materials. Before I could reach the chair, someone picked up the box and placed it on the coffee table in the middle of the room. Many of my former friends were gathering there. Unsure if I should go and take one, I hesitated. Anna, Christopher' wife, greeted me. We exchanged pleasantries. I relaxed a little.

While we were talking, I felt a hand on my shoulder. I assumed it was Rev. Julie, but when I turned around I discovered it was Joe. We had attended Bible study together prior to my dechurching. Joe had also been a member of the church council. He was one of the "innocent bystanders."

Distressed by the physical intrusion, I recoiled. "I would be happy to greet and speak with you after we sit down with Rev. Julie."

"What?" he said.

I repeated what I said. He stormed off.

Shaking and upset I turned back to Anna and apologized to her.

"Would you like a hug?" Anna asked.

Frozen by my distress, I didn't answer right away. I was uncertain what to say. Finally finding my voice, I said yes. We hugged. When we stepped back I could see tears in Anna's eyes.

"I wish I knew how I can help you," she said.

We talked a bit. I quoted Bruno Bettleheim, "That which cannot be talked about, can never be put to rest."

Anna then told me how she had dealt indirectly with a conflict she had with a coworker. She also didn't think Joe understood.

"I won't pretend there is nothing between Joe and me," I said. "Keeping up appearances is what he and the rest want. It will get me nothing."

Mallory joined us. Before I could say anything, Anna told me Mallory hadn't been around in awhile. She had been in a car accident. After I expressed my concern there was a long, awkward silence.

"I'm sorry if I interrupted your conversation," Mallory said.

"I don't know how to respond to you. Are you aware Rev. Julie is trying to set up a meeting?"

"Yes," Mallory replied.

"I'm unwilling to speak to you until then," I told her.

"Not even to say hello?" she asked indignantly. Her face was full of disgust. It was clear she was fully in the other camp. Her soul appeared dark and ugly to me.

"Yes," I replied.

Mallory turned to Anna and proceeded to talk as if I wasn't there. Seeing a clear path to the box, I walked over and grabbed a copy of the study materials, then left quickly out of the side door.

Once in my car, my body shook and the tears welled up in my eyes. What to do? Go home, or go food shopping as planned? Distraught, I drove to the supermarket and parked. I sat in the car for a quarter of an hour. Fearing a meltdown, I considered calling Lyndon or Dr. Emmett, but I was able to pull myself together. I decided the distraction of shopping would be good for me.

I went into the market, and began feeling pretty good about standing up for myself. I was enjoying picking out produce for Sunday dinner when Dorrie greeted me.

"Maggie," her voice was filled with concern, "how are you?"

I stared blankly at her. "I don't know what to say given the situation."

With a look of disgust and anger on her face, she stormed off. Shaken, I grabbed my cart and walked off in the opposite direction.

Unable to sleep Sunday night, I thought about all that had transpired. My former friends from Immanuel continued to refuse to give me what I needed, while insisting I accept their crumbs. They were angry that I wouldn't keep up appearances. Sitting down with me would involve discussing deeper emotional issues. They, on the other hand, were all surface. Perhaps they believed there was only surface. My passion, my emotional demonstrativeness angered and threatened them.

Dr. Emmett attempted to reframe Joe and Mallory's behavior as "friendly." I felt it was merely civil, a front. Joe invaded my space and became angry when I suggested we sit down and talk with Rev. Julie. I conceded to Dr. Emmett that I couldn't be sure what their true intentions were. However, I did know they hadn't called me in three years, and were refusing to meet with Rev. Julie and me. Their "civil" behavior was confusing, and raised the false hope that they would talk to me and mend our "friendship." It just added more pain to my grief.

Fear again overwhelmed me, and I had an intense desire to curl up into a fetal position. I longed to curl up under the trees and wither with the autumn leaves. It was difficult to face my demons and press on for some small piece of justice. I had spent three years since James left in emotional turmoil. I desperately needed respite.

I wanted to confront all those who had demeaned me, disrespected me and analyzed my behavior without looking at themselves. I knew I was right, but I was out of step with the prevailing church culture. I wasn't part of the keeping-up-appearances crowd. I demanded and wanted more from relationships. I didn't have time to waste on superficiality.

A week later, I attended Holy Week services at Immanuel. The passing of the Peace was awkward. Should I shake the hands of my detractors, or do I refuse? I attempted to avoid the problem by sitting up front, away from everyone. Unfortunately, one of the members of Bible study sat behind me. I shook the hand of the woman in front of me and didn't turn around. The communion assistant walked past, avoiding eye contact. When Rev. Julie came near, I extended my hand and she shook it.

Colleen was the usher on Maundy Thursday. During communion, she ignored me and invited people behind me to the communion rail. The woman in front of me was confused. Uninvited, I got up and went to the communion rail. I found Marlene next to me. The previous summer, we had sat together at the outdoor service. Our eyes met. We gave communion to each other. Marlene always respected my space and never violated my boundaries. I felt grateful.

At the end of the Maundy Thursday service, everyone is supposed to exit the church in silence. As I walked past, Colleen greeted me. I looked right past her. Why did she keep pushing the issue in public ways but continue to refuse to sit down with me? I was so weary of people not respecting my boundaries.

The Easter Sunday service at Immanuel was done well. I sat up front and was surrounded by people I didn't know. Ruth sat across the aisle with a Sudanese man. Recognizing me, he waved. I wasn't sure who he was. I turned my back.

I felt tears fill my eyes. James, I thought, chose Ruth and her friends as his American family while rejecting us. He chose the adults who catered to him, gave him gifts and didn't hold him accountable. While Ruth and the others might have been attached to him, they didn't love him enough to discipline him and risk losing him as I had. There was nothing I could do about it. It was too late. I just had to accept it as it was.

During communion, I could no longer stifle my tears, and they gushed down my face. I searched desperately for a tissue while I tried to hide my weeping. I was forced to turn to the stranger on my left.

"Oh, dear," she gasped, and quickly obtained a paper towel from her elderly mother. She asked no questions.

Monday night I telephoned Christopher. I was anxious because I hadn't heard from him since the confrontation with Joe. We talked much longer than I wanted to. Christopher tried to convince me to make small talk with my former friends. He hoped that would encourage them to sit down and discuss things with me. I refused, explaining I had already tried that approach by inviting them to my twenty-fifth wedding anniversary party. It hadn't worked.

"I can't pretend everything is okay when it isn't," I told him. Doing that, I thought, could lead to explosions at unexpected and inappropriate times.

Christopher and Rev. Julie claimed to be taking a neutral stance, but I suspected that since they saw my former friends more frequently than they did me, they had a closer relationship with them than with me. Later, Christopher would claim he spoke with me by phone and in person far more often than he did with my former friends.

I didn't believe Christopher and Rev. Julie fully comprehended how abusive the situation was and how devastating it was to me. They didn't understand there was wrongdoing here that required a different approach than the one they were taking.

I met with Christopher and Rev. Julie on Monday, April 26, 2004. Christopher handed me a letter he had prepared on behalf of the church council. The council threw me a small crumb by acknowledging my family's generosity in welcoming James into our home. They did not acknowledge we were good parents. The council denied any wrongdoing and my request for restitution.

"I'm not surprised by their response," I said. "But it's unacceptable. I am angry and hurt. It's hard for me to believe people care when they refuse to meet as I've requested and they continue to violate my physical boundaries contrary to my wishes. It feels like harassment to me."

Even though Christopher and Rev. Julie had always been respectful of my physical boundaries, neither acknowledged my right to determine who did or did not touch me. Christopher kept focusing on what he believed Joe and the others' intentions were. "Joe didn't intend any harm."

"Since Joe has refused to sit down and talk, we don't know for sure what his intentions are."

Instead of reassuring me that I would be safe and my boundaries respected, Christopher asked, "What are you going to do about your church membership?"

"How are you going to reintegrate me into the church community?" I countered.

No answer.

I said, "You should look beyond people's excuses for refusing to meet with me and ask why such a reasonable request is being denied. I am the one who is willing to meet and talk. I am the one attempting reconciliation."

Shortly after the meeting, I contacted my lawyer, Michael Lustig, and instructed him to move ahead with filing the insurance claim against Immanuel for breach of confidentiality and defamation of character. I contacted Christopher and asked him for copies of the church council minutes dating back to when James lived with us. Christopher cooperated fully, and I was allowed to go over to the church office and copy them.

In reviewing the minutes, it appeared the bishop's assistant had advised the church council to deny me a meeting and to initiate disciplinary actions if I didn't submit to their will. Rev. David, the interim minister, appeared to have advised a less drastic, fairer approach.

I didn't want to spread the pain as I sought to heal my own. However, I was well aware that holding people accountable for their actions would upset them. I continued to hope that at the end of this conflict there would be reconciliation and healing. I hoped for a stronger, healthier congregation at Immanuel, one that excluded and marginalized no one.

On June 10, at Christopher' request, we met one last time in Rev. Julie's office. Shortly after we arrived, it became clear to me that the meeting was more to meet Christopher's needs than mine. It was a brief meeting. Christopher presented me with a letter informing me there wasn't anything more he could do for me. He was moving to Colorado.

"I have done my best," he said. "I feel extremely sad to be dealing with a situation that seems to have nothing but loss for everyone. I am very disappointed that things didn't work out."

"I am disappointed, too."

"I see no possibility of reintegrating you into the church community," he went on. "It is unhealthy for you to stay. I suggest you leave Immanuel."

"I have carefully thought out my return," I said. "It has given me the opportunity to face my fears and overcome them. I don't plan on leaving. Good luck in your new home."

Sunday morning, I went to church at Immanuel. Although I was tempted to just walk away, I thought it was better to stay as long as possible while building relationships outside of church. At the beginning of the year, I had started taking ice skating lessons. Eventually I would join a book club.

As had become my habit, I sat in the front, pulpit side. I didn't shake the hands of any of my enemies during the Peace. After church, Anna greeted me. We spoke briefly about her impending move to Colorado. She told me she admired my courage to sit in front when everyone else sits in the back. At the end of our conversation, I told her I would welcome contact with her via email. From the expression on her face, I could see that she didn't want to do that, and was perhaps suspicious of my motives. I left thinking I was tired of people's "kindness" while they continued to refuse me true friendship and fellowship.

A few days later, my attorney emailed me informing me he had contacted Immanuel. I decided it would be better to attend church at St. Matthew's until the insurance claim was settled. However, Rev. Julie's husband was selected as St. Matt's interim minister. I feared that since his wife must have told him about the conflict at Immanuel, he wouldn't allow me to fully participate at St. Matt's. I felt too uncomfortable to continue attending church there.

It was time to move on. There wasn't any way I could be a full participating member of Immanuel again unless other members reached out far more than they were willing. They never considered the impact of their behavior on me. Casting me as either sick or evil, they denied their culpability. I believed I was just as deserving of acceptance as anyone else. During the summer, I followed Rev. Rick to his new church and became a member there the following December.

# Breaking the Silence

Whenever I find myself near World War I Park, I drive past the petting zoo and up the hill to where I took James the morning after he arrived from Africa. Sitting on the rocks overlooking the Attleboros, I remember pointing out to him the water tower in the distance. The unexpectedly warm and sunny day in November 2000 had filled me with hope and love. I was certain God was blessing our new son and that he would become a permanent member of our family.

With bitter sorrow, I remember the unfulfilled promise of that day. In my mind's eye I see James standing there, thin, dark and handsome. I stretch out my hand to caress his cheek. He pulls away and disappears into the mist. I sigh. I cannot change it. I cannot have him back. Brokenhearted, I return to my car.

Life slowly returned to normal, but normal was now different. I lost a certain innocence. Reading Thompson and O'Neill's *Best Friends, Worst Enemies*, I learned that social science research has identified five basic types of children within schools. A child can be popular, accepted, neglected, rejected or controversial. My dechurchings made me painfully aware that these social distinctions continue beyond childhood. Over the years my place in the social strata moved between the rejected and the neglected group.

Starting in kindergarten, my peers rejected me. I was rarely invited anywhere by anyone, and my invitations or overtures for friendship weren't accepted. Things improved a little when I went to college. I moved from being rejected to being marginally accepted.

While raising my children, I had the most social connections. There was some reciprocity. But looking back on it now, those relationships were more important to me than to the people I considered friends. None of those relationships survived the move to New England or my dechurchings.

Each dechurching was progressively worse. The verbal and emotional assault escalated to include not only attacks on my character but also attacks on my husband and children's characters. I was proud that I created a life for myself and my children that was free of the abuse and neglect I suffered when I was a child. All that I accomplished was harshly criticized by other church members either directly or by innuendo, calling into question the value of my entire life. As devastating as that was, the extremity of the attack made me realize it wasn't I who was at fault. Rather, all religious communities, regardless of denomination, at some point in their history have engaged in abusive behavior. I was merely a pawn in the drama.

In *Trauma and Recovery*, Judith Herman listed three stages of recovery from trauma: establishing safety, reconstructing the trauma story and restoring the connection between survivors and their community. In my own experience, these tasks didn't follow a nice, neat, linear pattern. Safety had to be established repeatedly in every environment I entered.

Dr. Emmett and Rev. Rick established safety for me by respecting my emotional and physical boundaries, by returning phone calls, and by being honest. This feeling of safety was quite fragile. It was easily lost whenever I was attacked or betrayed by someone outside the relationship.

Immanuel's church leadership failed to establish a safe place for me. Instead of assuring me that my physical and emotional boundaries would be respected, they criticized me for not accepting handshakes and hugs from my former friends. I could never be certain my detractors wouldn't invade my space and that they wouldn't continue to advocate my removal from Immanuel.

Herman's *Trauma and Recovery* affirmed my conviction that remembering and truth telling needed to occur before there could be real peace. I needed and deserved an opportunity to speak my truth to the religious communities that harmed me. The true cause of my suffering needed to be formally acknowledged. Individuals needed to be held accountable for the part they played whether they were the perpetrator, collaborator or bystander.

If religious communities want to avoid reliving past conflicts, then people must remember, grieve and atone for their own sins without scapegoating others. If I and others like me had no hope for justice, there was also no hope for a true peace, no hope for reconciliation.

As is common with trauma survivors, my life in many ways became constricted. My contacts and interactions with others declined. While some of this was due to my fear of social contact, a large part was due to rejection and neglect by others. Once victimized, you are easily re-victimized. My parent's neglect left me vulnerable. Unprotected and needy, I was easy prey for pedophiles and bullies. I lacked the necessary social skills to adequately protect myself.

During calmer moments when I was more centered, I realized that I had internalized abusive messages. I replayed them over and over. The message that I was unlikable and would never have friends was actually a version of my father's message that I was unlovable. It was the same message of my abusive classmates. I heard it so much, I came to believe it. It was never true.

I squandered my time and energy on people who devalued emotions and preferred to keep up appearances. They were never worthy of my friendship. I resolved to be more selective in the future.

Rather than engaging in an honest dialogue with me about the problem, church members made me the problem and attempted to impose a solution. When I quite naturally protested, I was threatened with disciplinary action and expulsion from the church community. They tried to break me while protecting those who had been abusive.

People at Immanuel wanted me to participate in their pretend peace. I wanted so much more than that. Every day, I prayed for God to open their hearts and minds. I prayed for Rev. Julie and Christopher to question more closely what my adversaries told them. I prayed for my adversaries to finally recognize their sin, repent and seek to make restitution. I longed to be fully reconciled and fully accepted into Immanuel's church community. Lacking adequate support from the church leadership, my hopes were never realized.

As time passed, I talked less about the church conflict even though it remained unresolved. I lost twenty-seven pounds, got a new haircut, and had fun purchasing a whole new wardrobe. I was glad I attempted to return to Immanuel, even though was hard and ultimately failed. Going back provided me with information that helped me put the pieces of the puzzle together. It also gave me a chance to face my detractors and overcome my fear.

I did achieve one small victory. On Saturday, February 26, 2005, I drove down to New York City with Lyndon, Melissa and her fiancée. We spent the day in Central Park looking at "The Gates," set up by artists Cristo and Jeanne Claude. Later that evening when we returned to our Attleboro house, I sorted the mail and found Immanuel's newsletter. "What's this?" I said to no one in particular. "I haven't gotten a newsletter from Immanuel since I transferred my membership to Our Redeemer last December."

My husband grunted and said nothing. The phone rang. It was my brother Rich. We had missed each other in New York. I took a seat on the couch in the family room. While I chatted with Rich, I skimmed the newsletter. As I hung up the phone, I spotted it. It was there, under the council news.

I whooped as I hopped down the hall and back. "I've won," I shouted. "I've won!"

Lyndon was sitting on the couch watching television. "What's going on?"

Holding up the newsletter, I read it to him, "The Council reviewed a draft harassment and misconduct policy. The Council will be adopting a harassment and misconduct policy as required by the insurance company."

Lyndon smiled.

"My filing an insurance claim must have triggered this," I said. I immediately called my brother back.

"It took the insurance company to get them to do something they should have done all along," Rich said with a snicker. "And they're admitting that? They're saying, we don't really want to do this but the insurance company's making us. You got to be kidding."

The next morning when I went to church, I asked Rev. Rick to offer a prayer for the survivors and perpetrators of spiritual abuse. As I exited the sanctuary, I told him what had happened and thanked him for his help.

"Can I give you a hug?" I asked, elated. He nodded assent.


My struggle with churches made me stronger. I now strive to accept things as they are, focusing on what I have, not on what I don't have and probably will never have. With no reputation and friends to lose, I am free to do what I want, pursue my own interests, say and think what I like. I am free to find my own way to live an authentic Christian life, unencumbered by unspoken rules and the false projections of others.

The knowledge and insights I gained into groups, and human evil, has aided me in my work as a psychologist. I know what it's like to be rejected, abandoned and used as an object to satisfy someone else's lust and power needs. God, in a peculiar kind of way, blessed me.

The religious communities I cherished silenced me and almost broke my spirit. The unbearable pain gave birth to an overwhelming need to be heard. While writing this book, I have striven to adhere to the truth as I know it without demonizing others. We all had our parts to play: victim, perpetrator, collaborator and bystander.

The telling has given me some distance and clarity. Whether I am accepted by a church community or not, I still belong to God. He will always accept me. By breaking the silence, I am triumphant.

# References

Battin, M.P. (1990). *Ethics in the Sanctuary: Examining the Practices of Organized Religion.* New Haven, CT: Yale University Press.

Benyei, C.R. (1998). *Understanding Clergy Misconduct in Religious Systems: Scapegoating, Family Secrets and the Abuse of Power.* Binghamton, NY: The Haworth Pastoral Press.

Blue, K. (1993). *Healing Spiritual Abuse: How to Break Free from Bad Church Experiences.* Downers Grove, IL: Intervarsity Press.

Boers, A.P. (1999). *Never Call Them Jerks.* US: Alban Institute, Inc.

Coloroso, B. (2004). *The Bully, the Bullied, and the Bystander.* New York: HarperCollins Publishers.

Evans, P. (1996). *The Verbally Abusive Relationship.* Holbrook, MA: Adams Media Corporation.

Fairbanks, C.B. (2002). *Hiding Behind the Collar.* Baltimore, MD: America House Book Publishers.

Fowler, J.W. (1981). *Stages of Faith: The Psychology of Human Development and the Quest for Meaning.* New York: HarperCollins Publishers.

Gula, R.M. (1996). *Ethics in Pastoral Ministry.* Mahwah, NJ: Paulist Press.

Hammond, Mary (2001). *The Church and the Dechurched.* St. Louis, Missouri: Chalice Press.

Haugk, K.C. (1988). *Antagonists in the Church: How to Identify and Deal with Destructive Conflict.* Minneapolis: Augsburg Publishing House.

Hill, A. (1997). *Speaking Truth to Power.* USA: First Anchor Books.

Johnson, D. & VanVonderen, J. (1991). *The Subtle Power of Spiritual Abuse: Recognizing and Escaping Spiritual Manipulation and False Spiritual Authority within the Church.* Minneapolis, MN: Bethany House Publishers.

Jones, O. Garfield (1971). *Parliamentary Procedure at a Glance.* New York: E.P. Dutton.

Katherine, A. (1991). *Boundaries.* New York: Simon & Schuster.

Lebacqz, K. & Driskill, J.D. (2000). *Ethics and Spiritual Care: A Guide for Pastors, Chaplains, and Spiritual Directors.* Nashville, TN: Abingdon Press.

Nickman, S.L. & Lewis, R.G. (1994). "Adoptive Families and Professionals: When the Experts Make Things Worse." *Journal of the American Academy of Child and Adolescent Psychiatry,* 33:5

Park, A.S. (1993). *The Wounded Heart of God*. Nashville, TN: Abingdon Press.

Peck, M.S. (1983). *People of the Lie*. New York, NY: Simon and Schuster.

Rediger, G.L. (1977). *Clergy Killers: Guidance for Pastors and Congregations Under Attack*. Louisville, Kentucky: Logos Productions, Inc.

Rupp, J. (1988). *Praying Our Goodbye*. USA: Ava Maria Press

Shaughnessy, M.A. (1998). *Ministry and the Law: What You Need to Know*. Mahwah, NJ: Paulist Press.

Simmons, R. (2002). *Odd Girl Out: The Hidden Culture of Aggression in Girls*. US: Harcourt Books.

Smedes, L.B. (1997). *The Art of Forgiving*. New York: Ballantine Books.

Swidler, L. (1996). *Toward a Catholic Constitution*. New York: The Crossroad Publishing Company.

The New English Bible with the Apocrypha. (1970). USA: Oxford University Press.

Thompson, M. & O'Neill-Grace, C. (2001). *Best Friends, Worst Enemies: Understanding the Social Lives of Children*. New York: Ballantine Books.

Walgren, J. (1998). *The Lost Boys of Natinga: A School for Sudan's Young Refugees*. Singapore: Houghton Mifflin Company.

Wiesenthal, S. (1998). *The Sunflower: On the Possibilities and Limits of Forgiveness*. New York: Schocken Books.

Zur, O. & Lazarus, A. (2002). *Dual Relationships and Psychotherapy*. New York: Springer Publishing Company.

# About the Author

MARGARET W. JONES, PhD was awarded her doctorate in psychology in 1986 from Hofstra University, and her professional background includes extensive work with both severely mentally ill and developmentally disabled clients.

In 1994, Dr. Jones went into private practice with her husband, Lyndon C. Jones, LICSW. Both believe that depression and anxiety is best overcome without the use of medication, and that these problems are not usually the result of a "chemical imbalance." Instead, through the use of cognitive behavioral therapy, they help individuals alter their responses to life challenges and achieve a healthy, balanced life. Having achieved marital fulfillment themselves, they are also committed to helping other couples, and offer premarital training as well as couples counseling. A trained life coach, Dr. Jones enjoys helping others achieve success in their careers and significant relationships.

Dr. Jones draws from her own recovery from trauma to assist other survivors to thrive, and founded Pluck Press to help survivors tell their stories. *Not of My Making*, the account of her survival of spiritual abuse, is her first book.

For more information, please visit www.adultchildcounseling.com or www.altheacoaching.com

# Quick Order Form

**Fax orders:** 781 341-0994  Send this form.

**Telephone orders:** 781 341-0993

**Email orders:** pluckpress@verizon.net

**Postal Orders:**

Pluck Press, PO Box 516, Stoughton, MA 02072-0516

**Please send:** *Not of My Making.* I may return this purchase for a full refund excluding shipping and handling within 30 days of purchase.

Name: _____

Address: _____

City: _____State: ____Zip:_____

Telephone: _____

Email: _____

**Sales tax:** Please add 5% for books shipped to Massachusetts.

**Payment:** $19.95 plus $4 for shipping and handling.

- o  Check enclosed
- o  Credit card

  Card number: _____

  Name on card: _____

  Expiration Date: _____